ASK THE ANIMALS

SEMEIA STUDIES

Jacqueline M. Hidalgo, General Editor

Editorial Board:
L. Juliana M. Claassens
Rhiannon Graybill
Raj Nadella
Emmanuel Nathan
Kenneth Ngwa
Shively T. J. Smith
Wei Hsien Wan

Number 104

ASK THE ANIMALS

Developing a Biblical Animal Hermeneutic

Edited by

Arthur W. Walker-Jones and Suzanna R. Millar

SBL PRESS

Atlanta

Copyright © 2024 by SBL Press

All rights reserved. No part of this work may be reproduced or transmitted in any form or by any means, electronic or mechanical, including photocopying and recording, or by means of any information storage or retrieval system, except as may be expressly permitted by the 1976 Copyright Act or in writing from the publisher. Requests for permission should be addressed in writing to the Rights and Permissions Office, SBL Press, 825 Houston Mill Road, Atlanta, GA 30329 USA.

Library of Congress Control Number: 2024937883

Contents

Acknowledgments ix
Abbreviations xi

Introduction: Difference, Identity, Indistinction
    Arthur Walker-Jones and Suzanna R. Millar 1

Part 1. Difference, Posthumanism, and Animality

Wild Christology: On Foxes, Birds, and the Son of Man
    William "Chip" Gruen 23

Monsters, Beasts, and Animals: The Taxonomy of Fierce
Creatureliness in the Biblical Text and Beyond
    Robert Paul Seesengood 39

"He Differed in Nothing from the Beasts": The Disruption of the
Human-Animal Difference in John Calvin's
Commentary on Daniel 4
    Peter Joshua Atkins 51

"Let Them Eat Straw": An Ecological Reevaluation of
Isaiah 11:6–8
    Jacob R. Evers 67

"The Fate of Humans and the Fate of Animals Is the Same":
Animality and Humanity in Qoheleth and the Hebrew Bible
    Ken Stone 83

Part 2. Identification and Animal Rights

Biblical Studies Meets the Humane Society: The Emergence of Animal Activist Exegesis
    Michael J. Gilmour 101

Attending to the Forest and Its Denizens in the Hebrew Bible
    Margaret Cohen..115

Recognizing the Gen(i)us of Animals: Jeremiah 8–9 as a Test Case
    Jaime L. Waters 131

Like Dogs That Return to Their Own Vomit: Ruminations on the (Re)production of Animalizing Hate in the Second Letter of Peter
    Dong Hyeon Jeong...143

Part 3. Indistinction and Alternative Stories

Human Obligation to Nonhuman Animals in Proverbs
    Timothy J. Sandoval...161

Mark's Parabolic Aviary: Reading Mark's Parabolic Birds Ecologically with and against Mark's Jesus
    Brian James Tipton...179

The Pasture and the Battlefield: Domesticated Animals in the Song of Songs
    Jared Beverly 195

The Donkey as Tamasoaalii: A *Fāgogo* Reading of Balaam and the Donkey in Numbers 22:22–35
    Brian Fiu Kolia..205

Miss Piggy and the Pretty Woman of Proverbs 11:22: Beauty, Animality, and Gender
    Anne Létourneau...219

Job and the Maggots
    Suzanna R. Millar 235

Responses

From Jumping Viruses to Job's Leviathan: A Response
    William P. Brown 255

Biblical and Other Cultural Zoontologies
    Robert McKay 263

Afterword: An Animal Hermeneutics? Research
Directions and Teaching Ideas
    Arthur Walker-Jones and Suzanna R. Millar 269

List of Contributors 277
Ancient Sources Index 281
Modern Authors Index 291

Acknowledgments

We are grateful for SBL Press for publishing this volume, in particular for the hard work and support of Steed Davidson, Shively Smith, and Jacqueline Hidalgo, who have overseen the project from proposal to book.

Of course, the volume would not have been possible without the hard work of our contributors, to whom we owe a debt of thanks: Peter Joshua Atkins, Jared Beverly, William Brown, Margaret Cohen, Jacob Evers, Michael Gilmour, William Gruen, Dong Hyeon Jeong, Brian Fiu Kolia, Anne Létourneau, Robert McKay, Timothy Sandoval, Robert Seesengood, Ken Stone, Brian Tipton, and Jaime Waters.

Some of the research for the introduction to this volume and Timothy Sandoval's contribution began as part of the Human Distinctiveness Seminar, generously funded by the Templeton Foundation and led by Celia Dean-Drummond and Agustín Fuentes.

Early versions of some of the chapters in this volume were presented at a conference on animals and religion—Polar Bears, Ponies, and Pets—at the University of Winnipeg, made possible in part by funding from the United Church of Canada Research Chair in Contemporary Theology.

Other chapters were first presented at the Animal Studies and the Bible Consultation of the Annual Meeting of the Society of Biblical Literature. The consultation included joint sessions with the Animals and Religion section of the American Academy of Religion and the Ecological Hermeneutics section of the Society of Biblical Literature. We are grateful to the Society of Biblical Literature for approving the Animal Studies and the Bible consultation and for the support of the Animals and Religion and Ecological Hermeneutics sections that brought the authors and editors of this volume together to collaborate.

Finally, we would like to add our personal thanks to our colleagues, friends, and families—too many to mention by name—who have supported us throughout this project. We are truly grateful.

Abbreviations

1QIsa^a	Isaiah^a
AAArch	Approaches to Anthropological Archaeology
AB	Anchor Bible
ABD	Freedman, David Noel, ed. *Anchor Bible Dictionary*. 6 vols. New York: Doubleday, 1992.
ACET	Athlone Contemporary European Thinkers
AJSP	*Association for Jewish Studies Perspectives*
ANET	Pritchard, James B., ed. *Ancient Near Eastern Texts Relating to the Old Testament*. 3rd ed. Princeton: Princeton University Press, 1969.
AnS	Animal Series
AOTC	Abingdon Old Testament Commentaries
AUSS	*Andrews University Seminary Studies*
AV	Authorized Version
B. Qam.	Bava Qamma
BASOR	*Bulletin of the American Schools of Oriental Research*
BBR	*Bulletin for Biblical Research*
BCT	*The Bible and Critical Theory*
BDB	Brown, Francis, S. R. Driver, and Charles A. Briggs. *A Hebrew and English Lexicon of the Old Testament*. Oxford: Clarendon, 1907.
BETL	Bibliotheca Ephemeridum Theologicarum Lovaniensium
Bib	*Biblica*
BibInt	*Biblical Interpretation*
BioN	*Biota Neotropica*
BJS	Brown Judaic Studies
B&P	*Biology & Philosophy*
BRT	*Behaviour Research and Therapy*
BT	*The Bible Translator*

BTB	*Biblical Theology Bulletin*
BZAW	*Beihefte zur Zeitschrift für die alttestamentliche Wissenschaft*
CBQ	*Catholic Biblical Quarterly*
CC	Continental Commentaries
CEHES	Cambridge Elements: Histories of Emotions and the Senses
ch(s).	chapter(s)
CI	*Critical Inquiry*
CIT	Current Issues in Theology
CLR	*Cultura, lenguaje y representación: revista de estudios culturales de la Universitat Jaume*
CNTC	Calvin's New Testament Commentaries
COTC	Calvin's Old Testament Commentaries
CRB	*Comptes Rendus Biologies*
CSHB	Critical Studies in the Hebrew Bible
CTC	*Culture, Theory, and Critique*
CurBio	*Current Biology*
CurBR	*Currents in Biblical Research*
DCH	Clines, David J. A., ed. *Dictionary of Classical Hebrew*. 9 vols. Sheffield: Sheffield Phoenix, 1993–2014.
DTMT	Dictionaries of Talmud, Midrash and Targum
Dtr	Deuteronomistic (History; writer); Deuteronomist
EarthB	Earth Bible
EC	Epworth Commentaries
EDNT	Balz, Horst, and Gerhard Schneider, eds. *Exegetical Dictionary of the New Testament*. ET. 3 vols. Grand Rapids: Eerdmans, 1990–1993.
EE	*Evolutionary Ecology*
ESV	English Standard Version
ET	English translation
FAT	Forschungen zum Alten Testament
FCI	Focus on Contemporary Issues
FM	*Frontiers in Microbiology*
fol(s).	folio(s)
Gos. Nic.	Gospel of Nicodemus
Gos. Pet.	Gospel of Peter
Gos. Thom.	Gospel of Thomas
HACL	History, Archaeology, and Culture of the Levant

HAR	*Hebrew Annual Review*
HBM	Hebrew Bible Monographs
HNTC	Harper's New Testament Commentaries
HS	*Hebrew Studies*
HT	Helps for Translators
HTS	Harvard Theological Studies
HvTSt	*Hervormde teologiese studies*
IBC	Interpretation: A Bible Commentary for Teaching and Preaching
ICC	International Critical Commentary
IDS	*In die Skriflig*
Int	*Interpretation*
IntF	*Interface Focus*
JAJSup	Journal of Ancient Judaism Supplement Series
JAVMA	*Journal of the American Veterinary Medical Association*
JBL	*Journal of Biblical Literature*
JBQ	*Jewish Bible Quarterly*
JCAS	*Journal for Critical Animal Studies*
JHerp	*Journal of Herpetology*
JHI	*Journal of the History of Ideas*
JME	*Journal of Medical Entomology*
JNSL	*Journal of Northwest Semitic Languages*
JPSBC	JPS Bible Commentary
JRP	*Journal of Research in Personality*
JS	*Journal for Semitics*
JSNT	*Journal for the Study of the New Testament*
JSOT	*Journal for the Study of the Old Testament*
JSOTSup	Journal for the Study of the Old Testament Supplement Series
JSP	*Journal for the Study of the Pseudepigrapha*
KJV	King James Version
LCC	Library of Christian Classics
LHBOTS	The Library of Hebrew Bible/Old Testament Studies
LM	*Le Museon*
LSJ	Liddell, Henry George, Robert Scott, Henry Stuart Jones. *A Greek-English Lexicon*. 9th ed. with revised supplement. Oxford: Clarendon, 1996.
LXX	Septuagint

MCA	Meridian, Crossing Aesthetics
MdB	Le Monde de la Bible
MoS	Moreshet Series
Mosaic	*Mosaic: An Interdisciplinary Critical Journal*
MT	Masoretic Text
NAB	New American Bible
NAC	New American Commentary
Natur	*Naturwissenschaften*
NEA	Near Eastern Archaeology
NIB	Keck, Leander E., ed. *The New Interpreter's Bible.* 12 vols. Nashville: Abingdon, 1994–2004.
NIV	New International Version
NJPS	Tanakh: The Holy Scriptures: The New JPS Translation according to the Traditional Hebrew Text
NKJV	New King James Version
NRSV	New Revised Standard Version
OBO	Orbis Biblicus et Orientalis
OJB	Orthodox Jewish Bible
OST	Oxford Shakespeare Topics
OTL	Old Testament Library
PB	*Plant Biology*
PCPS	Perspectives in Continental Philosophy Series
PILR	*Pace International Law Review*
Pirqe R. El.	Pirqe Rabbi Eliezer
PMLA	*Publications of the Modern Language Association of America*
Postm	*Postmedieval: A Journal of Medieval Cultural Studies*
PQ	*The Philosophical Quarterly*
Praec. ger. reip.	Plutarch, *Praecepta gerendae reipublicae*
Prog.	Aphthonius, *Progymnasmata*
RBS	Resources for Biblical Study
RC	Routledge Classics
RC	*Religion Compass*
RevExp	*Review and Expositor*
RSV	Revised Standard Version
S&A	*Society & Animals*
ScEs	*Science et esprit*
SemeiaSt	Semeia Studies
SHBC	Smyth & Helwys Bible Commentary

SJOT	*Scandinavian Journal of the Old Testament*
SocRev	*Socialist Review*
Song. Rab.	Song of Songs Rabbah
SPJNZ	*Social Policy Journal of New Zealand*
SR	*Studies in Religion*
StBr	Stanford Briefs
SymS	Symposium Series
T. Job	Testament of Job
TEAS	Twayne's English Authors Series
TS	*Theological Studies*
TScot	*Theology in Scotland*
TTC	Transdisciplinary Theological Colloquia
USQR	*Union Seminary Quarterly Review*
v(v).	verse(s)
VC	*Vigiliae Chrisianae*
VeE	*Verbum et Ecclesia*
VRev	*Victorian Review*
VT	*Vetus Testamentum*
VTSup	Supplements to Vetus Testamentum
Vulg.	Vulgate
WBC	Word Biblical Commentary
WBComp	Westminster Bible Companion
WisdC	Wisdom Commentary
YCS	Yale Classical Studies
ZAW	*Zeitschrift für die alttestamentliche Wissenschaft*
ZDPV	*Zeitschrift des Deutschen Palästina-Vereins*

Introduction:
Difference, Identity, Indistinction

Arthur Walker-Jones and Suzanna R. Millar

The Bible teems with birds, beasts, and creeping things. There are snakes, sheep, goats, cattle, oxen, camels, donkeys, mules, horses, pigs, dogs, foxes, jackals, wolves, ostriches, sparrows, nighthawks, seagulls, sand grouse, storks, hawks, eagles, vultures, ospreys, buzzards, kites, sparrows, ravens, and crows. There are locusts, crickets, grasshoppers, ants, mice, rock hyraxes, lions, leopards, mountain goats, gazelles, aurochs, and onagers.[1] Some, such as nighthawks, appear only once; others, such as sheep, hundreds of times. Barely a biblical book is without other creatures. They slither, creep, walk, run, and fly through the pages. They give birth (Job 39:2–3), build homes (Ps 104:17), suffer want (Joel 1:17–18), and fast in sackcloth (Jon 4:7–9). Lions roar, birds sing, wild asses and horses laugh (Job 39:7, 22). They cry out to God (Job 38:41, Joel 1:20), seek food from God (Ps 104:21, 27), and are watched over by God (Matt 10:29 // Luke 12:6). They are God's covenant partners (Gen 9:9–10, Hos 2:18), and some, such as Balaam's ass (Num 22:22–30), seem to have an individual relationship with God. Leading figures in Judaism and Christianity lived much of their lives with other animals: Abraham, Moses, and David were shepherds, and Jesus's life and teachings are full of nonhuman animals.

Yet such creatures have received sparse attention in biblical studies. Considered to be mere metaphors, passive objects, or background embellishment, they are often skipped over, as scholars hurry on to the human story. Since evolutionary biologists and anthropologists understand humans as coevolving with other species (e.g., Pierotti and Fogg

---

1. Not all of these identifications are certain, as there has been limited research to identify the referents of individual Hebrew and Greek terms.

2017), historical and literary criticism that largely ignores these other species appears anthropocentric and unscientific. This volume shows the importance of attending to these nonhuman animals in their own right. It does so in conversation with the interdisciplinary field of animal studies.[2] Animal studies scholar and historian of religion Aaron S. Gross (2012, 1) argues for a "multifaceted, critical 'animal hermeneutics.'" The present volume traces the contours of a biblical animal hermeneutics and the contributions it can make to both biblical interpretation and animal studies.

In this introduction, we first explain the background that has framed biblical studies. We then discuss biblical animals and animal studies and the interaction between them. Finally, we introduce the framework of approaches that will structure the volume—difference, identity, and indistinction. We explain each approach, survey the biblical scholarship that has so far emerged, and indicate how the chapters of this volume contribute to the conversation.

Human Superiority and Anthropocentrism

Nonhuman animals have been too often overlooked in biblical studies. Underlying this neglect is an assumption of human superiority, such that nonhuman entities become superfluous. This ideology has deep roots in the Western scientific, philosophical, and theological traditions. Until quite recently, Western science largely followed René Descartes, who held that animals were without thought, language, or self-consciousness and operated like automata. It is a short step from this to the view of subsequent Cartesian philosophers that animals could not feel pain or suffer. As Nicolas Malebranche (1638–1715) puts it: "They eat without pleasure, cry without pain, grow without knowing it; they desire nothing, fear nothing, know nothing" (Harrison 1992, 219). Such a view justified scientific experimentation on other species. In the nineteenth century, vivisection became popular—dissecting individuals while they were still alive.

Science, however, is undermining the anthropocentric assumption that certain human characteristics—such as Descartes's triad of thought,

---

2. Some use different names for the field, or overlapping fields. For instance, *critical animal studies* often indicates an ethical commitment to veganism, and *animality studies* may indicate a focus on what it means to understand humans as animals. The editors have chosen *animal studies* as the most inclusive designation and have not required contributors to use particular terminology for the field.

language, and self-consciousness—are unique. Even theological criteria such as religion and morality find parallels in other species. Consider this memory test: The numbers one to nine are displayed randomly on a touch screen. When you touch the number one, the other numbers are hidden by squares. Now you must touch the squares concealing two to nine in ascending order, and if you succeed, you will receive a reward. When this game was played by chimpanzees and humans, the former were, in general, better than the latter. One chimpanzee was even more adept than graduate students (Inoue and Matsuzawa 2007). In this particular area of intelligence, then, humans cannot claim total superiority. Researchers have also found what appears to be altruism in rats. They placed rats in pens with two cages—one with treats and one with another rat. Rather than keep the treats for themselves, most rats released their caged companion and shared the bounty (Jabr 2012). We should thus consider carefully the empirical evidence before we claim certain characteristics as uniquely human.

But if the characteristics themselves are not uniquely superior, perhaps the forms they take in humans are? Arguments like this are often circular: human intelligence is assumed as the norm; other species do not display this kind of intelligence; therefore, nonhuman intelligence is nonnormative and inferior. The argument arrives back at the premise with which it began. By this reasoning, the superior intelligences of other species, such as the navigational intelligence of pigeons, is denigrated or ignored. Many biologists now recognize that using human language and cognition as a norm is anthropocentric, and they seek to understand not the level of humanlike language or intelligence attainable by other species but the language and intelligence of those species on their own terms (Fudge 2002, 113–50).

Despite the scientific evidence casting serious doubt over any straightforward assumption of human superiority, this assumption lingers on in society and in biblical scholarship. Western, human culture has a unique, complex, and deeply ambiguous relationship with other species.[3] Yet these material and cultural relations are largely invisible to most Westerners. Their main awareness of relationship with other species may be through

---

3. The dominant scholarly tradition has been primarily Western in orientation, and the editors of this book both write from a Western social location. As noted later in this introduction, non-Western societies may offer alternative ways of understanding nonhuman animals that are vital for correcting the anthropocentrism of the academy.

their pets. The current culture of keeping pets developed in Europe as people moved away from farms and extended families and into cities and nuclear families during the industrial revolution. Recently, a multibillion-dollar pet care industry has developed, providing food, treats, toys, clothes, veterinary care, and even health insurance for these pets. Yet this relationship remains anthropocentric because pets tend to be included in human families as honorary humans. The love and care lavished on them is not generally extended to other species or even to other members of the same species. Those who include a purebred dog in their family seldom extend that care to the other members of the breed that may suffer from genetic diseases caused by breeding, or the dogs of all breeds that suffer in scientific experiments. Moreover, the beloved pet dog under the table does not generally cause people to reflect ethically on the chickens, pigs, and cattle on their table (Fudge 2002, 9–10). They get their meat and groceries from a supermarket and have no relationship with the animals that produce their food.

Western cultures and languages facilitate the invisibility of other species and obscure the ethical issues. We are "human"; they are "animal." Jacques Derrida (2008, x, 34, 47–51) notes the absurdity that this word *animal* claims to sum up the great diversity of other-than-human species. Such usage underscores human superiority and facilitates the exploitation of all other species as well as of humans identified with nonhuman animals. We are "flesh"; they are "meat." Carol Adams (1993, 41) and Erica Fudge (2002, 36) observe that this obscures how we are eating the flesh of other sentient beings. Examples could be multiplied. We have "skin"; they have "hide." We are "murdered"; they are "slaughtered." We are "he" and "she";[4] they are "it." The English language thus helps create a social reality that maintains the superiority of humans and denies the suffering of other species. We have limited resources to circumvent this, but terminology that moves beyond the binary can be helpful. In this volume, many contributors speak of "other-than-human animals," "nonhuman animals," or "other animals." *Homo sapiens* are, after all, also animals.

The anthropocentrism of Western society and language is intertwined with other oppressive ideologies. Nonhuman animals are embedded in the wider matrices of relations that structure society, participating in kyriarchal

---

4. As we problematize the human-animal binary in language, we must also note the problems of the male-female binary inherent in these human pronouns.

and colonial power dynamics. These power dynamics are realized through multiple media—physical, institutional, and ideological. And the media that subjugate marginalized people groups (e.g., women and ethnic minorities) mimic and are entangled with those that subjugate animals. To take a historical example, in the sedentary lifestyle offered by the agricultural revolution, the domestication of nonhuman animals in the fields went hand in hand with the domestication of women at home. The one for husbandry, the other for her husband—speciesism intertwined with sexism. Throughout history, a negative association with animal nature has justified the oppression of women and so-called primitive peoples. These mutually reinforcing oppressions linger on in society and must be mutually dismantled.

Biblical Studies and Animals

Identity-based and ideological criticisms stress the fundamental necessity of acknowledging the social location and biases of biblical writers and readers. Patriarchal cultures have produced patriarchal texts and interpretations, harmful to women. Imperialist cultures have produced imperialist texts and interpretations, harmful to the colonized. And, we stress, anthropocentric cultures have produced anthropocentric texts and interpretations, harmful to nonhumans. The Bible is the product of human authors, writing largely in their own human interest. The voices of nonhumans (if heard at all) will be muted, mediated, and distorted, and we are justified in reading with a hermeneutic of suspicion. On the other hand, though, those authors probably lived much closer to nonhuman animals than do most modern Western biblical scholars. The worldview of biblical authors was not freighted with the conceptual baggage of Cartesian dualisms or the daily realities of sanitized, postindustrial living that shape the perspectives of its interpreters. The Bible may thus provide forgotten insights into animal lives.

Attention to animals may have deep ramifications across biblical studies. We must attend to nonhuman animals to better understand Israelite history and material culture (constituted by the realia and dynamics of an agricultural-pastoral society), imagery and figurative language (populated by multiple species), theology and anthropology (as writers imagine their God and themselves through animal others), language and translation (with the identification of many species still uncertain). Animal studies must also enter conversation with ecological, feminist, and postcolonial biblical interpreters, to condemn the entangled oppressions of animals, earth, women, the colonized, and others. Until recently, nonhuman animals have been largely ignored within biblical scholarship. As shown in the survey of scholarship below, however, this is beginning to change. Particularly significant has been the recent rise of animal studies—a field with great potential for productive interaction with biblical studies.

Animal Studies

Animal studies is a growing interdisciplinary field of inquiry that critically analyzes the nature and role of nonhuman animals and human-animal relationships across literature, culture, media, politics, and society. It has established itself through dedicated academic programs, journals, and conferences. Several universities worldwide now offer qualifications in animal studies and related fields, and law schools provide degrees with animal-rights specializations.[5] Some schools have animal studies institutes or centers.[6] There are now two dozen animal studies journals, many academic publishers have animal studies series, and textbooks and handbooks are available (Waldau 2013; McCance 2013; Kalof 2017).[7] Animal studies has made its presence felt in the study of religion: the American Academic of Religion hosts a productive Animals and Religion section, whose participants have produced many books in this area (e.g.,

---

5. Yale Law School (n.d.), for instance, has a Law, Ethics, and Animals Program. Animal studies programs are offered by Michigan State University (n.d.; master's and doctoral specializations) and New York University (n.d.; undergraduate minor and MA program).

6. Sheffield University, for example, has an Animal Studies Research Centre (Sheffield Animal Studies Research Centre n.d.)

7. For animal studies journals, see Animals and Society Institute n.d. Publishers that have animal studies series include Baylor University Press, Berghahn, Bloomsbury, Brill, Columbia University Press, Duke University Press, Johns Hopkins University Press, Oneworld, Oxford University Press, Palgrave Macmillan, Penn State University Press, Routledge, SCM, State University of New York Press, Temple University Press, University of Chicago Press, University of Georgia Press, University of Hawaii Press, University of Illinois Press, University of Michigan Press, University of Minnesota Press, University of Scranton Press, University of Sydney Press, University of Tennessee Press, and University of Virginia Press. Reaktion Books published both Erica Fudge's (2002) *Animal*, a very accessible introduction to animal studies, and a series of volumes on various individual species, for example, *Dog* (McHugh 2004), *Pigeon* (Allen 2009), *Lion* (Jackson 2010), and *Sheep* (Armstrong 2016).

Deane-Drummond and Clough 2009; Gross 2015; Hobgood-Oster 2008; Waldau and Patton 2006).

The Bible is often cited in animal studies literature, from basic introductions to the foundational works of key theorists. Primary attention is usually given to the primeval history (Gen 1–11), especially the creation narratives. Following Lynn White Jr. (1967), many animal studies scholars interpret the creation of humanity in the image of God and the human "dominion" over other species (Gen 1:26–28) to sanctify the human exploitation of animals. Adam's naming of other species is taken as an expression of power—one that intertwines with his oppressive naming of the woman (Adams 1993, 85) and leads to violence in the story of Cain and Abel (Derrida 2008, 42). This interpretation is taken as representative; indeed, in the Bible there is "nothing to challenge the over-all view, set down in Genesis, that man is the pinnacle of creation, that all the other creatures have been delivered into his hands" (Singer 1975, 195). This alleged ideology of Genesis is thought to have passed largely unaltered into Christian tradition, resulting almost inevitably in the Cartesian dualisms of human and animal, culture and nature (207–9; Haraway 1985, 66–68), making Christianity "the most anthropocentric religion the world had ever seen" (White 1967, 1205). The creation myths are thought to still underlie contemporary anthropocentrism; indeed, "much of the naturalized morality of our culture comes from this source" (Fudge 2002, 13).

The role of the Bible in perpetuating Western anthropocentrism must, of course, be taken very seriously. Yet, the narrative outlined above hugely oversimplifies both the biblical text and the history of its interpretation. While not all animal studies scholars accept it in precisely this form (e.g., see comments in McCance 2013, esp. 206–8; Waldau 2013, 173), it still predominates. The Genesis stories, though held to have huge repercussions for contemporary understandings of animals, are rarely treated in more than a cursory manner, and biblical texts other than Genesis are not often engaged. Biblical scholars have rarely entered these discussions but could have a crucial role in correcting the oversimplification. The chapters in this volume show how biblical studies can contribute significantly to animal studies and add much ambiguity, depth, breadth, and nuance to these uses of the Bible.

Until recently, biblical scholars seldom studied animals or discussed the ethics of human relations with nonhuman animals and their intersection with other oppressions. Several works summarize the historical, literary, and cultural evidence concerning nonhuman animals in the Bible (Bodenheimer 1935, 1960; Cansdale 1970; Hope 2005; Riede 2002). These, however, tend to include limited or outdated biological information. Richard Whitekettle (2001a, 2001b, 2002, 2003, 2005a, 2005b, 2006, 2008, 2009a, 2009b, 2011, 2014) is one of the few who has given thought to biblical Hebrew zoological taxonomy. Arthur Walker-Jones (2005) shows that translations may not accurately identify a species, and biological information can help to correct this. A few book-length studies of particular species have appeared—notably Brent Strawn (2005) on lions, Kenneth Way (2011) on donkeys, and Martin Heide and Joris Peters (2021) on camels. These studies make use of zooarchaeology—a burgeoning field whose rich resources are rarely tapped by biblical scholars (Strawn 2005, 77–128; Way 2011, 106–59; Heide and Peters 2021, 27–192; see also Collins 2001; Borowski 1998; Sasson 2010). These authors also attend to symbolic meanings, as does Tova Forti (2008, 2018), who examines animal symbolism in the books of Proverbs and Psalms. Strawn (2005, 289) has a brief reflection on the plight of contemporary lions, but generally these works do not raise the justice of human relations with other species. In sum, only a few biblical scholars have attended to nonhuman animals, the studies that use natural history and biology are dated, zooarchaeology is seldom discussed, and few analyze the justice of human relations with other species.

This has begun to change, particularly with the rise of animal studies and its influence on biblical studies. Pro-animal philosopher Matthew Calarco (2015) divides animal studies into three approaches—difference, identity, and indistinction. The parts of this book are organized around these approaches, modified to suit biblical studies. Calarco (e.g., 2015, 5) suggests the indistinction approach has the greatest political potential but recognizes the strengths of the difference and identity approaches and includes elements of each in his work. While his categories are not mutually exclusive, they have heuristic value as an overview of theorists in animal studies. We modify Calarco's categories and organize the chapters by emphasizing certain elements within Calarco's description of each. These modified emphases give us the titles for the parts of this book: (1) "Difference, Posthumanism, and Animality," (2) "Identification and Animal Rights," and (3) "Indistinction and Alternative Stories." These modifications are intended to indicate a movement away from anthropocentrism and highlight areas of current and potential research in biblical studies. The following section explains these approaches, reviews the literature in animal studies and biblical studies, and indicates how the chapters in this volume contribute to the discussion.[8]

Difference, Posthumanism, and Animality

We treat Calarco's difference approach first because this is the animal studies approach biblical scholars have engaged the most so far. Coming out of Continental philosophy, this approach rejects humanism's notion of a fixed human nature and an ethics based on that nature. Instead, it understands human nature as historical and socially conditioned and emphasizes the differences between humans. It is those differences—that encounter with the Other—that provide foundations for ethics. Nonhuman animals have been brought into this discussion in two main ways, seminally by Jacques Derrida (2008) in *The Animal That Therefore I Am*. First, as Derrida shows, Western philosophers have commonly (and problematically) defined human nature over against animal nature. But, second, if we must acknowledge the manifold differences between humans, how much more the differences between animals! There is no single dividing line between humans and animals but many dividing lines between and within species, many of which cut across each other. In this volume, we broaden the difference approach to include discussions of posthumanism and human animality, many of which follow in the spirit of Derrida. Several biblical scholars (including in this volume) have made contributions in this area, furthering the discussions in ways helpful for both animal studies and biblical studies. It should be noted, though, that this approach is often anthropocentric, in the sense that it is primarily concerned with what the study of animals tells us about humans. This primary concern with humans may contribute to this approach having been, as Calarco (2015, 46) notes, "somewhat removed from broader policy and political debates" about nonhuman animals.

This is true of the work of many biblical scholars within this approach. In Jennifer Koosed's (2014) *The Bible and Posthumanism*, the contributions by Ken Stone and Robert Seesengood centralize other animals, but most of the other chapters focus on human animality. Denise Kimber Buell,

---

8. In this introduction and the chapters that follow, we engage with literature available at the time of writing. Due to delays in publication, we regret that not all the literature available at the time of publication has been integrated into this volume. Notable examples include Atkins 2023; Jeong 2023; Olyan 2023; Waters 2022.

Heidi Epstein, Rhiannon Graybill, and George Aichele focus on humans. Hannah Strømmen, Benjamin Dunning, and Eric Meyer discuss the blurring of the line between humans and other animals, but primarily insofar as it affects our understanding of humanity. Hugh Pyper focuses on divinity, and Yvonne Sherwood and Stephen Moore on both humanity and divinity. Similarly, animal studies is only one of several perspectives and methods that Moore includes within what he calls "the nonhuman turn" in theory. As with Koosed's volume, Moore's (2017) *Gospel Jesuses and Other Nonhumans* focuses on human animality without much consideration of the animals themselves. Hannah Strømmen's (2018) *Biblical Animality after Jacques Derrida* is primarily concerned with posthumanism. She follows Derrida in interrogating how animals define what it means to be human. She shows that in a few key texts where the characterizations of the human, animal, and divine "might be fixed as detrimental to animal life lie also the possibilities of seeing animals radically otherwise" (1).

The essays in the difference part of this volume show that animal studies can continue and extend the conversation about posthumanism and animality in the Bible. Robert Seesengood draws on Derrida to argue that humans and monsters are alike in their transcendence over rudimentary animals. He expands Derrida's concept of the beast and the sovereign, finding this analogous to the relationship of the monstrous and the divine. Divine-human-animal relationships are also important for William Gruen, as he explores how animal symbolism is used to elucidate the identity of Jesus in Matthew and Luke. The animals reveal Jesus to be categorically problematic: he disrupts conventional boundary lines and provokes us to reconsider which differences are significant. Similarly, Peter Atkins examines the various perceived physical and mental differences that establish or cut across the human-animal boundary. He focusses on how John Calvin negotiates these issues in his interpretation of Dan 4. The differences between species are significant in Jacob Evers's interpretation of Isa 11. If ethics begins with my encounter with the Other, then I should not force that Other to conform to my norms but rather allow them to flourish in all their difference from me. Evers shows the ethical problems that emerge when animals' differences are ignored and their lives are conformed to human society.

Differences, of course, do not always run parallel to species lines. In his exploration of Ecclesiastes, Ken Stone shows how the human-animal distinction itself can have an ideological function internally to the human category, separating off some humans as being more closely related to animals than others. Stone's focus on animality places his chapter within this section of the volume; however, his conclusion could equally place him in Calarco's indistinction category. He notes that reflection on shared creaturely mortality could lead "to greater acknowledgment that all mortal creatures wish to enjoy the modest life God has given" and could lead us to work to foster their mutual flourishing. While this is an identification with animals, it is subtly different from the type of identification highlighted by identity theorists (see further below). Indeed, the fear of mortality is typically a driver of the human/animal binary (e.g., Alderman 2020). Instead, this is the type of identification that Calarco (2015, 4–5) refers to when he says that indistinction theorist note "the surprising ways in which human beings find themselves to be like animals." Stone's chapter thus intimates how an indistinction approach can, on the one hand, contribute to posthumanism and animality studies, and, on the other hand, lead to an ethical concern for better lived relations with other species.

Identity and Animal Rights

Biblical scholars have engaged less with the identity and indistinction approaches. The articles in these sections showcase the new conversations these approaches make possible—the cutting-edge ethical questions and new biblical interpretations. In contrast to the difference approach, which centralizes the differences between humans and between animals, the identity approach "founds its ethical and political frameworks on human-animal identity" (Calarco 2015, 3). As noted in the brief scientific overview above, the separation and superiority of the human species is an illusion. What is more (argue identity theorists), the similarities between humans and nonhuman animals (e.g., sentience and suffering) are ethically relevant. Humans should extend their moral sphere to include an equal consideration of the interests of all partners that are relevantly alike. In this approach, Calarco includes the major philosophical works commonly associated with the animal rights movement: Peter Singer's (2009) *Animal Liberation*, Tom Regan's (2004) *The Case for Animal Rights*, and Paola Cavalieri's (2001) *The Animal Question: Why Nonhuman Animals Deserve Human Rights*.

Only a few biblical scholars have related biblical interpretation to animal rights. An early contribution was Heather McKay's (2002) "Through the Eyes of Horses." She warns of "the human-centredness of literature and literary criticism" and that animals can "be abused by the pen of a human writer, or the mind of a human reader ... more often than we realize" (1). In particular, "Equines are demeaned by their perceived 'lack' of human qualities and their appropriate equine qualities are purloined to warn or insult humans. Other of the animals' qualities that could be admired, respected, and emulated are ignored, except, perhaps in the one story of Balaam's ass" (14). McKay was an early adopter of animal studies and recognized that the Bible and biblical interpretation are anthropocentric and ignore or devalue animal qualities to avoid identification and ethical responsibility.

The issue of animal justice, however, was slow to gain traction in biblical studies. Only in 2014 did chapters by Ken Stone and Robert Seesengood again raise the question (in Koosed 2014). In the same year, Michael Gilmour (2014) explored the biblical resources for a Christian animal-rights ethic in *Eden's Other Residents*. Recently, Saul Olyan (2019; Olyan and Rosenblum 2021) has given attention to animal ethics of biblical legal codes. Given this paucity, there is room for many contributions to biblical studies. These contributions would be significant for animal studies because of the history and ongoing influence of biblical interpretation in animal-rights activism.

Michael Gilmour's chapter that begins the identity section traces the interpretation of the Bible in animal activist circles going back to the 1800s as either "blood-soaked" or "animal-friendly." He hopes this is a first step in developing within biblical scholarship an activist animal hermeneutics. Likewise, Margaret Cohen notes that "the moral sphere surrounding humans should logically expand to include other species that are relatively alike." She investigates texts about forests, highlighting the "shared living-being-ness" of creatures (human, animal, and even plant) and its ethical repercussions. Jaime Waters, too, stresses the importance of empathy for nonhuman animals, which are not so very different from humans. Indeed, even characteristics held to be quintessentially human, such as intelligence, may be found in other species. In texts such as Jer 8–9, nonhuman animals "sometimes even have more understanding than humans." Waters's reading of this text has implications for contemporary animal welfare and ecological degradation. Calarco limits his discussion to this positive identification of humans with animals, but identification—if it is accompanied by devaluation—can also have a sinister side. There is a long history across cultures of identifying outsiders with animals to legitimate hatred, oppression, and war. In his chapter, Dong Hyeon Jeong explores the complex role of imperialism in the negative identification with animals in 2 Peter. Feminist and postcolonial criticism rightly urges a deconstruction of such dehumanization. But, for the animal studies scholar, such deconstruction must also entail the revaluation of the nonhuman (see Millar 2022a).

Indistinction and Alternative Stories

The final section of this volume deals with indistinction. Calarco takes this concept from Gilles Deleuze (1987) and Giorgio Agamben (2004) and modifies it with the work of Rosi Braidotti (2013), Val Plumwood (1993), and Donna Haraway (1985). These theorists attempt to remove the human as the starting point for ethical reflection, to move beyond the human-animal binary, and to find new ways of thinking and doing that promote the mutual flourishing of all species. Haraway, herself trained as both a scientist and a philosopher, appreciates Derrida's recognition that such disciplines have treated animals as objects and his attention to the real cat looking at him. "Yet," she notes, "he did not seriously consider an alternative form of engagement ... one that risked knowing something more about cats and *how to look back*, perhaps even scientifically, biologically, and *therefore* also philosophically and intimately." "He came right to the edge of respect," she continues, but "he did not become curious about what the cat might actually be doing, feeling, thinking, or perhaps making available to him" (Haraway 2008, 20). Derrida's approach may remain anthropocentric in this respect. Haraway is typical of these indistinction theorists in wanting to move beyond binaries, hopeful that "positive knowledge of and with animals might just be possible ... if it is not built on the Great Divides" (21). She seeks to develop new stories and practices of respectful and responsible relationship with companion species that go beyond philosophical abstraction or scientific objectivity: "Why did Derrida not ask, even in principle, if a Gregory Bateson or Jane Goodall or Marc Bekoff or Barbara Smuts or many others have met the gaze of living, diverse animals and in response undone and redone themselves and their sciences?" (21). Haraway here refers to the work of scientists such as Barbara Smuts, who wanted to be the neutral, scientific observer of a baboon troop but had to change her methodology when she realized the baboons wanted to interact with her. Such scientists have engaged members of other species as subjects and been changed by the encounter.

Few biblical scholars have engaged these theorists or this approach. Haraway's ideas are brought into recent interpretations of Gen 2–3

(Walker-Jones 2008; Midson 2019) and Job (Millar 2022b), and Ken Stone's (2018) *Reading the Hebrew Bible with Animal Studies* owes much to her work. Stone shows how zooarchaeology and the growing body of biological research on animal affect, language, intelligence, morality, and religion might illuminate biblical history and literature. As erudite and methodologically sophisticated as his work is, it is far from the last word. It is, rather, a model of animal hermeneutics that has many applications.

Moving beyond binaries has implications for the understanding of metaphor: the line between tenor and vehicle becomes indistinct or blurred. In her contribution to this volume, Anne Létourneau examines the reverberating connotations within the metaphorical structure, the back-and-forth interplay between the various images that defies any unidirectional understanding of metaphor. Similarly, Jared Beverly notes the blurring of tenor and vehicle—of human and animal—in the Song of Songs's depictions of shepherd and sheep, challenging a straightforward binary understanding. For Haraway (2008, 4), animal "figures are at the same time creatures of imagined possibility and creatures of fierce and ordinary reality; the dimensions tangle and require response." Literary encounters with animals are always tied up with the writers' and readers' encounters with actual animals. The prevalence of the imagery of sheep and goats in the Bible depends on relationships with real sheep and goats. Thus, Brian Tipton's chapter uses Rosi Braidotti's "neoliteral" reading strategy, which aims to liberate animals from the "empire of the sign," and reads parabolic birds as real birds in the Gospel of Mark. Tipton emphasizes the entanglement of human and nonhuman lives: both are "siblings in the 'kin-dom' of God." Such entanglements are stressed by Timothy Sandoval, too, as he examines the biological realities of coevolution and niche construction between humans and livestock. These insights into interspecies relationships illuminate Proverbs' exhortations to animal welfare. Suzanna Millar also examines biological entanglements, focusing on maggots, which break down physical and conceptual boundaries in Job. Though generally considered insignificant and detestable, they are productive thinking partners for reflection on human-animal indistinction.

Indistinction theorists seek overlooked practices and stories that might support the flourishing of all creatures. In this regard, Indigenous peoples may have better ways of thinking and being with other species. In this volume, Brian Fiu Kolia offers Samoan storytelling as a means to explore the story of Balaam's ass, alongside the Samoan tale of a shark who was given the honorific, chiefly title Tamasoaalii. He demonstrates how other species can be understood as agents and can communicate ethics and values.

Conclusion

Human superiority cannot be taken as a given, and uncritical anthropocentrism must be challenged within biblical studies. In dialogue with animal studies, this volume seeks to do this. It continues the productive conversations that have already been started by biblical scholars engaging with difference approaches to animal studies. It also makes new inroads into the identity and indistinction approaches, where biblical contributions have so far been lacking. Two responses conclude the volume—from a Hebrew Bible scholar (William P. Brown) and an animal studies scholar (Robert R. MacKay). Each reflects on the potential of these discussions to influence their respective disciplines. We end with an afterword, suggesting areas for further research and reflecting on the pedagogical implications of this volume. We hope the volume offers an animal hermeneutics that supports the flourishing of all creatures.

Works Cited

Adams, Carol J. 1993. *The Sexual Politics of Meat: A Feminist-Vegetarian Critical Theory*. New York: Continuum.
Agamben, Giorgio. 2004. *The Open: Man and Animal*. MCA. Stanford, CA: Stanford University Press.
Alderman, Isaac. 2020. *The Animal at Unease with Itself: Death Anxiety and the Animal-Human Boundary in Genesis 2–3*. Lanham, MD: Lexington Books/Fortress Academic.
Allen, Barbara. 2009. *Pigeon*. AnS. London: Reaktion.
Animals and Society Institute. N.d. "Human-Animal Studies Journals." https://www.animalsandsociety.org/human-animal-studies/human-animal-studies-journals.
Armstrong, Philip. 2016. *Sheep*. AnS. London: Reaktion.
Atkins, Peter Joshua. 2023. *The Animalising Affliction of Nebuchadnezzar in Daniel 4*. LHBOTS 733. London: Bloomsbury T&T Clark.
Bodenheimer, Friedrich S. 1935. *Animal Life in Palestine: An Introduction to the Problems of Animal Ecology and Zoogeography*. Jerusalem: Mayer.
———. 1960. *Animals and Man in Bible Lands*. Leiden: Brill.

Borowski, Oded. 1998. *Every Living Thing: Daily Use of Animals in Ancient Israel*. Walnut Creek, CA: Altamira.
Braidotti, Rosi. 2013. *The Posthuman*. Cambridge: Polity.
Calarco, Matthew. 2015. *Thinking through Animals: Identity, Difference, Indistinction*. StBr. Stanford, CA: Stanford University Press.
Cansdale, George S. 1970. *All the Animals of the Bible Lands*. Grand Rapids: Zondervan.
Cavalieri, Paola. 2001. *The Animal Question: Why Nonhuman Animals Deserve Human Rights*. New York: Oxford University Press.
Collins, Billie Jean. 2001. *A History of the Animal World in the Ancient Near East*. Leiden: Brill.
Deane-Drummond, Celia, and David Clough, eds. 2009. *Creaturely Theology: On God, Humans and Other Animals*. London: SCM.
Deleuze, Gilles, and Guattari Félix. 1987. *A Thousand Plateaus: Capitalism and Schizophrenia*. Translated by Brian Massumi. Minneapolis: University of Minnesota Press.
Derrida, Jacques. 2008. *The Animal That Therefore I Am*. Edited by Marie-Louise Mallet. Translated by David Wills. PCPS. New York: Fordham University Press.
Forti, Tova. 2008. *Animal Imagery in the Book of Proverbs*. Leiden: Brill.
———. 2018. *"Like a Lone Bird on a Roof": Animal Imagery and the Structure of Psalms*. CSHB 10. University Park, PA: Eisenbrauns.
Fudge, Erica. 2002. *Animal*. FCI. London: Reaktion.
Gilmour, Michael J. 2014. *Eden's Other Residents: The Bible and Animals*. Eugene, OR: Cascade.
Gross, Aaron S. 2012. "Introduction and Overview." Pages 1–23 in *Animals and the Human Imagination: A Companion to Animal Studies*. Edited by Aaron S. Gross and Anne Vallely. New York: Columbia University Press.
———. 2015. *The Question of the Animal and Religion: Theoretical Stakes, Practical Implications*. New York: Columbia University Press.
Haraway, Donna. 1985. "A Cyborg Manifesto: Science, Technology, and Socialist Feminism in the 1980s." *SocRev* 80:65–107.
———. 2008. *When Species Meet*. Minneapolis: University of Minnesota Press.
Harrison, Peter. 1992. "Descartes on Animals." *PQ* 42:219–27.
Heide, Martin, and Joris Peters. 2021. *Camels in the Biblical World*. HACL 10. University Park, PA: Eisenbrauns.

Hobgood-Oster, Laura. 2008. *Holy Dogs and Asses: Animals in the Christian Tradition*. Champaign: University of Illinois Press.

Hope, Edward R. 2005. *All Creatures Great and Small: Living Things in the Bible*. HT. New York: United Bible Societies.

Inoue, Sana, and Tetsuro Matsuzawa. 2007. "Working Memory of Numerals in Chimpanzees." *CurBio* 17:1004–5. https://doi.org/10.1016/j.cub.2007.10.027.

Jabr, Ferris. 2012. "Rats Display Altruism." *Scientific American Mind*. https://tinyurl.com/SBL06107b.

Jackson, Deirdre. 2010. *Lion*. AnS. London: Reaktion.

Jeong, Dong Hyeon. 2023. *With the Wild Beasts, Learning from Trees*. Semeia. Atlanta: SBL Press.

Kalof, Linda, ed. 2017. *The Oxford Handbook of Animal Studies*. New York: Oxford University Press.

Koosed, Jennifer L. 2014. *The Bible and Posthumanism*. SemeiaSt 74. Atlanta: SBL Press.

McCance, Dawne. 2013. *Animal Studies: An Introduction*. Albany: State University of New York Press.

McHugh, Susan. 2004. *Dog*. London: Reaktion.

McKay, Heather A. 2002. "Through the Eyes of Horses: Representation of the Horse Family in the Hebrew Bible." Pages 127–41 in *Sense and Sensitivity: Essays on Reading the Bible in Memory of Robert Carrol*. Edited by Alastair G. Hunter and Philip R. Davies. Sheffield: Sheffield Academic.

Michigan State University. N.d. "Graduate Certificate in Animal Studies: Social Science and Humanities Perspectives." https://tinyurl.com/SBL06107a.

Midson, Scott. 2019. "Humus and Sky Gods: Partnership and Post/Humans in Genesis 2 and the Chthulucene." *Sophia* 58:689–98.

Millar, Suzanna R. 2022a. "Dehumanisation as Derision or Delight? Countering Class-Prejudice and Species-Prejudice in Job." *BibInt* 30:150–70.

———. 2022b. "The Ecology of Death in the Book of Job." *BibInt* 30:265–93.

Moore, Stephen D. 2017. *Gospel Jesuses and Other Nonhumans: Biblical Criticism Post-Poststructuralism*. SemeiaSt 89. Atlanta: SBL Press.

New York University. N.d. "NYU Animal Studies." http://as.nyu.edu/environment/animal-studies.html.

Olyan, Saul M. 2019. "Are There Legal Texts in the Hebrew Bible That Evince a Concern for Animal Rights?" *BibInt* 27:321–39.

———. 2023. *Animal Rights in the Hebrew Bible*. Oxford: Oxford University Press.

Olyan, Saul M., and Jordan D. Rosenblum. 2021. *Animals and the Law in Antiquity*. BJS 368. Providence, RI: Brown Judaic Studies.

Pierotti, Raymond John, and Brandy R. Fogg. 2017. *The First Domestication: How Wolves and Humans Coevolved*. New Haven: Yale University Press.

Plumwood, Val. 1993. *Feminism and the Mastery of Nature*. New York: Routledge.

Regan, Tom. 2004. *The Case for Animal Rights: Updated with a New Preface*. Berkeley: University of California Press.

Riede, Peter. 2002. *Im Spiegel der Tiere: Studien zum Verhältnis von Mensch und Tiere im alten Israel*. Schweiz: Universitätsverlag Freiburg; Göttingen: Vandenhoeck & Ruprecht.

Sasson, Aharon. 2010. *Animal Husbandry in Ancient Israel: A Zooarchaeological Perspective on Livestock Exploitation, Herd Management and Economic Strategies*. AAArch. London: Equinox.

Sheffield University. N.d. "Sheffield Animal Studies Research Centre." http://sheffieldanimals.group.shef.ac.uk/.

Singer, Peter. 1975. *Animal Liberation: A New Ethics for Our Treatment of Animals*. New York: Avon Books.

———. 2009. *Animal Liberation: The Definitive Classic of the Animal Movement*. Updated ed. New York: Ecco Book/Harper Perennial.

Stone, Ken. 2018. *Reading the Hebrew Bible with Animal Studies*. Stanford, CA: Stanford University Press.

Strawn, Brent A. 2005. *What Is Stronger Than a Lion? Leonine Image and Metaphor in the Hebrew Bible and the Ancient Near East*. OBO 212. Fribourg: Academic Press.

Strømmen, Hannah M. 2018. *Biblical Animality after Jacques Derrida*. SemeiaSt 91. Atlanta: SBL Press.

Waldau, Paul. 2013. *Animal Studies: An Introduction*. Oxford: Oxford University Press.

Waldau, Paul, and Kimberley Patton, eds. 2006. *A Communion of Subjects: Animals in Religion, Science, and Ethics*. New York: Columbia University Press.

Walker-Jones, Arthur. 2005. "The So-Called Ostrich in the God Speeches of the Book of Job (Job 39, 13–18)." *Bib* 86:494–510.

———. 2008. "Eden for Cyborgs: Ecocriticism and Genesis 2–3." *BibInt* 16:263–93.

Waters, Jaime L. 2022. *What Does the Bible Say about Animals?* Hyde Park, NY: New City.
Way, Kenneth C. 2011. *Donkeys in the Biblical World: Ceremony and Symbol.* HACL 2. Winona Lake, IN: Eisenbrauns.
White, Lynn, Jr. 1967. "The Historical Roots of Our Ecologic Crisis." *Science* 155:1203–7.
Whitekettle, Richard. 2001a. "Rats Are Like Snakes, and Hares Are Like Goats: A Study in Israelite Land Animal Taxonomy." *Bib* 82:345–62.
———. 2001b. "Where the Wild Things Are: Primary Level Taxa in Israelite Zoological Thought." *JSOT* 25:17–37.
———. 2002. "All Creatures Great and Small: Intermediate Level Taxa in Israelite Zoological Thought." *SJOT* 16:163–83.
———. 2003. "Of Mice and Wren: Terminal Level Taxa in Israelite Zoological Thought." *SJOT* 17:163–82.
———. 2005a. "Bugs, Bunny, or Boar? Identifying *Zîz* Animals of Psalms 50 and 80." *CBQ* 67:250–64.
———. 2005b. "The Raven as Kind and Kinds of Ravens: A Study in the Zoological Nomenclature of Leviticus 11,2–23." *ZAW* 117:509–28.
———. 2006. "Taming the Shrew, Shrike, and Shrimp: The Form and Function of Zoological Classification in Psalm 8." *JBL* 125:749–65.
———. 2008. "Forensic Zoology: Animal Taxonomy and Rhetorical Persuasion in Psalm l[50]." *VT* 58:404–19.
———. 2009a. "One if by and: Conjunctions, Taxonomic Development, and the Animals of Leviticus 11,26." *ZAW* 121:481–97.
———. 2009b. "Oxen Can Plow, but Women Can Ruminate: Animal Classification and the Helper in Genesis 2.18–24." *SJOT* 23:243–56.
———. 2011. "A Communion of Subjects: Zoological Classification and Human/Animal Relations in Psalm 104." *BBR* 21:173–87.
———. 2014. "Like a Fish and Shrimp out of Water: Identifying the *Dāg* and *Remeś* Animals of Habakkuk 1:14." *BBR* 24:491–503.
Yale Law School. N.d. "The Law, Ethics & Animals Program." https://law.yale.edu/animals.

Part 1
Difference, Posthumanism, and Animality

Wild Christology:
On Foxes, Birds, and the Son of Man

William "Chip" Gruen

The most common interpretation of Jesus's aphorism "Foxes have holes, and birds of the air have nests; but the Son of Man has nowhere to lay his head" understands the saying as a description of the hardships of Jesus's own itinerant mission.[1] Indeed, the narrative context of each Synoptic telling (Matt 8:19–21; Luke 9:57–59) shows Jesus using the saying to warn a potential disciple about the perils of life on the road. However, stepping back from this narrative situation and examining the animals used in the saying (i.e., foxes and birds) leads to additional interpretive possibilities. This paper postulates that the juxtaposition of the bird as a celestial animal and the fox as a chthonic animal can be read as symbolically potent. To unpack this possibility, this study explores other meanings for these animals using comparative and anthropological approaches.

Considering the bird and the fox in the symbol, myth, and ritual of a variety of religious and cultural contexts demonstrates their symbolic potency. Because these animals cross boundaries (biologically or behaviorally), each can be identified with liminal states of being, social relationships, and religious practices. Upon unpacking the verdant array of meanings connected to each animal, these associations are reintroduced into the context of Jesus's life and mission in the saying itself. This aphorism, and the use of the animal images within it, offers an opportunity for thought about Christology and cosmology for both ancient and modern readers of the text.

If one considers the animal imagery of the New Testament and other ancient Christian literature, one will see that pastoral animals such as

---

1. Unless otherwise stated, all biblical quotations follow the RSV.

lambs, sheep, and goats receive a great deal of attention. From very early in the history of reception, Jesus is both the "lamb of God" and "the good shepherd," providing significant grist for thinking about Christology, highlighting claims made about Jesus's ontological and functional attributes. In the history of interpretation, the texts containing these and other domesticated animals have inspired considerable scholarly scrutiny, while other texts, particularly those that reference undomesticated or wild animals, receive significantly less attention. Upon consideration of these less noticed wild animals, one might notice that they are given meanings that are often more complex and nuanced than the simple economic relationships of the domesticated animals. These complex meanings can be imagined as analogous to other identities and relationships, including consideration of the divine.

Before examining the particular sayings traditions in question, however, it is important to think about how this chapter fits into this volume and the field of animal studies more generally. The structure of this book uses Matthew Calarco's (2015, 3–5) rubric of animal studies, in particular the categories identity, difference, and indistinction. The *difference* approach—in which this chapter is situated—is influenced by posthumanism, particularly the way that representations of nonhuman animals are used to clarify human identities. This chapter takes this further, reflecting on how foxes and birds contribute to the depiction of Jesus's humanity and divinity as he disrupts conventional categorizations and provokes new ones. Indeed, the symbolic and metaphorical use of animals can contribute a great deal to understanding the historical and cultural understanding of gods, humans, and nonhuman animals over time. This understanding can in turn help to unpack the place of animals in the worldviews of human communities. These worldviews are not only artifacts of past beliefs and practices but also the antecedents to the current conversation, including issues of animal rights and animal justice. Sometimes these antecedents are foundations to be built on, and sometimes they are relics to be undone by a new generation. Nevertheless, to fully understand human-mediated conversations on animals, the context and history of those discursive structures is key.

By understanding the complexities of the use of animals, both wild and domestic, in primary-source texts, one can consider how human communities try to comprehend that which is most difficult to explain on its own. If one admits the possibility for a more nuanced view of nonhuman animals in these texts, one can start to see that nonhuman animals represent more than simply a commodity that can be bought, sold, and consumed. Instead, the use of nonhuman animal symbols is a way for communities to consider that which might otherwise be ineffable, such as divinity. Disjunction, a concept drawn from Jonathan Z. Smith's (1978, 309) *Map Is Not Territory*, provides an opportunity for the contemplation of some of the most difficult concepts in religious traditions. In this case, the disjunctions can be found between the wild and domestic, the nonhuman animal and the human, and the animal and the divine.

In this essay, I am interested in the complicated process of discerning christological theologies in nascent Christianity. I argue that the use of particular animal symbols is not random but represents human cultural negotiations of ideas that are difficult to express. For this reason, the tradition turns to metaphor, which relies heavily on symbols from the natural world, that is, foxes and birds.[2] However, the implications of this argument reach beyond christological controversies of ancient Christians into territory that may be of interest to animal studies more generally. This analysis helps in understanding the long history of meditation on animals, their meaning, and their connections to the rest of the cosmos. Nothing comes from nowhere, and the roots of present conversations on the dignity and sacredness of nonhuman animals lie in the distant past—a distant past that is evidenced by the cultural productions of antiquity, including biblical materials.

Sayings, Oral Traditions, and Incorporation into the Gospel Tradition

Before proceeding any further, here are the textual witnesses to the tradition from the extant gospel traditions:

> And a scribe came up and said to him, "Teacher, I will follow you wherever you go." And Jesus said to him, "*Foxes have holes, and birds of the air have nests; but the Son of man has nowhere to lay his head.*" Another of the disciples said to him, "Lord, let me first go and bury my father." But Jesus said to him, "Follow me, and leave the dead to bury their own dead." (Matt 8:19–22)

---

2. Though there is not room to deal with it here, it should be noted that a similar animal dyad is used in Matt 10:16 when Jesus tells his disciples to "be wise as serpents and innocent as doves." Here one gets the same juxtaposition of the chthonic and celestial, though as a metaphor for his followers rather than christological formulation.

As they were going along the road, a man said to him, "I will follow you wherever you go." And Jesus said to him, *"Foxes have holes, and birds of the air have nests; but the Son of man has nowhere to lay his head."* To another he said, "Follow me." But he said, "Lord, let me first go and bury my father." But he said to him, "Leave the dead to bury their own dead; but as for you, go and proclaim the kingdom of God." Another said, "I will follow you, Lord; but let me first say farewell to those at my home." Jesus said to him, "No one who puts his hand to the plow and looks back is fit for the kingdom of God." (Luke 9:57–62)

Jesus said: [The foxes have] the[ir holes] and the birds have [their] nest, but the Son of Man has no place to lay his head and rest. (Gos. Thom. 86)

Although there are some differences in how the saying is contextualized, the Q twosome, Matthew and Luke, incorporate the saying in a narrative about discipleship. Following a shared source, both stories follow the aphorism with a potential disciple's request that he be able to bury his father before joining Jesus's mission. Central to the discursive strategy in Q is the radical eschatology of the anticipation of the coming of the kingdom of God. Though the initial read of this sayings tradition might lead one to understand it as a departure from that eschatological focus, favoring a more worldly reading on homelessness, the use of the "Son of Man" language in the symbolic triad (foxes, birds, and Son of Man) reinforces the eschatological potential of the passage. That it may be about more than itinerancy and discipleship is further strengthened by the pairing of the urgency of the task at hand, that is, "let the dead bury their own dead," bringing the tradition more in line with Q eschatology.

Nevertheless, the history of the interpretation of the textual tradition is not particularly interesting, following the general theme of the hardship of being a disciple. A representative example of this facile interpretation comes from Ulrich Luz, in a commentary on Matthew. The author writes,

> By means of a sharp paradox Jesus points out the difficulty of discipleship. The coming judge of the world, the Son of Man, does not even have on earth what the foxes and the birds of the heaven take for granted. Although Matthew seems to be familiar with a tradition about Jesus' permanent residence, he will describe Jesus as constantly on the move. (Luz 2001, 17)

Likewise, in a commentary on the Lukan version, Eric Franklin (2001, 160) writes, "Discipleship now meant journeying with the Son of Man, who had nowhere to lay his head." Additionally, comments are often made about the callousness of Jesus's demand that a would-be disciple not bury his father, which demonstrates disregard for social obligations. Insofar as this Jesus saying serves a narrative role within Matthew and Luke, the gospel writers seem to understand the aphorism in a similar way. In particular, Luke follows this saying with the sending of the Seventy on a similarly itinerant mission; they are commanded to go out with "no purse, no bag, no sandals" (Luke 10:4).

However, it has long been recognized that many of the pithy sayings of Jesus, the so-called apophthegmata or pronouncement sayings, may have circulated independently of the literary contexts of the gospel traditions (Robbins 1992, 307). In fact, Rudolf Bultmann (1963, 28) speculates about this very saying that "it is plain that the dominical saying could have circulated without any framework." A related school of thought places these sayings in a specific tradition of Greek rhetoric, in particular the use of *chreia*. According to ancient Greek rhetorician Apthonius (*Prog.* 2–4), "a chreia is a concise remembrance aptly attributed to some person" (Gowler 2006, 133). David Gowler uses this particular aspect of Greek rhetorical and pedagogical practice to provide a context for the transmission and elaboration of the sayings tradition. This practice, he writes, includes the freedom of speakers or authors to "vary the wording, details, and dynamics of *chreiai* according to their ideological and rhetorical interests. Speakers/authors were taught and encouraged to make minor and/or major changes to bring clarity and persuasiveness to the point they wanted to make with a *chreia* in specific contexts" (Gowler 2006, 134). One type of embellishment he points to is expansion: "expanding a *chreia* by reciting or writing it at greater length and enlarging on the questions and responses expressed in it" (139).

This potential context echoes Claude Levi-Strauss's (1966, 19) concept of bricolage, which posits that the cultural creator, or in this case the compiler of a gospel tradition, makes use of materials at hand, incorporating them in a new and potentially creative way to create meaning. Inevitably, these new uses will sometimes reincorporate materials in a way that obscures their original or previous intent. Thus, the standard rhetorical practice of the time provides a context in which sayings could circulate free of narrative context only to be incorporated or reincorporated into a larger framework at the behest of the speaker/author. Thus, one can see Luke expanding the saying into a narrative context of itinerancy, Matthew placing the saying in the context of the calling and commission of the twelve disciples, and Thomas, keeping with the form of the sayings gospel, leaving the quote without narrative context.

Over time, these contexts become part of the written tradition and grow to be both conventional and expected. However, placing these sayings in the *chreia* tradition brings a number of other questions to light. If the narrative contexts of these sayings are embellished, how else might the sayings have been understood before they were incorporated in their current narrative form? What other interpretive possibilities exist that might make better sense of some of the details of the sayings that have often been glossed over or ignored in the reception of the tradition? Upon further reflection, the theme of itinerancy can be seen as secondary to other meanings that explain the selection of the fox and the bird.

The Synoptic Gospels tradition does not lack in animal allusions: ox and donkey, sheep and goats, swine, fish, and so on. Many of these animal images arise from the context of the economic realities of agro-pastoralist, first-century Galilee and Judea. Wild animals, such as the fox, are less often present. In fact, the fox only appears one other time in the New Testament, in an unrelated diatribe by Jesus against King Herod (Luke 13:32). Similarly, aside from Gos. Thom. 86, the fox does not appear in the Nag Hammadi Library. Likewise, the fox only makes a handful of appearances in the Hebrew Bible and noncanonical early Christian literature, none of which are germane to this analysis. When the fox does make the rare appearance in any of these collections, those references are, without exception, negative. The neutrality of the association of the fox in this saying stands out.

So, how should one understand the enigmatic use of this animal symbol?

Imagining the World

Before continuing with the analysis of the passages in question, it will be helpful to offer up a different context for understanding the tradition, one not strictly rooted in biblical studies but one that draws more broadly on the methodological tools provided by religious studies.

Though the work of the godfather of religious studies, Mircea Eliade, has been refined, refuted, and otherwise digested by the field, there are a number of his comparative observations that eloquently describe not universal similarities but commonalities that are worth keeping in mind as one encounters and describes myriad religious traditions. One such observation is the *imago mundi*, more specifically, the frequency with which religious systems divide that world into three levels.

In his discussion of hierophany, the eruption of the sacred into the profane world, Eliade (1957, 36) writes: "Where the break-through from plane to plane has been effected by a hierophany, there too an opening has been made, either upward (the divine world) or downward (the underworld, the world of the dead). The three cosmic levels—earth, heaven, underworld—have been put in communication."

An examination of cosmologies across cultural landscapes of religious traditions yields a variety of spatial relationships that seek to explain the structure of the cosmos through this tripartite model. Though Eliade goes to great lengths to demonstrate this three-story cosmos as a phenomenon of far-flung religious traditions, it is enough for one to recognize it in several of the traditions of the ancient Mediterranean. Broadly considered, from sacrifices and libations, to prayers and curses, to burial and cremation practices, one is continually reminded that some things belong to the celestial sphere above (apotheosized emperors on the wings of eagles, or prayers directed to the heavens), while others belong to the chthonic sphere below (inhumated bodies, or curses written and buried).

Common among many of these models are descriptions of the familiar world, the terrestrial, alongside imagined places above and below. The nonterrestrial realms can map onto a dichotomy of good and evil or heaven and hell, that is, gods in the heavens and demons of the underworld, but those associations are culture dependent and need not follow that pattern. Depending on the particularities of the religious system and community in question, the gods may live above or below; likewise, the ultimate destiny of human afterlife might be in the underworld or in the heavens. What does it mean when one cremates rather than buries? In fact, this tripartite system is explicitly referenced in the epistolary tradition preserved in the New Testament in Philippians, where Jesus is described: "Therefore God exalted him to the highest place and gave him the name that is above every name, that at the name of Jesus every knee should bow, in heaven and on earth and under the earth" (Phil 2:9–10 NIV).

The three-story universe, though in no way ubiquitous, is common in various cultural and religious settings around the world in both ancient and contemporary settings. The practical implications for the life of a community can also be far reaching and affect a myriad of human concerns. When such a model for the cosmos exists, it is often attested to in both myth and ritual of the accompanying religious systems. For example, consider the associations of caves with the worship of chthonic deities, or the mountaintops as imagined homes of the gods. Likewise, the worship of celestial gods by burning incense or the offering of smoky sacrifice makes spatial sense, as the smoke ascends, reaching the imagined abode of the gods; likewise, pouring a libation onto the ground, or burying a petition that supplicates the underworld gods, serves the equally practical purpose of delivering the materials of the ritual to the underworld, the place of the chthonic deities. The tripartite universe helps individuals and communities organize and explain the world in which they need to meaningfully dwell (Eliade 1957, 47).

Animals and the Three-Tiered Cosmos

What, then, does this have to do with the animal symbols used in the aphorism in question? Humans see themselves as living in the terrestrial plain of the three-tiered cosmos. However, the boundaries of the three cosmic stories are imagined as permeable, often through particular ritual processes used to supplicate the gods above or below. Likewise, it is possible for special, liminal entities to cross the boundaries between worlds, like Elijah on his golden chariot of fire or Persephone on her annual trip to the underworld. Likewise, either mythically or ritually, animals might also be endowed with the ability to cross over from one world to the next.

Swedish anthropologist Ake Hultkrantz (1979, 221) recognizes this pattern of integration and describes it in "Ecology of Religion: Its Scope and Methodology." He labels the use of aspects of the natural, physical world within the beliefs and practices of a religious community "morphological integration." He uses this term to consider not only the way that the natural environment in toto affects the way that a community lives and worships but also how particular elements of that environment might be used to describe particularities within the cultural or religious system. He defines the term:

> Morphological integration: the covering of religious features with forms taken from the physical and biological environment. Religious concepts and rites are by their very nature traditional but borrow their formal appearance from phenomena within the actual biotope.... The choice of forms is not arbitrary but is related to the symbolism that is inherent in them. For instance, the bird dress of a shaman tells us of the bird-like supernatural powers of the shaman. (228)

His example of the shaman in this example is closely related to the bird imagery that is present in many religions of the ancient Mediterranean. The spirit of God descends in the form of a dove (Matt 3:16, Mark 1:10,

Luke 3:22, John 1:32), and the Israelites are delivered from Egypt "on eagles' wings" (Exod 19:4), to name just two examples. Perhaps the most familiar of these images is the way that heavenly messengers, that is, angels, are imagined with wings—a kind of hybrid creature that is able to cross the boundaries between the terrestrial and celestial—the respective abodes of humans and God.

If there are animals that can easily be identified with heavenly places and the deities that reside in them, are there similar underworld associations? Though Hultkrantz does not include an example of underworld imagery, we can extrapolate from his theoretical framework and consider other classes of animals besides birds. For example, anything that lives below ground in a den, burrows in the earth, or inhabits a cave might easily be associated with a cosmological underworld. The most prevalent of these underworld animals is the snake, which (depending on region and species) often lives belowground and therefore might be imagined as a consort of underworld beings. However, just like the bird, these animals rarely reside exclusively underground and out of sight. Instead, they traverse the boundaries, moving between the terrestrial world and the subterranean. This boundary crossing between the two worlds symbolically serves the same purpose of the birds of the heavens, demonstrating an ability to navigate the place of human habitation and another world.

Though the examples are not as prevalent as bird imagery, one sees a similar pattern of morphological integration of the fox into myth and symbol cross-culturally. From the Near Eastern goddess Ninhursag, who is a "mother-earth" figure associated with the fox (Dickson 2007, 26), to the Scottish goddess Dia Griene, the daughter of the sun who is held captive in the underworld and only allowed to visit the earth in the form of a fox (Mailahn 2015, 152–53), to the boundary-breaking fox spirits of Chinese folklore (Kang 2006, 17), one can see cross-cultural associations with the fox and the religious ideas of the subterranean. Admittedly, fox references in the immediate context under discussion are few and far between. However, the quotation in question contains in itself the recognition of the fox as a burrowing animal, with access to the lowest tier of the three-story cosmos, that is, "foxes have holes."

Application of the Theory to the Passage

Bearing these comparisons in mind, in returning to the saying itself, new possibilities emerge. By reflecting on the animal symbols used, one can read this not only as a passage about the hardships of following Jesus on his itinerant mission but also as a metaphor that highlights christological possibilities. The two animals that are used in the passage are representative of the two kinds of spatial liminality mentioned above. The bird, though present in the terrestrial world, can ascend to the heavens. Likewise, the fox, though similarly present in our world, can descend to the subterranean world. Both are liminal; both are capable of transcending the permeable boundaries of the cosmos. However, the saying does not end there. Instead, there is a third category introduced, a third being as part of the equation, the Son of Man. Perhaps the gist of the passage is that even those boundary-crossing animals the bird and fox are in the end rooted to two planes of existence. However, the Son of Man is even more of a boundary crosser, even more categorically problematic and uncanny than these symbolically potent animals.

In order to consider this possibility, it is imperative that one sees Christology not as a topic to be explained in these traditions but a conversation to be explored. That is to say, at the time when this saying was circulating, before being concretized in the Gospels of Matthew, Luke, and Thomas, who Jesus was and why he was significant were open questions for nascent Christianity. In fact, in the earliest extant telling of Jesus's life, the Gospel of Mark, Jesus asks his disciples, "Who do people say that I am?" (Mark 8:27 NRSV), a tradition that is replicated in the other Synoptic Gospels as well (Matt 16:5; Luke 9:18). The answers provided by the disciples are not satisfactory. Even Peter's answer, "You are the Messiah," which initially seems to hit the mark, is presented as a fundamental misunderstanding, as his definition of the functions of a Messiah do not align with Jesus's own understanding. Even if one sticks to the canon (to say nothing of the Nag Hammadi Library or other apocryphal traditions), the gospels offer an astoundingly broad array of titles to describe who Jesus is and why he is important. How exactly the categories and names such as Messiah, Christ, Lord, Son of God, Son of Man, Son of David, and so on fit together to describe a single cosmological figure is unclear in any one of these texts, much less seen together as a part of a single textual tradition. Thus, the question of who Jesus is, his ontology, and what he does, his function, remains unresolved. In fact, the gospels within the canon play with the inconsistencies of Jesus's ontology continually, with disciples mistaking him for a ghost (Matt 14:26; Mark 6:49; Luke 24:37), not recognizing him while traveling the road to Emmaus (Luke 24:13), or wondering at his entry into the upper room through locked doors and windows (John 20:19).

The christological questions and the implications for the myriad possibilities offered continued to be asked and answered in written traditions for centuries to come. From stories of the precocious child Jesus in the Infancy Gospel of Thomas to the role of Jesus as simultaneously sacrificial victim and priest in the Epistle to the Hebrews, the speculation about Jesus's ontology and function is both wide and varied. Attempts were made to craft a more unified understanding that answered these questions, a process that continued at the Council of Nicaea in the early fourth century and beyond.

It is within the context of this very early debate over Christology, which was being contested in oral and written traditions, that I would like to place this aphorism that juxtaposes the Son of Man with foxes and birds. Instead of simply driving the narrative of Jesus's itinerant mission, this saying was using the associations with the fox and the bird to consider possibilities for the ontology and function of Jesus at a time when those questions were still very much debated.

Ascent/Descent

Placing Jesus within the context of the liminal foxes and birds can be seen as an attempt to make a claim about how and why this figure, Jesus, is significant. If one considers these two animal associations from a spatial perspective, the distinctive feature is their ability to cross the boundaries between this world and the celestial realm above and the chthonic realm below. Looking to both canonical and noncanonical texts that describe Jesus as a cosmological figure, he is not infrequently described as ascending to the heavens or descending to the underworld. However, unlike the animal referents that are offered as comparison, he is not limited in what parts of the three-tiered cosmos he can inhabit, but he has the ability to cross both celestial and chthonic boundaries.

Jesus's ability to ascend to the heavens is the easier spatial association to see, as it is explicitly present in multiple gospel traditions. Luke-Acts details the narrative of the ascension in two places, Luke 24:51 and Acts 1:9–11. The Gospel of John also features dialogue that describes this ascent on multiple occasions. John 3:13 reads, "No one has ascended into heaven but he who descended from heaven, the Son of man." Likewise, John 6:62 reads, "Then what if you were to see the Son of man ascending to where he was before?" Each of these two examples places Jesus's ascension against his original descent from above to earth. Finally, in John 20:17 Jesus warns

Mary Magdalene, "Do not hold on to me, because I have not yet ascended to the Father. But go to my brothers and say to them, 'I am ascending to my Father and your Father, to my God and your God'" (NRSV).

Though the epistolary tradition does not explicitly reference the ascension in a narrative context, there are many places that reference Jesus's place in heaven, implying a similar spatial relationship, that is, the transcendence of this world to a place in the kingdom of heaven (Rom 8:34; Eph 1:19; Col 3:1; 1 Tim 3:16; 1 Pet 3:22). That these epistolary references come from a variety of contexts (authentic Paul, deutero-Paul, Pastorals, and Petrine literature) is an indication that the Christology of ascension is not merely a preoccupation of a particular author but a theme that runs fairly consistently through the apostolic and postapostolic period.

The best textual evidence for this tradition of ascent in the epistolary tradition also includes the tradition of descent, providing evidence for the three-tiered cosmos and Jesus's ability to transcend boundaries to inhabit all three cosmic planes: "When it says, 'He ascended,' what does it mean but that he had also descended into the lower parts of the earth? He who descended is the same one who ascended far above all the heavens, so that he might fill all things" (Eph 4:9–10 NRSV). Though not as explicit as Eph 4, 1 Pet 4:6 describes the descent by stating that the "gospel was preached even to the dead." Likewise, the noncanonical Gospel of Peter includes a voice that asks the risen Christ whether the "good news was proclaimed to those who sleep?" and the answer comes in the affirmative, "Yes!" echoing a tradition of descent to the underworld between the crucifixion and resurrection (Gos. Pet. 41–42). Though it is a later text, the Gospel of Nicodemus also picks up on this tradition and even offers a more complete telling of the descent: "The brazen gates were shattered, and the iron bars broken, and all the dead who had been bound came out of the prisons ... and the King of glory came in the form of a man, and all of the dark places of Hades were lighted up" (Gos. Nic. 5).

In addition to these scriptural referents to decent, many later Christian authors picked up on the tradition, including Clement of Alexandria and Origen (Turner 1966, 174). Finally, these traditions of ascent and descent were also highlighted and repeatedly used in later creedal traditions, underscoring the centrality of this idea in the developing orthodox tradition. In Rufinus's commentary on the Apostles' Creed, circa 404, Jesus's passion is described: "(Jesus) *descended into hell, rose again from the dead on the third day, ascended into heaven*, and is seated at the right hand of God the Father almighty" (Connell 2001, 266). Why is Jesus significant? One prominent answer is his unique ability to traverse the three planes of existence—he is chthonic, terrestrial, and celestial. This ability to transgress the boundaries of space is matched only by his own categorical problematic-ness.

Conclusions

The extant ancient texts in question are inherently layered; not only is one dependent on the ancient scribes to faithfully preserve them, but the gospels themselves incorporate aphorisms, narrative elements, and other oral and written sources in order to compose a story that conveys the meaning of Jesus for their own communities. For this reason, it is sometimes necessary to perform a kind of archaeology on the text that may reveal strata of meaning.

The aphorism in question here, "foxes have holes," has accrued a dominant interpretive framework that was encouraged by its placement in the narrative of canonical gospel traditions. However, this way of understanding the saying may have obscured other associations and implications for the passage. This saying may have also been an attempt to grapple with the complicated christological formulations that were being hashed out in nascent Christian circles. Who is the Son of Man, and why is he important? The answer that is obliquely offered by this aphorism is that the Son of Man is important in ways that are best understood through an animal metaphor. Birds are celestial; foxes are chthonic; the Son of Man transcends all of the boundaries.

The implications for this reading are not just about animals and animal images. Instead, a deeper reading of this passage might help us to notice how ancient Christianities wrestled with both the ontology and function of Jesus, leading ultimately to a summation of orthodoxy that rests on paradox and, perhaps, irony. The dominant tradition holds that Jesus triumphs through suffering, that he is both fully divine and fully human, and that he is simultaneously distinct from the Father, yet God. If one looks at these juxtapositions as instances of Jesus's categorical problematic-ness, perhaps one can consider this unexpected animal association as another expression of boundary crossing. The association of Jesus with these wild animals may not make ancient Christian christological understandings clear, but it may let us see another layer to the complexity of both the questions posed and the answers proposed in the extant sources.

Finally, there are implications for our understanding of the cultural relationships of humans, nonhuman animals, and their relationships to the divine, concerns that are of interest to animal studies more generally. There are many ways that humans use nonhuman animals: as food, clothing, entertainment, and companionship, to name just a few. The use of animals in symbol and metaphor can be seen as the intellectual extension of the human use of nonhuman animals. It may also be that the use of animals as metaphors for the divine also says something more about those very animals. The fox and the bird are imagined as wild animals, not in the immediate control of humans; they are neither domestic nor domesticated. Juxtaposing the foxes and the birds with the lamb, for example, may sharpen one's understanding of how different animals were considered in this world, and how that reflected on understandings of divinity—and helped to shape the illogical and impractical theology that developed around the Son of Man.

The use of wild animals in metaphor is something different—and rare—in this body of texts. That the Son of Man is understood in the content of the uncontrolled members of the animal kingdom expresses a sense of unknowableness and mystery, both characteristics that will be familiar when considering christological formulations. These wild animals retain some dignity in the context of the aphorism and can therefore be appropriate ways to think about other wild and ultimately unknowable beings, such as the Son of Man.

Works Cited

Blatz, Beate. 1991. "The Coptic Gospel of Thomas." Pages in 110–33 in *New Testament Apocrypha*. Edited by Wilhelm Schneemelcher. Translated by R. McL. Wilson. Louisville: Westminster John Knox.

Bultmann, Rudolf. 1963. *History of the Synoptic Tradition*. Translated by Basil Blackwell. New York: Harper & Row.

Calarco, Matthew. 2015. *Thinking through Animals: Identity, Difference, Indistinction*. StBr. Stanford, CA: Stanford University Press.

Connell, Martin F. 2001. "Descensus Christi ad Inferos: Christ's Descent to the Dead." *TS* 62:262–82.

Dickson, Keith. 2007. "Enki and Ninhursag: The Trickster in Paradise." *JNES* 66:1–32.

Ehrman, Bart. 2003. "The Gospel of Peter." Pages 124–26 in *The New Testament and Other Early Christian Writings*. Oxford: Oxford University Press.

Eliade, Mircea. 1957. *The Sacred and the Profane: The Nature of Religion*. Translated by Willard R. Trask. New York: Harper & Row.

Franklin, Eric. 2001. "Luke." Pages 134–85 in *The Oxford Bible Commentary: The Gospels*. Edited by John Muddiman and John Barton. Oxford: Oxford University Press.

Gowler, David B. 2006. "The Chreia." Pages 132–48 in *The Historical Jesus in Context*. Edited by Amy-Jill Levine, Dale C. Allison Jr., and John Dominic Crossan. Princeton: Princeton University Press.

Hultkrantz, Ake. 1979. "Ecology of Religion: Its Scope and Methodology." Pages 221–36 in *Science of Religion: Studies in Methodology*. The Hague: Mouton.

Kang, Xiaofei. 2006. *The Cult of the Fox: Power, Gender, and Popular Religion in Late Imperial and Modern China*. New York: Columbia University Press.

Levi-Strauss, Claude. 1966. *The Savage Mind*. Chicago: University of Chicago Press.

Luz, Ulrich. 2001. *Matthew 8–20: A Commentary on the Gospel of Matthew*. Edited by Helmut Koester. Minneapolis: Augsburg Fortress.

Mailahn, Klaus. 2015. *Der Fuchs und die Göttin*. Hamburg: Disserta Verlag.

Robbins, Vernon K. 1992. "Apophthegm." *ABD* 1:307–9.

Smith, Jonathan Z. 1978. *Map Is Not Territory*. Chicago: University of Chicago Press.

Turner, Ralph V. 1966. "Descendit Ad Infernos: Medieval Views on Christ's Descent into Hell and the Salvation of the Just." *JHI* 27:173–94.

Walker, Alexander. 1886. "The Gospel of Nicodemus, Part II: The Descent into Hell, Greek Form." Pages 435–38 in vol. 8 of *Ante-Nicene Fathers*. Edited by Alexander Roberts, James Donaldson, and A. Cleveland Coxe. Buffalo, NY: Christian Literature Publishing.

Monsters, Beasts, and Animals: The Taxonomy of Fierce Creatureliness in the Biblical Text and Beyond

Robert Paul Seesengood

Introduction

What makes an animal a beast? Or a beast a monster? We might answer that the beast or monster has increasing degrees of unique ferocity or somehow transcends nature. It is tempting to suggest that fabulous monsters were something populating the world of prescientific modernity. The monster or the beast, from our safe distance of (post)modernity, was a savage but misunderstood animal or simply a character of fantasy. Indeed, the modern sophisticate, armed with sturdy zoology and taxonomy textbooks, seems hard-pressed to find any true beasts or monsters anymore. Monsters are merely misunderstood animals.

This paper will explore the possibility that the categories of human and monster share an affinity in being, each, transcendent over the rudimentary *animal*. Humans are a type of animal. As I will show, scholarship in animality has argued that the categories of the human and the beast remain separate in terms of ferocity and wildness (the beast) in contrast to reason and restraint (the human). But where does the category of monster, creatures often also animals (though, admittedly, singular and fantastic), fit on this continuum? I will argue that, as the (reasoning) human is the polar, transcendent opposite of the beast, the (reasoning) divine is the transcendent Other to the chaotic monster. Beasts (and monsters) parallel humans (and divine) in ascendency (or degeneracy) over generic animals via the ascription of volition and cleverness (if not sentience). To have a will (whether a wild or a reasoned one), not necessarily awareness or intelligence, was the determinate for transcendence from animality. Finally, this paper will suggest that, following Jacques Derrida as analogy, as the sovereign is the extreme expression of beastliness, God becomes the singular antipode of the monstrous. The beast and the sovereign anticipates God and the monstrous.

Leviathan and Behemoth:
Turning Untamable Monsters into Rowdy Animals

I am considering Behemoth. It is a bright, brisk, early October day in Philadelphia, and I am standing next to the hippopotamus enclosure in the nation's oldest zoological garden. We are members of the zoo, and we are here for "Boo at the Zoo," where children arrive in costume and, as they visit the animals, are given candy donated by area patrons. My son, dressed as Harry Potter in his wizard robes, Gryffindor tie, and scarf, is turning circles beside me; around us are an array of ghouls, superheroes, vampires, a werewolf, a Philadelphia Eagle, and more. Roughly an hour before, we were regarding Leviathan, tucked for the winter indoors at the herpetarium, lying immobile on the bottom of his pool, grinning luridly at a memory or joke only he knew. The hippo nearest me, fully submerged, rose to the water's surface with astonishing grace given her bulk and snorted a spray of water vapor and snot from her nostrils. My son found this hilarious.

Throughout the day, I have had snippets of Job and, more precisely, commentary on Job's infamous monsters rattling through my mind alongside Natan Slifkin's (2011) fascinating book *Sacred Monsters* (published by Zoo Torah). Invoked as codas to God's whirlwind speech (whirlwind rebuke?) in Job 40:7–41:26, Leviathan and Behemoth enjoy their primary exposure to readers, with brief cameos by Leviathan in Psalms and the prophets (Job 3:8, Amos 9:3, Ps 74:13–23, 104:26, Isa 27:1; note Balentine 1998; Schlobin 1992, 25–32; Pope 1965, 265–79). Leviathan and Behemoth have sparked a long literature of scholarly criticism, a significant portion of which is attempting to find a strong enough hook to wrangle them, according to the divine challenge—if not from frothing primeval seas, then at least from the realm of the monstrous and back into the world of "savage beasts" (Slifkin 2011, 169–200; Beal 2001; especially Day 1985, 1992). An array of antecedents has been suggested. Leviathan as crocodile, whale, serpent; Behemoth as elephant, crocodile (apparently a Hebrew's nightmare critter), water buffalo (from an ingenious interpretation of *behem*), or, most commonly, hippopotamus (Silfkin 2011). Young-earth creationists have argued these are references to dinosaurs, with some positing that a possible sauropod, though rare, still roams the earth somehow still defying discovery by science (bear in mind that Answers in Genesis, the source, does not have an extensive reputation for high regard for science; see Steel 2001; Slifkin 2011, 190–91, is most decisively not impressed). Similar moves to normalize Hebrew Bible monsters surround Gen 1:21's *tannînim* ("sea monsters," often rendered "whales," in a move first suggested by the LXX and Vulgate) or Isa 34:14's Lilith (boringly reduced to "screech owl"; Slifkin 2011, 171–80). Since 1663 and Samuel Bochart's persuasive monograph, critics have generally agreed on crocodile and hippopotamus for Leviathan and Behemoth, respectively (Day 1992). The crux of such criticism is the assumption that primitive, prescientific Hebrews regarded natural animals as monsters. A biblical monster, then, is a (abnormally noxious or savage, rare) beast, a savage animal, as yet unnamed by ancients, who were lacking rational science (not a real, living monster appearing in a broader fantasy tale).

Yet talmudic rabbinic traditions surrounding Leviathan recognize him, or her (or both), as monstrous and not simply another beast. Rabbinic midrash has a sporting pair of Leviathan (forgive me, I am unsure of the plural form in English) made on the fourth day of creation (Day 1985; Beal 2001). Lordly in the churning seas of chaos, God subdues them as God moves on to create the more ordered universe of land and sky animals (a conquest reflected in Ps 74). Leviathan's mate is killed promptly, and she is contained, stored away until the great day of the messianic banquet in the world to come. The principal dish at that banquet will be the flesh of Leviathan, the battle between God and disorder concluded and marked by a cosmic, monstrous Thanksgiving roast. Leviathan will be considered kosher, despite her reptilian nature, by the nature of the messianic age, a bit of *treyf* eaten with permission in God's presence being part of the fun. The skins of Leviathan will be stretched into Sukkot booths large (or numerous) enough for everyone to gather inside.

Postmodern Monsters: Irrational Beasts and Where to Find Them

Scholarship that demonsters the biblical text reassures us in our modern, postmythological world and results in a biblical text more palatable to modernity. Yet it also smacks of a *Tendenz* to demythologize, politely coughing into our hands over the unfortunately exuberant rhetoric of biblical authors, an exuberance surely forgivable by context. Many modern believers—and many rational, scientific modern scholars—struggle to accept that the miraculous and supernatural things in the Bible could exist, or to concede that these elements' impossibility indelibly marks the Bible as fantasy literature. Others, who want to continue to affirm the Bible's inerrancy, but very aware monsters do not exist, craft animal studies apologia for them. For both, biblical monsters are only as-yet-to-be-documented animals. Modern people know better than to believe in monsters.

Do they? Consider the chupacabra. The chupacabra, or "goat sucker," is described by witnesses as four feet high, walking erect on small hind legs, hairless, reptilian and scaled, gray, with large bright eyes and spines or ridges running down its back (for this and what follows, see BBC 2016; Wagner 2004). It has a long proboscis tongue and savage teeth. It moves at night and is a cunning hunter. The chupacabra kills domestic animals: chickens, sheep, pigs, goats, dogs—and consumes their blood (apparently only their blood). Its calling cards are the completely bloodless bodies of its victims. The chupacabra was described in March 1995 outside Orocovis, Puerto Rico, a few miles from a closed-access US Air Force installation and observatory. Between 1995 and 1998, there were dozens of sightings across Puerto Rico. They seem to have ceased with the turn of the century.

That is, they ceased in Puerto Rico. The chupacabra emerged roughly synonymous with the rise of the internet, and it may well be the internet's first monster, sharing the horrible pantheon with the likes of Slender Man. The sightings of the chupacabra spread over the internet, first to South America (Brazil and then Chile) and then northward to Mexico (where most twenty-first-century sightings take place). There have been claims of sightings as far away as Russia. Conspiracy theorist Art Bell did much to popularize interest, establishing early on a popular idea that the chupacabra was an extraterrestrial, crashed on earth, and was captured by the government but escaped (perhaps the second-most popular theory is that the chupacabra is an escaped secret government genetic experiment). The entire mythos of the chupacabra has emerged within the hyperconnected, documented, extremely scientific modern age of the internet. Technology and communication have not quelled interest in it or demystified it. Indeed, just the opposite. People still want their monsters; the category of monster—not just stories about monsters, or simulacrums of monsters, or theoretical and fictional monsters, but assertions of actual, active, physical monsters in our world alongside us—must still address some human social need even in our age of hypercommunications, broad general education, and explosive technology. Indeed, these benchmarks of intellectual sophistication, as tools for communication and shared content, seem to have enabled even more rapid spread of monster mythology.

The chupacabra has attracted the attention of renowned cryptobiologist Benjamin Radford. As a field, cryptobiology seeks to hunt down monsters, such as Sasquatch or Nessie, and determine their proper animal taxonomy. Such has, in fact, happened in our modern age. Fishers in 1938 famously caught a monstrous-looking fish, the coelacanth, believed to have been extinct since the late Devonian but found, quite alive and well and happily oblivious to why anyone would be surprised, living in the deep, deep ocean off the coast of South Africa. Similarly, there is mounting evidence for the survival of sea serpents, which are gigantic, deep-ocean species of squid or oarfish of unusual size. Radford has examined some dozen corpses of chupacabra shot or discovered by farmers in rural Mexico. Rather than a mystical monster, he has discovered, time and again, the body is actually a raccoon or feral dog infected with sarcoptic mange and rendered grotesquely hairless.

Yet none of this data, often cited side by side with lurid and goose-pimpling narratives of late-night monster attacks, has quelled interest in the chupacabra. In fact, in more than a few examples, the dissemination of rational explanations for chupacabra sightings, or the necropathic analysis of corpses proving the animal in question to be a dog, often only accelerates interest and germinates conspiracy logics. Chupacabra loyalists insist, contrary to the evidence (if not, indeed, *because of* the counterevidence) that any rational explanation or evidence is a government plant designed to throw off the faithful. The legend of the chupacabra continues in our modern age of documentation and information because information that is rational only serves, perversely, to fuel speculation. In a sense, the critics are correct. Whatever animal is discovered by chupacabra hunters, if it is an animal, it is, to an equal degree, *not* a chupacabra. The irony is that both skeptic and believer can assert with equal conviction and vigor that the chupacabra transcends embodiment and has no natural, earthly, animal physiology.

The Beast and the Sovereign; the Monster and the Animal

The tendency to reduce Leviathan, Behemoth, sea monsters, and Lilith to ordinary crocodiles, hippos, whales, and screech owls reveals the unease invoked by the monster, a symbol of the unknown and irrational. Yet, I would insist that monsters are persistent. They evade the rational evidence of "science" and reason, most definitely, and are not merely unclassified beasts. The monster exists, and persists, in ways and spaces that beasts and animals do not.

In his last university lectures, Derrida (2009) posited that a beast was an animal that transcended law and rule, eluding domestication, beyond restraint. Beasts, Derrida argued, shared this status with kings and sovereigns. Above the law (because they made the law), sovereigns are equally unpredictable and unstable (and potentially savage). Beasts are to ordinary animals as sovereigns are to citizen humans.

Like sovereigns, monsters are on a continuum intersecting with beasts, particularly regarding their savagery and lawlessness, but, also like sovereigns, monsters are antipode. Beasts are the antithesis of human and civil, but monsters disrupt reality and cosmology. Monsters are chaotic, singular, and sinister, hidden things that are malevolently intelligent and suddenly revealed. Monsters are the embodiment of chaos and of what we do not know. But, perhaps more frightening, they are, in their embodiment, reminders of both the persistence of chaos and that, despite ever-burgeoning information, there stubbornly remain things we do not know, that there is a limit to knowledge, because knowledge presumes at least some predictability and order. What order we have in this universe is tenuous and hard fought, and it is by no means permanent. Monsters are creatures of chaos but also serve as revelations of an ineffable (divine?) mysteriousness that lies just beyond our vision.

Bible Animals, Biblical Beasts, the Monsters of Scripture

To speak of ineffable, mysterious, revelation, and the divine, of course, is to venture into territory of religion and the biblical. Beasts, particularly religious and biblical ones can certainly act in monstrous ways. Stephen Moore (note, for now, 2014a, 2014b) has returned repeatedly to the theme of the beastly creatures within John's Revelation. Moore (2014a, 197) observes the ways John links animality and divinity and steeps both in affective rhetoric.

Moore surveys the beasts as beasts (he does not call any "monster"), though his analysis surely notes their terrible quality. "Revelation's *therion*, its 'beast,' is also a 'wild animal.' Not only does the Greek admit both meanings, but 'wild animal' is what *therion* most often meant according to most Greek lexicons" (2014a, 201). In the end (or is it "at the end"?), Moore notes that the triumph of the Lamb over the dragon and beasts is not a bloodless coup; in Revelation, the Lamb matches the beast in its ferocity.

John's beastly metaphors were spawned in the dank headwaters of Daniel. Robert Seesengood and Jennifer Koosed (2014) note how, there, Daniel's savage beasts most resemble (and, in some cases explicitly are) the Derridian sovereign. As in Revelation, in Daniel these beasts are ciphers for sovereigns. As in Revelation, God defeats these false sovereigns by "out-savaging" them; God conquers by out-beasting the beasts.

Timothy Beal deals with monsters as monsters explicitly. Creeping around both Revelation's end-times horror and Job's Leviathan and Behemoth, he notes, monsters are indeed very often tied to the divine. Existing on the opposite end of the continuum of order and chaos, monsters are "chaos gods" (2001, 13–22). Beal reads God's challenge to Job from the whirlwind, noting the role of the monster as symbol of chaos (and God's assertions of order, but of an order that transcends human sense) and concluding that God is, in implying Job's nondivinity, acknowledging the antidivinity inherent in the chaos of the monster. God's power lies in out-savaging the savageness of challenges to order, of chaos, be they Leviathan, Behemoth, or even Job himself. Beal notes:

> Job is drawn to the monstrous as a violent invasion of unaccountable excess within God's established order of creation. These monsters are forces of un-creation and, as such, potential threats to the creator. Still, Job has little hope of seriously challenging the creator God with or without their help. Although he identifies with chaos monsters, even representing his voice of pain as a monster's embodiment of chaos within God's world, he fully expects that God will smash him down just as God has smashed down other chaos monsters who threatened the divine rule. Job identifies himself among the monsters but sees God as the ultimate monster killer … a God who does not slay or banish the Chaos monster but glories in it and identifies with it as an embodiment of cosmic horror.… God out-monsters Job. (2001, 47–48)

In other words, Job depicts God responding to theodicy, to questions about God's reason, control, and management of divine order (in the particular case, insuring the proper distribution of blessing and curse), not with reasoned explanation but with the assertion of God's (savage) power over (chaos) monsters.

Beast, Monster, Sovereign, Deity: What's in a Name?

Etymologically, because questions of taxonomy are always a bit etymological, there is no word, generically, for *monster* in Hebrew (Slifkin 2011); there is no Hebrew equivalent for *monster*. Fantastic creatures are singular and often properly named. The Latin *monstrum*, unlike the benign *beastiari* or generic *anima*, derives from *moneo*, for "sign" or "omen" (see Huet 1993). The *monstrum* is frightening but also warning (Beal 2001, 18–19; Asma 2009, 1–19).

The Greek *thērion* refers to "beasts" both savage, such as a lion, and dull and mindless, such as an ox (for this and what follows see LSJ, s.v. "θηρίον"; Balz 2003). In the New Testament, *thērion* is used forty-six times; thirty-nine occur in Revelation. There, it exclusively refers to terrible polyform creatures under the control of Python the dragon (the "beast from the sea" and the "beast from the land"), a usage following Dan 7 (Collins 1976). Of the other eight uses, all refer to animals, generally. Yet there is also a Greek word for monster; *teras* refers to "signs" generically (as if "from heaven" or of war; Balz 2003, 350; LSJ). It appears this way in biblical text, always in plural and often appearing with *semeia*. Henry Liddell, Robert Scott, and Henry Jones also note that *teras* may be used "in a concrete sense" for "monster" (LSJ) When used this way in broader Greek literature, it refers to gorgons, serpent/dragons, Typhoeus, Cerberus, the chimera, and others. These supernatural, unique creatures are "portentous" and often harbingers of the divine. In Hebrew, Latin, and Greek, the monster is unique, sui generis, and often named. Leviathan and Behemoth are always already transcendent of ordinary reality, encroaching on God's space (and, in Ps 74, in need of God's restraining). As Rudolph Otto (1958; see also Freud 1955) famously observed, *mysterium tremendum*, terror and fear, chaos and chaos restrained, very often share company.

Theorists of horror observe that horror is the fearful rending and consumption of our bodies, but also the rending of the ordered, reasoned, comprehensible world (Carroll 1990; Schlobin 1992). Horror is the revelation of what lies hidden as it suddenly bursts forth. Like Michel Foucault's fold, reality is shown to have a depth, and a depth that conceals some secret and terrible something capable of bubbling up, of bursting out and showing itself. Horror is the awareness that chaos is peering in at the window. Even more horrible, however, is the fear captured in Sigmund Freud's (1958) *unheimlich*—the (permanent) Other within ourselves. Monsters are the embodiment and the persistence of chaos.

They are markers of otherness that disrupts our world. They are terrible because they are warning omens, exposing the limits of order and the throbbing nearness of chaos, but also perhaps revealing, as well, that God or reason is not as immune from monstrosity as one might hope. Friedrich Nietzsche knew the terrible, transformative costs of battling with monsters and staring into abysses.

If a beast, as Derrida has argued, is the limit of the civil and the human(e), the monster is the limit of order. Beasts are antithesis of civil and human. Monsters are antithesis of divine and rationality. Monsters, like deities, are singular poles of (dis)order. Derrida defines the beast as the opposite of lawfulness and rule. Sovereigns, he argues are the center of lawfulness, civilization, and rule. These emanate out of them. Yet, as the radial origin of law, they are also, like beasts, outside law. Beasts become sovereign. Monsters, in turn, are chaotic, the opposite of ordered cosmology. Deity, in Western classical and Judeo-Christian thought, is the center of order, structure, and cosmology, which emanate out of the divine, radiating from *theos* into *cosmos*. Yet, as the origin point of order, the divine is also monstrous, outside order, primal chaos. Gods are monsters, and monsters are divine. Beast is to sovereign as monster is to God.

Conclusion: Does It Matter Whether It's a Beast or a Monster if (When?) It Eats You?

This fall, a few weeks before Halloween, on Yom Kippur we chanted the questions, "Who by fire?," "Who by strangling?," "Who by wild beast?," pondering together who among our community might die this year and how. I am always struck by the antiquity and primacy of these questions, an oddity in some ways to the modern ear and also somewhat strange to the occasion. Who looks around at annual celebrations and events—birthday parties, sacred occasions, Annual Meetings of the Society of Biblical Literature—and wonders who in the present room will be dead by next year? (OK, sometimes I do.) And is death by strangulation or wild animal such a common thing we should expect it of someone next year? But I do find the prayer's interest in beasts interesting, reflecting, as it does, a very different, more natural (and agrarian) way of being in the world from my own. It recalls a people who understood both eating and being eaten by animals.

And not to be too harsh, but the terrors of this prayer are ours, really, as well. This essay met the broader public, leapt from the shadows of my hard drive and into a room full of innocents, as a November presentation during the Annual Meeting of the Society of Biblical Literature in Denver. Within the state of Colorado, if not the city of Denver, the month (day?) I read this draft, there was very possibly someone who indeed died by strangulation. When it happened, she (and it was, sadly, likely a she) was afraid. The last person with her, the last person to touch her, was her killer, perhaps someone, based on the terrible statistics of domestic violence, she both knew and trusted. We, as we moved through the city that week and conference, may very likely have seen her. The darkness of chaos and the monster surrounds, even now. We do not see it, but it is here; that is how monsters work, is it not?

To the eaten and torn, the question "By whom?" is irrelevant. But to the remnant, to those left behind, it matters significantly. Beasts differ from monsters in both scale and system. Beasts are ordinary and common. Monsters are unique and ominous. Beasts destroy with a thoughtless savagery and disrupt the borders of civilization. Monsters consume us with a sort of sentient savagery, with a malevolent intention to disrupt the borders of order. Beasts are thoughtless and neutral. Monsters are intentional and, to a worldview that emphasizes order and community as good, evil.

The question posed to Job is not one of the mastery of the ordered world. It is an acknowledgment of the inability to master chaos. The presence of the dragon in John's Revelation, alongside its minion monsters, is the persistent presence of disruptive, anticosmogony. The challenge of the monster is the codification, the collection of chaos. Monsters are warped points in the fabric of the universal order, chaotic singularities, black holes, drawing the disorder into themselves, into a disruptive pinpoint of disorder and chaos. The best, the only, hope against them, the biblical text suggests, is God. Yet God beats monsters by being, Godself, at least a touch monstrous. God moves in mysterious and monstrous ways.

Consider Leviathan carefully.

Works Cited

Asma, Stephen T. 2009. *On Monsters: An Unnatural History of Our Worst Fears*. New York: Oxford.

Balentine, Samuel E. 1998. "'What Are Human Beings, That You Make So Much of Them?' Divine Disclosure from the Whirlwind: 'Look at Behemoth.'" Pages 259–78 in *God in the Fray: A Tribute to Walter*

Brueggemann. Edited by Tod Linafelt and Timothy K. Beal. Minneapolis: Fortress.

Balz, Horst. 2003. "*teras, aatos, to*." *EDNT* 3:350.

BBC. 2016. "The Truth about a Strange Blood-Sucking Monster." 10 November.

Beal, Timothy K. 2001. *Religion and Its Monsters*. New York: Routledge.

Bochart, Samuel. 1663. *Hierozoicon (or Hierozoici) Sive biparti Operis De Animalibus Scripturae*. London: Thomas Roycroft.

Carroll, Noel. 1990. *The Philosophy of Horror*. New York: Routledge.

Collins, Adela Yarbro. 1976. *Combat Myth in the Book of Revelation*. Atlanta: Scholars Press.

Day, John. 1985. *God's Conflict with the Dragon and the Sea: Echoes of a Canaanite Myth in the Old Testament*. Cambridge: Cambridge University Press.

———. 1992. "Leviathan." *ABD* 4:295–96.

Derrida, Jacques. 2009. *The Beast and the Sovereign*. Vol. 1. Translated by Geoffrey Bennington. Chicago: University of Chicago Press.

Freud, Sigmund. 1955. "The Uncanny." Pages 219–33 in *The Standard Edition of the Complete Psychological Works of Sigmund Freud*. Vol. 17. Edited and translated by James Strachey with Anna Freud. London: Hogarth.

Huet, Marie-Helene. 1993. *Monstrous Imagination*. Cambridge: Harvard University Press.

Moore, Stephen D. 2014a. "Ecotherology." Pages 196–209 in *Divinanimality: Animal Theory, Creaturely Theology*. Edited by Stephen D. Moore. New York: Fordham University Press.

———. 2014b. "Ruminations on Revelation's Ruminant, Quadrupedal Christ; or the Even-Toed, Ungulate That Therefore I Am." Pages 301–26 in *The Bible and Post-Humanism*. Edited by Jennifer L. Koosed. SemeiaSt 74. Atlanta: Society of Biblical Literature.

Otto, Rudolph. 1958. *The Idea of the Holy*. 2nd ed. New York: Oxford University Press.

Pope, Marvin H. 1965. *Job: Introduction, Translation and Notes*. AB 15. New York: Doubleday.

Schlobin, Roger C. 1992. "Prototypic Horror: The Genre of the Book of Job." *Semeia* 60:23–38.

Seesengood, Robert, and Jennifer L. Koosed. 2014. "Daniel's Animal Apocalypse." Pages 182–95 In *Divinanimality: Animal Theory, Crea-*

turely Theology. Edited by Stephen D. Moore. New York: Fordham University Press.

Slifkin, Natan. 2011. *Sacred Monsters: Mysterious and Mythical Creatures of Scripture, Talmud and Midrash*. Springfield, NJ: Gefen Books.

Steel, Allan. 2001. "Could Behemoth Have Been a Dinosaur?" *Creation* 15.2:42–45.

Wagner, Lloyd. 2004. *El Chupacabras: The Trail of the Goatsucker*. New York: iUniverse.

"He Differed in Nothing from the Beasts": The Disruption of the Human-Animal Difference in John Calvin's Commentary on Daniel 4

Peter Joshua Atkins

The narrative in Dan 4 contains a seemingly bizarre event: Nebuchadnezzar, king of Babylon, experiences a divine affliction that causes him to resemble an animal. The specifics of this bestial transformation are never fully described, and due to this, later commentators have struggled to understand this event. In his lectures on Daniel, John Calvin (1509–1564) eventually came to interpret this passage too; however, despite being seemingly untroubled by metamorphoses elsewhere in the Bible, he considered it "absurd" to suggest that Nebuchadnezzar had changed shape into an animal. This inconsistency in his interpretation is puzzling. This chapter will attempt to resolve this issue by proposing that Calvin likely interpreted the Danielic metamorphosis differently from others to make Nebuchadnezzar's punishment as severe as possible. Additionally, using the work of difference theorists and critical animal theory, this chapter will then examine how Calvin's specific interpretation of Dan 4 may counteract his intention to deny the animalization of Nebuchadnezzar. While he thinks of Nebuchadnezzar as remaining essentially human, Calvin's alternative explanation reveals the manifold complexities of the differences between beings and the reductive nature of a simplistic human-animal boundary.

Nebuchadnezzar's Transformation in Daniel 4

Daniel 4 recounts the narrative of King Nebuchadnezzar's dream followed by its eventual fulfillment in the second half of the narrative. Nebuchadnezzar sees a tree that grows up over the whole world until it is chopped down by command of an angelic "watcher" (Dan 4:1–14).[1] Daniel is the only one able to interpret the dream and reluctantly explains that the tree symbolizes Nebuchadnezzar himself. God will take his kingdom away from him and make him live in the wilderness (4:16–24). This subsequently comes to pass (4:25–30). After a fixed period of time is completed and Nebuchadnezzar acknowledges God, his kingdom is then restored to him (4:31–34).

A major aspect of this affliction is that Nebuchadnezzar is changed into an animal-like state. In his dream, the watcher commands that Nebuchadnezzar's "heart be changed from that of a human, and let the heart of an animal be given to it" (4:13). Later in the narrative, he is "driven out and he was eating grass like oxen and his body was wet from the dew of the heavens, until when his hair grew long like that of eagles and his nails were like those of birds" (4:30). However, the precise details of this animal transformation are not absolutely clear. When Nebuchadnezzar's heart is replaced with an animal heart (4:13), the text could be suggesting a physiological change whereby the beating heart of an animal is given to Nebuchadnezzar (and his body will then be partly animal); or this may be a reference to the heart as that which controls and dictates the actions and thoughts of an individual, and thus it involves only a behavioral or psychological modification to resemble a nonhuman animal. Both understandings are reflected in other parts of the Hebrew Bible/Old Testament (e.g., 2 Kgs 9:24, Prov 18:15; see also Wolff 1974, 40–58) and in Aramaic more generally (Sokoloff 2002, 616b).

Thus, the animal heart in the Danielic text may be read as either a physical or a psychological feature, or indeed incorporate both aspects. Elsewhere in Dan 4, both possible understandings of Nebuchadnezzar's affliction are seemingly supported. After Nebuchadnezzar's exile ends, his "reason" returns to him (4:31, 33) suggesting the affliction was psychological. Nevertheless, some physical changes do take place to make Nebuchadnezzar more physically animal-like (e.g., 4:30). Several of these changes are merely similes (i.e., Nebuchadnezzar gains characteristics that were animal-like and did not, for example, literally gain bird's claws), but they still describe some physical alteration of the king. The precise nature of Nebuchadnezzar's animal transformation in the narrative is therefore

---

1. I follow the verse numbering found in the MT in this essay. Any English translations of the text of Daniel are my own unless otherwise stated.

unclear and has left open two interpretative possibilities: he changed either physiologically or psychologically.

This ambiguity is borne out in the text's interpretation in the early modern period. Some interpreters understood the narrative as describing the literal change of Nebuchadnezzar into the form of an animal. The suggestion of a bovine metamorphosis in Dan 4 was prominent during the fifteenth and sixteenth centuries, when there was a resurgence of interest in lycanthropy. French philosopher Jean Bodin (1580, 101) writes, "[Lycanthropy] seems incredible and almost impossible to human sense. And nonetheless it is quite certain, that this is confirmed by the sacred history of King Nebuchadnezzar, about whom the Prophet Daniel speaks, he was converted and transformed into an ox."[2] For Bodin, such metamorphoses involve only a physical change. The mind and "reason," which Bodin considered the essentially human features (102), were unaffected. Several other philosophers proposed similar arguments that Nebuchadnezzar physically and substantially changed into an animal (Goclenius 1591, 86; Thomasius 1667, fol. C2rf).

Other early modern commentators concluded that Nebuchadnezzar was stricken with some form of frenzy that made him act like an animal. Andrew Willet (1610, 131–32) and William Pemble (1631, 62) adamantly deny that Nebuchadnezzar changed shape into a beast. John Mayer (1652, 533) writes that Nebuchadnezzar's affliction was "in his minde, and not in the transmutation of his body." These commentators decided Nebuchadnezzar did not physiologically transform into an animal and that a psychological understanding of the transformation should be adopted.[3]

John Calvin's Interpretation of Nebuchadnezzar and Daniel 4

It is amid this wider context of the early modern period that John Calvin's interpretation is situated. Calvin gave a series of lectures on the book of Daniel, which were then published in 1561 under the title *Praelectiones in Librum Prophetiarum Danielis*.[4] When faced with the issue of how to understand the bestial affliction in Dan 4, Calvin (1993, 189–90) acknowledged other commentators thought that Nebuchadnezzar changed shape

---

2. Translations of this text are my own.
3. For a fuller discussion of various interpretations of Nebuchadnezzar's affliction in the early modern period, see Atkins 2023.
4. For further detail on Calvin's lectures on Daniel, see Pitkin 2007.

into an animal; however, he decided this was not an appropriate interpretation: "Some think that Nebuchadnezzar was changed into an animal, but that is too harsh and absurd. So we are not to imagine some metamorphosis. But he was so rejected from human society that, save for his human shape, he differed nothing from the brute beasts."

He then proceeds to state that, while Nebuchadnezzar was changed to the same *status* as the other animals, his human shape was the one quality that was not affected. He emphasizes his decision later, stating: "God left him his human shape" (190). When confronted with passages describing Nebuchadnezzar's hair as like eagle's feathers or nails like the claws of a bird, Calvin is forced to concede that some physical change did take place. However, he is also careful to state that aside from these *likenesses* to other animals, overall the king kept his human shape (190). Moreover, Calvin explicitly rejects any proposal that Nebuchadnezzar actually became an animal, noting, "Nebuchadnezzar, although not changed into a beast, was yet deposed from the community of men and his whole body deformed" (229). Calvin concludes that Nebuchadnezzar "had been cast into ignominy of being like the wild beasts" (199). Therefore Calvin's understanding of the passage is simply that, while Nebuchadnezzar became *like* a beast, he was not changed *into* a beast.

Instead, Calvin adopts a psychological understanding of the narrative's events, and thus Nebuchadnezzar merely lost his human understanding and was seized with madness.[5] Calvin explains, "Either Nebuchadnezzar was seized by insanity, or while he was mad he left human society" (190). The loss of his reason was part of Nebuchadnezzar's overall punishment, so he would "be despoiled not only of his empire but also of human understanding, so that he would differ in nothing from the beasts" (165). Not only did he lose his kingdom and his place in society, but he lost his sanity too. In this insane state, Nebuchadnezzar lived like one of the animals, feeding alongside them, and became estranged from the human community (199). Only once "he had recovered his sanity" did Nebuchadnezzar return to his empire (199).

Calvin is quite clear in demonstrating his opinion that a physiological metamorphosis in Dan 4 is absurd, and in this he seems to be in accord with other commentators writing around the early modern period. He

---

5. However, Calvin (1993, 194) is forced to admit Nebuchadnezzar retained some remnant of intelligence, otherwise he would have been unaware of the torment inflicted on him.

advocates the idea that Nebuchadnezzar was afflicted psychologically with a bout of insanity where he lost all reason and human understanding and thus became like one of the beasts.

Understanding Calvin's Interpretation

While Calvin repeatedly reasserts his interpretation of Dan 4, beyond stating that a physiological transformation was absurd, his precise reasons for it are not immediately apparent. Indeed, his other writings suggest he should have no problem with the occurrence of a physiological metamorphosis. For example, in Gen 19, as Lot and his family flee from Sodom, his wife looks back and immediately becomes a pillar of salt. In his commentary on Genesis, Calvin (1948, 1:513) refers to this event as a metamorphosis and speaks of it in relation to the metamorphoses in the writings of Ovid. Calvin declares: "Since God created men out of nothing, why may he not, if he sees fit, reduce them again to nothing? If this is granted, as it must be; why, if he should please, may he not turn them into stones?" (1:513). Calvin even defends this transformation against other commentators, whom he calls "captious and perverse men," who denied the validity of this metamorphosis (1:513). He explains that people accept miracles in nature, such as an animal generating from a seed or a bird from an egg, so should not also deny this miraculous change of woman into salt. Calvin further explains that, as God can reduce humans back to that from which they were created, the transformation of her flesh into a saline corpse is only slightly different from that which normally happens to people when they die (1:513). Though he carefully states that her human soul remained intact, Calvin was resolved that Lot's wife nevertheless physiologically transformed into a pillar of salt.

Calvin is also content to find a physiological transformation in Exod 7, where Aaron's wooden staff is transformed into a living snake when he casts it onto the ground. Calvin (1852, 145) views this in a similar light to Gen 19: "But, because the rod was changed into a serpent in an extraordinary manner, and contrary to the course of nature, we must form the same judgement of it as of the change of Lot's wife into a pillar of salt; except that the rod soon after returned into its original nature."

Calvin can then state he is "confidently persuaded" the transformation was true because "there is no more difficulty with God to change the forms of things, than there was to create heaven and earth out of nothing" (1852, 145). Calvin is even able to ascribe the Egyptian magicians' ability to transform their staffs into snakes in Exod 7:11–12 to the power of God: "Such liberty was conceded to them by God, not that they should create one body out of another, but that they should set forth the work of God as being their own" (146). In this second example of a physical metamorphosis, Calvin again has no problems with accepting the truth of such transformations.

Therefore, it seems Calvin was content to believe in scriptural metamorphoses because of either the prevalence of transformations in nature or the omnipotence of God. Yet his assessment of Nebuchadnezzar's transformation clearly contrasts with how he deals with these other biblical transformations. To understand why Calvin may have adopted a different position regarding Nebuchadnezzar's transformation, this section will suggest that the implications of a psychological interpretation were, for Calvin, more important.

An appropriate starting point to identify the implications of Calvin's interpretation of Dan 4 is to examine the reason for Nebuchadnezzar's transformation. Calvin (1993, 152) explains that the primary cause of Nebuchadnezzar's affliction was that he was consumed by pride and "glories in himself as a king of kings, and in Babylon as the queen of the whole world!" In a later passage, Calvin characterizes Nebuchadnezzar's pride as "his disease" (192). This pride thus seems to be the primary failing of the king and the cause of his subsequent punishment. If pride was the "disease," Calvin later explains the cure:

> Just as the remedy is difficult and lengthy when some vital part is corrupt, almost wasted away, so, because pride is deeply infixed in men's hearts and invades their innermost being and infects everything within the soul, it is not easily eradicated—and this is important to note. We are also taught that God so worked within King Nebuchadnezzar. (192)

Unlike bodily illnesses, Calvin spoke of pride as an infection of the soul that needed curing. However, while bodily sickness requires a medical cure, the soul needs a divine cure.

This cure for pride seems to be found in the transformation of Nebuchadnezzar. Calvin (1993, 200) later imagines a statement by Nebuchadnezzar: "I was swollen with pride; God corrected it with such a terrible punishment." This appears to confirm the idea that, in Calvin's interpretation, Nebuchadnezzar's affliction was a divinely ordained cure for his pride. Thus, if Calvin saw Nebuchadnezzar's pride as an illness of the soul, the remedy and punishment must also affect his soul (and not his body). A physiological transformation of the king could not adequately address his pride (as it would only affect his body); therefore Calvin must advocate a psychological transformation in Dan 4.

When it comes to describing this psychological transformation, Calvin explains that Nebuchadnezzar loses a specific component of his soul: his human reason. In Calvin's thought, reason was one of the soul's two main faculties, and thus by losing this characteristic Nebuchadnezzar received an appropriate remedy for his soul's affliction (Voorster 2014, 4). However, it is also clear that losing his human reason would be a very effective humbling experience to rectify the royal pride. For Calvin, the capacity to reason most significantly distinguishes humans from and elevates them above nonhuman animals. In his *Institutes of the Christian Religion*, Calvin (1960, 2.2.17) states, "We see among all mankind that reason is proper to our nature; it distinguishes us from brute beasts,"[6] and elsewhere he claims, "We know that men have this unique quality above the other animals, that they are endued with reason and intelligence" (Calvin 1959, 18). Moreover, even in his commentary on Dan 4, Calvin (1993, 229) states, "We know that the chief difference between men and the brute animals is that men understand and judge but brute animals are carried away by their senses." Reason therefore seems to be the principal characteristic that differentiates humans from other animals in Calvin's thought (see also the discussions in Voorster 2014, 4; Engel 2002, 49; Niesel 1956, 65). The physiological distinctiveness of humanity (e.g., the human form) is less important for Calvin (1960, 1.15.3), as he admits, "God's glory shines forth in the outer man," but "the image of God, which is seen or glows in these outward marks, is spiritual." While Calvin recognized the existence of a physically recognizable difference between humans and other animals, this was only a manifestation of the true difference in the human soul, of which reason was a principal part.

Thus the implication of Calvin's interpretative decision regarding Dan 4 is that God inflicted on Nebuchadnezzar, at least in Calvin's eyes, a far harsher punishment. While Nebuchadnezzar may have looked physically different if he had been changed into the form of an animal, his position above the rest of creation would have been more secure. However, with his

---

6. The English translation of Calvin's *Institutes* used throughout this essay is Calvin 1960.

reason gone, Nebuchadnezzar lost a key identifier of his humanity. Calvin (1993, 229, 177) himself states that God "gave a memorable example" by reducing him to "the utmost shame, differing nothing from the brute beasts." This more plainly humiliates Nebuchadnezzar, as, in Calvin's view, his punishment was more severe if his soul and not his body was affected.

Calvin's psychological interpretation of Nebuchadnezzar's transformation in Dan 4 may be seen to be motivated by two factors. First, by losing his reason, Nebuchadnezzar receives an appropriate punishment that affects his soul, just as the pride that caused his punishment originated in his soul. Second, in Calvin's thought, a psychological transformation was a much harsher punishment for the king, which more effectively humbled the proud monarch.

The Animalization of Nebuchadnezzar by John Calvin

While I have examined the reasons for Calvin's interpretation of Dan 4, his understanding of the biblical narrative has further implications for his conception of the human-animal boundary and the way in which it can be conceived. Before these implications are assessed, it will be useful to briefly note the work of critical animal theorists on the difference (or differences) between humans and animals. In his volume *Thinking through Animals*, Matthew Calarco (2015, 28–47) notes the work of scholars who attend to the difference between the human and the animal. Such "difference theorists" work toward deconstructing traditional notions of a human-animal binary but also "seek to undercut the notion that there is a simple, single barrier separating human beings from animals" (38). To do this, the difference between humans and animals is complicated and multiplied through an acknowledgment of the various differences that exist between individual humans, but also those between individual animals. For example, those characteristics (such as reason or language) that are typically seen as uniquely human are themselves found in varying degrees among human and nonhuman animals. Rather than a single human-animal difference, it might be better to reflect on the various *differences* that separate individuals within, as well as between, species.

The difference theorist whose work on the human-animal binary has perhaps been the most influential is Jacques Derrida. In his work he is suspicious of traditional Western philosophical accounts of the construction of the human, and he sees the animal as having a central role in how such ideas are determined (Derrida and Roudinesco 2004, 63). The human is traditionally constructed in opposition to the category of "the animal" in order to determine what is proper to human nature. Derrida (2002, 399) critiques this idea and suggests that in opposition to the human there is not a homogenous grouping that shares something of "animality," but rather an entirely heterogenous group including a "multiplicity of the living, or more precisely (since to say 'the living' is already to say too much or not enough) a multiplicity of organizations of relations between living and dead.... These relations are at once close and abyssal, and they can never be totally objectified."

The recognition of this multiplicity and heterogeneity of what has been called "the animal" has implications for how the human-animal boundary is viewed. The traditional division between the human and the animal seems reductive as, instead of attending to the richness of human or animal life, it imagines a group of animals that are somehow associated by a shared essence. One might, like Calarco (2008, 142), ask: "Do not 'human beings' belong to this multiplicity of beings and relations? Are we to believe that humans are somehow exempt from the play of differences and forces, of becomings and relations? Are not 'human beings' sliding constantly along a series of differences, including those that are thought to separate human from animal, animal from plant, and life in general from death?" The idea of a clear and clean boundary between the human and animal is not possible due to the essential plurality of different beings, and due to the varying relations between them.

Returning to Calvin's (1993, 189–90, 199, 229) commentary, he emphasizes multiple times that Nebuchadnezzar did not actually turn into an animal and makes his intention to deny a physical transformation abundantly obvious. However, the consequence of his decision to interpret Nebuchadnezzar's affliction differently from other similar metamorphic accounts is that Nebuchadnezzar's essential status as a human can legitimately be called into question. While Calvin categorically denies that the king was deprived of his human form, in so doing it is also clear that Nebuchadnezzar's human form was the only remaining part of his essential humanity. Calvin states, "Save for his human shape, he differed in nothing from the brute beasts" (189–90). The single distinctively human feature that Nebuchadnezzar retained was his human physical shape—he was animal in every way except his appearance. This implies that all other distinctively human qualities that made Nebuchadnezzar different from animals (including reason, which Calvin explicitly mentions being removed) must be absent. Thus in Calvin's interpretation, by losing reason and other distinctively human faculties, Nebuchadnezzar's soul must effectively be changed into that of an animal, albeit with his body remaining human. His interpretation of the narrative therefore results not in an essentially human Nebuchadnezzar in animal form but instead in a genuinely animal Nebuchadnezzar who appears physically human. Within his own framework, Calvin (perhaps unintentionally) ends up suggesting that Nebuchadnezzar actually *does* transform into an animal.

Furthermore, within Calvin's own thought, when Nebuchadnezzar loses the spiritual distinctiveness of humanity (reason), he is in danger of also losing the image of God. For Calvin (1851, 24; 1960, 1.15.3), the image of God was specifically linked with the capacity of reason—"They [humans] are endued with mind and intelligence, and so far they bear some likeness to God"—and is specifically located in the soul: "It is not absurd for man, in respect to his soul, to be called God's image." If Nebuchadnezzar is to lose reason, understanding, and other human features of the soul, then he inevitably also loses the image of God (see the similar discussion in Zachman 2012, 45). Calvin (1960, 1.15.3) is willing to allow that some physical characteristics may be included under the image of God, but the fundamental aspects of it, which he considers to be spiritual and rational (Zachman 2012, 43–44), would be missing from the irrational Nebuchadnezzar.

While these appear to be the implications of Calvin's interpretation when situated within his wider thought, he resists them and continues to insist on Nebuchadnezzar's essential human status. However, in so doing, Calvin's interpretation demonstrates the ultimate breakdown of a simplistic understanding of the difference between human and animal. As Calvin suggests Nebuchadnezzar's human reason disappeared in the narrative, he must rely on another element to continue contending that Nebuchadnezzar was essentially human. In his own interpretation of the narrative, Calvin (1993, 190) states that the only trace of Nebuchadnezzar's humanity that remained was his human form. It therefore seems that his physical human form fulfills the function of marking Nebuchadnezzar's human status.

Based on his writings elsewhere, it may seem unreasonable for Calvin to expect that the human physical form is enough on its own to cause an individual to be categorized as human, when all other features are essentially animal. In his *Institutes of the Christian Religion*, Calvin (1960, 1.15.3) writes of the human shape as being only a manifestation or "display" of the divine glory of the human soul, or as a way in which the spiritual image of God is made conspicuous. He does not speak of the human form as being

"He Differed in Nothing from the Beasts" 61

able to distinguish humans from animals on its own; only the spiritual aspects of the human can do this (Shih 2004, 263). However, his reliance on the human form in Dan 4 appears to give a peculiar prominence to the physical distinctiveness of humanity in marking out the human-animal boundary. The efficacy of reason alone as the human "unique quality" that sets them "above the other animals" is seemingly laid bare, as it does not ultimately make the crucial difference to an individual's categorization in Calvin's (1959, 18) thought. His interpretation essentially demonstrates that the human-animal binary is governed by not one but multiple features. In the context of his commentary on Dan 4, Calvin cannot rely only on reason as the distinguishing human feature but must acknowledge the role of additional factors in determining the limit of the human. This demonstrates what Derrida might call a fold in the human-animal boundary. Based on Calvin's reading of Dan 4, some humans can evidently lack reason and yet still be essentially human. There are different humans who relate to this concept in varying ways or, as Derrida (2002, 399) would say, there is "a heterogenous multiplicity" of humankind. The use of the phrase "the human" disguises the diversity of humankind, who may vary in their individual relation to a traditional human-animal binary.

This awareness of the "many fractures, heterogeneities, differential structures" within humanity might even be found in Calvin's wider writings (Derrida and Roudinesco 2004, 66). He was evidently not unaware of the potential problems associated with using reason as a defining characteristic of humanity, as he recognizes numerous examples of situations where it can be diminished or threatened. He notes that some people "lack reason" as a result of some defect from birth; excessive consumption of alcohol can lead people to deprive themselves of it; and others are simply labeled by him as "imbeciles" who lack basic reason (Calvin 1960, 2.2.17; 1948, 1:301; 1960, 2.2.14). However, when considering cases where humans lack reason, Calvin (1960, 2.2.17; see also 2.2.13) concludes, "Still, we see in this diversity some remaining traces of the image of God, which distinguish the entire human race from the other creatures." He seems uncomfortable with the idea that some humans may entirely descend to the level of the beasts and reluctant to see them as relinquishing the image of God. Instead, he proposes that some traces of the image of God continue to keep those individuals distinct from animals.[7] Thus, despite

---

7. Julie Canlis notes that the distinction between human and animal has, for

apparently lacking reason, Calvin still defends these individuals' essential human nature from a possible descent to animality, relying on additional markers of humanity, thereby tacitly acknowledging the multiplicity of the human-animal difference.

It is not only on the human side of the binary where this multiplicity of difference can be found, though. While Calvin is clear that Nebuchadnezzar was made to differ in nothing from the beasts, the change he underwent was not only centered on his loss of rationality. There were other changes to Nebuchadnezzar that acknowledged the multiplicity of the animal creatures on the other side of the binary—for example, his nails are likened to an eagle's, his hair to bird's feathers, and his diet to an ox's (Dan 4:30). These references in the biblical passage provide evidence that we cannot "speak of 'the animal' as of a single set that can be opposed to 'us,' 'humans'" (Derrida 2002, 90). The inherent multiplicity of features within the animal world and "the infinite space that separates" the eagle from the ox means that there is no single difference between human and animal (34). Instead, there are multiple points of difference between humans and the other animals—for example, one way eagles differ from humans is the form of their nails, whereas one way oxen differ is by their diet. Nebuchadnezzar is becoming like some animals, but not like all of them. Calvin might be seen to homogenize some of these varieties of change in Nebuchadnezzar, for example, when Nebuchadnezzar is told he will eat grass like oxen. Calvin (1993, 190) comments that he will "eat grass as if you were a brute beast," perhaps implying all animals eat grass. However, the text itself acknowledges the existence of a variety of different creatures that make up the category "animal." Nebuchadnezzar is not simply living as another member of a vast homogenous group of animals that all possess the same characteristics; rather, he is cohabiting with many creatures. Indeed, as the king's transformation includes a variety of changes that cause him to become increasingly similar to a diverse selection of animals, he might almost be thought of as a personification of the multiplicity inherent to the animals. Essentially, while Calvin might insist in his interpretation that Nebuchadnezzar did not become *an animal*, through assuming various features resembling a bird, an ox, and an eagle,

---

Calvin, a qualitative dimension. It is crucial that the "excellence" of humankind is turned toward God (Canlis 2009, 95–96). However, this also cannot be said of Nebuchadnezzar in Dan 4 and thus cannot distinguish him from the animals there.

the king might become one of the *animals* (or, as Derrida [2002, 47] might say, *animot*).

Therefore, Calvin's commentary on the narrative of Dan 4 can help us reflect critically on the construction of a human-animal boundary. If, as he claims, reason is the defining human characteristic, then, despite his ostensible protestations to the contrary, Calvin provides an example of an individual who spends time on both sides of the human-animal divide. While he is adamant that Nebuchadnezzar did not become an animal and did not change form, by counterproposing that he lost his reason, Calvin's Nebuchadnezzar may transgress this boundary in a far more significant way. Calvin's particular interpretative strategy with regard to the narrative of Dan 4 thus may result (perhaps unintentionally) in a significantly more striking transformation, one with potentially far-reaching consequences for the perceived fluidity of the human-animal boundary. However, if Nebuchadnezzar does remain human, as Calvin insists, we can find a useful example of the multiplicity and heterogeneity implicit within a construction of the human-animal boundary. Nebuchadnezzar becomes different, but, if he remains human, his change reveals the differences within humanity, just as the various kinds of animal-like changes he undergoes reveal the range of differences between animals. He may not change into an animal, but neither does he remain the same human. Instead, Nebuchadnezzar has been "sliding constantly along a series of differences, including those that are thought to separate human from animal" (Calarco 2008, 142).

Conclusion

In his commentary on Daniel, Calvin tries to deny that Nebuchadnezzar changed into an animal by suggesting instead that his reason was taken away. Some have argued that Calvin's psychological reading of the passage results in a more appropriate punishment for Nebuchadnezzar's pride but also a far harsher treatment of the king. As Calvin conceived of reason as being the primary unique property of humanity, by robbing him of it, God punishes Nebuchadnezzar far more severely than by causing him to change form.

However, coupled with this effect is that Calvin's interpretation causes Nebuchadnezzar to move far more significantly toward being an animal than if he had merely taken the form of one. Within his own theological worldview, reason is intrinsically linked to the image of God and an individual's status as a human. By understanding Nebuchadnezzar's punishment as a loss of reason, Calvin is, intentionally or not, advocating that Nebuchadnezzar lost his humanity and was reduced to the status of an animal. It is precisely in his attempt to deny the ostensible animalization of Nebuchadnezzar that Calvin is nonetheless forced to construct a situation whereby Nebuchadnezzar did in fact become an animal.

Nevertheless, through his continued attempts to deny that Nebuchadnezzar became categorically an animal, Calvin maintains that the king remained human throughout his affliction even after losing (in Calvin's eyes) the uniquely human characteristic of reason. This interpretation of the text favored by Calvin reveals that the difference between the human and the animal is not one single line or point of division (as suggested in Calvin 1959, 18). Rather, there are multiple lines, or multiple differences, between (and within) humans and other animals. Reason may indicate one difference; the human form may indicate another. Thus, by claiming that Nebuchadnezzar retained his humanity but also "differed in nothing from the beasts," Calvin (1993, 190) shows the complicated nature of human-animal *differences* and the reductive nature of a simplistic division between humans and other animals.

Works Cited

Atkins, Peter Joshua. 2023. *The Animalising Affliction of Nebuchadnezzar in Daniel 4: Reading across the Human-Animal Boundary*. LHBOTS. London: Bloomsbury.
Bodin, Jean. 1580. *De la démonanie des sorciers*. Paris: Jacques Du Puys.
Calarco, Matthew. 2008. *Zoographies: The Question of the Animal from Heidegger to Derrida*. New York: Columbia University Press.
———. 2015. *Thinking through Animals: Identity, Difference, Indistinction*. StBr. Stanford, CA: Stanford University Press.
Calvin, John. 1851. *Commentaries on the Book of the Prophet Jeremiah and Lamentations*. Translated by John Owen. Vol. 2. Edinburgh: Calvin Translation Society.
———. 1852. *Commentaries on the Four Last Books of Moses Arranged in the Form of a Harmony*. Translated by Charles William Bingham. Vol. 1. Edinburgh: Calvin Translation Society.
———. 1948. *Commentaries on the First Book of Moses Called Genesis*. Translated by John King. 2 vols. Grand Rapids: Eerdmans.
———. 1959. *The Gospel according to St John 1–10*. Translated by T. H. L. Parker. CNTC 4. Edinburgh: Saint Andrew Press.

———. 1960. *Institutes of the Christian Religion*. Edited by John T. McNeill. Translated by Ford Lewis Battles. 2 vols. LCC 20. Louisville: Westminster John Knox.

———. 1993. *Daniel I: Chapters 1–6*. Translated by T. H. L. Parker. COTC 20. Grand Rapids: Eerdmans.

Canlis, Julie. 2009. "What Does It Mean to Be Human? John Calvin's Surprising Answer." *TScot* 16:93–106.

Derrida, Jacques. 2002. "The Animal That Therefore I Am (More to Follow)." Translated by David Wills. *CI* 28:369–418.

Derrida, Jacques, and Elisabeth Roudinesco. 2004. "Violence against Animals." Pages 62–76 in *For What Tomorrow…: A Dialogue*. Translated by Jeff Fort. Stanford, CA: Stanford University Press.

Engel, Mary P. 2002. *John Calvin's Perspectival Anthropology*. Eugene, OR: Wipf & Stock.

Goclenius, Rudolph. 1591. *Scholae seu Disputations Physicae, More Academic Fere Propositae et Haitae Plaeraeque Omnes in Schola Illustri Cattorum*. Marburg: Egenolphus.

Mayer, John. 1652. *A Commentary upon All the Prophets Both Great and Small*. London: Miller and Cotes.

Niesel, Wilhelm. 1956. *The Theology of Calvin*. Translated by Harold Knight. London: Lutterworth.

Pemble, William. 1631. *The Period of the Persian Monarchie*. London: Capel.

Pitkin, Barbara. 2007. "Prophecy and History in Calvin's Lectures on Daniel (1561)." Pages 323–47 in *Die Geschichte der Daniel-Auslegung in Judentum, Christentum und Islam: Studien zur Kommentierung des Danielbuches in Literatur und Kunst*. Edited by Katharina Bracht and David DuToit. Berlin: de Gruyter.

Shih, Shu-Ying. 2004. "The Development of Calvin's Understanding of the *Imago Dei* in the *Institutes of the Christian Religion* from 1536 to 1559." PhD diss., Ruprecht Karls University of Heidelberg.

Sokoloff, Michael. 2002. *A Dictionary of Jewish Babylonian Aramaic of the Talmudic and Geonic Periods*. DTMT 3. London: Johns Hopkins University Press.

Thomasius, Jacobus. 1667. *De Transformatione Hominum in Bruta Dissertationem Philosophicam*. Leipzig: Hahnius.

Voorster, Nicolaas. 2014. "Calvin on Human Reason." *IDS* 48:1–9.

Willet, Andrew. 1610. *Hexapla In Danielem*. Cambridge: Cambridge University Press.

Wolff, Hans Walter. 1974. *Anthropology of the Old Testament*. Philadelphia: Fortress.

Zachman, Randall C. 2012. *Reconsidering John Calvin*. CIT 9. Cambridge: Cambridge University Press.

"Let Them Eat Straw":
An Ecological Reevaluation of Isaiah 11:6–8

Jacob R. Evers

And wolf will sojourn with lamb
and leopard lie down with kid
And calf and young lion and fattened ox together
and a little child leading them
And cow and bear will graze
together their young will lie down
and like cattle, lion will eat straw
And nursing child will play on a serpent's hole,
And on a viper's light-hole weaned child putting its hand. (Isa 11:6–8)[1]

Commentators frequently explicate the vision described in Isa 11:6–8 using terms such as *peace* and *harmony*, as though the vison conveyed an ideal state of affairs. The text, they say, evinces the motif of return to an ideal past, to Edenic paradise (e.g., Smith 2007, 273; Tull 2010, 232–33; Roberts 2015, 180), or, alternatively, the motif of promised ideal future brought about through a righteous ruler (e.g., Wildberger 1991, 481; Childs 2001, 103; Van Ee 2018, 319–37). While I would not exclude the possibility that the images in the vision are related to creation theology or royal ideology, the widespread construal of the vision as a peaceful or ideal scenario warrants scrutiny. To arrive at such an understanding, interpreters focus selectively on certain aspects of the portrayal, to the neglect of others. After introducing my approach and summarizing potential problems with traditional readings, I will analyze the passage itself with a focus on the

---

1. For the purposes of this essay I translate the MT, as it presents difficulties that pertain to the concerns that guide my analysis. I have consulted other textual traditions to illuminate the obscurities of the MT. See the notes included with my analysis of the text for further discussion of translation decisions that are significant for interpretation.

oft-neglected elements. As I will show, these elements primarily concern the depiction of nonhuman animals. Furthermore, I will discuss how the construal of the vision as an ideal scenario may yield fraught ideological implications when used as a resource for contemporary ethics—especially given the ecological disruption and predator depletion caused by modern human activity. In a concluding proposal, I will suggest we reconsider reading the vision as an allegory for the purposes of retrieval.

In the analysis that follows, I discern overlooked aspects of the text by attending closely to the portrayal of nonhuman animals, with empathy for the wildlife depicted. These aspects of the text could well be observed by any interpreter; it just happens that the lens I apply brings them into particular focus and so opens fruitful lines of investigation. A few words on this lens. In reading with empathy for nonhuman animals, I rely on interpretive strategies developed by the Earth Bible Project, particularly the strategy of identification (Habel 2000, 25–37; 2008, 4–5; see also Balabanski 2013, 20–31). As I adopt it, this strategy involves examining the text in light of the experiences and interests of nonhuman animals. Broadly, some of my guiding concerns include how nonhuman animals fare in the envisioned events, and how (and why) nonhuman animals are characterized the way they are.

Insofar as I grant ethical consideration to nonhuman animals in the process of interpretation, my approach also relies on previous work in the discipline of animal studies. Recognition of animals' moral agency or subjectivity (as a property shared with humans) is associated with what Matthew Calarco (2015, 13–19) calls the identity approach. I attend also to the question of how the biblical text may reflect or promote certain ways of relating to nonhuman animals. Prompting this interrogation is my own recognition of the ways in which human practices and institutions govern and exploit the lives of nonhuman animals in the contemporary world. For Calarco, consideration of such power dynamics, along with the political ramifications of human violence against animals, figures prominently in the indistinction approach (63–67). Finally, as will become apparent in the analysis, my reading of the vision in Isa 11:6–8 raises a variety of questions surrounding the anthropocentric bias of the text *and* its interpreters.[2]

---

2. Although I attempt an interpretation that does not privilege human interests, I do so using a framework that assumes anthropocentric conceptions of agency and subjectivity. Critical animal studies theorists have rightly shown that humans remain at the center when ethical reflection is grounded in human-animal identification (see Calarco 2015, 49–51).

"Let Them Eat Straw"   69

Interpreters, of course, have extensively discussed the general portrait of nonhuman animals in Isa 11:6–8. But traditional construals of Isa 11:6–8 as a glimpse of a new (or renewed), peaceful world do tend to be forged from a selective handling of details in the text. Taking for granted certain assumptions about the relationship between human and nonhuman animals, interpreters do not comment on the power dynamics, or conflict between species, embedded in the imagery. It is as though the vision, once pegged as that of a peaceable and ideal order, is simply too enticing to scrutinize—even for those who read the passage with evident concern for the nonhuman. Take Walter Brueggemann (1998) as a representative example. Brueggemann recognizes in the text an interest in the way the human exercise of power negatively affects the created order ("adversarial human transactions foul the nest for all creatures" [102]). But no further does he probe the power relations in the vision or the notions about interspecies relations that characterize his own worldview. Underpinning his interpretation of the text is an affirmation of God-ordained human dominion over creation, whereby "God fully authorizes the right human agents" to "make it possible for the earth to function fruitfully" (102–3). Neither does Brueggemann appear to question whether the relations between species depicted in Isa 11:6–8 actually make for the kind of world he describes. On what grounds, one might ask, can the envisioned state of affairs be deemed fruitful, safe, healthy, and free of domination (Brueggemann 1998, 103)? Or, more pointedly, for whom is this state of affairs fruitful, safe, healthy, and free?

Even those who adopt a more explicitly suspicious stance toward the text seem to be enticed by this conception of the vision as a world in harmony. In a contribution to the Earth Bible series, John W. Olley (2001, 227), who attempts to read from an animal perspective, praises the inclusiveness of the vision in Isa 11:6–8 as that of an earth "made right." Olley concludes, "Just as young human children will be in the future kingdom, so too will the whole animal family.... Wild or domestic, their integrity and diversity is affirmed" (227). While it is true that both wild and domesticated animals make an appearance in the vision, the text does not indicate that all species will participate; it depicts a small, curated selection. The nonhuman animals that do make an appearance engage in markedly novel relations, yet they also conform to a not-so-novel system of human agriculture. It would scarcely be an exaggeration to characterize the portrayal as one of domestication taken to an extreme. There is also quite a contrast in the agency of human figures as compared to that afforded to the nonhuman animals in the text. One might expect an interpreter reading from an animal perspective to remark on the centrality of human beings in the vision, on the place of domestication in the supposedly harmonious interspecies relations depicted, or on the gaps in the text. How exactly were these predators domesticated? Which species benefit from the envisioned arrangement? How might other species—and the larger environment—be affected?

Let us proceed, then, to an analysis of the text that grapples with the questions that arise when the vision and its implicit ideology are put under scrutiny. The content of the passage itself is clear enough in some respects. First, various groupings of animals are described in a manner that suggests the creatures shall dwell together (Isa 11:6); the descriptions further imply a transformation that will enable a common diet (v. 7) and that will apparently eliminate the need for aggression in resolving interspecies conflict (v. 8). The presentation conveys a seeming end of hostilities by its pattern of references to predators alongside would-be victims. Pairs include wolf and lamb (v. 6aα), leopard and kid (v. 6aβ), bear and cow (v. 7aα), lion and ox (v. 7b), snake and human child (v. 8).

The few portions of the oracle in which such pairing is not evident function to amplify this portrait of (supposedly) harmonious relations. In verse 6b, following the MT,[3] the word order is such that reference to the young lion is encased by references to the calf and fattened ox, the structure of the line thereby imaging that which the words portray. In the next line, one finds a little child driving this band of animals—a scenario marked by the absence of the threat typically posed by predators (v. 6bβ). The reference in verse 7 to the grouping of young calves and cubs presses the point further still: even the smallest offspring of livestock—the weakest, the most immobile and inexperienced, the most vulnerable to predation—will be safe enough to rest together with the offspring of a bear (v. 7aβ). So much for the proverbial ferocity of a protective bear sow (2 Sam 17:8, Hos 13:8, Prov 17:12).

However, adopting the lens described above, one also finds several indications of residual conflict that bespeak a less than ideal outcome. For the reader empathetic toward nonhumans, a striking feature of Isa 11:6–8 is the prominence of humanity. The references to calf, young lion, and

---

3. 1QIsa^a, however, has *ymrw* (a verb, "they will grow fat") rather than the MT's noun *mry'* ("fattened ox"). The line would thus conform to the pattern of depicting an unlikely pair of animals engaged in shared activity.

fattened ox in verse 6 follow after two parallel lines that each consist of a subject of one creature, a verb, and a prepositional phrase referring to a second creature ("wolf will sojourn with lamb, and leopard lie down with kid," v. 6a). The line with the triad of creatures (calf, lion, fattened ox) thus diverges from the pattern of the preceding lines not just by number of animals but also by its lack of explicit verb. So reading, as one follows this development, searching perhaps for the expected verb, one comes to the end of the verse and finds only a participle with not a beast but a human as its lone subject: "a little child leading them" (v. 6bβ). Semantically, one might note that this description of the human child's action stands in contrast to the more static descriptions of the nonhumans. From the onset, then, both form and content seem to highlight human agency.

Similarly, at the end of the portrayal in verse 8, one finds human figures in a place of prominence. The idea here is that serpents have become harmless, but nursing child and weaned child are the respective subjects of the verbs (v. 8). By contrast, the wildlife is mentioned only in prepositional phrases that refer to its dwelling (signifying "cavern" and "nest," according to the LXX). As with the calf, young lion, and fattened ox, the snakes are referenced apart from any direct relation to the action of the verbs. The imagery is consequently that of agile hunters atypically characterized by restraint and passivity before human actors.

But alongside the creatures that populate the grammatical background, some nonhuman animals are presented as active subjects in the vision. These include the wolf, leopard, cow, and bear (Isa 11:6–7). Yet of the five verbs of which these animals are the subject, two are forms of the same word denoting the act of lying down to rest (*rbṣ* in vv. 6aβ and 7aβ). While relaying such an act is not necessarily significant on its own (see, e.g., Gen 49:9), the repetition is conspicuous, given the emphasis on the passive docility of wild beasts in the portrayal as a whole. It may then connote not the satisfied lying down of lions in their den as after the hunt (Ps 104:20–22) but the fatigued respite of the oppressed (see, e.g., Exod 23:5, Isa 14:30). Accordingly, two other verbs with predators as their subjects are used in expressions of activity reserved for livestock: grazing (*rʿh*) in Isa 11:7aα and eating straw (*ʾkl*) in 7b.[4]

---

4. Not to mention "growing fat" (*mrʾ*) in v. 6bα, if one follows 1QIsaᵃ. Regarding *rʿh*, this interpretation applies if one follows the LXX in reading a passive form of *rʿh* I, with *yḥdw* ("together") being an *apokoinou* construction (Roberts 2015, 178). *Rʿh* may describe human shepherding, but in describing nonmetaphorical feeding, its use

The remaining verb, "dwelling as alien" (*gwr*), indicates that the wolf will stay with the lamb, just as the stranger depends on the resident for refuge (Isa 11:6aα). That the wolf (and lamb, for that matter) should comply with such an arrangement is remarkable. Questions arise, however, from the representation of the addressees' own social norms in this portrayal of interspecies relations. Does the depiction suggest nonhuman animals will actually conform to the customs on which the scenario draws—conform, that is, to human culture? The wolf, as sojourner, was previously an outsider to the domain of human life but has now been brought into the fold. Are the words, then, an acknowledgment of the wolf's agency, or perhaps an indicator of the creature's desperation for survival? The lamb found a place in the human sphere, so the wolf follows suit and submits to human imposition, just as refugees submit to the one who provides shelter (Gen 12:10–13, 19:1–9, 26:1–7, Ps 120:5–7). The expression of the predators' (in)activity in the following lines may confirm the suspicion that their apparent agency here has been leveraged to serve human interests.

So even where humans are not mentioned explicitly in Isa 11:6–8, their influence over the nonhuman looms in the portrayal. Word choice is telling in that respect. In addition to the verb reflecting human customs for resident aliens, one finds the mention of straw (*tbl*). This signals the text's assumption of a particular ecological order that functions to sustain a way of life advantageous for human beings—one that involves cultivating plants and domesticating animals. Straw is convenient feed for farm animals because it is a byproduct of human grain farming; it is not, however, a nutritious feed. In the Old Testament itself, other references to providing straw for domesticated animals indicate that it was given alongside actual fodder that would include grain.[5] In this vision, though, it is just the straw that is to be consumed—and not only by domesticated ruminants but even by the now-tamed predators (v. 7b).

---

is restricted to the activity of livestock. Though see the rhetorical use of *rʿh* to describe the "grazing" of humans alongside livestock in Jonah 3:7.

5. With *mspwʾ* ("fodder") in Gen 24:25, 32; Judg 19:19. With *śʿrh* ("barley") in 1 Kgs 5:8. See also the distinction between *tbl* and *br* ("grain") assumed by the rhetorical question in Jer 23:28. For modern cattle farmers the use of straw for feed is a matter of resource management and often a cost-saving mechanism. The pertinent questions addressed by agricultural institutions become, how much straw may be safely fed to animals? See, e.g., Alberta Agriculture and Forestry Ministry 2007.

Of course, felids as they exist in the world are incapable of surviving on a diet consisting exclusively of vegetation (see, e.g., Zoran 2002, 1559–67), a fact that again may tempt the reader to take the vision in terms of an ideal past or ideal world to come. But what one finds here is not some alternative, paradisaical order. The emergence of predators who eat *straw*, in particular, bespeaks a scenario in which certain nonhuman animals conform completely to a real-world system of human agriculture. Not only do the beasts refrain from hunting livestock (thereby saving humans resources otherwise used to protect the flocks and herds), but they actively participate in human agricultural efforts by consuming—presumably to the detriment of their health—crop residues, the refuse that must be removed after threshing has been completed. The depiction implies that the likes of lions and bears shall essentially become livestock themselves, beasts of burden akin to the bovines that were raised primarily for hauling, plowing, and threshing (Boer 2015, 64–65).

That the shape of the portrayal in Isa 11:6-7 revolves around the security of human agrarian society is also evident from the specific creatures listed. Notably, there is no mention of the wild creatures on whom wolves, bears, and wildcats prey. These would likely have included ruminants such as the ibex, deer, onager, or aurochs, but also small mammals such as the hare, and birds such as the swallow. Thus, it is not necessarily the case that the text offers a vision of peace between animals generally, or among all species of animals. As it stands, the text mentions only domesticated animals and human beings in its presentation of those that shall coexist happily with predators. If the vision suggests what Edward Young (1972, 389) calls a "reversal of nature," it is a limited reversal and one that expressly profits humans. Together with the previously discussed straw, the reference to a bovine fattened for slaughter (*mry'*) would seem to reflect the concern for the prosperity of human agriculture. Animals raised for human consumption, or for sacrifice to the deity as a benefit to humans,[6] shall be safe from the interference of wildlife. What is in view, then, is not the problem of predation *generally* but that of specific animal behaviors that disrupt or threaten human interests. The imagery in the text effectively resituates the wild carnivores in such a way that they fit neatly into the human agricultural order, destabilizing it no longer. Accordingly,

---

6. See, however, Morgan (2010, 32–45), who questions whether sacrifice is best understood as an anthropocentric practice.

if the scenario invokes the agency of the creatures, it does so to communicate not the natural majesty of their self-determination but their docility before human conquerors. The ideal animal is that which has been tamed.

As regards the serpents (*ptn* and *ṣpʿwny*) mentioned in connection with human offspring in Isa 11:8, their presence is perhaps not surprising, given the realities of village life in agrarian societies.[7] The human transformation of wildland into farmland creates conditions that are enticing for such carnivorous reptiles, as the concomitant crops, animal carcasses, and waste attract a myriad of insects and rodents on which snakes may prey. The establishment of human settlements entails the removal of predators that would otherwise control snake populations in the area (see, e.g., Santos 2013), thereby necessitating human management. But a healthy population of small snakes is in fact useful to humans, since the vermin on which the reptiles prey may harm crops and carry disease. The text seems to assume this much by proposing a scenario in which the serpents will remain; notably, unlike the bear and lion, no mention is made of changes to the snake's diet.

We might note that in a similar depiction in Isa 65, the diet of the snake (*nḥš* in that case) *will* have changed so that it too conforms to human needs: by consuming dust (*ʿpr*), the snake will essentially be turning the soil and so aiding cultivation (65:21–25). In Isa 11:8, though, the point is rather that serpents will no longer bite the children that harass them for amusement (v. 8), will no longer be threatened by humans reaching down to grab them as a predator might. So the snakes too appear to have been domesticated, like the lion, bear, and wolf in the preceding verses. Again, the outcome depicted amounts to a shift away from the negative impact of animal behavior on humans as experienced in the real world. Ultimately, then, it would be imprecise to classify the scenario in Isa 11:6–8 as one of harmony between species. The text rather appears to hold up a situation

---

7. Each of these terms occurs elsewhere in parallel with the more common term for snake, *nḥš* (see Ps 58:4, Prov 23:32). However, the terms here are relatively rare, making further classification uncertain. In a rare comment on actual animals, Watts (2015, 212) discusses snakebite mortalities in modern-day India (presumably because its economy, like ancient Israel's, is agrarian). Determining the extent to which snakes were a danger to humans in Israel is difficult. Portrayals in the Old Testament emphasize the threat posed by unexpected bites from the snake's place of shelter (Gen 49:17, Amos 5:19, Prov 30:19). While human behavior in relation to snakes varies by culture, modern studies have shown that humans are more likely to approach/attack snakes than the reverse. See, e.g., Whitaker and Shine 2000.

in which there has been a removal of undesirable behaviors in previously indomitable species known to disrupt the human order. The creatures that once interfered with human interests have now been made to serve them.

But the vision does not trouble itself with explaining how the likes of apex predators were tamed. Interpreters who discuss the transformation tend assume the deity supernaturally alters the creatures. Michael Chan and Maria Metzler (2014, 221), for instance, conclude that the prophet's message emphasizes the power of YHWH to "make kings gentle and lions eat straw." Hilary Marlow (2009, 242) suggests the vision is one of transformation "initiated and maintained by YHWH himself." The prophet's perspective may well have allowed for such an exercise of divine power. One finds a pronouncement just a few verses later in the chapter that YHWH will modify major waterways (Isa 11:15–16). But the situation described in Isa 11:6–8 is, by comparison, noticeably absent of references to supernatural activity. Even the mention of the Spirit of YHWH in the preceding section serves to describe inspired *human* activity (Isa 11:1–5).

So rather than assuming the prophet is merely being uncharacteristically shy about affirming divine agency, I propose we reckon with the creaturely agency evident in the portrayal. Humans, as seen here, act by leading and having their way with predators. Nonhuman animals, on the other hand, act by conforming to the demands of a particular human cultural order. To suggest that the stronger creatures have merely accommodated themselves to the weaker is to ignore the vision's human-oriented outlook (Williamson 2018, 661). The lion's new diet, as specified in the text, is particularly telling. Crop residues are feed for animals that human beings have domesticated. Given that the text is not more forthcoming about how exactly this came to pass, one might presume the process is not unlike any other act of domestication: humans have imposed on the species a way of life that benefits humans.[8] In light of such interspecies relations, one might rightly ask whether such an outcome assumes the use or threat of force, coercion, or even violence in the process. Though allegorical, the lament in Ezek 19:1–9 describes how predators might be brought into the human sphere: through domination, by means of hooks, nets, pits, and cages. The realities of any domestication process leading to

---

8. An oversimplification, of course. For a brief synopsis of competing understandings of domestication in the broader philosophical discussion of power negotiations between humans and animals, see Russell 2002, 285–302.

the outcome described in Isa 11:6–8 seem likely to undermine the claim of harmonious relations between humans and animal others.

Contemporary readers need not look far for evidence that such a state of affairs—absurd as it is—would be undesirable even if it could be achieved (so Clements 1999). We know that the removal of predators has a cascading effect on the food chain and thus on the ecosystem. If humans were to domesticate the species mentioned in the text, they would inevitably be forced to take on the management of other animal populations. What of the former prey of the straw-eating lion? Damage due to overgrazing by exploding prey populations seems a likely consequence. And what of other predators—hippopotamus, crocodile, birds of prey? A variety of species would need to be tamed, were they to take the lion's place in the food chain. And that is not to mention the issue of genetic diversity in any newly domesticated species. All this amounts to substantial responsibility. In practice, it is known all too well how demanding such responsibility can be, with disaster looming as a possible consequence of mismanagement (see Balvanera 2019, esp. 109–10, 119).

But even if the vision were still construed as idyllic, as it often is, there remains the matter of the theological and ethical implications of such an understanding. If these verses convey an ideal scenario, representing an outcome the deity too desires, then it could be argued that human control over animal populations is an acceptable cost of human flourishing, that God elevates the value and interests of human beings, even to the detriment of nonhuman animals. Such rationalization is not far from what one finds among some circles today (see, e.g., Raymond 2016).

It strikes me as ironic that certain features of the vision now obtain in the contemporary world, given that commentators describe the vision as an unobtainable ideal (noting, for instance, that a straw-eating lion is in fact no longer a lion at all; Oswalt 1986, 283). The wolf may not be just another animal on the farm, but human control over the species is quite extensive even in the aftermath of a centuries-long crusade to rid the land of gray wolves entirely (see Robinson 2005). Any talk of the small wolf populations that have been reintroduced in my home state of Oregon evokes fervent debate around control measures (Hernandez 2021).[9] The

---

9. While the question of federal protections for gray wolves continues to be litigated, in Oregon the species remains protected under statute. See Oregon Department of Fish and Wildlife 2021 for a record of measures taken to control the species while complying with protections.

narrowly construed interests that led to this point are not dissimilar from those in Isa 11:6–8: the security and stability of the human agricultural and economic order. As it turns out, our concern over the implications of the vision, with its conflict and complexities, is not merely theoretical. Reading the vision literally, as an ideal scenario, can become a recursive justification for the domination of actual nonhuman animals.

As an alternative, an allegorical reading of Isa 11:6–8 becomes somewhat attractive for the reader empathetic toward the wildlife. While the imagery itself is inescapably anthropocentric, I propose the significance of the vision is less ecologically problematic when the nonhuman animals are taken as symbolic representations of human beings. Read this way, the text yields implications not primarily for interspecies relations but for relations among humans. Such meaning-making is not foreign to the text of Isaiah. One finds humans compared to nonhumans by use of figurative language elsewhere in the book, such as when Israel and Judah are a vineyard in Isa 5:1–7, or foreign nations are likened to lions in Isa 5:29. Admittedly, it is difficult to determine the real-world referent of the creatures in Isa 11:6–8. Unlike the song in Isa 5:1–7, no explanation of the components is offered. There are also details that complicate the symbolism here, such as the use of terms that specify the age of creatures, and the reference to humans in the portrayal.

Still, the juxtaposition of the visions in Isa 11:6–8 and 11:1–5 offers some guidance. The portrait of a secure human agricultural order, built on an unprecedented degree of domestication, corresponds to the anticipation of a secure divine order, built on an unprecedented degree of righteousness and justice. The predators would then represent dominant nations—such as Assyria—while the domesticated animals represent those vulnerable to being conquered, as Israel and Judah were (see also Seitz 1993; cf. Goldingay 2014). As I have discussed, both groups of creatures are depicted in the text as having conformed to the order of human life, just as Judah and Assyria are expected to conform to YHWH's order. The mention of the human children in the vision may then refer to leaders, as it does in a few other instances in Isa 1–12 (e.g., 7:14, 9:5). Here, they are leaders who faithfully represent the values of the deity, as set out in Isa 11:1–5. This fits with the subsequent development in verses 9–10 as well. All nations will be "domesticated" by the knowledge of YHWH, as faithful representatives of YHWH take a place of leadership among them.

The vision, as metaphor for a new order among human beings, also coheres well with other material in Isa 1–12. In these chapters, it is human beings (not nonhuman animals) who must change if there is to be peace between nations under the ultimate rule of the deity; humans are the ones engaging in mistreatment and destruction (Isa 11:9a). The prophet has previously made clear that the people of YHWH are included among these human beings who mistreat ($rʿʿ$) and who destroy ($šḥt$; see, e.g., Isa 1:4). Hence Israel-Judah must submit to YHWH like the ox submits to its owner (1:2–3). Assyria, meanwhile, is obligated to acknowledge the deity before whom the powers stand accountable (10:12–19). Indeed, both the people of God and Assyria are plagued by oppressive leaders (2:13–15, 10:1–11). And if the addressees should defend themselves against the prophet's call to turn from their way of life, arguing that violence is inevitable, that domination of the weak by the strong is a fact of life on earth? Well, then this allegorical portrayal functions to disrupt such assumptions by suggesting that YHWH may bring about a state of affairs in which even natural enemies such as wolf and lamb (and Assyria and Judah) may dwell together.

This understanding of the vision is certainly not without its own ethical difficulties. Were one to inquire, *à la manière de* David J. A. Clines, as to whose interests are reflected in this vision, one would be remiss to ignore the details in the surrounding verses that point to the nation of Judah (Jesse in Isa 11:1, 10; YHWH's holy mountain in 11:9). To the extent that the new, peaceful order will be forged through violence against those outside Judah (see 11:4b, 12–16), it would appear to be people of foreign nations (represented by domesticated wildlife) who stand to suffer domination.

One must also reckon with the counterintuitive notion that it should be preferable to read the nonhuman animals in Isa 11:6–8 metaphorically. The interpretive approach of the Earth Bible Project (see esp. 2001) has been to regard the nonhuman components of the natural world as subjects and active agents, and to critique portrayals of Earth that relegate it to mere setting or symbol for human activity. Similarly, the reduction of nonhuman animals to mere representations of humans (or human attributes/values) has been shown to be problematic by animal studies scholars (see Braidotti 2013, esp. 67–76). However, the matter of a text's use or rhetorical function complicates the calculus—especially with the prophets, who were wont to reach their audience through ugly and disturbing means (see Sherwood 2009). Of what use is the ideological evaluation of the content of prophetic words, if that content was shaped in the service of impact? Regardless of whether they are taken literally or allegorically, the very images of Isa 11:6–8 enshrine human interests related to the negotiation of power with nonhuman animals. As an allegory, however, the vision yields new implications that may point in more ecologically positive directions.[10]

Adhering, then, to the strategy of reading with empathy for the nonhuman, I propose readers affirm the vision's implied criticism of the oppressive human powers that be. Their ongoing engagement in warfare yields ecological devastation—a reality of which one finds hints elsewhere in Isa 1–12 (see 5:8–17, 6:11–13, 7:18–25, 10:18–21). That the text does not concern itself with the mechanics of domesticating wildlife suggests it does not intend to mobilize its addressees for the objective of conquering the wild (or the nations), as though the audience could neutralize every creature that might disturb the customs of human civilization (or every foreign power that might threaten Judah). Rather, in exploring figuratively what it might look like for there to be leadership that embodies the values of the deity, the text effectively invites the addressees to critique the arrangement under which they find themselves for its failure to measure up. The amalgamation in the portrayal of fantastic elements with concrete details from agrarian life therefore has a disillusioning effect, even as it may engender hope for a state of affairs that surpasses what the monarchy has produced. In that respect, the text serves to highlight the grave human shortcomings that stand in the way of a more equitable order. Perhaps that is why, even today, it may be easier to imagine a lion reversing its ferocious nature than human leaders reversing theirs.

Works Cited

Alberta Agriculture and Forestry Ministry. 2007. "Winter Feeding Programs for Beef Cows and Calves." Agri-Facts, revised December 2007. https://tinyurl.com/SBL06107c.

Balabanski, Vicky. 2013. "The Step of 'Identification' in Norman Habel's Ecological Hermeneutics: Hermeneutical Reflections on 'Ecological Conversion.'" Pages 20–31 in *Where the Wild Ox Roams: Biblical Essays in Honour of Norman C. Habel*. Edited by Alan H. Cadwallader and Peter L. Trudinger. HBM 59. Sheffield: Sheffield Phoenix.

---

10. Some may well choose to ignore or reject the vision in response to the problematic ideology of interspecies relations I have discussed. But for those committed to retrieval, or for those of traditions in which the biblical text is to serve a formative function, reading the vision allegorically may prove the most ethical course available.

Balvanera, Patricia, et. al. 2019. "Status and Trends—Drivers of Change." In *Global Assessment Report of the Intergovernmental Science-Policy Platform on Biodiversity and Ecosystem Services.* Edited by Eduardo S. Brondízio, Josef Settele, Sandra Díaz, and Hien T. Ngo. Bonn: IPBES Secretariat.

Boer, Roland. 2015. *The Sacred Economy of Ancient Israel.* Louisville: Westminster John Knox.

Braidotti, Rosi. 2013. *The Posthuman.* Cambridge: Polity.

Brueggemann, Walter. 1998. *Isaiah 1–39.* WBC. Louisville: Westminster John Knox.

Calarco, Matthew. 2015. *Thinking through Animals: Identity, Difference, Indistinction.* StBr. Stanford, CA: Stanford University Press.

Chan, Michael J., and Maria Metzler. 2014. "Lions and Leopards and Bears, O My: Re-reading Isaiah 11:6–9 in Light of Comparative Iconographic and Literary Evidence." Pages 196–225 in *Image, Text, and Exegesis: Iconographic Interpretation and the Hebrew Bible.* Edited by Izaak J. de Hulste and Joel M. LeMon. London: Bloomsbury.

Childs, Brevard S. 2001. *Isaiah.* OTL. Louisville: Westminster John Knox.

Clements, Ronald E. 1999. "The Wolf Shall Live with the Lamb: Reading Isaiah 11:6–9 Today." Pages 83–99 in *New Heaven and New Earth: Prophecy and the Millennium; Essays in Honour of Anthony Gelston.* Edited by Peter J. Harland and Robert Hayward. VTSup 77. Leiden: Brill.

Earth Bible Project. 2001. "The Voice of Earth: More than Metaphor?" Pages 23–28 in *The Earth Story in the Psalms and the Prophets.* Edited by Norman C. Habel. EarthB 4. Sheffield: Sheffield Academic.

Goldingay, John. 2014. *The Theology of the Book of Isaiah.* Downers Grove, IL: InterVarsity.

Habel, Norman C. 2000. "Introducing the Earth Bible." Pages 25–37 in *Readings from the Perspective of Earth.* Edited by Norman C. Habel. EarthB 1. Sheffield: Sheffield Academic.

———. 2008. "Introducing Ecological Hermeneutics." Pages 1–8 in *Exploring Ecological Hermeneutics.* Edited by Norman C. Habel and Peter L. Trudinger. SymS 46. Atlanta: Society of Biblical Literature.

Hernandez, Rolando. 2021. "Wolves Spark Debate as Environmentalists Want Protections and Ranchers Want to Keep Their Cattle Safe." *Oregon Public Broadcasting,* 2 December. https://tinyurl.com/SBL06107d.

Marlow, Hilary. 2009. *Biblical Prophets and Contemporary Environmental Ethics: Re-reading Amos, Hosea, and First Isaiah*. Oxford: Oxford University Press.
Morgan, Jonathan. 2010. "Sacrifice in Leviticus: Eco-friendly Ritual or Unholy Waste?" Pages 32–45 in *Ecological Hermeneutics: Biblical, Historical and Theological Perspectives*. Edited by David G. Horrell, Cherryl Hunt, Christopher Southgate, and Francesca Stavrakopoulou. London: T&T Clark.
Olley, John. 2001. "'The Wolf, the Lamb, and a Little Child': Transforming the Diverse Earth Community in Isaiah." Pages 219–29 in *The Earth Story in the Psalms and the Prophets*. Edited by Norman C. Habel. EarthB 4. Sheffield: Sheffield Academic.
Oregon Department of Fish and Wildlife. 2021. "Wolf Program Updates." Updated August 2021. https://tinyurl.com/SBL06107e.
Oswalt, John N. 1986. *The Book of Isaiah, Chapters 1–39*. NICOT. Grand Rapids: Eerdmans.
Raymond, Erik. 2016. "Why Do They Care More about Dogs than People?" The Gospel Coalition, 22 August 2016. https://tinyurl.com/SBL06107f.
Roberts, Jimmy J. M. 2015. *First Isaiah*. Hermeneia. Minneapolis: Fortress.
Robinson, Michael J. 2005. *Predatory Bureaucracy: The Extermination of Wolves and the Transformation of the West*. Boulder: University Press of Colorado.
Russell, Nerissa. 2002. "The Wild Side of Animal Domestication." *S&A* 10:285–302.
Santos, Maurício B., et al. 2013. "Does Human Influence on Coastal Grasslands Habitats Affect Predation Pressure on Snakes?" *BioN* 13:366–70.
Seitz, Christopher R. 1993. *Isaiah 1–39*. IBC. Louisville: John Knox.
Sherwood, Yvonne. 2009. "The Baroque Prophets: An Encounter between Hebrew Prophets and John Donne." Pages 115–40 in *Sacred Tropes: Tanakh, New Testament, and Qur'an as Literature and Culture*. Edited by Roberta Sterman Sabbath. Leiden: Brill.
Smith, Gary. 2007. *Isaiah 1–39*. NAC. Nashville: B&H.
Tull, Patricia K. 2010. *Isaiah 1–39*. SHBC. Macon, GA: Smyth & Helwys.
Van Ee, Joshua J. 2018. "Wolf and Lamb as Hyperbolic Blessing: Reassessing Creational Connections in Isaiah 11:6–8." *JBL* 137:319–37.
Watts, John D. W. 2015. *Isaiah 1–33*. Rev. ed. WBC. Grand Rapids: Zondervan.
Whitaker, Patrick B., and Richard Shine. 2000. "Sources of Mortality of Large Elapid Snakes in an Agricultural Landscape." *JHerp* 34:121–28.

Wildberger, Hans. 1991. *Isaiah 1–12: A Commentary*. CC. Minneapolis: Fortress.
Williamson, Hugh G. M. 2018. *Isaiah 6–12*. ICC. London: T&T Clark.
Young, Edward J. 1972. *The Book of Isaiah*. Vol. 1. Grand Rapids: Eerdmans.
Zoran, Debra. 2002. "The Carnivore Connection to Nutrition in Cats." *JAVMA* 221:1559–67.

"The Fate of Humans and the Fate of Animals Is the Same": Animality and Humanity in Qoheleth and the Hebrew Bible

Ken Stone

Introduction

"Ecclesiastes is a strange and disquieting book." These words open Michael Fox's (2004, ix) commentary on Ecclesiastes. Fox is hardly alone in emphasizing the unusual nature of Ecclesiastes or, to use its Hebrew title, Qoheleth. Elias Bickerman (1967) famously includes it among what he calls *Four Strange Books of the Bible*. In his study of Bible, science, and ecology, William Brown (2010, 177) observes that this "unorthodox" book "contains the most unconventional perspective on creation in the Bible," while Marie Turner's (2017, 6) Earth Bible Commentary on Ecclesiastes refers to it as "an enigmatic and ambiguous work," the meaning of which is often "indeterminable." Lisa Wolfe (2020, xlii; see Koosed 2012) argues in her feminist commentary that "Qoheleth insistently questions doctrinal beliefs" and "fosters and encourages a hermeneutic of suspicion toward much of ancient Israelite theology." I even suggest that, when read in dialogue with queer theory, one may discover that Ecclesiastes is "surely ... a 'queer' biblical text" (Stone 2005, 145).

But what makes Ecclesiastes so unusual? How does its strange and disquieting nature relate to its views on animality and the human/animal distinction? What might happen if one reconsidered it in dialogue with contemporary animal studies, as scholars are beginning to do with other biblical texts (Stone 2018; Strømmen 2018; Sherman 2020)? Does Ecclesiastes promote strange ideas about animals, or about what Matthew Calarco (2015, 4), in his overview of "critical animal studies," calls "traditional ideas about the human/animal distinction and ethical relations with animals"? Or does it rather help one understand the multiplicity of views on nonhuman animals found across the Bible?

The uneasy fit of Ecclesiastes with much biblical theology, signaled by the adjectives used to describe it, can be seen in the terminology that is often taken as the book's motto: *hebel* or *hăbēl hăbālîm* (Crenshaw 1987, 57–59; Fox 1989, 161–63). Traditionally rendered into English as "vanity," *hebel* more literally means something like "vapor" or "breath," and has connotations of something that is ephemeral or fleeting. Among its translations, Fox (2004, xix) underscores the words "'senseless' or 'absurd,' not in the sense of ludicrous" but rather in the book's catalog of "contradictions in the world, which violate rational expectations." In many cases, the expectations that Ecclesiastes violates are found in other parts of biblical literature.

As unusual as Ecclesiastes is, however, its differences from other biblical books are not absolute. Nearly all scholars associate it with wisdom literature, for example, even while acknowledging that it represents what Katharine Dell (1994, 303) calls "wisdom at its limits in the way it provides a critique of the wisdom tradition and remains outside the main development of wisdom thought." Qoheleth, a term I will use, as do other scholars (Fox 2004, x; Turner 2017), to refer to the primary speaking voice or persona in the book of Ecclesiastes, follows a kind of wisdom method when drawing conclusions, a method that consists of making empirical observations about the world and human experience and articulating possible consequences of such observations for Qoheleth's understanding of God, humanity, and the nature of life and death.

Ecclesiastes also refers to animals, though less frequently than the wisdom books Proverbs and Job, which both contain numerous animal images (Forti 2008; Schifferdecker 2008; Walsh 2017; Stone 2018, 130–39). Because the arguments in Ecclesiastes do not always proceed in a linear fashion, I discuss the book's animal references here in a few categories rather than following the order of the book's sections. In spite of the book's strange nature, Qoheleth's animal observations are both similar to and different from ideas that one finds across the Hebrew Bible with respect to animals, human and nonhuman alike.

Domesticated Animals and Wealth in Ecclesiastes

Early in the book of Ecclesiastes, when adopting the persona of a "king over Israel in Jerusalem" (Eccl 1:12), Qoheleth describes how the search for "what is good for humans to do under the heavens for the few days of their lives" (2:3) led to the pursuit of wisdom and the accumulation of possessions.[1] Among these possessions are living creatures, including male and female slaves and also "livestock," such as "herds" of cattle and "flocks" of sheep and goats (2:7). There is nothing unusual about Qoheleth's association between flocks and herds and the acquisition of wealth. Domesticated animals played a prominent role in what Donna Haraway (2003, 2008) calls "companion species," whose interactions with humans shaped the lives and literature of the Israelites and Judahites, as one sees from both textual and archaeological evidence. The stories about Israel's ancestors in Genesis thus represent the patriarchs' wealth and prestige in part through references to their livestock, especially in the case of Jacob (Stone 2018, 28–33) but also throughout stories about Abraham (Gen 12:16; 13:2, 5–7; 21:27–30; 24:10). Perhaps more relevant to Ecclesiastes are biblical references to kings, both positive and negative. When Samuel warns Israel about consequences of asking for a king in 1 Sam 8, he notes that kings will take "the best of your donkeys" and "your flocks" (1 Sam 8:16–17). Even closer to Qoheleth's association with Solomon, 1 Kgs 4:22–28 calls attention to numerous oxen, cattle, flocks, gazelles, roebucks, and fatted fowl who are brought to Solomon daily, as well as horses who fill his stalls (see 1 Kgs 8:62–64, 10:26). Qoheleth's acquisition of animals as part of a quest to amass possessions is therefore typical of biblical imagery.

Typical, too, is the reference to "male slaves and female slaves and slaves born in my house" in the same verse as herds and flocks (Eccl 2:7). While this juxtaposition of slaves with animals also has parallels in stories about Israel's ancestors, it appears in other texts including both versions of the Ten Commandments. Thus Exod 20:17 warns a male audience: "You will not covet the house of your neighbor. You will not covet the woman of your neighbor, or his male slave, or his female slave, or his ox, or his donkey, or anything that belongs to your neighbor." This prohibition and its parallel in Deut 5:21 list things belonging to one male Israelite that another might desire, including women, slaves, and animals. It is therefore wrong to suggest that the Hebrew Bible generally, or Ecclesiastes specifically, understands all animals to exist in a category that is entirely separate from, and subordinated to, the category of humans. The human-animal distinction does not simply cordon off humanity but divides it inter-

---

1. Except where noted, all translations of Scripture are mine.

nally, differentiating some humans from others and associating particular humans more closely with animality. These associations are made through processes and structures that Carol Adams (1995, 71–84) calls "interlocking systems of domination" and that Jacques Derrida (1995, 277–84) refers to as the "sacrificial structure" of "carnophallogocentrism" or "carnivorous virility." Both Adams and Derrida underscore a recurring tendency to disparage and subjugate other humans by turning them into beasts who can be treated like animals. Ecclesiastes reflects a version of this tendency in its summary of Qoheleth's acquisition of goods, but similar dynamics are found in other biblical texts (Stone 2016; 2017; 2018, 40–44).

In Eccl 2, then, animals appear in a traditional biblical role. They are included among goods and living beings that powerful, prestigious men accumulate to demonstrate their wealth. Animals are distinguished from these powerful men, but not from human beings as such, since some humans are also considered the property of those with power and wealth. Where Ecclesiastes differs from other biblical texts is not in its use of animals and subjugated humans to signify wealth, but rather in Qoheleth's frank admission that the accumulation of goods, including living goods, does not ultimately satisfy or supply a meaning for life. To borrow language from Eccl 5:10, "one who loves money is not satisfied with money, nor whoever loves abundance," including an abundance of domesticated animals and slaves, "with gain. This also is *hebel*."

Qoheleth's Animal Proverbs

In her study *Animal Imagery in the Book of Proverbs*, Tova Forti (2008, 138) devotes one chapter to two "aphorisms that involve animal imagery" that appear in Ecclesiastes. Like other scholars, Forti calls attention to "dissonance between conservative statements that relate to various phenomena of life, on the one hand, and skeptical observations that contradict traditional views, on the other hand" (137). By including a chapter on Qoheleth's animal sayings in a book on Proverbs, however, Forti acknowledges the kinship between Ecclesiastes and other wisdom texts.

In Eccl 10:1, one finds this saying: "Dead flies give the perfumer's ointment a foul stench, A little folly outweighs wisdom and honor." Although commentaries render this verse in various ways, its point is clear. Qoheleth's focus is on the danger that even small amounts of folly, which one might be tempted to consider harmless, actually present to wisdom. In that respect Eccl 10:1 coheres with the verse that precedes it in 9:18, where one reads: "Wisdom is better than weapons of war, but one offender destroys much good." In distinction from 10:1, where two parts of the proverb make a similar point, 9:18 contains two statements that seem antithetical to each other. Both verses, however, emphasize that "a single or a little thing that is bad may outweigh a whole lot of good" (Seow 1997, 311). In each case, Qoheleth makes use of "analogies" that, in Forti's (2008, 146) words, "qualify the superior status of wisdom because they propose a sober examination of reality, in which sin and folly (the primary natural enemies of wisdom) are likely to prevail." To make this argument in 10:1, Qoheleth appeals to an animal observation that is less about the inherent evil of flies and more about negative consequences of folly. While the implication of wisdom's relative weakness may alarm conventional adherents of the wisdom tradition, the attention to wisdom and folly and the use of animal proverbs are both characteristic of that tradition.

The second animal proverb discussed by Forti appears in Eccl 9:4, and its focus is closer to other themes I wish to highlight here. One of several topics that Qoheleth explores in chapters 8 and 9 is the matter of death, which no one can predict. In 8:8 Qoheleth notes, "No person has power over the wind [*rûaḥ*] to restrain the wind [*rûaḥ*], or power over the day of death." Fox (2004, 56) suggests that, since *rûaḥ* can mean not only "wind" but also "breath" or "lifebreath," as it does elsewhere in Ecclesiastes, the first part of 8:8 might be translated, "no man has authority over the lifebreath—to hold back the lifebreath." Even "the righteous and the wise" cannot fully understand why things happen, what fate lies ahead, or when "the day of death" (8:8) will arrive, for such matters lie "in the hand of God" (9:1). As Fox (2004, 61) summarizes the quandary with which Qoheleth wrestles, "The righteous and wise might be expected to shape their future by righteous deeds and wise choices. That, after all, is what wisdom is for. But God's enigmatic control of human destiny cripples wisdom's ability to do so." Indeed, Qoheleth observes, "There is one fate for all, for the righteous and the wicked" (9:2); and that fate is death: "This is the evil that happens under the sun, there is one fate for all ... and after that, [they go] to the dead" (9:3). Death is inescapable, we cannot know when it is going to happen, but it happens to everyone whether they are wise or foolish, righteous or wicked.

While Forti (2008, 151) refers here to "Qoheleth's gloomy observation of life," she notes that Qoheleth makes a comment about animals in 9:4 that partly alleviates the gloom: "But whoever is found among all the living has hope, for a living dog is better than a dead lion." This animal proverb "is woven into [Qoheleth's] discussion in order to illustrate the superiority of life to death" (153). The saying does contradict the claim in 4:2 that the dead are better off than the living. But it leads toward Qoheleth's recommendation, in 9:7–10 and elsewhere in the book, to enjoy modest pleasures in life even though—or precisely because—we all share the same fate in the end.

The animals included in this proverb—dogs and lions—are chosen with specific rhetorical goals in mind. Although biblical scholars sometimes overstate the negative connotations of dogs in the Hebrew Bible, it is true that dogs are viewed with some ambivalence, probably because of the ways in which their lives and actions blur boundaries between domesticated and wild, human habitation and the desolation of wilderness, grazing and scavenging, and so forth (Stone 2018, 45–65). Their appetites (Isa 56:11) may even obscure the line between humans and other animals, since their willingness to scavenge both carrion torn by animals (Exod 22:30 [ET 22:31]) and the bodies and blood of members of Israel's royal houses (1 Kgs 14:11; 16:4; 21:23–24; 22:38; 2 Kgs 9:10, 35–37) reveals that human bodies are composed of animal meat. The phrase "dead dog" also appears in the Bible as a symbol for those of low status (2 Sam 9:8) or as an insult (2 Sam 16:9; see 2 Sam 3:8, 1 Sam 24:14).

Though lions, too, may kill and eat humans, their fierce nature and strength make lion symbolism "polyvalent—open to multiple uses," as Brent Strawn (2005, 284) puts it. They can represent both "power and threat"; and in the ancient world they symbolize both human kings and deities, though Strawn points out that, inside the Bible, lions more often refer to Israel's God than to Israel's kings. The force of lion symbolism usually depends, however, on the lion's being alive. A dead lion may demonstrate the power of the human who killed it, such as Samson (Judg 14:5–6); but its death is not envied.

Qoheleth's assertion that "a living dog is better than a dead lion" therefore modifies connotations traditionally associated with each of these species: dogs inhabit the more desirable position here, while lions are represented negatively. The parable also qualifies Qoheleth's tendency to suggest that the living have no advantage over the dead. The living do have some hope (Eccl 9:4) and know they are going to die, whereas the dead know nothing (9:5) "and will never again have any share in all that happens under the sun" (9:6). The certainty of death reinforces Qoheleth's admonitions to enjoy life while we can. The underlying assumption behind the animal symbolism remains stark, however. Like lions and dogs, all of us are going to die. The lives and deaths of nonhuman animals are used to shed light on our own lives and deaths, and on the common fate that we share as mortal creatures in a world of *hăbēl hăbālîm*.

"Like Fish Caught in a Terrible Net": Animality and the Cruelty of Chance

Several animal references in Ecclesiastes point toward not simply the inevitability of death but also the recurrence of chance, accident, and tragic mishap. A number of biblical traditions, including the wisdom tradition, encourage the view that those who are wise, good, or obedient will experience positive consequences. Qoheleth points out several times, however, that this is not always the case. Not only folly and wickedness but also chance and unexpected circumstances can lead to situations in which one's plans are disrupted, sometimes with disastrous results. At least some of Qoheleth's examples involve animals.

In 10:6–8, for example, Qoheleth calls attention to situations that reverse expectations about folly, social status, and honor or recognition. The problem that concerns Qoheleth is summarized in 10:6: "The fool is set in high places, and the rich sit in a low place." Presumably Qoheleth believes that, if the rich are rich because of their wisdom and skill, they ought to be rewarded for it. Instead, the fool is elevated. In Choon-Leong Seow's (1997, 315) view, Ecclesiastes is "speaking of a topsy-turvy world in which the incompetent are in positions of power and influence, whereas the elite are in lowly positions." That Qoheleth is concerned with "the elite" is apparent from the animal-related example that follows in 10:7: "I have seen slaves on horses, and princes walking like slaves on the ground." Slaves are again associated with animals, but the context is different from the one in chapter 2. In this case, slaves are not included alongside domesticated animals among a rich man's property but rather are riding on such animals. The specification of horses is significant, since horses are associated in the Hebrew Bible with armies and members of royal houses, including Pharaoh (Exod 14:9, 23; 15:1, 19, 21), Absalom (2 Sam 15:1), Solomon (1 Kgs 4:26, 28; 10:26–29), Ben-Hadad of Aram (1 Kgs 20:1, 20) and Qoheleth's persona as "king" in Eccl 1–2 (McKay 2002). In Eccl 10, slaves, rather than being subjugated like animals, are riding on animals reserved for royalty, while princes walk. Some commentators find hints in this chapter of what Lisa Wolfe (2020, 153) calls a "critique of hierarchy," since "Wisdom does not necessarily correspond to a high station in society." Whether one understands this as a critique of hierarchy or simply another "evil under the sun" (10:5), "things are not turning out according to expectations," as Seow puts it. Qoheleth finds "no order in society or in the cosmos," as evidenced by the fact that slaves ride on horses while princes walk (Seow 1997, 325).

In Eccl 10:8, one reads that "one who digs a pit will fall into it, and one who breaks through a wall will be bitten by a snake." Here there is no hint that folly or wickedness are at work. Digging pits and breaking walls are understood as normal activities. While the animal reference in the second part of the verse is obvious, Seow (1997, 326) notes that the first part of the verse probably refers to "the practice of excavating pits as traps for animals, pits that were then camouflaged with a net." The wall, on the other hand, "refers not to the residential wall or city wall, but to the low stone fences built to define the areas of an orchard or a vineyard." Such walls make excellent hiding places for snakes. Seow thus considers both of these examples, as well as activities in 10:9 that do not involve animals but also lead to injury or worse (quarrying stone, splitting logs), to be "occupational hazards," used by Qoheleth to make the point "that accidents happen in all walks of life." No one is or "can be exempt from the dangers in life." Such dangers may or may not involve animals, but they are more likely to do so where humans frequently encounter animals, as was true in ancient Israel.

There are other references to animals in chapter 10 as well. In a strange saying in 10:11 one reads: "If a snake bites before it is charmed, there is no advantage in being a master charmer." Once again, an encounter with an animal provides an occasion for misfortune. The second half of 10:20, on the other hand, warns against cursing the king or the rich, since a "bird of the air" or some other "winged" creature might spread the news (Seow [1997, 334] references the still-contemporary saying, "a little bird told me so").

A more unsettling reference to birds is found in chapter 9. Eccl 9:7–10 contains one of Qohehet's admonitions about enjoying one's life, work, and modest pleasures "under the sun" (9:9) while one can, since this is one's "lot in life" (9:9) and all are headed toward Sheol, where none of these things are experienced (9:10). This admonition is followed by a better-known verse in 9:11: "Further I saw under the sun that the race is not to the swift, nor the battle to the strong, nor bread to the wise, nor wealth to the intelligent, nor favor to the knowledgeable. For time and chance happen to all." Qoheleth acknowledges here what William Brown (2000, 96) calls "the indomitable hegemony of chance." Contrary to assumptions made in numerous biblical texts and among interpreters, Qoheleth recognizes that wisdom and skill are not always sufficient to ensure success. Rather, as Brown puts it, "Next to death, the only guarantee in life is that accidents will happen, and no one knows where and whom they will strike" (96).

In 9:12, then, one finds the following verse with two striking animal references: "For no person knows their time. Like fish caught in a terrible net, and like birds caught in a snare, so humans are snared at a terrible time when it falls on them suddenly." As is true for the horse in 10:7, or the snake in 10:8, the fish and birds in 9:12 are represented as actual creatures in situations where they interact with human beings. The scenarios in 9:12 were probably familiar to Qoheleth's audience, since they involve activities of procuring food. To the extent that such an audience had actually seen fish in nets and birds in snares, they may have had some awareness of the physical signs and sounds of suffering that result. Today, awareness of the suffering (still often denied) of fish—not to speak of the suffering of massive numbers of marine animals trapped in nets as "bycatch" under industrial fishing, and awareness of the suffering endured not only by snared animals that humans are trying to catch but also animals that wander into snares accidentally—should give one pause when one reads this verse. Securing food may be necessary, but it still creates suffering for animals, arguably more so now than in the time of Qoheleth because of the massive scale of contemporary food production.

Ecclesiastes 9:12 does not simply call attention to fish and birds, however. It also invites one to identify with them. Reflecting on fish in nets and birds in snares, one may be reminded that none of them plan to be caught. Nor have they arrived in nets and snares because they are evil or foolish. To the contrary, Qoheleth describes the nets themselves as "evil," using a Hebrew word, $rā'â$, that I translate as "terrible" (following Seow 1997, 306, 308, 320–21). That humans use those nets to catch food does not remove their cruelty. So too the snare, though also used to secure human food, is cast in a negative light by such passages as Prov 7:23, which uses the image of a bird and a snare metaphorically to refer to a young man who does not realize that he, like the bird, is about to lose his life (*nepeš*). What is striking about Eccl 9:12 is that the human vulnerability to "chance and calamity" (Brown 2000, 96) is acknowledged as being similar to that of nonhuman animals, and not simply animals that one might recognize as being similar to humans (primates, for example) but rather fish and birds, which are hunted by humans using methods that cause suffering. Qoheleth's comparison sheds light on the role that sudden disaster can play in anyone's life, with a "timing" that is "utterly unpredictable" (Seow 1997, 321). But it also underscores that one's susceptibility to unpredictable disaster erases the distinction between humans and other animals. Like fish and birds, humans are subject to finding themselves trapped in terrible situations that result in suffering and death.

The Fate of Humans and the Fate of Animals

Although Ecclesiastes contains other passing references to animals (for example, 12:4–5), the representation of fish and birds in circumstances that lead to death brings me to the final passage from Ecclesiastes I consider here. After the famous poem on "times" in 3:1-8 and additional comments in 3:9–15 about time, work, and enjoyment, Qoheleth observes in 3:16–22 (NRSV, modified):

> Moreover I saw under the sun that in the place of justice, wickedness was there, and in the place of righteousness, wickedness was there as well.
> I said in my heart, God will judge the righteous and the wicked, for God has appointed a time for every matter, and for every work.
> I said in my heart with regard to human beings that God is testing them to show that they are but animals.
> For the fate of humans and the fate of animals is the same; as one dies, so dies the other.
> They all have the same breath [*rûaḥ*], and humans have no advantage over the animals; for all is *hebel*.
> All go to one place; all are from the dust, and all turn to dust again.
> Who knows whether the human spirit [*rûaḥ*] goes upward and the spirit [*rûaḥ*] of animals goes downward to the earth?
> So I saw that there is nothing better than that all should enjoy their work, for that is their lot; who can bring them to see what will be after them?

This passage highlights themes that are raised elsewhere in the book, including that humans cannot always figure out what God is up to (although, as 3:11 points out, God has made humans want to do exactly that) and the conclusion that the best response is to enjoy one's work and one's lot in life. Qoheleth does go further here than in some sections of the book "to apply a hermeneutic of suspicion to religious tradition," as Lisa

Wolfe (2020, 56) puts it: "The sage is unwilling to ignore the dissonance of a religious belief such as retributive justice that does not coincide with lived experience."

For my purposes, the significance of Eccl 3:16–22 lies in its suggestion that humans "are but animals" (3:18). The text and translation are difficult here (Seow 1997, 167–68; Fox 2004, 25–26), but the rhetorical flow of the passage, and the role of animality within it, is not. Just as Qoheleth sees that there is no meaningful distinction between the fate of the fool and the fate of the wise (2:15–16), and just as Qoheleth sees that there is no meaningful distinction between the fate of the righteous and the fate of the wicked (7:15–17), so also Qoheleth sees that there is no meaningful distinction between the fate of humans and the fate of animals: "For the fate of humans and the fate of animals is the same; as one dies, so dies the other" (3:19a).

Brown (2000, 47) suggests that, in context, this "reference to animals is pejorative; humans are no better than animals, morally or otherwise." After all, when Ecclesiastes argues that there is little advantage to being righteous rather than wicked, or wise rather than foolish, the argument is hardly a commendation of wickedness and folly. If Qoheleth's rhetoric deflates the reputation of righteousness and wisdom by comparing them to evil and folly, so also Qoheleth's blurring of distinctions between humanity and animality could be understood as assuming a negative view of animality.

Where might this negative view come from? The distinction between humans and animals is partly rooted in biblical texts that suggest that all humans, and apparently only humans, are created "in the image of God" (Gen 1:27), with "dominion" or "rule" over other living creatures (Gen 1:26, 28; Ps 8:5–8), which God has given to humans for food and which rightly "fear" humans as they multiply across the earth (Gen 9:1–7). From a contemporary "humanist" perspective, this distinction between humans and animals is often understood as contributing to human welfare, rights, and dignity.

I have already shown, however, that distinctions between humans and animals do not ensure equitable treatment among humans. In the Hebrew Bible, slaves, women, children, and enemies are all associated at various points with animals as part of their subjugation to other humans. Nor is the Bible exceptional here. Like Adams and Derrida, animal studies scholar Cary Wolfe (2003, 8, emphasis original) insists,

> As long as it is institutionally taken for granted that it is all right to systematically exploit and kill nonhuman animals simply because of their

species, then the humanist discourse of species will always be available for use by some humans against other humans as well, to countenance violence against the social other of *whatever* species—or gender, or race, or class, or sexual difference.

Jennifer Koosed (2012, 244), however, argues that, rather than reinforcing the human/animal boundary, readers of Ecclesiastes might choose to take Qoheleth's blurring of boundaries further for feminist reasons:

> Feminism begins with the dismantling of the fundamental binary oppositions between male and female, masculine and feminine. If the differences and distinctions between human and animal can be questioned because both die equally, cannot we also question the differences and distinctions between men and women? They are as ephemeral as the wind.

As for the relationship between Qoheleth's undermining of the human/animal distinction and other biblical texts, it is crucial to recognize that Eccl 3 does take a different position on this distinction from such passages as Gen 1:26–28, 9:1–7, and Ps 8:5–8, while relying on vocabulary and ideas found in other biblical texts. The emphasis in 3:19 on the *rûaḥ*, "breath" or "spirit," shared by humans and animals recalls, for example, Ps 104, which is one of the least anthropocentric chapters in the Bible (Stone 2019). There one finds references to *rûaḥ* as both the breath given to all creatures by God when they are created (104:30) and the breath taken from all creatures by God when they die (104:29). Although Ecclesiastes introduces a novel element into this picture by referring to a theory that perhaps the spirit of humans "goes up" and the spirit of animals "goes down" (3:21), Qoheleth does not commit to this idea and finds no comfort in it. The emphasis here, as in Ps 104, lies rather on what humans and animals share, specifically the breath given and taken by God. As Turner (2017, 62) argues, Qoheleth "does not divide the possibility of an afterlife with God between human and animal," even if many later readers do, "but is more interested in [their] common fate." Moreover, the attention to *rûaḥ* as something shared by humans and animals resonates with the book's emphasis on *hebel*, which can also mean "breath" and is associated explicitly with *rûaḥ* in Eccl 1:14 ("all is *hebel* and a chasing after *rûaḥ*") and 4:4 ("This also is *hebel*, and a chasing after *rûaḥ*"). Indeed, they appear together here in 3:19 ("They all have the same *rûaḥ*, and humans have no advantage over the animals; for all is *hebel*").

The language used in Eccl 3:16–22 to discuss humans and animals overlaps with other biblical texts as well. The observation that "all" humans and animals "go to one place; all are from the dust, and all turn to dust again" uses a word for dust, *ʿāpār*, that is also used for the dust from which humans and animals are created and to which they return (see Gen 2:7, 3:19, Ps 103:14, 104:29, Job 34:15). The recognition of the shared fates of humans and animals resonates with numerous biblical passages that refer to both the salvation and the judgment of humans and animals, from the stories of flood, plagues, and the exodus from Egypt to such prophetic books as Jeremiah, Ezekiel, and Jonah (see Stone 2018, 154–63). Even Qoheleth's recurring admonition to accept one's lot in life by enjoying God's gifts of food and drink may remind one of the point made throughout Ps 104 that humans and animals all look to God for sustenance (Stone 2019). Thus, while Ecclesiastes challenges human exceptionalism by blurring distinctions between humans and animals, it does not do so from a position that is completely at odds with the rest of the Bible. Rather, it makes observations and draws conclusions that are consistent with nonpejorative strands of biblical literature that also associate humans with other living creatures.

Conclusion

In *Thinking through Animals*, Calarco (2015, 6) divides approaches to "the human/animal distinction," and the contemporary "breakdown" of that distinction, into three categories: identity, difference, and indistinction. Although indistinction is the least clearly defined among Calarco's categories, it is also the approach that Calarco prefers. In his own words, the indistinction approach "aims to think about human-animal relations in a manner that deemphasizes the importance of human uniqueness and the human/animal distinction. Indistinction theorists and activists explore some of the surprising ways in which human beings find themselves to be like animals" (4–5; see also 45–69).

"Indistinction" hardly sounds like a biblical idea. The anthropocentrism that has shaped biblical interpretation for centuries is partly based on commitments to "the importance of human uniqueness and the human/animal distinction," commitments that are defended by appeals to biblical texts. As I have shown, however, the book of Ecclesiastes does identify several "surprising ways in which human beings find themselves to be like animals." In particular, Ecclesiastes emphasizes the vulnerability of humans and animals alike to chance, suffering, and death, and casts doubt on the reality of an afterlife that would be available to humans but not to animals.

These emphases can no doubt be understood as examples of the "strange and disquieting" (Fox), and even "gloomy" (Forti), nature of Ecclesiastes. Yet Qoheleth's animal references do connect to other biblical texts, including texts that are far less "gloomy," such as Ps 104. Ecclesiastes is often characterized in terms of its contradictions, and understandably so. Even its perspectives on animals can seem contradictory to one another if, for example, one compares passages that imply indistinction with passages that understand animals as property. Yet the animal contradictions found in Ecclesiastes are related to contradictory views about animals that are found across the Bible as a whole and across its history of interpretation. Perhaps it is the Bible, and not the book of Ecclesiastes, that is "strange and disquieting" where animals are concerned.

But let me end on a different note. Ellen Davis argues that while it is important to reflect carefully on Qoheleth's "observation that humans are mere animals with respect to death," this "blunt statement should not be heard as mere cynicism." It is, rather, "crucial" to acknowledge "our physicality" and that "we are as ephemeral … as the beasts of the field." After all, she continues:

> We live in an age when human activity is wantonly destroying countless others of God's creatures. The accelerated rate of species endangerment and destruction for animals is often cited.… Such destruction as we have already wrought is possible only because we have largely forgotten this most basic fact of our existence, our common creaturehood. (Davis 2000, 187)

"Our common creaturehood" is not always comforting. It can be unsettling, and even terrifying, when one reflects on such matters as chance, accident, and the certainty of death. But if attention to Ecclesiastes and its views on the "common creaturehood" of animals and humans can lead to greater acknowledgment that all mortal creatures wish to enjoy the modest life that God has given as our lot in life, one may come to understand that one's work as a human includes a commitment to fostering the conditions that contribute to such enjoyment during one's fleeting days under the sun.

Works Cited

Adams, Carol J. 1995. *Neither Man nor Beast: Feminism and the Defense of Animals*. New York: Continuum.

Bickerman, Elias. 1967. *Four Strange Books of the Bible: Jonah, Daniel, Koheleth, Esther*. New York: Schocken Books.

Brown, William P. 2000. *Ecclesiastes*. IBC. Louisville: Westminster John Knox.

———. 2010. *The Seven Pillars of Creation: The Bible, Science, and the Ecology of Wonder*. New York: Oxford University Press.

Calarco, Matthew. 2015. *Thinking through Animals: Identity, Difference, Indistinction*. StBr. Stanford, CA: Stanford University Press.

Crenshaw, James L. 1987. *Ecclesiastes: A Commentary*. Philadelphia: Westminster.

Davis, Ellen F. 2000. *Proverbs, Ecclesiastes, and the Song of Songs*. WBComp. Louisville: Westminster John Knox.

Dell, Katharine. 1994. "Ecclesiastes as Wisdom: Consulting Early Interpreters." *VT* 44:301–29.

Derrida, Jacques. 1995. "'Eating Well,' or the Calculation of the Subject." Pages 255–87 in *Points...: Interviews, 1974–1994*. Edited by Elizabeth Weber. Translated by Peggy Kamuf. Stanford, CA: Stanford University Press.

Forti, Tova L. 2008. *Animal Imagery in the Book of Proverbs*. Leiden: Brill.

Fox, Michael V. 1989. *Qohelet and His Contradictions*. Sheffield: Sheffield Academic.

———. 2004. *Ecclesiastes*. JPSBC. Philadelphia: Jewish Publication Society.

Haraway, Donna. 2003. *The Companion Species Manifesto: Dogs, People, and Significant Otherness*. Chicago: Prickly Paradigm.

———. 2008. *When Species Meet*. Minneapolis: University of Minnesota Press.

Koosed, Jennifer L. 2012. "Ecclesiastes." Pages 243–46 in *Women's Bible Commentary*. Rev. and updated twentieth anniversary ed. Edited by Carol A. Newsom, Sharon H. Ringe, and Jacqueline E. Lapsley. Louisville: Westminster John Knox.

McKay, Heather A. 2002. "Through the Eyes of Horses: Representation of the Horse Family in the Hebrew Bible." Pages 127–41 in *Sense and Sensitivity: Essays on Reading the Bible in Memory of Robert Carroll*. Edited by Alastair G. Hunter and Philip R. Davies. Sheffield: Sheffield Academic.

Schifferdecker, Kathryn. 2008. *Out of the Whirlwind: Creation Theology in the Book of Job*. Cambridge: Harvard University Press.

Seow, Choon-Leong. 1997. *Ecclesiastes: A New Translation with Introduction and Commentary*. AB 18C. New York: Doubleday.

Sherman, Phillip. 2020. "The Hebrew Bible and the 'Animal Turn.'" *CurBR* 19:36–63.

Stone, Ken. 2005. *Practicing Safer Texts: Food, Sex and Bible in Queer Perspective*. London: T&T Clark.

———. 2016. "Animal Difference, Sexual Difference, and the Daughter of Jephthah." *BibInt* 24:1–16.

———. 2017. "Judges 3 and the Queer Hermeneutics of Carnophallogocentrism." Pages 261–76 in *The Bible and Feminism: Remapping the Field*. Edited by Yvonne Sherwood. Oxford: Oxford University Press.

———. 2018. *Reading the Hebrew Bible with Animal Studies*. Stanford, CA: Stanford University Press.

———. 2019. "'All These Look to You': Reading Psalm 104 with Animals in the Anthropocene Epoch." *Int* 27:236–47.

Strawn, Brent A. 2005. *What Is Stronger Than a Lion? Leonine Image and Metaphor in the Hebrew Bible and the Ancient Near East*. Göttingen: Vandenhoeck & Ruprecht.

Strømmen, Hannah M. 2018. *Biblical Animality after Jacques Derrida*. Atlanta: SBL Press.

Turner, Marie. 2017. *Ecclesiastes: Qoheleth's Eternal Earth*. EarthB. London: T&T Clark.

Walsh, Carey. 2017. "The Beasts of Wisdom: Ecological Hermeneutics of the Wild." *BibInt* 25:135–48.

Wolfe, Cary. 2003. *Animal Rites: American Culture, the Discourse of Species, and Posthumanist Theory*. Chicago: University of Chicago Press.

Wolfe, Lisa Michele. 2020. *Qoheleth (Ecclesiastes)*. WisdC. Collegeville, MN: Liturgical Press.

Part 2
Identification and Animal Rights

Biblical Studies Meets the Humane Society: The Emergence of Animal Activist Exegesis

Michael J. Gilmour

Veterinary surgeon David Williams observes a resemblance between the "five freedoms" proposed by the (British) Farm Animal Welfare Council and Ps 23. The council calls for (1) freedom from thirst, hunger, and malnutrition; (2) freedom from discomfort; (3) freedom from pain, injury, and disease; (4) freedom to express normal behavior; and (5) freedom from fear and distress. Psalm 23, according to Williams (2008, 22; as cited in Bauckham 2010, 138),

> reads just like a poetic vision of the FAWC freedoms ... needs met, appropriate environment, sufficient food and water, even protection at the hour of death. The shepherd's rod and staff (which could quite easily be seen [as] agents of domination) are comforting guides showing how dominion, properly executed, is beneficial for the animal. Surely goodness and mercy will follow the animal properly cared for throughout its life. Here is a paradigm of good animal welfare practice in Old Testament times, in Jesus' day and today.

I am intrigued that no less an exegete than Richard Bauckham writes favorably of this beautiful reading of the psalm. At least on this one occasion, in my opinion, a champion of animal welfare and amateur exegete succeeds in crossing that hermeneutical divide between ancient text and modern concern. It gives me hope the pursuit of a credible, biblically informed animal ethic is not merely a fool's errand. But it will not be easy. For one thing, as the introduction to this volume shows, academic biblical studies is anthropocentric, with deep roots in philosophical (see, e.g., various essays in Beauchamp and Frey 2011) and theological (see, e.g., Clough 2012) traditions largely disinterested or otherwise interested with respect to animals. For another, the Bible is a highly contested space within welfare discourses. Many within protectionist circles identify it as the root of the problem, maintaining the Bible gives divine sanction for any and all forms of use and exploitation. Others argue the reverse, invoking the Bible's authority in defense of animals. For scholars approaching the Bible with attention to ethics, who carry the prophets in one hand and a placard in the other, there is need for caution but also much to contribute through participation in these conversations, not least by challenging dubious readings and exploring new interpretive possibilities.

Biblical scholarship tends to be myopic, but, as seen time and again, new approaches—for example, feminist, postcolonial, queer, ecocritical—disrupt habits of thought in useful ways. The emerging convergence of critical animal studies and the Bible is late in coming but promises to do the same. This is a welcome step forward and indeed urgently needed. Quite apart from animal well-being, our interactions with other species have far-reaching implications for human health and environmental protection, and since the Bible is religiously authoritative for so many, it is in humanity's collective best interest and strategically sensible to scrutinize uses of it that dismiss nonhuman life as expendable and merely utilitarian, no more than a backdrop to the human story.

For the most part, I do not look directly at biblical texts in this essay but instead at a few uses of the Bible within advocacy debates of the last two hundred or so years, corresponding loosely with the founding of the first humane society in 1824. Especially in the century after the establishment of the Royal Society for the Prevention of Cruelty to Animals (it received Queen Victoria's patronage in 1840), reformers invoked the Bible often in their efforts to promote compassion and urge better legal protections. They apparently found something in their Bibles very few modern-day readers, scholarly or otherwise, see. Histories documenting the religious roots of modern advocacy, such as Janet M. Davis's (2016) *The Gospel of Kindness: Animal Welfare and the Making of Modern America*, present a fascinating story of Bible-reading reformers who played an integral part in modern animal-welfare movements. In time, humane societies moved away from their religious roots, but the very existence of an animal-sensitive approach to Christian (my focus) teaching in the nineteenth century and beyond, largely among laity engaged with reform efforts, suggests new possibilities for academics exploring the intersection of animal ethics and biblical interpretation.

The reformers I refer to reject(ed) the anthropocentrism described in the introduction. Their Bibles insist human and nonhuman animals are all creatures of the same God (an identity approach to human-animal relations and ethics), capable of suffering, and deserving of kindness. They find in the Old and New Testaments a mandate to care, and their sermons, school curricula, children's club programming, political arguments, pamphlets, poetry, and novels appeal to the Bible as they urge an end to cruel practices. There is not space here to discuss the wide spectrum of biblically and theologically grounded arguments in defense of animals produced by reformers. A great deal of this material is available in archives (e.g., the open-access John Ptak Collection of Animal Rights and Animal Welfare Printed Education Materials 1882–1937, housed in the North Carolina State University Library). As far as I am aware, there is no book-length analysis of engagements with the Bible in this material. What follows are only a few illustrations of this nonspecialist, animal-friendly approach to it. I also include examples of those invoking biblical support to oppose such calls for reform. The emphasis falls on the former because compassion-motivated exegesis is typically underrepresented.

An Equine and Canine Hermeneutic

One finds the most compelling occurrences of animal-friendly Bible reading in fiction, and Anna Sewell's 1877 novel *Black Beauty* is perhaps the most important instance of this kind of storytelling exegesis. This influential book is a spirited call to animal compassion that is explicitly Christian and biblically informed. Sewell was "a natural storyteller, motivated and trained by religious thought to make a moral argument out of all the injustices she saw" (Smiley 2011, x). Any number of comments in the story give a sense of this ethical sensibility. As one character puts it:

> If we saw any one who took pleasure in cruelty, we might know who he belonged to, for the devil was a murderer from the beginning, and a tormentor to the end. On the other hand, where we saw people who loved their neighbours, and were kind to man and beast, we might know that was God's mark, for [as it says in 1 John 4:8] "God is Love." (Sewell 1877, 51)

Another offers practical advice on the proper treatment of animals with an easy slide into the cadences of Prov 22:6 in the Authorized Version. Horses "are like children, train 'em up in the way they should go, as the good book says, and when they are old they will not depart from it" (Sewell 1877, 57). Sewell's influence on animal-welfare efforts proved to be considerable, as later writers recognized the potential of good storytelling for inspiring love for animals and loathing for abusive behaviors. Hers was not the first novel to use the Bible this way, as part of the strategy to compel reform, nor was it the last.

In the early 1890s, George T. Angell of the American Humane Education Society published *Black Beauty* in America to raise awareness of animal suffering. He also advertised a competition for a novel along the same lines as Sewell's. *Black Beauty* tells a horse's story from a horse's point of view, and Angell wanted another book to help promote compassion among other species. The winner of that Humane Society book prize was a Nova Scotia author named Margaret Marshall Saunders, whose novel *Beautiful Joe* first appeared in 1894, published by the American Humane Education Society. Like Sewell's *Black Beauty*, it too is an animal autobiography. Joe is an abused dog, mutilated by a cruel owner who chops off his ears and tail with an axe. The rescue of this dog and his subsequent adventures in the home of an animal-friendly Christian family provide occasion for a series of accessible lessons on the proper care of pets, farm animals, and wildlife.

Beautiful Joe is unambiguously Christian in perspective, with biblical passages regularly introduced as a basis for its ethical instruction. Its principal human character is the daughter of a minister, and she and others in the story regularly align kind treatment of animals with a wide range of more traditional Christian virtues such as care for the poor, honesty, and temperance. One advocate in the story speaks of God's judgment on those cruel to animals and evokes Paul when she says, "Our whole dumb creation [is] groaning together in pain, and would continue to groan, unless merciful human beings were willing to help them" (Saunders 1894, 138; see Rom 8:22). One crucial scene involves three friends committing to protect all creatures. They admit there are some unanswered theological questions but agree this is no basis to ignore what they do know: "'There's nothing definite about their immortality,' said Mr. Harry. 'However, we've got nothing to do with that. If it's right for them to be in heaven, we'll find them there. All we have to do now is to deal with the present, and the Bible plainly tells us that 'a righteous man regardeth the life of his beast'" (238). For them, Prov 12:10 (AV) is a sufficiently clear mandate to care for other species.

It seems likely Saunders's explicitly religious and biblical approach to the topic helped her win the contest. In 1893, a member of the Humane Society prize committee who selected her book insisted, "The church owes it to her mission to preach and to teach the enforcement of the 'bird's nest commandment' [in Deut 22:6–7]; the principle recognized by Moses in the Hebrew world" (in Saunders 1894, 47–48). If one is a person of faith, this Humane Society member insists, one is under obligation to let the mother bird go free, as it says in Deut 22:6–7—shorthand for insisting the Bible urges kindness to all species.

The alignment of animal compassion and the Bible by Sewell and Saunders—just two of many possible illustrations of creative writers using their platforms to promote compassion—reflects a dilemma facing many, past and present, troubled by cruelty and convinced it ought to be a matter of religious import. The church's and the religious academy's widespread indifference to animals left few options for advocates to express what they understood to be obvious: animals are theologically consequential; cruelty is sin; and kindness to all species is a Christian obligation. But talk of animals in religious contexts is not always welcome, then or now. Saunders's follow-up novel, 1902's *Beautiful Joe's Paradise, or, the Island of Brotherly Love*, was not nearly as successful as her first book. As the title suggests, it is an imagined depiction of animals in the afterlife and an obvious answer to a question raised (see above) in *Beautiful Joe*. Was this a theological step too far for readers? If so, she was not alone. The inclusion of animals in speculative theology and biblical interpretation is risky. When Victorian fantasist and children's author George MacDonald was a young minister in Sussex, he was charged with heresy for merely suggesting an animal afterlife (Shelley and Pierce 2014, 11 n. 1). C. S. Lewis faced similar hostility when addressing ethical questions from a theological point of view. His decision to include a chapter on animal suffering in 1940's *The Problem of Pain* resulted in ridicule, as did his outspoken antivivisectionist stance. As Alister McGrath (2013, 237) notes, "Lewis's views on this matter lost him many friends at Oxford and elsewhere, as vivisection was then widely regarded as morally justified by its outcomes. Animal pain was the price paid for human progress." But for these two, opposition did not force a retreat from their ideas. Instead, they re-presented them in fiction. One finds in MacDonald's fairy tales, such as 1871's *At the Back of the North Wind*, and in Lewis's science fiction, poetry, and children's books of the mid-twentieth century, some of these writers' more theologically robust arguments in support of animal compassion. Their most developed, sustained, and compelling visions of inclusivity appear in their biblically informed creative writing, not MacDonald's pulpit or Lewis's university podium.

Of course, not all uses of the Bible in animal-welfare debates occur in fiction. England's SPCA was initially a religious reform movement. The Christian convictions of some of its founders, among them the Anglican clergyman Arthur Broome, provided the moral basis for their work. He described the new organization as a Christian society based on Christian principles (see Linzey 1995, 19, 36, 160 n. 17). The English movement proved to be "an inspiration and a model for American reformers," many of whom also viewed their work on behalf of animals as a fundamental Christian duty (Beers 2006, 23). Henry Bergh, founder of the American SPCA in 1866, insisted that the treatment of animals "is a moral question in all its aspects.... It is a solemn recognition of the greatest attribute of the Almighty Ruler of the Universe, mercy" (cited in Beers 2006, 44). Christian faith and biblical teachings are also explicit in the writings of other early proponents of the American humane movement. Angell, mentioned above, founded the Massachusetts SPCA in 1868, and Caroline Earle White, a Quaker turned Roman Catholic, helped start the Pennsylvania SPCA in 1867 and the American Anti-Vivisection Society in 1883. In his autobiography, Angell mentions an 1871 invitation from White to speak in the Church of the Unity in Boston. He suspects this was "probably the first church in America, and perhaps the first in the world, in which a lecture on cruelty to animals was ever given by a layman on [the] Lord's Day" (Angell 1892, 39).

There are dissenting opinions, of course. While many view the Bible as a basis for compassion, other animal advocates insist it is blood-soaked, offering nothing to the cause. There is one prominent example of this in the writings of South African novelist and later Nobel laureate John Coetzee, who delivered the Tanner Lectures at Princeton University in 1997. Departing from conventional delivery, his talks were fictional in form. (He later integrated these lectures, first published in *The Lives of Animals* [Coetzee 1999], in his novel *Elizabeth Costello* [Coetzee 2003]). He tells the story of an aging novelist and vegetarian named Elizabeth Costello, who is herself asked to give guest lectures at a prestigious university. Her topic is animal suffering and humanity's indifference to it. Coetzee's provocative short story includes a sarcastic, offhand remark by Costello about the relationship of the Bible to human attitudes toward animals. "'Perhaps that is the origin of the gods,' says his mother. A silence falls. 'Perhaps we invented gods so that we could put the blame on them. They gave us permission to eat flesh. They gave us permission to play with unclean things. It's not our fault, it's theirs. We're just their children'" (Coetzee 1999, 41). When pressed to explain, she answers by referring to Gen 9:3: "'And God said: Every moving thing that liveth shall be meat for you,' his mother quotes. 'It's convenient. God told us it was OK'" (41). Coetzee is himself vegetarian and an outspoken proponent of animal rights, often using his public platform to speak to the issues. Genesis 9, he finds, is little more than a thinly veiled license for carnivorousness.

In 1967, physicist Charles D. Niven, who organized the Eastern Ontario SPCA (now part of the Ontario SPCA), published *History of the Humane Movement*. Like Coetzee, he finds more violence than kindness in the pages of the Bible, especially the New Testament. Niven begins with a survey of teachings about animals in pre-Christian religious thought, including a cursory overview of Moses, Isaiah, Zoroaster, Mahavira, Gautama, and Pythagoras, and then he turns to Christianity, tracing episodically its attitudes toward the nonhuman from Paul through to the twentieth century. He finds little help here. To understand the history of the humane movement, he insists, "we have to face squarely the fact that there is no *explicit* statement on the part of Jesus recorded in the Gospels that cruelty to animals is one of the great sins" (Niven 1967, 23, emphasis original). His critique of Jesus's early followers is equally harsh. The "worst feature" of the early Jesus movement is that "the man who was to be most active as a missionary of the early Christian Church, was intuitively neither tolerant nor humane." His evidence is 1 Cor 9:9, Paul's citation of the injunction in Deut 25:4 not to muzzle an ox while it treads grain. By saying the passage refers to people, Paul "completely failed to understand the motives which prompted the insertion of this clause in the early Israelite code." Furthermore, "those six words 'Doth God take care for oxen?' which are now a part of Holy Writ have had an exceedingly disastrous effect on the animal welfare movement" (Niven 1967, 24–25).

While some animal welfarists blame the Bible for atrocities, others commit atrocities citing the Bible as justification. An article appearing in *Popular Science Monthly* in 1874 by Cambridge University physiologist Sir Michael Foster is illustrative when he finds in humanity's "dominion" over other species permission for human-caused animal suffering, including vivisection.

> If we believe that man is to govern the world, and he must either govern or succumb, then we must be prepared to use animals selfishly, if you

please to call it so—to use animals for our advantage—to kill them when we have need of their deaths—to kill them with pain when the pain is for our benefit; and, inasmuch as the greater includes the less, to inflict pain without death where their pain does us good. Our good is, in fact, the rule of our conduct towards animals. (cited in Saunders 2015, 280–81)

Apparently claiming biblical dominion covers a multitude of sins.

Doctor Dolittle Reads Genesis

As Calarco explains, the philosophers employing an identity approach to critical animal studies emphasize the shared evolutionary history of human and nonhuman animals. On this basis, pro-animal philosophers such as Peter Singer, Tom Regan, and Paola Cavalieri, whose work he discusses, stress deep continuities across species lines, such as sentience and cognition. This provides the basis for developing ethical arguments rooted in the principle of equal consideration of interests (Calarco 2015, 11–14). Though the premises obviously differ, there is a resemblance in the structure of thinking found in many of the mythic and poetic accounts of humans and nonhumans in the Bible. Land animals and humans appear on the same day (Gen 1:24–26), emerge from the same soil (Gen 2:7, 19), and depend alike on God for sustenance (Ps 104:10–30). God cares about the people *and* animals of Nineveh (Jonah 4:11), and even sends rain to places where no humans live, which implies concern for other-than-human life (Job 38:26). Though a prooftext approach is hardly sufficient, such textual moments at least hint at the possibility of a compassionate, ethically robust identity hermeneutic. What devout activists and amateur exegetes of a century ago emphasized was the shared history of all creatures in the creative work of God, who declared them all good (Gen 1:31). They found in this foundational premise reason enough to act in defense of others. That the world and everything in it has its origins in God's creative work is also a presupposition shared by all biblical writers. Of course there are ambiguities and ambivalence within the Bible—the disparate writings of the Hebrew Bible and Christian Testament do not offer a singular vision of animals—but in many instances, texts assumed to rule out an animal-friendly interpretation do not withstand scrutiny. Michael Gilmour (2014, 65–67, 92–112, 83–87, 28–36), for one, discusses various texts and subjects thought to rule out the Bible as an animal-friendly resource—among them the permission to eat meat in Gen 9:2–3, animal sacrifice, the death of the Gadarene swine, and Paul's remarks about muzzling oxen in 1 Cor 9:9–10—and finds the Bible is not so indifferent to animals as many suppose.

Biblical scholarship is a relative newcomer to critical animal studies and only rarely a participant in conversations about animal ethics. But as the very few examples above illustrate, the Bible has long been bandied about in this context. Is it animal friendly or blood-soaked? The pattern of claim/counterclaim seems unending. Most engaged in these debates on both sides are not biblical scholars or theologians, and they often find in the Bible justifications for positions already taken on other grounds. They often read the same texts but reach wildly divergent conclusions. Emotion and selectivity are the rhetorical weapons of choice.

The meeting of formal biblical studies with the humane society is potentially productive even if fraught. Theologian and activist Stephen Webb finds two stories about animals in the Bible—one God's divine plan, the other a story of human use and abuse. "The Hebrew prophets insist that in the end God will restore the world to its original peace and harmony," he writes, "a vision confirmed by the message of the New Testament. [But] If God's ultimate plan for animals is not kept in mind, then the Bible can seem to legitimate all sorts of practices that many would find abhorrent today" (Webb 2013, 243). Is there a way out of this dilemma? Confronting the philosophical and theological biases contributing to the speciesism of biblical scholarship is a crucial first step. Another is for scholars to formulate an inclusive hermeneutic with room to address welfarists' concerns.

One potential resource for biblical scholars engaged with this progressive agenda is the work of those bringing a feminist ethic of care to their analyses of texts (see Calarco's [2015, 23] brief remarks on the feminist approaches to animals). This conception of morality stresses relationality, something easily accommodated within the language of many biblical writers. When integrated to animal ethics, this approach disrupts anthropocentric ways of thinking by engaging in what literary critic Josephine Donovan (2016, 95–96) refers to as an animal-standpoint criticism, which deconstructs ideologies of exploitation and dominance. It begins with the premise that animals are subjects, not objects, "individuals with stories/biographies of their own, not undifferentiated masses; that they dislike pain, enjoy pleasures; that they want to live and thrive; that in short they have identifiable desires and needs" (99; see too Adams, 2018, 34). This approach identifies "authorial and critical blindness that often accompanies animal representation, questioning the absences and elisions, the lapses and lacunae in texts where animals appear" (Donovan 2016, 99).

By attending to "the emotional meaning" of literary works, she challenges the dominant Kantian approach to ethics with its emphasis on decision-making "based on abstract universalizable principles disconnected from particular contexts and purged of emotional and personal evaluation" (Donovan 2016, 1–2). As Calarco (2015, 23) puts it when summarizing feminist approaches to animals, the "privileging of reason over emotion is, from this feminist perspective, a continuation of the logocentrism of human centered and male-centered thinking and a pernicious dogma that the identity discourse needs to question more thoroughly." He defines logocentrism as an "uncritical focus and overemphasis on *logos*, understood here as reason and its associated capacities and faculties (language, consciousness, subjectivity, and so on)" (22). Logocentrism occurs among identity-based thinkers when arguments for extending ethics to animals appeal to reason and argumentation alone, thus allowing no place for emotion or pity (22–23).

Empathy and emotional connection with suffering animals involves acknowledgment of common experience, a recognition of a shared creatureliness. For biblical scholars, there are numerous opportunities to explore such overlaps. The ark preserves human and animal life; Israelite legislation protects orphans and widows and strangers in the land, but in the near context the well-being of oxen (Deut 25:4). Humans and animals alike are to rest on the Sabbath (Exod 20:10). Jesus speaks of sparrows and people in the same breath (Matt 10:29–31). The list goes on. A shift in thinking, a disruption in habituated animal-*exclusive* reading, one that emphasizes a shared mythic origin and creaturely experience, would open the way for an *inclusive* hermeneutic that is ethically relevant for twenty-first-century readers.

I conclude with an odd illustration of an identity approach to biblical writing that reflects the sensibilities of a feminist ethic of care. Hugh Lofting's 1923 novel *Doctor Dolittle's Post Office* involves a subtle engagement with a biblical text that illustrates the potential of an animal-sensitive hermeneutic. While visiting a remote coastal town, residents tell Dolittle of a nearby island filled with fire-breathing dragons. They warn him to avoid this terrible place, appropriately named No Man's Land. Naturally Dolittle is curious, and he decides to swim to the island with his companion dog, Jip. They get into trouble owing to strong currents, but help comes unexpectedly from below as a large dinosaur-like creature rises and carries them on its back to the island. It is a piffilosaurus. When they arrive, the friendly creature shows them around and explains the unusual circumstances of the place's diverse species. (Dolittle, of course, speaks animal languages.) The island's residents fear humanity's destructive ways and exploitative tendencies, and the ancient lore about fire-breathing dragons serves to protect them from unwanted intrusions. From the animal's point of view, this island is paradise on earth.

Those living there know Dolittle's reputation as a friend to animals, and they welcome him gladly. He is in fact the island's first human visitor in a thousand years. The secret to their preservation lies in the absence of human interference: "'We didn't want the locals to see us,' said the strange beast. 'They think we are dragons—and we let them go on thinking it. Because then they don't come near the island and we have our country to ourselves…. They think we live on men and breathe fire! But all we ever really eat is bananas'" (Lofting 2019, 478–79). This is the only place in the world where they can live in peace because humans are such a serious threat: "Whatever happens, we mustn't be seen from the shore and have the [locals] coming here. It would be the end of us if that should ever happen" (480).

Lofting clearly models this chapter, titled "The Animals' Paradise," on the biblical story of Eden. It is not a stretch to propose Genesis is in view. His 1948 novel *Doctor Dolittle and the Secret Lake* includes the story of an ancient turtle named Mudface, the last living survivor of the great flood and a passenger on Noah's ark. Dolittle and his friends listen as Mudface relates the story of Noah and life in the aftermath of the flood.

As in Genesis, this paradise is no longer accessible to people (see Gen 3:24), but instead of a *fiery* sword, the lore about *fiery* dragons keeps visitors away. Furthermore, the island is populated entirely by harmless, vegetable-feeding creatures. "If we had the others," the piffilosaurus continues, "we wouldn't last long" (Lofting 2019, 480). The scene, with its absence of predation and emphasis on vegetation, recalls the first biblical creation story: "God said, 'See, I have given you every plant yielding seed that is upon the face of all the earth, and every tree with seed in its fruit; you shall have them for food. And to every beast of the earth, and to every bird of the air, and to everything that creeps on the earth, everything that has the breath of life, I have given every green plant for food.' And it was so" (Gen 1:29–30 NRSV). Lofting (2019, 481) stresses the plant-eating character of this strange island:

> Down by the banks of the streams the Doctor was shown great herds of hippopotami, feeding on the luscious reeds that grew at the water's

edge. In the wide fields of high grass there were elephants and rhinoceri browsing. On the slopes where the forests were sparse he spied long-necked giraffes, nibbling from the trees. Monkeys and deer of all kinds were plentiful. And birds swarmed everywhere. In fact, every kind of creature that does not eat meat was there, living peaceably and happily with the others in this land where vegetable food abounded and the disturbing tread of man was never heard.

The absence of predation also echoes the prophet Isaiah, who writes of a kingdom of peace involving people and animals (Isa 11:1–9). As the lone human in this vegetation rich animal paradise, Dolittle is in effect another Adam: "out of the ground the Lord God formed every animal of the field and every bird of the air, and brought them to the man" (Gen 2:19 NRSV). Within this imaginative space, Lofting (2019, 482) alludes to the common origin of all creatures (created by God) by drawing on Genesis, and as the Genesis animals approach Adam, so too the piffilosaurus and others living there approach the Adam-like Doctor: "He was kept busy from morning to night with all the animals who wanted to consult him about different things."

The capacity of stories to create worlds that do not exist is part of the magic of fiction. There is an ethical message in Lofting's writings as well.[1] We are not able to hide animals from harm, as in Lofting's tale, to create spaces for them beyond human reach—human-caused climate change, for instance, touches all living things on earth—but the ability to imagine safe places where animals flourish is an evidence of sorts that people can do *some things* to ameliorate conditions for *some animals*. While standing on a hill with Jip and the piffilosaurus, the doctor gazes at the island and its contented residents, and sighs. His emotional engagement with the island's residents and willingness to see the situation from their point of view, his efforts to care for their needs and his longing to preserve their safe haven, all reflect an identity approach to animals rooted in an ethic of care. Dolittle then pronounces what amounts to a benediction: "This beautiful land could also have been called the 'Animals' Paradise,' he mur-

---

1. Lofting created his famous character while on the battlefields of World War I. Not wanting to write letters to his children about the horrors around him, and troubled by the suffering of horses and other animals caught up in the conflict, he retreated into an imaginative world with a doctor whose priority is care for animals in need. On this, see, e.g., Schmidt 1992, 13–14, 51–52.

mured. 'Long may they enjoy it to themselves! May this, indeed, be *No Man's Land* forever!'" (Lofting 2019, 481).

Biblical scholarship is inescapably anthropocentric, and as such woefully out of step with pressing issues of the day. The climate crisis, growing awareness and revulsion at industrial-scale factory farming, habitat destruction, and pollution, in addition to myriad other ways humans oppress other animals and harm the environments they depend on, are unavoidable realities demanding attention. To dismiss biblical literature as irrelevant to these conversations is shortsighted and even irresponsible. The Bible speaks often of animals and the earth—to ignore this is to give tacit approval to those who flippantly equate dominion with despotism and with license to do whatever they want with animals and the earth. The pious welfare advocates of previous generations, however imperfect as exegetes, were surprisingly insightful. They saw fins, feathers, and fur everywhere in their Bibles, and it awakened an ethical impulse. We have much to learn from them.

Works Cited

Adams, Carol J. 2018. *Neither Man nor Beast: Feminism and the Defense of Animals*. London: Bloomsbury.

Angell, George T. 1892. *Autobiographical Sketches and Personal Recollections*. Boston: American Humane Education Society.

Bauckham, Richard. 2010. *Bible and Ecology: Rediscovering the Community of Creation*. Waco, TX: Baylor University Press.

Beauchamp, Tom L., and Ray G. Frey, eds. 2011. *The Oxford Handbook of Animal Ethics*. Oxford: Oxford University Press.

Beers, Diane L. 2006. *For the Prevention of Cruelty: The History and Legacy of Animal Rights Activism in the United States*. Athens: Swallow; Ohio University Press.

Calarco, Matthew. 2015. *Thinking through Animals: Identity, Difference, Indistinction*. StBr. Stanford, CA: Stanford University Press.

Clough, David L. 2012. *On Animals*. Vol. 1 of *Systematic Theology*. London: Bloomsbury.

Coetzee, J. M. 1999. *The Lives of Animals*. Princeton: Princeton University Press.

———. 2003. *Elizabeth Costello: Eight Lessons*. London: Vintage.

Davis, Janet M. 2016. *The Gospel of Kindness: Animal Welfare and the Making of Modern America*. New York: Oxford University Press.

Donovan, Josephine. 2016. *The Aesthetics of Care: On the Literary Treatment of Animals*. New York: Bloomsbury.

Gilmour, Michael J. 2014. *Eden's Other Residents: The Bible and Animals*. Eugene, OR: Cascade.

King, Shelley, and John B. Pierce. 2014. "Introduction." Pages 9–35 in *The Princess and the Goblin and Other Fairy Tales*, by George MacDonald. Edited by Shelley King and John B. Pierce. Peterborough, UK: Broadview.

Linzey, Andrew. 1995. *Animal Theology*. Urbana: University of Illinois Press.

Lofting, Hugh. 2019. *Doctor Dolittle's Post Office*. Pages 427–709 in *Doctor Dolittle: The Complete Collection*. Vol. 1. New York: Aladdin.

McGrath, Alister. 2013. *C. S. Lewis: A Life*. Carol Stream, IL: Tyndale.

Niven, Charles D. 1967. *History of the Humane Movement*. London: Johnson.

Saunders, Margaret Marshall. 1894. *Beautiful Joe*. Edited by Keridiana Chez. Peterborough, UK: Broadview, 2015.

Schmidt, Gary D. 1992. *Hugh Lofting*. TEAS 496. New York: Twayne.

Sewell, Anna. 2011. *Black Beauty*. New York: Penguin. Originally 1877.

Smiley, Jane. 2011. "Foreword." Pages ix–xiii in *Black Beauty*, by Anna Sewell. New York: Penguin.

Webb, Stephen H. 2013. "Animals in the Bible." Pages 243–44 in *The Global Guide to Animal Protection*. Edited by Andrew Linzey. Urbana: University of Illinois Press.

Williams, David. 2008. *Animal Rights, Human Responsibilities*. Cambridge: Grove Booklet E151.

Attending to the Forest and Its Denizens in the Hebrew Bible

Margaret Cohen

Introduction

Animal studies has much to offer biblical investigations by pushing us to consider the biblical text through an array of new lenses: considering other species on their own terms, complicating the relationships between human and nonhuman animals, and considering the ethical implications of how anthropocentrism, often rooted in the biblical text, has affected various forms of oppression. Conversely, rigorous work in biblical studies can offer those nonbiblicists in animal studies a rich set of sources from the ancient world. The biblical text is complex and varied and has its own history of growth and change. Attention to these details offers an opportunity to understand deeply the natural world in the Bible, including the life of animals and their depictions in antiquity.

This essay examines a particular environment, the biblical forest, the *yaʿar*, both in its existence and in its destruction. Standing trees occur in all sorts of places in the Hebrew Bible and are often imbued with cultic, aesthetic, and even didactic significances. There are also examples of the felling of trees and the destruction of forest habitats in addition to the use of various types of deforestation imagery to convey ominous messages. Further, denizens of the forest are present in numerous passages and factor prominently in several narratives. Using the tools of philological and textual study, one can reconstruct the multiple facets within the biblical concept of the forest, of wooded areas, their ecosystems, and their maintenance or destruction. Reading texts about the forest with this conceptual framework not only, in the traditional vein, offers a fuller historical-critical analysis of the narrative but also lays the groundwork for an ecological hermeneutic that can bring attention to the earth, the environment, and the dynamic relationship that all species within an ecosystem share.

Of the instances in the biblical text that demonstrate a clear and particular connotation, the most frequent semantic focus of forest/*yaʿar* is as a place where trees are procured for the purpose of using their wood for construction or artisanal activity. So, for example, Jer 10:3, "For it is the work of a craftsman's hands. He cuts down a tree in the forest with an ax."[1] This use resonates with the typically English sense of the term, a wooded space with a critical density of standing trees. The next most frequent semantic focus is that of a place that is something between an open field and a full-growth forest—something like a brush land, or even perhaps a forest that has not reached its climax vegetation. For example, Isa 9:17, "It has kindled the thickets of the forest, which have turned into billowing smoke." This semantic field also includes references to vines and other kinds of nontall tree growth. The term appears almost as frequently as the explicit abode of animals, particularly bears and lions. So, Ps 50:10, "For mine is every animal of the forest," or Mic 5:7, "Like a lion among beasts of the forest." A smaller but noticeable group comprises instances in which the forest is a place housing something cultic or a location with a particular access to the divine. This language is more subtle and often poetic, as in Ps 83:15, where the anger of Yahweh is cast as a fiery storm in the forest. The variability of the possible semantic range requires nuanced readings of passages dealing with the forest, including those dealing with destruction, and one can use this variability to more fully engage with the agrarian worldview of the biblical authors, whose familiarity with the natural world is apparent. The authors demonstrate that they understand multiple senses of the term and the physical realities of forest habitat in the region (e.g., the different types of vegetation, the animal species present, the common occurrence of forest fire).

This kind of examination is by itself productive, but one can also delve further by using the philological descriptions of the biblical forest to more fully attend to the nonhuman beings present in the biblical text. While language can and does obscure ethical issues (see the introduction to this volume), it can also conversely reveal, in the biblical authors' choices, ancient views about the very nature of trees and forests, the animals that live in the forest world, and, if one looks carefully, certain fundamental

---

1. Unless otherwise stated, all biblical translations are my own.

similarities between trees, forest animals, and humans (Stone 2018, 74–82, similarly investigates language around sacrifice). These revelations can both demonstrate the complexity of the ancient ethic and allow one to reconsider reception of the biblical text and how it has—often negatively—affected modern views of anthropocentrism and attitudes toward animals and the natural world (Strømmen 2018, 10–17, on "biblical blame"; see also introduction). As I will show in three biblical passages below, the forest and its inhabitants share certain characteristics with humans that lead to ethical questions regarding habitat destruction and the agency of animals (see Calarco's [2015, 20] identity theorists).

In the narratives presented here, the trees and woody areas directly affect the driving factors of the action. However, the trees and the forest are also a location of encounters with the category of animal, both literal animals, such as the bears in the Elisha story, and animal-ness, especially in narratives where the locations of human endeavors, such as cities, are contrasted with natural habitats, such as forests. In these encounters, and through careful examination of the text, one can see certain similarities among human animals, nonhuman animals, and even the trees of the forests in which they dwell. A biblical concept of a shared living-being-ness among creatures in the natural world is to be found in the language of the authors.

Phillip Sherman (2020, 56), in a recent review of the state of research at the intersection of biblical and animal studies, suggests that one productive avenue of investigation may be in the consideration of diachronic change in biblical attitudes toward the "question of the animal." Here, three biblical narratives, one from the Deuteronomic Code, another from the Elijah/Elisha cycle, and one from Joshua's settlement account, are examined in this regard. The passages are discussed in roughly compositional order,[2] and one can see some tentative indications of differences and change in the biblical understanding of the animal question. In a legal discussion from Deuteronomy, one sees that trees are coded with a kind of human animality. In the Elijah/Elisha cycles, one sees that trees and the forest stand in contrast to the city and that they are the place of divine

---

2. Debate regarding composition of the Deuteronomistic History, as traditionally understood, is robust. I will follow some consensus opinions here, such as they are. The increasingly contradictory nature of the debate can be readily seen in recent collections such as Knoppers and McConville 2000; and Dozeman, Römer, and Schmid 2011.

sanction. By means of their other-than-human animals, they are agents of Yahweh. In both of these narratives one sees a complex perspective on trees and the woods, and one that holds somewhat contradictory points simultaneously. In a passage from Joshua, there is less complexity in the author's attitude toward the forest and trees—they are cleared for human settlement without much consideration.

Deuteronomy 20: Cutting Down Trees in War

The first passage comes from the Deuteronomic Code, considered to be the heart of what is now the book of Deuteronomy (Van Seters 1998, 16), and the material that influenced and guided the hands that later crafted the huge project of the Deuteronomistic History, the narrative of Israel's story, which stretches from Joshua to 2 Kings. The compositional history of this material is the subject of much scholarly debate (Knoppers and McConville 2000; Römer and de Pury 1996). The diversity of proposals, some specific to certain verses and others relating to wide swaths of text and ideology, cannot be fully retold here. However, generally speaking, the verses below are considered to be older legal material forming the nucleus out of which Deuteronomy grew as well as influencing later growth of the larger corpus of Deuteronomistic works.

> When you set siege against a city for many days to wage war against it, to seize it, you will not destroy its trees, to cast an axe against them, because from it, you can eat it, so you won't cut [it down]. Because are the trees of the field human, to go from before you into the enclosure? Only trees which you know that it is not a tree for food, it you will destroy and cut and build siege works against the city which is the one making war with you, until its fall. (Deut 20:19–20)[3]

Deuteronomy 20:19–20 details the legal ruling regarding cutting down trees during war, but even as these verses are didactic, they also contain ambiguities (Uval 2000). This set of instructions forbids destroying fruit trees during siege warfare. However, it is not a blanket prohibition; tree destruction is permitted under certain conditions. But perhaps the most unusual part of this passage, and one troubling commentators from Ibn

---

3. I have translated to specifically highlight the points under discussion even if the result is somewhat awkward in English.

Ezra to now (see Shacter 2003), is the rhetorical question, "Are the trees of the field human?" This locution is presumably meant to explain that the trees do not have the protection of walls to avoid the destructiveness of warfare. They are rooted on the field of battle and cannot withdraw to safer ground. But why should the author even comment on such a characterization? The inclusion of the question implies that there is deep thought over the very nature of the trees. First, they are living beings. The text does not, for example, suggest that warring soldiers avoid destroying rocks or other inanimate impediments in their path. Second, however, despite the similarity of being alive, trees are somehow distinct from humans. They lack a human concept of mobility and cannot travel from their positions in the open to safety behind city walls.

There is a subtle change in the scenario from verse 19 to verse 20 regarding the warring parties. In verse 19, the people being addressed are waging war against the people in the besieged city, but in verse 20, the extra relative clause explains that it is the city that is making war against the addressees. Here, those on the defensive may cut down trees for wood to besiege the enemy city "until its fall." Further, the ruling distinguishes between trees, forbidding the cutting down of those that produce food for humans and allowing the felling of those that humans "know" are not "food trees." The textual details mitigate the destruction of the trees—only certain types, only for defensive measures, and only until the city falls—a kind of minimum level of destruction for human needs. But these stipulations also reveal a deep understanding of the trees' nature. From the human perspective, tree fruits are food; however, from the tree perspective, fruits are their seed containers, holders of offspring. The prohibition against destroying a living being with its offspring is a familiar one in the biblical imagination.

J. Gordon McConville (1984) and others point out that this tree law has connections to two other legal prohibitions: the prohibition against taking a mother bird together with her fledglings (Deut 22:6–7) and the prohibition against cooking a kid in its mother's milk (Deut 14:21, Exod 23:19, 34:26; see Wright 2008). The prohibition in each of these cases, including Deut 20, is against the destruction of a life-giving being with its life-product (Wright 2008, 456). The legal analogy recognizes the animal-ness of the tree; that is, the tree, like the mother bird or mother goat, is fulfilling one of the fundamental aspects of life, reproduction. The offspring, too, in this case the seed in the fruit of a fruit tree, like the fledglings and the kid, has a life force, an animality, and the legal prohibition, then, views their wanton destruction together as unethical.

Despite the overall formulaic and legalistic nature of the Deuteronomic Code, in this passage we see perhaps a glimpse of something more emotional and abstract. The self-reflective commentary of this question suggests that the author(s) understands some intrinsic quality of trees that is comparable with humans, even as it is also distinct. The living-being-ness of the tree requires the author to use a (hu)man as comparanda. The living-being-ness is further amplified, by comparison with the other legal rulings about parents and offspring, in the reminder that trees have what one might even call a concern with reproduction. Ultimately, this passage does not protect every tree, and they are clearly still expendable to serve human needs under various conditions. But the unusual rhetorical question demands explanation, and one can see in its inclusion some notion of the ethical connections between living beings across species.

The Elisha Cycle:
Humans Cutting Down Woods, Bears Cutting Down Humans

In 2 Kings, there is a long series of accounts regarding the prophet Elisha. The Elijah and Elisha material presumably circulated independently as stories of the prophets and was incorporated as an addition to the Kings text (McKenzie 1991, 95; Miller 1966). It is difficult to say with certainty when such a collection of stories may have been added, but it is likely that they came to the attention of Deuteronomistic author(s) after the fall of the Northern Kingdom (Halpern and Vanderhooft 2009, 287). Regardless of an exact date for the incorporation into the Deuteronomistic History, the written additions concerning the careers of these prophets should be understood to postdate the original legal heart of Deuteronomy.

The constellation of natural details in this cycle of stories not only is an indication of the primacy of agrarian concerns in the biblical narrative in general but also highlights Elisha's strong connection to nature, as Laura Feldt (2013) and others more thoroughly demonstrate elsewhere. These narratives have careful craftsmanship, and the person of Elisha is portrayed with intentional detail. That Elisha has a nonnormative body, for example, is particularly relevant when one comes to meet the bears at the heart of the story. Rhiannon Graybill (2019) suggests that his lack of hair perhaps removes some of his virile animal-ness, and such depiction may serve to highlight the female bears, which are (presumably) quite hairy and (explicitly) powerful. That Elisha defies the category of human is of note when one considers his relationship with actual animals as well as the biblical worldview that the wilderness is a place of special divinity and a locale in which Yahweh can be manifest (Feldt 2013, 345). Feldt demonstrates how Elisha occupies an other-than-human or more-than-human space, which confuses the typical categories of deity, human, and animal (324).

> [Elisha] went up from there to Beth-el and when he was going up on the road, young lads came out from the town and they mocked him, and they said to him, "Go on up, baldy, go on up, baldy!" And he turned behind him and he looked at them and he cursed them in the name of Yahweh, and then two she-bears came out from the forest, and they cleaved to pieces from them forty-two children. (2 Kgs 2:23–24)

The Elisha cycle is filled with details of flora and fauna, and in this particular section the author draws on the complex and vivid meaning of the forest to send a coded message in this scene. The bears emerge from the forest, *yʿr*, and the children emerge from the city, *ʿyr*. This is a clever play to encourage contrasting the two actors in the story and their habitats. Bethel, the city, is the subject here of some derision by the Deuteronomistic Historian, who favors Jerusalem over competitor locations for centralizing worship, such as Bethel (Burnett 2010; Bodner 2013). The natural animal habitat of the forest contrasts with the settled human activity in the city. But the city gets a negative portrayal by the narrator, and the wild bears of the woods are the heroes as they, presumably urged on by some divine sanction, eliminate Elisha's tormentors (who may or may not be children; see Burnett 2010 on the meaning of the "young lads").

The forest/*yaʿar* is the habitat of bears and large predatory animals, and this domain is invoked in the biblical text as dangerous and frightening to humans. Bears are thought to lay in wait for their prey (Lam 3:10) and cause havoc for shepherds (1 Sam 17:34). And what of these bears of the Bethel forest? Most notably, they "cleave" (*bqʿ*) the children, just as one "cleaves" wood (e.g., 1 Sam 6:14). This verb choice is an interesting kind of anthropomorphizing of the bears. They perform a task that a human typically performs against the natural world (trees), but here they, denizens of the natural world, perform it against humans. Bears have a certain unpredictability in the biblical imagination (Beard 2020, 6), so this kind of role reversal (animals taking on a human sense) is fitting. Elisha's bears are female, made clear by the gendered verbs. There is a repeated biblical image of a bear "robbed of her whelps," used in various metaphorical ways to make literary and theological points in the text but, given that biblical authors seem to have easy access to this image, it may reflect a known reality of their natural world. In depicting this reality, texts describe she-bears as "bereaved," *šākûl* (*škl*; 2 Sam 17:8, Prov 17:12, Hos 13:8). It is no coincidence, then, that this encounter comes on the heels of Elisha's healing of the bad waters (2 Kgs 2:21), in which he declares they will no longer cause "bereavement" (*məšakālet, škl*). The bears of 2 Kgs 2:24, too, are not bereaved; rather, they are powerful. They are true animals in their woodland home, which is unspoiled (in contrast to Bethel, spoiled perhaps both physically and spiritually); they are, like humans, active, living agents and indeed killers (in contrast to other biblical bears whose whelps are taken and in comparison to humans who also "cleave"); and they are, like Elisha, more-than-human (animal) beings, acutely able to access the divine and operate in its realm.

In another part of the Elisha cycle, in 2 Kgs 6, wooded land is again a source of miraculous deeds.

> And [Elisha] went with them. And they came to the Jordan and they cut down the trees. And, while one guy was felling a trunk, the iron [tool] fell into the water and he cried out, saying, "Oh no, my lord, it was even a borrowed one." And the Man-of-God said, "Where did it fall?" And he showed him the place, and then he cut off a piece of wood, and threw it there, and he caused the iron [tool] to flow [up/over to where he could reach it]. (2 Kgs 6:4–6)

In this account, the "sons of the prophets," that is, the followers or disciples who have most recently been mentioned in the hill country of Ephraim (2 Kgs 5:22), complain to Elisha that the place they are living is too restrained for them. They wish to go to the Jordan, a river valley, and there to cut beams or trunks (*qôrâ*) with which to build houses (2 Kgs 6:2). Based on what will be seen in Josh 17 below, one might assume that the area in which they currently live, the woody hill country of Ephraim, has already been cleared to accommodate their settlement. However, they now feel it is too cramped for them. They travel to the open space of the river valley, where they must seek out trees to cut for beams to build new homes. The trees would seem to fall victim to human settlement both in the hills and in the valley.

The author's choices to convey the semantic field "cut" are unusual, and as was the case in Deut 20, unusual language can alert one to a prevailing attitude toward the subject matter. Elsewhere in biblical texts, trees are cut down with the common verb for cutting, *kārat* (e.g., Num 13:23, Isa 44:14). Simply "cutting" down trees is a semantic option in the Hebrew Bible, and one can be confident an author could choose it. However, the verbs in this passage are not common ones for cutting wood. Instead, they point to humans and animals. The lexeme that is used, *gāzar*, typically means "to be separated from, cut off metaphorically," but here it seems to mean literally "cut." Another verb, *qāṣab*, a rare term perhaps related to shearing sheep, is the choice to describe what Elisha does to the tree or branch. Comparison with the attitude toward trees in Deut 20 is instructive. As was the case there, in the 2 Kings passage here, the language points to the living-being-ness, and even the animal-ness, of the trees. Since there were more common and literal lexemes available to the authors to mean simply "cut," it seems curious that both here and in Josh 17, the verbs chosen are nuanced and bring with them connotations from other domains. The authors convey complex views concerning the cutting of trees when language usually reserved for animals is applied to trees. Yet, ultimately the characters in the story pursue clearing trees as a divinely sanctioned human right. Trees are recognized in their life force, their animality, even, but, as with many biblical animals, are nonetheless under the power of humans.

Joshua 17: Cutting Down Canaanite Trees

Martin Noth (1981, 66–68) thought that the end of the book of Joshua (chs. 13–22) was a later addition to the Deuteronomistic History, and generally this view of "lateness" persists. Even as scholarly debate around the nature (or perhaps even existence) of the Deuteronomistic History has taken many trajectories in recent decades, one still finds that the material in Joshua is often given a rather late date of composition and/or redaction. Even scholars who move far from Noth's approach tend to place Joshua well into the later periods, the fourth and third centuries BCE (Albertz 2007) or even reaching into the Hasmonean period (Knauf 2007). Here I consider a passage from the outline of tribal allotments, one of the main foci of Joshua: "So the hill country will be yours. Because it is a forest you will make it [suitable] and it will be yours to its borders, for you will dispossess the Canaanite though he has the iron chariot" (Josh 17:18).

A clear depiction of forest destruction is found in Josh 17, in which land allotments are being distributed to the clans of Manasseh. The "Josephites," that is, Ephraim and Manasseh, complain to Joshua that they are too many people for the size of their allotted land (Josh 17:14). In response, Joshua assures them that they can have more space and that they should "go up to the forest country and clear an area for yourselves there, in the territory of the Perizzites and the Rephaim, seeing that you are cramped in the hill country of Ephraim" (Josh 17:15). These instructions provide not only plot points but much insight into the biblical perspective on this local habitat. The human need for space (see Demsky 2000 on the tribal struggles over space), and likely agricultural space, is the primary focus. The destruction of plant species (trees, i.e., nonagricultural ones), or the disruption to the animal species that require them, is not a critical factor in Joshua's solution. One sees this perspective also in the larger context of this account, where the descriptions of the territories, which are extensive, rely almost solely on town names and the humans who reside there (e.g., Josh 17:6–7). Receiving territorial allotments, while ostensibly about that natural landscape and its topography, is really quite significantly about human endeavor. For most of this section of Joshua, humans and their settlements are the points of reference rather than the uncultivated wilderness. So, in this sense, the presence of the descriptive terms *hill* country, the *valley*, and the *forest* land, in verses 15–18 is conspicuous.

Again, one must consider the lexical choices of the author and how they reveal attitudes toward the natural world. As noted above, there are common, literal semantic options for cutting down trees. But here one finds twice (Josh 17:15, 18) the special term used for divine creation, *br'*, describing this human terraforming. This lexeme, most famously appearing in Gen 1:1, implies that the destruction of the forest habitat is, for the humans, a new creation—a land suitable for settlement, farm or pasture. Their creation destroys an entire habitat and community of nonhumans, a habitat that does not serve the immediate human societal need. The human need for food and space is prioritized over the need of food and space for any other species, and the choice of verb emphasizes that this priority comes with divine sanction (Nelson 1997, 204–5).

At least a century of scholarship has explored the root *br'* as the term for divine creative activity (Böhl 1913; more recently, see van Wolde 2017). Johannes van der Ploeg (1946) suggests that the use may be dependent on a semantic identification with cutting based on some Semitic cognates. So, to view the forest through the human lens, one might see the flicker of creation as relevant in the phraseology of "clearing forest" or "fashioning a new source of food by paring." But the most salient aspect of this term is its connection to the divine actor. As a vehicle of the action, it suggests that the subject is godlike; in this case the humans who clear the trees of the forest do so as though they were divine beings, wielding power over the earth.

The sense of comparability between the human and the tree in Deuteronomy is missing here. In fact, the comparability is taken to the other extreme: humans are likened to the gods through the way in which they interact with the forest habitat. In the Joshua passage, the forest is completely subjected to the needs of humans and subjugated by the power of humans. The concept of the forest as a natural locale of divine accessibility is turned on its head. Instead of the *yaʿar* as a site of Yahweh's sacredness, it is here a site of human sacredness. The humans, albeit through divine sanction, have become the creators, though instead of creation as one has come to expect it (e.g., Gen 1:11–12), in Josh 17 creation is a destruction of nature.

Discussion

In the biblical world, and indeed much of the ancient world, the relationships between humans and animals are largely focused on the phenomenon of sacrifice and feasting, and one must consider these activities in any examination of the biblical animal (Sherwood 2014). The "religious" aspects of the biblical narrative place a heavy political and social import on meat eating, on ritual slaughter, and on dominion of humans over creation. Even when these aspects are nuanced through compassion, exception, or unexpected accounts, the human role of killing livestock for meat, other products, and religious requirements is undeniable (Stone 2018, 74–82; Gross 2015). By extension, then, the logistical scenarios that support these roles must also be considered to rise to this level of import. Those who tend and grow the herds participate in this sacred work. To ensure the animals will be in place for their role in this cultural schema (Gross 2015, 201), the land on which the herds live is a necessary requirement. Land manipulation and use, including deforestation for the purpose of human settlement, then, participates in the larger religious and culturally significant display of human power, raising animals and killing them for meat.

The interaction between humans and forests, whether as they stand and live or in their destruction and death, directly addresses issues of power and vulnerability, and "killability" (Strømmen 2018, and especially 135–39 on the ambiguity in these themes). A concept Jacques Derrida

(1997, 2008) already developed, and others building on his work have forwarded within biblical sources (Carr 2021), the prioritization of the meat-eating male human (Derrida's carnophallogocentrism) is evident in a passage such as Josh 17. David Carr (2021, 262, 268) argues that, within the primeval history, the Priestly source, in contrast to non-Priestly material, is focused on a binary system between god and godlike humans on one side and animals on the other, in which animals then necessarily must be more attended to, despite the fact that a major focus of that attention is on their killability and role as food. Non-Priestly materials, he contends, perceive the world in a series of binaries (male-female, human-nonhuman, Hebrew-other ethnic groups) in which the function and worth of animals is diminished. The Josh 17 passage, despite its presence in the Deuteronomistic History, shares these features with the Priestly source: godlike humans have dominion over the world of plants and animals, and their manipulation of the environment is for the purpose of creating space for human food production, either crop planting, herd keeping, or a combination of both. Such complexity in the Hebrew Bible should not be a surprise—and even paradoxical views on the question of anthropocentrism and the place of nonhuman animals should be expected (Strømmen 2018, 18).

Actual forests are dynamic systems and have many characteristics in common with human systems. Plants (and fungi) exhibit such similarities to (human) animals as kin recognition, protection from danger, and communication (Asay 2013; Peng et al. 2011; Ninkovic and Baluška 2010). If one considers these biological functions seriously, the moral sphere surrounding humans should logically expand to include other species that are relatively alike (Calarco 2015). So, in the instruction of Deut 20, the alike-ness of trees and (human) animals forces the biblical author to outline legal guidelines on the killability of trees. These guidelines are not absolute, and their mitigation does ultimately prioritize human needs, but they do offer a critical window into the ancient and modern ethical questions. The Elisha cycle hints at fundamental similarities between bears and "more-than-humans" in the person of Elisha, and similarities between trees and animals in language applied to the cutting of wood. These provocative comparanda point to a biblical worldview in which similarities exist between the human living beings and many other kinds of living beings in the natural world (both plants and animals). That similarities are also explored between plants and nonhuman animals is especially compelling. Trees, like the mother bird or the mother goat, are imbued with an animality that the biblical authors, even as they allow for destruction, cannot help but recognize. Aaron Gross (2015, 201) writes, "We also revise myths ... when animals confront us and we always have," but the rhetorical question in Deut 20:19 gives us pause—trees also may confront and transform us.

Works Cited

Albertz, Rainer. 2007. "Die kanonische Anpassung des Josuabuches: Eine Neubewertung seiner sogenannten 'priesterschriftlichen Texte.'" Pages 199–216 in *Les dernières rédactions du Pentateuque, de l'Hexateuque et de l'Ennéateuque*. Edited by Thomas Römer and Konrad Schmid. BETL 203. Leuven: Leuven University Press; Peeters.

Asay, Amanda Karlene. 2013. "Mycorrhizal Facilitation of Kin Recognition in Interior Douglas-Fir (Pseudotsuga Menziesii Var. Glauca)." Master's thesis, University of British Columbia.

Beard, Brady Alan. 2020. "Snatched from the Hand of the Bear: A Comparative Perspective on the Bear in David's Speech in 1 Sam 17:34-37." *JNSL* 46:1–20.

Bodner, Keith. 2013. *Elisha's Profile in the Book of Kings: The Double Agent*. Oxford: Oxford University Press.

Böhl, Franz. 1913. "*bārā*, als Terminus der Weltschöpfung im Alttestamentlichen Sprachgebrauch." Pages 42–60 in *Alttestamentliche studien Rudolf Kittel dargebracht*. Leipzig.

Burnett, Joel S. 2010. "'Going Down' to Bethel: Elijah and Elisha in the Theological Geography of the Deuteronomistic History." *JBL* 129:281–97.

Calarco, Matthew. 2015. *Thinking through Animals: Identity, Difference, Indistinction*. StBr. Stanford, CA: Stanford University Press.

Carr, David M. 2021. "Competing Construals of Human Relations with 'Animal' Others in the Primeval History (Genesis 1–11)." *JBL* 140:251–69.

Demsky, Aaron. 2000. "The Chronicler's Description of the Common Border of Ephraim and Manasseh." Pages 8–13 in *Studies in Historical Geography and Biblical Historiography Presented to Zecharia Kallai*. Edited by Gershon Galil and Moshe Weinfeld. Leiden: Brill.

Derrida, Jacques. 2008. *The Animal That Therefore I Am*. Edited by Marie-Louise Mallet. Translated by David Wills. PCPS. New York: Fordham University Press.

Dozeman, Thomas B., Thomas Römer, and Konrad Schmid, eds. 2011. *Pentateuch, Hexateuch, or Enneateuch? Identifying Literary Works in Genesis through Kings*. Atlanta: Society of Biblical Literature.

Feldt, Laura. 2013. "Wild and Wondrous Men: Elijah and Elisha in the Hebrew Bible." Pages 322–52 in *Credible-Incredible: The Miraculous in the Ancient Mediterranean*. Edited by Janet E. Spittler and Tobias Nicklas. Tübingen: Mohr Siebeck.

Graybill, Rhiannon. 2019. "Elisha's Body and the Queer Touch of Prophecy." *BTB* 49:32–40.

Gross, Aaron S. 2015. *The Question of the Animal and Religion: Theoretical Stakes, Practical Implications*. New York: Columbia University Press.

Halpern, Baruch, and David Vanderhooft. 2009. "The Editions of Kings in the Sixth-Seventh Centuries BCE." Pages 228–96 in *From Gods to God: Essays on the Social and Political Dynamics of Cosmologies in the Iron Age by Baruch Halpern*. Edited by Matthew J. Adams. FAT 63. Tübingen: Mohr Siebeck.

Knauf, Ernst Axel. 2007. "Buchschlüsse in Josua." Pages 217–24 in *Les dernières rédactions du Pentateuque, de l'Hexateuque et de l'Ennéateuque*. Edited by Thomas Römer and Konrad Schmid. BETL 203. Leuven: Leuven University Press and Peeters.

Knoppers, Gary N., and J. Gordon McConville, eds. 2000. *Reconsidering Israel and Judah: Recent Studies on the Deuteronomistic History*. Winona Lake, IN: Eisenbrauns.

McConville, J. Gordon. 1984. *Law and Theology in Deuteronomy*. JSOTSup 33. Sheffield: JSOT Press.

McKenzie, Steven. 1991. *The Trouble with Kings: The Composition of the Book of Kings in the Deuteronomistic History*. VTSup 42. Leiden: Brill.

Miller, J. Maxwell. 1966. "The Elisha Cycle and the Accounts of the Omride Wars." *JBL* 85:441–54.

Nelson, Richard. 1997. *Joshua: A Commentary*. OTL. Louisville: Westminster John Knox.

Ninkovic, Velemir, and František Baluška. 2010. *Plant Communication from an Ecological Perspective*. Berlin: Springer.

Noth, Martin. 1981. *The Deuteronomistic History*. Translated by Jane Doull. JSOTSup 15. Sheffield: JSOT Press.

Peng, Jun Zhang, Joop J. A. van Loon, Si-Jun Zheng, and Marcel Dicke. 2011. "Herbivore-Induced Volatiles of Cabbage (Brassica oleracea) Prime Defence Responses in Neighbouring Intact Plants." *PB* 13:276–84.

Ploeg, Johannes van der. 1946. "Le sens du verbe hébreu *bara*." *LM* 59:143–57.
Römer, Thomas, and Albert de Pury. 1996. "L'historiographie deutéronomiste (HD): Histoire de la recherche et enjeux du débat." Pages 9–120 in *Israël construit son histoire: L'historiographie deutéronomiste à la lumière des recherches récentes*. Edited by Albert de Pury, Thomas Römer, and Jean-Daniel Macchi. MdB 34. Geneva: Labor et Fides.
Shachter, Jay F. 2003. *Deuteronomy*. Vol. 5 of *The Commentary of Abraham ibn Ezra on the Pentateuch*. Hoboken, NJ: KTAV.
Sherman, Phillip. 2020. "The Hebrew Bible and the 'Animal Turn.'" *CurBR* 19:36–63.
Sherwood, Yvonne. 2014. "Cutting Up 'Life': Sacrifice as a Device for Clarifying—and Tormenting—Fundamental Distinctions between Human, Animal and Divine." Pages 247–97 in *The Bible and Posthumanism*. Edited by Jennifer Koosed. SemeiaSt 74. Atlanta: Society of Biblical Literature.
Stone, Ken. 2018. *Reading the Hebrew Bible with Animal Studies*. Stanford, CA: Stanford University Press.
Strømmen, Hannah M. 2018. *Biblical Animality after Jacques Derrida*. SemeiaSt 91. Atlanta: SBL Press.
Uval, Beth. 2000. "Ecology in the Bible." *JBQ* 28:260–63.
Van Seters, John. 1998. "The Pentateuch." Pages 3–52 in *The Hebrew Bible Today: An Introduction to Critical Issues*. Edited by Steven L. McKenzie and Matt Patrick Graham. Louisville: Westminster John Knox.
Wolde, Ellen van. 2017. "Separation and Creation in Genesis 1 and Psalm 104, A Continuation of the Discussion of the Verb ברא." *VT* 67:611–47.
Wright, Jacob L. 2008. "Warfare and Wanton Destruction: A Reexamination of Deuteronomy 20:19–20 in Relation to Ancient Siegecraft." *JBL* 127:423–58.

Recognizing the Gen(i)us of Animals: Jeremiah 8–9 as a Test Case

Jaime L. Waters

As the editors of this volume rightly note, anthropocentric interests dominate much of biblical scholarship today. To counter these tendencies, broaden interpretive strategies, and infuse a fresh and needed perspective into biblical studies, ecological hermeneutics has emerged as an attempt to go beyond anthropocentric views to reveal ecological voices and perspectives within the Bible. While expanding the avenues of inquiry for biblical studies, reading with an ecological hermeneutic can also inform animal studies by offering depth, nuance, and complexity to ideas about animals in biblical literature.

In this study, I examine Jer 8:4–9:11 using ecological hermeneutics. These verses are a poetic literary unit that depicts causes and methods of invasion, physical and emotional traumas of war, and corresponding ecological degradation. This treatment focuses especially on the presence, voices, and behaviors of the animals[1] highlighted in the unit, voices that are often overlooked, quickly glossed, interpreted metaphorically, or simply minimized in scholarly treatments. By reading with an animal-focused ecological hermeneutic, this study will reveal new insights for biblical and animal studies, especially for expanding and correcting ideas about animals in the Bible.

An Ecological Animal Hermeneutic

This study uses a threefold methodology of suspicion-identification-retrieval that has been prominent in ecological hermeneutics (Habel and

---

1. I recognize the important critiques of the word *animal*. Although I use *animal* throughout the study for ease and simplicity, the meaning "nonhuman animals" is intended.

Trudinger 2008). The framework is effective and adaptable for reading with an animal focus. It affirms that interpreters (1) should hold a suspicion that biblical texts are characteristically anthropocentric and have been read as such; (2) should identify the nonhuman elements[2] in a text, empathizing and reading with mindfulness of ecological impacts; and (3) should expose dimensions of texts that reflect or could be useful for discerning the voice of the earth community. In the case of Jer 8–9, commentaries on these chapters often analyze this unit as a prophetic or divine lament that expounds on human failings and their contribution to instability in the land (Holladay 1986; Stulman 2005; Allen 2008). These studies often place anthropocentric or theocentric attitudes in the foreground and miss or minimize animal-centric interests or experiences. This study offers animal perspectives on crises that are articulated in Jer 8–9. It identifies, listens to, and reads with the animals of the texts to offer a less anthropocentric reading. After a close reading of animal actions, retrieval of the animal voice will be somewhat easy, as the animal voice is hardly lost but rather simply requires careful articulation.

One of the prominent features of this literary unit is its description of ecological degradation and its impact on animal populations. To further understanding of this topic, the end of this chapter will explore a modern example of the impact of ecological instability on avian behavior. This chapter uses an animal-focused ecological hermeneutic to broaden ways of reading biblical texts, add detail and depth to ideas about animals in the Bible, and inform modern discussions of ecological crises and their impact on animals. These goals offer another dimension to biblical and animal studies and are complementary to others studies in this volume.

Identifying the Nonhuman Animals

Jeremiah 8:4–9:11 contains a lengthy poetic oracle of judgment that highlights the moral and religious failings of the people of Judah and the consequences of their actions, namely, the Babylonian invasion, destruction of the temple and kingdom, and exile. Perpetual backsliding is to blame, which includes wickedness, deception, failure to heed warnings, and continued refusal to follow divine law. The communal and prophetic

---

2. Nonhuman elements are often referred to as the earth community in studies using ecological hermeneutics. For this study, nonhuman animals are the primary focus. Environmental changes and their impact on animals will also be explored.

suffering and corresponding divine emotional frustration are the focal points of many commentaries on this text, but destruction of the land obviously affected animal life too, as it destabilized the environment, destroyed habitats, and compromised food and water sources. Within this extended judgment oracle, wild and domesticated animals are explicitly referenced for their connection to these destructions. Some animals facilitate and even benefit from destruction, while others clearly suffer hardships because of invasion and environmental instability in the land. The named animals in this poem are horses, snakes, jackals, cattle, and birds.

Horse (*sûs*)

Horses are mentioned twice in this text. Jeremiah 8:14–15 describes people fleeing towns for fortified cities, reflecting the impending destruction in the land. Verse 16 describes the imminent arrival of attackers, which is signaled with the sound of horses. While the Babylonians are not mentioned by name, the animals with them are highlighted:

> The snorting of their horses is heard from Dan;
> at the sound of the neighing of their stallions
> the whole land quakes.
> They come and devour the land and all its fullness,
> the city and those who live in it.[3]

The horses are loud and expressive, with their voices snorting and neighing on their approach. The sound of the horses is a signal of attack, and the horses' power causes people to flee and the land to quake. Horses were used in warfare with riders and to draw chariots, and this passage recalls the sound of the horses as a sign of war. The arrival of horses affects the land, as they devour all that fills it, feeding on the vegetation, which sets into motion habitat and food loss for other animals in the land.

The other reference to horses is metaphorical and deals more with human behavior than animal. When describing how humans consistently behave, the text says, "All [humans] turn to their course, like a horse plunging into war" (Jer 8:6b). This reference shows some of the similarities of human and horse behavior, particularly in their focus and power to

---

3. All translations are mine, unless otherwise noted. Verse numbers follow the MT. Variations in English numbers are noted in brackets.

advance forward, particularly during battle. In the case of the horse, the behavior is an assessment of their natural strength and abilities, but the metaphor is used to highlight the stubbornness of humans who have not listened but instead proceed forward on their corrupt path.

Snakes (*nəḥāšîm*)

The other animals highlighted as part of the invasion and destruction are snakes. Also called poisonous vipers (*ṣipʿōnîm*), snakes are depicted under divine control, as Yahweh sends them to attack the people of Judah, which has echoes of Yahweh sending snakes to attack during the wilderness period (Num 21:6–7). Unlike humans, snakes follow divine rule and order: "See, I am sending snakes among you, poisonous vipers that cannot be charmed, and they will bite you, says Yahweh" (Jer 8:17).

Walter Brueggemann (1998), Jack Lundbom (2008), and Leslie Allen (2008) interpret the snake reference as a metaphor for the Babylonian army. Yet, there is reason to consider these as real animal attacks, since several other real animals are described in the text. Real snakes would certainly elicit fear among the people of Judah, especially as they are unable to be controlled by humans. By coming out and biting, the snakes live out their natural tendances and facilitate divine justice.

As for animal agency, the horses and snakes participate in the attacking, although they are not depicted as the only agents. The horses are called "their horses," suggesting that humans are riding or at least have some amount of control, so there are human agents involved. The horses, however, devour the land, which is a natural horse behavior that could have damaging ecological effects. Similarly, there is a divine element integrated into the release of the snakes, and yet the snakes initiate biting, showing their participatory role in the attacks. As for the voices of the horses and snakes, they can be heard in the texts. The horses speak with their snorts and neighing, conveying their intensity and presence in the land. The snakes communicate through their movements in the land, biting, and making their presence known and felt.

Jackals (*tannîm*)

While the horses and snakes are animals in a position of power during the attack, jackals reap positive outcomes of war, while livestock and birds reveal the negative impacts on animal populations. Destruction and environmental degradation are generally deleterious to animals because of loss of habitat, food sources, and protection from humans, especially for domesticated animals. According to Jeremiah, cities in Judah had become desolate wastelands as a result of war. Human and nonhuman animals are victims, with some dying in battle, others fleeing, and still others being taken as treasures of war or as exiles. Jackals, however, benefit from these circumstances, as destruction and loss of life allow them to roam freely, scavenge food, and take advantage of the instability.

Oded Borowski (1998) describes the creatures as doglike scavengers that are omnivorous, nocturnal pack hunters. In the midst of environmental and societal instability, jackals thrive. Jeremiah affirms Yahweh, declaring, "I will give [*ntn*] Jerusalem as a heap, a home [*māʿōn*] of jackals; and the cities of Judah, I will give [*ntn*] as a desolation without inhabitant" (Jer 9:10[9]). Although *ntn* is typically translated as "I will make" in this verse, its primary meaning is "to give or present." If "give" is rendered, the sense could be that Yahweh gives the destroyed lands over to the jackals to inhabit and enjoy, consuming the decaying life and potentially offering additional destruction. The agency and voice of the jackals is not fully articulated in the text, but it can be inferred that if the cities become a dwelling (*māʿōn*) or a lair for jackals, they are able to capitalize on the freedom to control the area.

Elsewhere in Jeremiah, jackals are indicators of destruction. As the depiction of destruction and exile continues into Jer 10, the desolate cities of Judah are again "a home of jackals" (Jer 10:22). Likewise, in the oracles against Kedar, Hazor, and Babylon, cities are described as wastelands without inhabitants that are overrun with jackals (Jer 49:33, 51:37). Similarly, Isa 34:11–15 describes judgment to the nations, and their cities are overrun with various wild animals including birds, hedgehogs, and jackals.

Cattle (*miqneh*)

Cattle experienced the effects of war, especially by habitat degradation and loss of vegetation. According to Jer 9:10[9], following the attacks, "the voice of cattle is not heard ... the animals [*bəhemâ*] have fled and gone." The lack of sound speaks volumes, as healthy countrysides should be alive with the voices of sheep, goats, and cattle. There are a few possibilities for why the cattle are no longer heard. Silence could signify the death of cattle and animals generally as casualties for war. Silence could also signify death due to lack of vegetation, which was compromised due to war. These realities highlight the interconnection between human and animal life, one of the ecojustice principles affirmed by the Earth Bible Project. Squabbles between the Babylonians and Judeans directly affect the lives of animals.

Another possibility for the silence in the land is that the animals have fled, leaving Judah in search of more sustainable lands. The flight could be triggered by invasion or by the loss of human life. Cattle fleeing could shed light on their close association with humans, as they are domesticated animals. By fleeing, the cattle demonstrate natural acts of agency and self-preservation, fleeing conflict in search of greener pastures. Still another reason cattle may be missing in the land could be because they were captured as spoils of war. Borowski (1998) notes that military campaigns from Mesopotamia and Egypt incorporated animal confiscation and deportation, especially of small and large cattle.

Birds

In addition to the absence of cattle, birds are missing during the conflict, and the text is clear on why they flee the destruction. According to Jeremiah, birds are astute and intuitive in their response to destruction: "Even the stork [*ḥăsîdâ*] in the heavens knows her seasons; and the turtledove [*tōr*], swift [*sîs*], and crane [*'āgûr*] observes the time of their coming; but my people do not know the ordinance of Yahweh"[4] (Jer 8:7).

The birds know the season, and they observe the time, suggesting that they understand the destruction that is upon the land. They react and respond in ways that humans are unable or unwilling to fully grasp. This point is stressed in the verses that follow, which juxtapose the knowledge of birds with the lack of knowledge of humans.[5] Birds understand Yahweh, while the people think they are wise yet show a lack of wisdom by rejecting the divine word.

---

4. In the MT, horse (*sûs*) is written instead of swift (*sîs*), which is likely a scribal error influenced by the similar spelling and close proximity to horse in 8:6. Swift (*sîs*) is read here since this is a list of birds. Ancient witnesses and translators understood this bird to be a swallow or crane (LXX: *chelidōn*; Vulg: *hirundo*). Following Arabic *sūs* (swift), "swift" is likely and read here. The precise bird intended by *'āgûr* is uncertain. "Crane" is a frequent translation (NRSV, NJPS, ESV, OJB). Other translations include "thrush" (NIV, NAB) and "swallow" (NKJV, KJV).

5. For readers interested in the difference approach as described in Calarco 2015, Jer 8:7–9 and similar passages in the biblical corpus might be worth further exploration.

Hilary Marlow (2009) posits that the statement about the birds knowing the times refers to bird migration seasons, which is compelling since these birds are migratory. Moreover, Marlow includes a parallel in Isa 1:2–3, in which the ox and donkey have knowledge that humans lack. Similar to Isaiah, in Jeremiah the animals "act according to their God-given instincts … [whereas humans] deliberately shun the divinely instituted moral order" (Marlow 2009, 209). The birds' flying and ultimately leaving is how they communicate their understanding of what is happening. Commentaries often gloss over the actions of the birds, but Lundbom (2008, 510) offers an insightful comment on their behavior: "The stork—also the other birds—are singled out because they are migratory and because their migrations bear witness to an ordered creation under Yahweh's control."

One of the ongoing assumptions that persists in animal studies is a view of the Bible as promoting and validating human superiority over animals. Lynn White (1967) is one of the oft-quoted thinkers in this regard. Emphasis is placed on the creation accounts of Genesis and the language of dominion as the foundation for anthropocentricism that is reiterated in biblical and religious traditions. Mary Midgley (1983) and Erica Fudge (2006) have examined many of the rationalist thinkers and their (over) emphasis on language and reason that also helped to rationalize and promote models of human domination over animals. Although texts and traditions have unfortunately been used with deleterious outcomes, the biblical tradition is rich and diverse. Jeremiah 8–9 reveals that the overly simplistic idea that animals are simply subordinate creatures in the Bible should be nuanced and expanded to account for the diversity in the tradition. Jeremiah 8–9 reflects on animals as being in close connection with their creator, possessing knowledge that is in tune with the divine order, and sometimes even having more understanding than humans. This treatment offers an example of how reading ecologically can move both biblical and animal studies forward in meaningful ways.

A Modern Example: Learning from Bird Migration

The migration of birds described in Jeremiah has parallels in modern times. According to the US Fish and Wildlife Service, there are many natural and human sources that threaten the lives and cycles of migratory birds. There are over one thousand species of birds protected under the Migratory Bird Treaty Act that are experiencing population declines due to increased threats to their habitats. Ninety-two bird species are listed as either endangered (meaning in danger of extinction throughout all or a significant portion of the species) or threatened (meaning they are likely to become endangered in the foreseeable future) under the US Endangered Species Act of 1973. Two hundred seventy-four species are on the Birds of Conservation Concern list. These include both migratory and nonmigratory birds, nongame birds, and game birds with designated hunting seasons.

Millions of acres of bird habitat are lost or degraded each year due to development, agriculture, and forestry practices. Landscape changes resulting from climate change can also exacerbate bird mortality. It is important to have habitat restoration and protection in order to mitigate loss of lives. A concerted effort from governments, conservation organizations, industry, and the general public is needed in order to slow habitat loss.

The 2022 "State of the Birds Report" produced by the North American Bird Conservation Initiative estimates that three billion birds have been lost in the United States and Canada since 1970; nearly 30 percent have disappeared in the last fifty years. Despite these numbers, the agency also has evidence of the positive impacts of investing in bird conservation projects. For instance, in 1970 only a few hundred bald eagle pairs existed in the lower forty-eight states. With federal and state legislation, there was an increase in the numbers of bald eagles. In 2007, the bald eagle was delisted as an endangered species, and today there are over thirty thousand eagle pairs in the United States.

Accelerated development and demands for food, space, and energy sources put a strain on the environment, causing habitat loss, degradation, change, or fragmentations, reducing the availability of resources to meet bird needs. A statement issued by the Intergovernmental Science-Policy Platform on Biodiversity and Ecosystem Services (IPBES) on World Migratory Bird Day 2018 asserted:

> Many of the most fragile and vulnerable ecosystems are essential elements of the flyways for migratory species. Wetlands, for instance, which are key habitats and sources of food, have seen global losses of 87% since the start of the modern era—with 54% lost since 1900.... [Likewise,] conversion of forests and rangelands for food production, timber, and urban development has also led to habitat loss and fragmentation.... The IPBES is now collaborating with the Convention on Migratory Species, the Agreement on the Conservation of African-Eurasian Migratory Waterbirds and Environment for the Americas to address cross-boundary challenges and address migratory bird conservation as one unified global voice.

Each of these groups demonstrates the impact of land degradation on migratory birds and sees the causes and solutions as being interconnected, particularly for birds that fly across human-made land boundaries. Considering Jeremiah alongside these modern phenomena can give insight into how Jeremiah and later communities interpreted land degradation. Both recognize humans as the primary agents for destruction. In antiquity and today, it is human behavior that is the impetus for many environmental problems, and animals must adapt, migrate, suffer, or die due to habitat loss. For animal-justice advocates, these realities and the ancient evidence preserved in Jeremiah call on changes in behavior for the sake of the entire earth community.

Consequences of Habitat Degradation in Jeremiah and Today

Jeremiah 8–9 paints a vivid picture of invasion, destruction, and the consequences for earth and all its inhabitants. The ecological degradation is articulated as the lands are laid waste, and the text affirms the ecojustice principle of interconnectedness: "Earth is a community of interconnected living things that are mutually dependent on each other for life and survival" (Habel and Trudinger 2008, 2). In Jer 8–9, land degradation and animal displacement are couched as the results of human misdeeds, showing the interconnectedness of human behavior on earth. The people have been deceptive to one another, speaking dishonestly, committing iniquities, and oppressing their neighbors (Jer 9:1–7[2–8]). More generally, the people of Judah, unlike the animals, have failed to follow divine commands. The land is filled with human misconduct and a breakdown of social cohesiveness that is interpreted as the impetus for destruction of the land. Allen (2008, 116) notes, "People and land were inextricably linked, and Yahweh was to preside over a collapse that would drag down people and land in a common fate."

After the description of destruction of land and its impact on animals, Jeremiah wonders why the land is ruined, laid to waste, and uninhabited (Jer 9:11[12]), showing even the prophetic inability to understand and comprehend the destruction. The prophet seeks clarity and culpability for the conditions, and Yahweh blames humans because of their failure to follow divine law. Human disobedience and failure to keep covenantal obligations are interpreted as causes for societal problems and impetuses for invasion and war.

While the damage primarily affects the land and animals, people also feel consequences. Cities are uninhabited, which means people have died, relocated to more sustainable lands, or been forced into exile. Like the cattle and birds, some humans abandon their homes and seek lands with more resources for their survival. This lack of resources is emphasized as humans are forced to consume wormwood and poisonous water: "I am feeding this people with wormwood [laʿănâ], and giving them poisonous water [mê rōʾš] to drink" (Jer 9:14b[15b]).

Several species of wormwood grow wild in Israel in arid regions. The most common is desert wormwood, a bitter herb often referenced as a punishment for bad behavior. Wormwood is also used in curses, so it is remembered in the biblical tradition for its unpleasant, bitter taste. For instance, false prophets are fed wormwood to eat in Jer 23:15. In Deut 29:18, both wormwood and poisonous water are used to root out poisonous people in Israel. Fittingly, in Jer 9, humans are blamed for land degradation, and their real or imagined punishment is to consume something bitter that comes from earth. Earth, who suffers, also participates in adjudicating and delivering punishment on behalf of the land and animals that are the victims of human misbehaviors. Just as the dire circumstance demonstrate the impact of humans on the livelihood of earth and its inhabitants, so too earth is connected to the consequence and correction of the people. Some animals, such as the horses and snakes, participate in the destruction. Later in Jeremiah, other animals such as dogs, birds, and wild animals are appointed to devour and destroy the people when they cause additional ecological instability through drought (see Jer 14:1–6, 15:3).

Another possible reading of the reference to wormwood and poisonous water is that the instability in the ecosystem creates circumstances in which bitter natural substances such as wormwood and poisonous plants must be consumed in desperate times. While the primary meaning of the text appears as punishment for failing to keep covenantal obligations, these elements may be referenced to further substantiate the unlivable conditions in the land.

Notably, there is evidence of wormwood being used for therapeutic reasons. Wormwood has similar properties to absinthe and can be used for medicinal purposes such as pain management and upset stomach. If wormwood has potential positive qualities, this could suggest it was both a punishment and a relief. Even though the biblical references are decidedly negative, perhaps wormwood has the ability to be read both negatively and positively.

When considering the topic of land degradation, one can draw insights from Jer 9:9–10, which envisions the land of Judah in ruins. Animal and human habits are laid bare. Both animals and humans have died, fled, or been captured. Cities and countrysides are affected, and only select animals, such as horses, snakes, and jackals, facilitate and benefit from destruction in the land. Other animals, especially those domesticated animals that lived in close proximity to humans, suffer some of the worst effects of war. As for the birds of the air, their behavior illustrates the effects through their migration to more tenable areas where there is food, water, and sustainable land. Bird migration due to land degradation has stark modern parallels of birds migrating to different lands and dying off because of loss of natural resources. In the United States, the statistics on changes in bird migration patterns are linked with habitat loss. Scientists assert that the full impact of habitat loss on birds is difficult to isolate, and loss of habitat affects animals in differing ways, in particular death and change in migration.

It is significant that Jeremiah pictures animals as having greater intelligence than humans. Moreover, animals have a relationship with God. The horses and snakes listen to God, while the humans have failed to listen. The birds have changed course and found locations because they recognize God's vision and read the times. Scholars who assume an exclusively negative portrayal of animals in the Bible should carefully consider Jer 8–9, which offers an important contribution and corrective to animal and biblical scholarship. Animal intelligence and an animal-divine relationship is present in different ways and with multiple species. In Jer 8–9, the animal-divine relationship is productive, as animals listen to and respond to their creator. On the other hand, the human-divine relationship has been damaged by human actions and failures to understand and listen.

If one is reading the Bible to critically engage the biblical text and seek insights into modern ecological problems, Jeremiah provides an ancient reflection on the calamities of land degradation, both physically and metaphorically. Physically, the earth can no longer serve as a home for its inhabitants. Metaphorically, the humans are punished and potentially healed by the earth's remaining resources. Animals play various roles as administrators of divine justice, beneficiaries of chaos, and unfortunately as innocent victims. Jeremiah provides an ancient glimpse at realities that people still face today. As in Jer 9, animals are speaking if one listens to their behaviors. Migration and silence communicate a message of animals that adapt to or succumb to the actions of humans. They are resilient in their adaption and show agency and control over their lives by adjusting to the conditions. Just as Jeremiah questions why the land is laid waste, we too can ask the same question. Hopefully, a recognition of the ongoing problems that have affected the earth community will propel people, agencies, and governments to make substantive changes to correct the damage that has been and continues to be done on the earth. The wise birds in Jer 8–9 can inspire us to recognize the times and change our behaviors for the survival of the earth community.

Works Cited

Allen, Leslie C. 2008. *Jeremiah: A Commentary*. OTL. Louisville: Westminster John Knox.
Borowski, Oded. 1998. *Every Living Thing: Daily Use of Animals in Ancient Israel*. Walnut Creek, CA: Altamira.
Brueggemann, Walter. 1998. *A Commentary on Jeremiah: Exile and Homecoming*. Grand Rapids: Eerdmans.
Calarco, Matthew. 2015. *Thinking through Animals: Identity, Difference, Indistinction*. StBr. Stanford, CA: Stanford University Press.
Fudge, Erica. 2006. *Brutal Reasoning: Animals, Rationality, and Humanity in Early Modern England*. Ithaca, NY: Cornell University Press.
Habel, Norman C., and Peter L. Trudinger, eds. 2008. *Exploring Ecological Hermeneutics*. SymS 46. Atlanta: Society of Biblical Literature.
Holladay, William Lee. 1986. *A Commentary on the Book of the Prophet Jeremiah, Chapters 1–26*. Hermeneia. Philadelphia: Fortress.
Larigauderie, Anne. 2018. "Biodiversity Decline and Land Degradation Puts Migratory Birds at Risk." Intergovernmental Science-Policy Platform on Biodiversity and Ecosystem Services (IPBES) on World Migratory Bird Day 2018.
Lundbom, Jack R. 2008. *Jeremiah 1–20: A New Translation with Introduction and Commentary*. AB. New Haven: Yale University Press.
Marlow, Hilary. 2009. *Biblical Prophets and Contemporary Environmental Ethics: Rereading Amos, Hosea, and First Isaiah*. Oxford: Oxford University Press.
Midgley, Mary. 1983. *Animals and Why They Matter*. Athens: University of Georgia Press.
Stulman, Louis. 2005. *Jeremiah*. AOTC. Nashville: Abingdon.
White, Lynn, Jr. 1967. "The Historical Roots of Our Ecologic Crisis." *Science* 155:1203–7.

Like Dogs That Return to Their Own Vomit: Ruminations on the (Re)production of Animalizing Hate in the Second Letter of Peter

Dong Hyeon Jeong

We have to address the elephant in the room: the colonial legacy of animalization of the other. From a (Continental) philosophical perspective, animal studies contributes in holistically caring for nonhumans by promulgating, among many other things, the importance of ontological fluidity: "the rejection of humanism's notion of a fixed human nature … in which human beings find themselves to be like animals" (see the introduction to this book). Inasmuch as ontological fluidity is liberating and revolutionary, it must respond to the obvious critical inquiry posed by many minoritized communities: animalization of the other. Even today, minoritized communities (communities minoritized along vectors of race and ethnicity, gender and sexuality, disability, indigeneity, and others) have been voicing out for full humanity in the face of various animalizing/oppressive systems. We/They have done so because racism, sexism, and other -isms have denied us/them of our/their full humanity. That is why arguing for ontological fluidity with nonhuman animals needs to address this conundrum, lest animal studies be misconstrued as oblivious to the struggles of many minoritized persons and communities.

My response to this conundrum is to put animal studies in conversation with Sara Ahmed (affect theory) and Frantz Fanon (postcolonialism). I do not engage a particular animal studies scholar in this essay; rather, I ruminate on animal studies' ontological fluidity with Ahmed's affect theory on hate and Fanon's perspective on colonial neurosis because

---

A shorter and more reflective version of this chapter is published in *AJSP* (Jeong 2020).

their works express the realities and intersections of animalization, racism, and affect. Ahmed and Fanon provide a pause to the category of identification/identity in animal studies because they demand an acknowledgment and serious engagement with the history of colonization through animalization. This pause also provides (an) intersectional space(s) beyond the impasse. Instead of antagonism and erasure of the complexity at hand, this pause provides spaces to identify with nonhumans because it further dismantles (human or a particular group of people's claims for) exceptionalism/superiority by being in solidarity with those who are marginalized, especially nonhumans. This solidarity, this embrace, manifests by acknowledging our common struggle (humans and nonhumans) against oppressive systems. Animal studies' ontological fluidity, seen from this pause, becomes a tool for liberation not just for nonhumans but also for minoritized and oppressed humans as well.

My version of acknowledging our common struggle and dismantling human exceptionalism as a biblical scholar is to find manifestations of ontological fluidity between, within, and without the pages of the Bible. Interestingly, I find this manifestation in the form of animalizing rhetoric in 2 Peter. The animalizing rhetoric found in 2 Peter, though, is discombobulating because it is expressed through crab mentality. When a crab in a bucket of crabs tries to climb out, it is said that the other crabs pull it back down into the pail. The author of 2 Peter uses animalizing rhetoric against his fellow followers of Christ, to his fellow colonized/enslaved persons and communities. Such crab mentality as expressed through animalization of the other is witnessed all throughout (colonial) history and even in the Bible. Second Peter is not an exception to this history. As a matter of fact, the author of 2 Peter explicitly and strategically uses animalizing/objectifying rhetoric in order to defeat and lambast his opponents. The false teachers (opponents of 2 Peter) or "these people" (*houtoi*) are described as "irrational animals, mere creatures of instinct, born to be caught and killed" (2:12).[1]

Robert Seesengood (2017, 43) expresses this crab mentality as "intra-mural conflict" or an infight between colonized persons. Seesengood argues that 2 Peter's community has to negotiate their identity and boundaries under the imperial gaze, which commodifies and/or dehu-

---

1. Unless otherwise stated, all biblical translations follow the NRSV.

manizes the colonized, such as themselves. Moreover, the presence of various dissenting voices in 2 Peter's community further exacerbates the difficult condition. Being pressured from both sides (imperial animalization and oppositions within his community), the author of 2 Peter seems to mimic the Roman Empire's "rhetoric of dehumanization" in order to legitimize his definition of the community's identity and boundaries (43). I agree with Seesengood in reading 2 Peter as a disheartening narrative of desperation in which the colonized/enslaved are forced to tear each other apart, even using animalizing rhetoric, in order to survive. Inspired by Seesengood, this chapter builds on Seesengood's argument on the rhetoric of dehumanization by providing an alternative expression to it: rhetoric of animalization.

Moreover, as mentioned above, I engage this rhetoric of animalization with Ahmed's take on the emotion of hate and Fanon's take on colonial neurosis. According to Ahmed (2015, 45), hate does not originate in certain bodies; rather, hate circulates among bodies. The more hate circulates, the more it becomes affective or sticks to bodies. This circulation, repetition, or overdetermination of hate then produces a rhetoric of differentiation, us versus them (48). Duane F. Watson (2014, 47–62) argues that 2 Peter uses several rhetorical devices—judicial (accuse and defend), deliberative (persuade and dissuade), and epideictic (praise and blame)—to convey its frustrations and anger. Second Peter's *animalizing* rhetoric is a heuristic combination of judicial, deliberative, and epideictic. As I will explain further below, the author of 2 Peter uses the rhetoric of animalization against the false teachers, vitriol that has been circulating or constantly used by the Roman Empire against the colonized, because he knows that this colonial strategy affectively circulates, or it is effective in dehumanizing the other. In other words, it sticks. Yet, working with Fanon's self-reflexive discourse on colonial neurosis, the author's use of this animalizing hateful rhetoric seems to reflect his own colonial neurosis or his own struggle to overcome his animalized self. For the author to animalize his opponents is his (un)conscious return to his own colonial vomit, or his unwanted and yet uncontrollable utilization of the colonizers' strategy of animalizing the other. His colonized mind is affectively ingrained to animalize in order to survive. Although the author does not narrate the aftermath of writing this hateful animalizing letter or testimony, following Ahmed (2015, 60), this chapter concludes with a rumination on the "effects of such encounters of hate on the bodies of others who become transformed into objects of hate."

Mappings of Affect[2]

But what is affect theory? Among many definitions conjectured, I find Donovan O. Schaefer's (2019, 1) simple, but never simplistic, definition helpful:

> Affect theory is an approach to history, politics, culture, and all other aspects of embodied life that emphasizes the role of nonlinguistic and non- or para-cognitive forces. As a method, affect theory asks *what bodies do*—what they want, where they go, what they think, how they decide—and especially how bodies are impelled by forces other than language and reason. It is, therefore, also a theory of power. For affect theory, feelings, emotions, affects, moods, and sensations are not cosmetic but rather the substance of subjectivity.

Schaefer's definition does not represent the universal and consolidated definition of affect theory. As Gregory J. Seigworth and Melissa Gregg (2010, 3–4) admonish, "There is no single, generalizable theory of affect: not yet, and (thankfully) there never will be. If anything, it is more tempting to imagine that there can only ever be infinitely multiple iterations of affect and theories of affect: theories as diverse and singularly delineated as their own highly particular encounters with bodies, affects, worlds." Perhaps the lack of consolidation is due to its relative newness to the academic field. According to Jennifer L. Koosed and Stephen D. Moore (2014, 382; see also Clough 2007; Thompson and Hoggett 2012), the so-called affective turn had its roots from the mid-1990s, but it would not begin to consolidate for another decade or so. Within the field of biblical interpretation, Erin Runions's (2008, 41–69) article is considered to be the first engagement with affect theory. Nevertheless, one can see the slow but surely increasing interest in affect theory, due to the need to engage texts, cultures, and experiences beyond the stranglehold of prior theories and methodologies that solely focus on and assume the primacy of language and reason (Koosed and Moore 2014, 382).

Moreover, the rise of affect theory is indebted to queer and feminist (biblical) theorists/interpreters who have long been deconstructing the sexist and colonial binarization between reason and emotion in which

---

2. Recently, a number of biblical interpreters have used affect theory: Runions 2011; Kotrosits 2011, 2012; Kotrosits and Taussig 2013; Koosed and Moore 2014; Moore 2017; Spencer 2017; Brintnall, Marchal, and Moore 2018; and Black and Koosed 2019.

women and the othered are historically stereotyped to be lesser because of being "too emotional." Following the admonition of Maia Kotrosits (2016), cisgender males like me should and must acknowledge this, lest we "Columbus" it again. Racism and colonization are dependent in many ways on "emotional" appeal/justification, in which one considers oneself better than the other. To combat these animosities, one has to understand the affective channels such utterances emerge from. As Karen Bray and Stephen D. Moore (2020, 5–6) propound, affect theory "depathologizes and deindividualizes 'negative feelings'… [not] as signs of sickness in the individual … but [an invitation] for social diagnosis." Ahmed's approach to affect/emotion primarily responds to this invitation for social diagnosis. My reading of 2 Peter is also a social diagnosis of the Petrine community. I chose animal studies, affect theory, and postcolonialism because the constellation of these theories assists in navigating and illuminating 2 Peter's "elisions, ruptures, gaps, and points of contradiction (ideological, aesthetic, structural, and formal)" (Brinkema 2014, 37). This does not neglect close reading at all; as a matter of fact, it reads closer the hauntings that are missed when biblical interpretation is atomized as a "scientific" (repeatable, hard evidence–based, "if I do not see, it does not count") endeavor.

(Second) Peter's Affective Economy of Animalizing Hatred and Disgust

Ahmed's affect theory helps in a number of ways to understand 2 Peter's animalizing hate. First, the author of 2 Peter hates because he loves, as problematic as this sounds. Ahmed (2015, 42) argues that "hate is generated as a defense against injury." One hates because one loves oneself, one's group, one's ideology, and even one's faith. The author of 2 Peter prefaces the letter by demonstrating the author's love for their faith. Second Peter 1:1 describes their faith and those who have received the same faith as theirs. The author describes their faith as "precious" (*isotimon*) and honorable/dignified. The author further describes their community as recipients of the divine power that provides everything they need for life and godliness (1:3). Second Peter 1:3–4 reiterates again the author's love for their "precious" (*timia*) community by declaring their community's capacity to fend off the corruption of this world by becoming participants of the divine. Enamored with those who have received the same faith as precious as theirs, the author even calls their listeners "beloved" (*agapētoi*). This term of endearment is repeated three more times, in 3:8, 14, and 17.

Moreover, according to Ahmed (2015, 51), there is an ambivalent relationship between love and hate. Inasmuch as the author hates them, the author of 2 Peter has vigorously recomposed and conserved the nature(s)/identities and stories of his opponents/the false teachers. Second Peter 2:20-21 demonstrates more than a simple acquaintance with the false teachers. The author knows their past intimately, recalling how the opponents were once part of the community who "escaped the defilements of the world through the knowledge of our Lord and Savior Jesus Christ" (2:20a). The author even confesses that there was a time when the false teachers were co-recipients of the "holy commandment" (2:21). However, their holiness fell into the trap of the corruption of the world, much to the dismay of the author of 2 Peter (2:20b). The author once loved them. All of this raises the question: If the author hates the false teachers so much, then why does the author spend the majority of the letter describing them? Ahmed (2015, 51, 55) argues, "For the destructive relation to the object to be maintained the object itself must be conserved in some form.... Hatred is a negative attachment to an other that one wishes to expel." For the author of 2 Peter's vitriol to stand, the author has to create and conserve the object of hate. The irony of it all is that the existence of the opponents has to be solidified so that the vitriol stands. In other words, hatred seeks to destroy the other, but it needs the other to survive in order to continue its hatred.

Second, Ahmed (2015, 43) argues that hate reconfigures the ordinary, but, this "ordinary is fantastic." Hate realizes the fantasy in which one's self or one's community is a victim of pain caused by the other (racially minoritized communities). This fantasy creates "pure bodies," in which the victims are constantly violated by the other, however that looks. Thus, it justifies hatred. The author of 2 Peter hates because the author is trying to protect—probably on a deathbed or just playing the role of the about-to-be-martyred Peter (1:12-15)—the precious faith that the author and their community has received (1:1). Apparently, 2 Peter as a farewell speech or testament perceives the author's community to be constantly attacked by corruption based on licentiousness (1:4). For this reason, they have to make every effort to support their faith through goodness, knowledge, self-control, endurance, godliness, mutual affection, and love (1:5-7). They have to be more than eager to confirm their call and election, lest they stumble (1:10). The author has to constantly remind them (1:12-13) of their victimization, their struggle in the midst of their corrupt opponents and the Roman Empire, and that apparently they are the only ones who are eyewitnesses to Jesus, the recipients of prophecy from the Holy Spirit (1:16–19).

Andrew M. Mbuvi (2015, 7) frames this hyperbolic spewing of unfounded negative description of the other in the form of stereotyping: "Such rhetoric not only seeks to paint the perceived enemy in as much a negative light as possible, it does not necessarily claim to be historically accurate in its portrayal of the perceived enemy." The more hate spewed, the less it is about the other and the more it is about oneself. The author's vitriol against the false teachers could have ended in the early part of chapter 2. Yet, following Mbuvi's point, the author's sustained and compounding vitriol against the false teachers incites suspicion, inviting the listeners/readers of their letter to question the veracity of this hate-filled animalizing rhetoric. Similarly, John N. D. Kelly (1969, 223) echoes this wariness in his discussion of the book of Jude. He notes the author's "one-sided emphasis and general mediocrity … and [is] put off by Jude's almost unrelievedly denunciatory tone" not against the Roman Empire per se but against fellow colonized followers of Jesus.

In a certain sense, delineating the identity and the so-called teachings of the author's opponents is hard to do because one hears only one side of the conversation of this seemingly intense struggle between these two camps. What one hears/reads are biased glimpses of the opponents' teachings from those who intensely disagree with them. First, the opponents promise "freedom" (2:19) from corruption and slavery, from whomever they or it may be. Peter H. Davids (2014, 211) conjectures that this freedom might be related to Pauline theology (1 Cor 6:12), in which this freedom is freedom from law. Another explanation for this freedom could be its connection with Epicureanism, the philosophy that negates divine providence, afterlife, and correspondingly divine judgment for earthly decisions. Instead, it promotes moderate enjoyment of life within the bounds of reason (Davids 2014, 211; Neyrey 1993, 122–28). Such philosophy might fit with 2 Peter's polemic against the opponents for scoffing at the belief of the second coming of the Lord and Savior (3:3–5).

Second, Charles H. Talbert (1966) argues that the accusations against the false prophets for promulgating licentiousness (2 Pet 2:2, 18), "cleverly devised myths" (1:16), "knowledge" (1:2–3, 5, 8, 12, 15, 19; 2:20–21; 3:1–2, 18), freedom from corruption (2:19), realized eschatology, and rejection of future parousia are identity markers for identifying them as gnostics. However, such markers fall short because they are circumstantial at best (anyone can have myths and knowledge, whatever they may be).

Moreover, Richard Bauckham insists that 2 Peter's opponents are not the gnostics because there is no textual evidence that portrays the opponents as relying on cosmological dualism in their worldview. Their "freedom and licentiousness (perhaps, antinomianism)" and skepticism of the parousia are not based on some form of realized eschatology (Bauckham 1983, 156–57; see also Fornberg 1977, passim; Neyrey 1980, 504–19). I agree with Michel Desjardins (1987, 96–97) that the portrayal of the opponents is exaggerated. George Aichele (2017, 54) perceives that they might have just relapsed into their "pagan" ways, concluding that "the hypothesis of gnosticism is unnecessary." Aichele even pushes the boundaries and provides a thought experiment in which the opponents could be considered the (proto-)orthodox followers of Jesus (77). In any case, Aichele suggests that 2 Peter is highly likely a premade template (perhaps preserved in its orality) for anyone who needs to write a scathing and vituperative letter against their opponents (and even their community) (19). In other words, the letter was meant to incite affective persuasions to protect/support the so-called beloved (whoever they may be, as dictated by the author) by turning the dissenting members of the community (as dictated again by the author) into the hated ones.

Third, as mentioned above, Ahmed argues that hate circulates within and between bodies. Hate does not originate within an individual or a group. Hate "is economic; it circulates between signifiers in relationships of difference and displacement" (Ahmed 2015, 44). That is, "emotions work as a form of capital ... but [hate] is produced as an effect of its circulation" (45). Hate compounds in its circulation. Hate accumulates over time. At one point, the false teachers were part of the author of 2 Peter's beloved community who knew the way of righteousness (2:21). But the accumulation of their dissension against the author of 2 Peter, their constant animalization of each other, "materialized through the process of intensification," generated contempt even and particularly on their bodies (Ahmed 2015, 46). The stickiness of hate has finally stuck with the false teachers. That is why the author has to constantly recall how licentious the false teachers are in multiple ways because hate does not and did not originate with the false teachers. The stickiness of hate has to be glued to the false teachers. Interestingly, though, the author warns their beloved community that hate could also stick to them. The author warns the beloved that they are one (or a few) mistake(s) away and could be "carried away with the error of lawless and lose your own stability" (3:17) from becoming part of the circulation of hate. If Jude speaks of having mercy, saving others, and snatching the beloved out of fire (Jude 22–23), 2 Peter does not provide such opportunities for reconciliation.

Among the various forms of hateful rhetoric being circulated, the author of 2 Peter resorts to animalizing hate multiple times. He does so because animalization "is what sticks" (Ahmed 2015, 54). Animalization of the other is one of the most affective and effective ways to denigrate the other—"most intense or intimate, as being closer to the skin" (54). The author of 2 Peter knows what sticks, its rhetorical impact. The animalization of the other was a common rhetorical device, even used by the author of 2 Peter, a colonized person, who probably was and is also a victim of this animalization. Animalization of the other had been circulating before and during (and even after) the time of 2 Peter. Following Jude 10, 2 Pet 2:12 compares the false teachers to "irrational animals" (*aloga zōa*). Expanding on Jude 11, 2 Pet 2:15–16 describes the false teachers as followers of Balaam son of Bosor because Balaam is pegged for being idolatrous, although the author is selective and biased in rehearsing Balaam's narrative (Num 22:1–40). The idolatrous false teachers will be rebuked through divine intervention (an angel) and a donkey with a human voice (or by the author with the scathing polemic). Like Balaam, the false teachers will be humiliated because they are and will be shamed by a "dumb beast" (Horrell 1998, 170). Finally, 2:22 compares the false teachers with dogs who return to their own vomit (Prov 26:11) and pigs who wallow in mud right after getting washed.

The Aristotelian logic of human hierarchy over nonhumans is anticipated here. In this speciesist logic, to be ontologically compared to animals is an affront to one's humanity. Terrance Callan's (2009, 113) article "Comparison of Humans to Animals in 2 Peter 2,10b–22" provides an excellent summary of ancient authors who compared humans to animals. Callan arranges these comparisons into three groups: neutral, positive, and negative. He concludes that 2 Peter falls in the negative group. To mention just two examples among many provided, Callan argues that Gaius Musonius Rufus likens gluttons to pigs or dogs (Lutz 1947, 116–17). In *Praec. ger. reip.* 5, Plutarch teaches Menemachus that not all beasts are the same. Some people are like wolves: one cannot lead them by holding them by their ears or force them into submission. But there are "irrational beasts" or irrational humans/mobs who could be herded by currying favor and pulling them by the belly (corruption).

Fanon's own struggle with animalization helps to understand better 2 Peter's choice to animalize his fellow colonized persons. Fanon (1952,

95), in *Black Skin, White Masks*, describes how Black bodies, no matter how much they try to overcome animalization, seem to reinscribe in their own bodies the very animalization and/or inferiority ingrained by the colonizers and racists. Fanon confides that such self-animalization turns into an inferiority complex that (un)consciously seeks the approval of the colonizers (90, 118). This self-animalization turns into a powerful feeling, an unbearable affect. It even causes one to believe that one does and should not exist. It justifies being hated and maligned—a form of self-imposed guilt. The only way out is to "explode, to weep" (119).

Ahmed narrates Audre Lorde's experience of animalizing hate when she was young. In *Sister Outsider*, Lorde recalls a train ride with her mother in Harlem. On that cold, wet, wintry day, Lorde sat beside a white woman with a sleek fur coat. But as soon as Lorde sat beside her, the white woman stared at Lorde with disdain, flaring her nostrils, and jerked her clothing away, as far away as possible, from Lorde. At first Lorde, being young and naive, did not understand the white woman's reaction. She thought there was a cockroach in between them. But she quickly realized that there was nothing between them—except the white woman's hatred (Lorde 1984, 147–48).

According to Ahmed (2015, 54), the white woman signified Lorde as "the roach—the impossible and phobic object—that threatens to crawl from one to the other." Hate circulates and slides. Lorde became the object of hate because racism coopted her Black body as part of the animalized. It is not that any body could be an object of hate; histories of circulation and repetition of associations of hate with certain bodies create the stickiness of hate to the point that the reason for such hate becomes lost or unfounded.

The author of 2 Peter is trying to create a community/empire under Jesus. This new community/empire, the new heavens and new earth, will be formed through the destruction of the contemporary heaven and earth through fire (3:7, 10–13). But the parousia of this new empire is hindered, apparently, from the perspective of the author of 2 Peter, by none other than their fellow colonized persons. Whether they were truly licentious, greedy, and corrupt might never be known. So, the author hates their fellow colonized people by utilizing animalizing rhetoric. The author chose, out of many other possible means of hate, to animalize because it reflects a deeper issue that haunts their community. The author of 2 Peter is struggling to overcome the Roman Empire's animalization.

Among many literary examples to choose from, here are two examples of such animalization. Strabo, in *Geography*, describes the colonized people of Kyrnos/Corsica as "wilder than animals" (Roller 2014, 229 (5.2.7 [224]). Sallust (1957, 69 [18.1]), in *Bellum Iugurtinum*, describes the North African people as brutes who feed like beasts. These are the kinds of animalization the colonized people would have heard/experienced from time to time. Since he was living through this, the author's use of this animalizing rhetoric reflects his colonial neurosis. That is, Fanon's definition of colonial neurosis suggests that the author animalized the false teachers because they struggled to overcome their animalized self. For the author of 2 Peter to animalize his opponents is his (un)conscious return to his own colonial vomit or use of the colonizers' strategy of animalizing the other. His colonized mind is affectively ingrained to animalize in order to survive. This interpretation echoes Aichele's (2017, 76) take on this hate/fear of the other: "The two authors' [Jude and 2 Peter] own fears of contamination may have themselves infected the Word of God, not with the opponents' heresies, but with their own fears of difference." The author of 2 Peter is so overdetermined by animalization that animalization of the other has become part of his default discourse. You are dogs and pigs because I am animalized as a dog and a pig. I am the dog who returns to his own vomit, the pig who wallows in the mud right after washing.

It is not known how the implied audience received 2 Peter's testament. It is also not known what happened to the false teachers after 2 Peter was read aloud to its audience. But as Ahmed (2015, 60) points out: "It is not the affective nature of hate speech that allows us to understand that whether such speech works or fails; to work is not really the important question. Rather, the important question is: *What effects do such encounters have on the bodies of others who become transformed into objects of hate?*" Second Peter provides glimpses of the struggles of the early church, specifically its struggles to express itself. Sometimes, it resorted to animalizing hate against its fellow church members. It did not have any qualms about using and/or mimicking the colonizers' tools against each other. It is not known how such animalization affected the bodies of those who were animalized by the author of 2 Peter. Yet 2 Peter compels one to ruminate over how using biblical passages actually affects material bodies. The rhetoric of animalization kills. It kills through the dispensability not just of the physical body but also of possibilities and multiplicities.

Conclusion: Ruminating the Embrace

A critique of my hermeneutical choice to work with affect theory (Ahmed) is that I could be accused of sticking the bodies of the author(s) of 2 Peter, his community, and the opponents with one emotion (hate) as if that were the only emotion circulating among them. The author of 2 Peter could be viewed as a good person who is just trying to genuinely protect his community's orthodox teachings from the heretical unbecoming of outside influencers (Desjardins 1987, 92–93). Obviously, I do not claim to be the final word on how they felt. Instead, following Ahmed (2015, 13), "I am not discussing emotion as being 'in' texts, but as effects of the very naming of emotions, which often works through attributions of causality." For those who are living under the trauma of imperial oppression, 2 Peter (or any other incendiary text) is meant to affectively jolt the other/reader/listener. As Kotrosits (2015, 8) puts it, "Studying this [biblical] literature is not simply a strategic cultural or political intervention or an antiquarian fascination.... It is work fraught with deep affective entanglements, threaded as the Bible, is into so many other attachments and burned injuriously into so many folks' skin." I read 2 Peter in this way because it reflects my own body's stickiness to the ongoing/resurgence of hateful, animalizing rhetoric against minoritized bodies with the assistance of biblical text(s). My body's stickiness, however, is not a proclamation that I own or possess the definition/nature of hatred. Rather, I am reflecting on how hate is also circulating in my own context/body. My body is also a "contact zone," as Ahmed (2015, 14) puts it, in the midst of various contacts forming, fading, and reemerging. Here, 2 Peter (and even the Bible as a whole) is also a contact zone that channels various emotions/affect unto those who tap into its chapters and verses. Unfortunately, many choose to tap into these channels for animalizing/oppressive purposes. That is why I read 2 Peter with animal studies, affect theory, and postcolonialism, in order to jolt or to dismantle and complicate anyone's desire to channel biblical passages for animalizing means. As Moore (2019, 187–207) effusively feels the joy of anachronism in reading texts with affect/emotion, I find joy and liberation in working with these theories because their anachronistic tendency muddies the givens, especially for those who hate with the Bible. Moreover, such an anachronistic tendency gives one pause to ruminate over the fluidity of the *ontos* that positively connects us (humans) with all of creations, one way or another. We embrace our differences while acknowledging that the embrace transgresses even our beings and belongings.

Works Cited

Ahmed, Sara. 2015. *The Cultural Politics of Emotion*. 2nd ed. London: Routledge.
Aichele, George. 2017. *Letters of Jude and Second Peter: An Introduction and Study Guide*. London: Bloomsbury T&T Clark.
Bauckham, Richard. 1983. *Jude, 2 Peter*. WBC 50. Waco, TX: Word.
Black, Fiona C., and Jennifer L. Koosed, eds. 2019. *Reading with Feeling: Affect Theory and the Bible*. SemeiaSt 95. Atlanta: SBL Press.
Bray, Karen, and Stephen D. Moore. 2020. "Introduction: Mappings and Crossings." Pages 1–18 in *Religion, Emotion, Sensation: Affect Theories and Theologies*. Edited by Karen Bray and Stephen D. Moore. TTC. New York: Fordham University Press.
Brinkema, Eugenie. 2014. *The Forms of the Affects*. Durham, NC: Duke University Press.
Brintnall, Kent L., Joseph A. Marchal, and Stephen D. Moore, eds. 2018. *Sexual Disorientations: Queer Temporalities, Affects, Theologies*. TTC. New York: Fordham University Press.
Callan, Terrance. 2009. "Comparison of Humans to Animals in 2 Peter 2, 10b–22." *Bib* 90:101–13.
Clough, Patricia T. ed. 2007. *The Affective Turn: Theorizing the Social*. Durham, NC: Duke University Press.
Davids, Peter H. 2014. "Are the Others Too Other? The Issue of 'Others' in Jude and 2 Peter." Pages 201–13 in *Reading 1–2 Peter and Jude: A Resource for Students*. Edited by Eric F. Mason and Troy W. Martin. RBS 77. Atlanta: SBL Press.
Desjardins, Michel. 1987. "The Portrayal of the Dissidents in 2 Peter and Jude: Does It Tell Us More about the 'Godly' than the 'Ungodly'?" *JSNT* 30:89–102.
Fanon, Frantz. 1952. *Black Skin, White Masks*. Translated by Richard Philcox. New York: Grove.
Fornberg, Tord. 1977. *An Early Church in a Pluralistic Society: A Study of 2 Peter*. Lund: Gleerup.
Horrell, David G. 1998. *The Epistle of Peter and Jude*. EC. London: Epworth.
Jeong, Dong Hyeon. 2020. "When the KKK Exegetes: Circulating Hate with 2nd Peter." *AJSP* (Spring): 17–19.
Kelly, John N. D. 1969. *The Epistles of Jude and of Peter*. HNTC. New York: Harper & Row.

Koosed, Jennifer L., and Stephen D. Moore. 2014. "Introduction: From Affect to Exegesis." *BibInt* 22:381–87.

Kotrosits, Maia. 2011. "The Rhetoric of Intimate Spaces: Affect and Performance in the Corinthian Correspondence." *USQR* 62:134–51.

———. 2012. "Romance and Danger at Nag Hammadi." *BCT* 8:29–52.

———. 2015. *Rethinking Early Christian Identity: Affect, Violence, and Belonging*. Minneapolis: Fortress.

———. 2016. *How Things Feel: Affect Theory, Biblical Studies, and the (Im)Personal*. Leiden: Brill.

Kotrosits, Maia, and Hal Taussig. 2013. *Re-reading the Gospel of Mark amidst Loss and Trauma*. New York: Palgrave Macmillan.

Lorde, Audre. 1984. *Sister Outsider: Essays and Speeches*. Trumansburg, NY: Crossing.

Lutz, Cora E. 1947. *Musonius Rufus "The Roman Socrates."* YCS 10. New Haven: Yale University Press.

Mbuvi, Andrew M. 2015. *Jude and 2 Peter: A New Covenant Commentary*. Eugene, OR: Cascade.

Moore, Stephen D. 2017. *Gospel Jesuses and Other Nonhumans: Biblical Criticism Post-poststructuralism*. SemeiaSt 89. Atlanta: SBL Press.

———. 2019. "The Rage for Method and the Joy of Anachronism: When Biblical Scholars Do Affect Theory." Pages 187–212 in *Reading with Feeling: Affect Theory and The Bible* Edited by Fiona Black and Jennifer L. Koosed. SemeiaSt 95. Atlanta: SBL Press.

Neyrey, Jerome H. 1980. "The Apologetic Use of the Transfiguration in 2 Peter 1:16–21." *CBQ* 42:504–19.

———. 1993. *2 Peter, Jude: A New Translation with Introduction and Commentary*. AB 37C. New York: Doubleday.

Roller, Duane W. 2014. *The Geography of Strabo*. Cambridge: Cambridge University Press.

Runions, Erin. 2008. "From Disgust to Humor: Rahab's Queer Affect." *Postscripts* 4:41–69.

———. 2011. "Prophetic Affect and the Promise of Change: A Response." Pages 235–42 in *Jeremiah (Dis)Placed: New Directions in Writing/Reading/Jeremiah*. Edited by A. R. Pete Diamond and Louis Stulman. LHBOTS 529. New York: T&T Clark.

Sallustius Crispus, Gaius. 1957. *Catilina, Iugurtha, Fragment Ampliora*, Edited by Alphons Kurfess. Leipzig: Teubner.

Schaefer, Donovan O. 2019. *The Evolution of Affect Theory: The Humanities, the Sciences, and the Study of Power.* CEHES. Cambridge: Cambridge University Press.

Seesengood, Robert. 2017. "Irrational Animals, Creatures of Instinct, Bred to Be Caught and Killed: Hybridity, Alterity, and Name-Calling in 2 Peter 2." Unpublished paper. https://tinyurl.com/SBL06107g.

Seigworth, Gregory J., and Melissa Gregg, eds. 2010. *The Affect Theory Reader.* Durham, NC: Duke University Press.

Spencer, F. Scott, ed. 2017. *Mixed Feelings and Vexed Passions: Exploring Emotions in Biblical Literature.* RBS 90. Atlanta: SBL Press.

Talbert, Charles H. 1966. "II Peter and the Delay of Parousia." *VC* 20:137–45.

Thompson, Simon, and Paul Hoggett, eds. 2012. *Politics and the Emotions: The Affective Turn in Contemporary Political Studies.* New York: Continuum.

Watson, Duane F. 2014. "The Epistolary Rhetoric of 1 Peter, 2 Peter, and Jude." In *Reading 1–2 Peter and Jude: A Resource for Students.* Edited by Eric F. Mason and Troy W. Martin. RBS 77. Atlanta: SBL Press.

Part 3
Indistinction and Alternative Stories

Human Obligation to Nonhuman Animals in Proverbs

Timothy J. Sandoval

Introduction

What biblical wisdom literature has to say about nonhuman animals is offered in the context of moral instruction and reflection for humans. However, conceptions of human morality, including biblical wisdom thinking, develop within broader ecological contexts that include human interactions with nonhuman creatures. The level of interaction with nonhuman animals experienced by those who produced, and who are imagined by, biblical texts was considerable. This is especially so when compared with the fairly limited exposure to nonhuman creatures enjoyed by many urban- and suburbanites in the modern West. Aspects of the wisdom texts in the Bible—for example, the short proverbs of Prov 10:1–22:16; 25–29— likely emerged from, and were deemed relevant to addressing, a primarily rural, agricultural, village context (see Fox 2009, 500–503) within which nonhuman animals, both of the domesticated and wild sort, were prominently present.

The final form of Proverbs, however, offers moral instruction for young, intellectually elite, males existing primarily in urban contexts. Still, the text remains under the moral influence of a tradition of a folk wisdom embedded especially in Prov 10–29. This village wisdom, despite its patriarchal and paternalistic character, appears to have valued more fully certain egalitarian and communitarian social arrangements and virtues than did the more urban, socially stratified contexts out of which the final form of the book emerged. These concerns remain evident, for example, in the priority the text places on cooperative social virtue (see Prov 1:3). What

---

This paper was first developed for the University of Notre Dame's Human Distinctiveness Summer Seminar (2015–2016), funded by the Luce Foundation.

is more, although situated in more urban environs (especially Jerusalem), the intellectually elite addressees of the book were likewise inextricably situated within a broader agricultural or husbandry-based society that was also porously bounded by significantly more uncultivated or wild regions than is typical in many modern Western contexts. Indeed, Proverbs itself can take as proverbial—common or not unexpected—that certain wild animals (lions and bears, for example) might roam the streets of towns (Prov 22:13, 26:13; see also 28:15).

It should thus come as no surprise that those who composed and transmitted Proverbs were in all likelihood people who knew and understood well the lives of animals and consequently drew abundantly on images of animals, both wild and not so wild, when offering moral instruction for humans.

Niche Construction

The concept of niche construction developed by anthropologists and others concerned to understand the evolutionary development of human and nonhuman animals will prove useful for understanding Proverbs' conception of human moral obligations to at least some nonhuman animals. Although niche construction theory is a technical and specialized discourse, most basically, as Agustín Fuentes (2017, 5) explains, a niche "is the structural, temporal and social context in which a species exists. It includes space, structure, climate, nutrients and other physical and social factors as they are experienced, and restructured by organisms, and via the presence of competitors, collaborators and other agents."

Human beings are widely regarded as the species that is most robustly engaged in niche construction; humans most fully develop a "spatial and social sphere" that includes "structural ecologies (*including other species*), social partners," and "larger local groups/population" (Fuentes 2017, 5, emphasis added). Through niche construction, humans "shape their own and other organisms' evolutionary trajectories" (Zeder 2016, 326). Proverbs, with all its talk of animals, reveals that humans in ancient Israel/Judah had constructed a niche in which they not only interfaced with a range of wild animals (e.g., ants, birds, lions, bears, etc.) in a range of ways (e.g., as prey, predators, pests, etc.). They also enjoyed more intimate relations with certain domesticated animals. Humans and at least some animals are, for Proverbs, entangled in a single ecological and social existence—a niche.

Nonhuman animals in Proverbs are, in other words, recognized as residing within the circle of those (humans) whom the wisdom tradition insists ought to be the cultivators and recipients of wisdom and justice. In particular, certain domesticates belong intimately to the niche that the wisdom tradition was concerned to organize conceptually for humans in moral terms; they are regarded as falling within the realm of human moral action and obligation. The moral vision Proverbs promotes, however, resists a sharp form of the domesticate/nondomesticate binary and intimates that domestication for the ancient sages was no mere domination of nonhuman animals for exclusive benefit of humans. Instead, nonhuman creatures can be said both to have coevolved with the human population that produced Proverbs and to have coconstructed the niche occupied by the people whom the book addresses.

As social anthropologist Tim Ingold (2011, 76) notes, "Those who are 'with' animals in their day-to-day lives ... can offer us some of the best possible indications" of how humans might well understand animals. The insights developed by those who intimately know nonhuman creatures—whether ancient sages or contemporary anthropologists—might also, one might add, assist in efforts to discern good and appropriate ways of constructing human relationships with nonhuman creatures in the different ecological and social contexts that humans and animals continue to share.

In Proverbs itself, several key verses make clear that those humans who would be wise and just must extend a level of care and concern to at least some nonhuman animals with whom they share a niche in order to ensure the well-being of both. Close attention to these verses can help clarify what the ancient sages regarded as the moral status for humans of (at least some) nonhuman animals and the moral obligation of humans toward these beings. Subsequently, it may be possible to gesture subtly to how the wisdom, or a life of virtue, that Proverbs promotes for humans is—more than is usually recognized—complexly related to humans' long and intimate relationships with some of the nonhuman animals of which the text speaks.

Human Obligation to Nonhuman Animals in Proverbs

A key text for discerning how Proverbs understands human obligation to animals and the moral status of (some) nonhuman creatures for humans is Prov 12:10.

A just person knows the "soul" of his animal;
but mercies of wicked people are cruel.[1]

yôdēaʿ ṣadîq nepeš bəhemtô / vəraḥămê rəšāʿîm ʾakzārî

It is possible to read this text in a minimalist way as exhorting a hearer to appropriate husbandry practices. "Soul" (*nepeš*) often simply means "appetite" in the Bible, and the verse may primarily be reminding a hearer that one should be an astute enough householder to know that one must feed one's animals and not cruelly withhold fodder from them. The instruction might in part be motivated by simple "humanitarian" moral impulses (Fox 2009, 551), but probably also more rudimentarily by knowledge of some unstated practical benefit that might accrue to persons who provide approved care of their animals. As Prov 27:23–27 (discussed further below) suggests, one ought to know and give attention to one's animals—to the flocks and herds (sheep and goats)—since doing so ultimately can produce specific benefits for humans, whether clothing (wool, leather; v. 26), exchange value (v. 26), or food (milk, meat; v. 27). This is simple prudence, the practice of an intelligent, competent householder.

Although in Prov 12:10 the animal in question may be any sort of domesticate known in ancient Israel, the term *bəhēmâ* sometimes refers explicitly to large livestock—especially oxen or bulls. In this case, a further benefit that might accrue to the one competent in husbandry, and who possesses large livestock, is the animal's labor power. This power might be harnessed for plowing and transportation, with the animal's dung used as fertilizer. In ancient Israel/Judah donkeys and mules might serve as draught animals too (Deut 22:10; Ps 32:9) while the strength and intelligence of another nonhuman creature, the horse, could be marshaled by humans for military purposes and for elite displays of power (e.g., 1 Kgs 4:26; Job 39:19–25; Ps 20:7; see also Esth 6:7–11).

The Just and the Wicked

But even if the minimalist interpretation of Prov 12:10 is not completely wrong, it is an underreading of the line. It does not tend much to the line's robustly moral rhetoric of the "just" person (*ṣadîq*) and "wicked" people (*rəšāʿîm*). These terms, however, constitute two key moral types

---

[1]. Translations from the Hebrew are mine, unless otherwise noted.

in Proverbs, and so their mention in 12:10 evokes the book's larger moral discourse, which is concerned with considerably more than husbandry. Indeed, justice or social virtue is arguably *the* central virtue of Proverbs' moral instruction (see the focus on *ṣedeq ûmišpāṭ ûmêšārîm* in Prov 1:3); and wickedness is its antithesis. Just and wicked persons in Proverbs are those human agents that typically embody the range of virtues, or vices, mentioned throughout the book.

Proverbs, in fact, speaks of the just person (*ṣadîq*) some sixty-six times, often to declare some advantage these individuals enjoy over the wicked. Yet specific aspects of their moral dispositions are also sketched. The righteous person's character is obviously consonant with the book's broader conception of social virtue. This social virtue places a premium on the ties of kinship and friendship (17:9, 17; 18:24; 27:10a) and should be demonstrated through kindness and generosity to the poor (14:31; 15:25; 17:5; 21:13; 22:9; 23:10–11; 28:27), fairness in the legal realm (22:22), honesty in market interactions (11:1; 16:11; 20:10, 23), and the limiting of domestic and social conflict (15:18; 20:3; 28:5), for example through appropriate speech (e.g., 10:11, 20, 21, 31–32; 11:9; 12:26). The just likewise oppose the wicked (21:12, 29:27; see also 25:26) and promote justice, rejoicing when it is accomplished (21:15; 29:7; see also 25:26; 28:1).

In contrast to a minimalist reading of Prov 12:10, an initial, somewhat thicker reading of the line might thus suggest that the verse is first and foremost concerned to highlight the virtues of the just person (in this case, implicitly, kindness or mercy), while censuring the corresponding vice of the wicked (cruelty). On such a reading it is possible to regard the just person's relation to that person's animal as incidental to a broader moral point, the promotion of kindness among humans. However, the line might also imagine that a person who is kind to animals is likely to be kind to humans, too, while the one who is cruel to animals is more likely to be vicious in that person's relationships with humans. That a person's good or bad character is revealed not merely through isolated acts but in the larger patterns of one's life—including a person's relations, attitudes, and behavior toward nonhuman creatures—is not an inconsiderable ethical insight. What is more, if one's typical attitudes, emotions, and actions in relation to different people and toward various goods reveal character, then, as Robert Wennberg (2002, 170) puts it, "To be cruel to an animal" is not only "to give expression to a bad character." Such cruel action also "contribute[s] to the formation of that bad character" and "is expressive of 'wickedness.' It is simply, and importantly, not the sort of thing a just person would do." By contrast, tend-ing to the "soul" of one's animal *is* the sort of conduct that characterizes a just person. Both the just person's *usual* kindness and the wicked person's *regular* cruelty with animals are constitutive of their characters, analogous to other contexts of moral discernment and action that likewise serve to establish and reveal one's disposition, whether for good or ill.

A reading of Prov 12:10 that focuses primarily on the nature of virtue exercised in human-human relations may also betray a typically modern bias of interpretation. For whatever philosophical or ethical-theological reasons (see introduction above), it may betray an interpretive orientation that presupposes a sharp moral-ontological distinction between humans and animals, one that has already decided that nonhuman animals are not full moral agents and consequently not of significant moral concern to humans. One might well wonder, though, whether the sages who preserved Proverbs from within a niche where animals were prominent would have conceptualized matters in that way.

The Soul of Another

Although an interpretation of Prov 12:10 that highlights the line's concern with human virtue is a helpful expansion of a minimalist interpretation of the line, both readings may pay too little attention to a further feature of the verse: that the just person's orientation toward a nonhuman animal is described by the evocative locution "to know the 'soul'" of something. As noted, one might well understand the term *nepeš* in the line simply as "appetite." But it might also be rendered as "soul" or "life"—the "complex of desires and feelings" that in part constitutes a living being (Fox 2009, 551). But if so, what does it mean "to know" the *nepeš* of another?

Two lines, one from Proverbs and one from Exodus, which use rhetoric similar to that of Prov 12:10, can fill in that verse's meaning. First, like Prov 12:10, Prov 29:7 speaks of the "just person," who, in contrast to a wicked person, "knows" something in relation to an Other: "A just person [*ṣadîq*] knows [*yōdēaʿ*] the rights [*dîn*] of poor people; a wicked person [*rešaʿ*] has no such understanding" (NRSV, adapted). In Exod 23:9 one finds essentially the same expression Prov 12:10 uses—"to know the soul." "You shall not oppress a sojourner—indeed you know the soul [*yədaʿtem ʾet-nepeš*] of the sojourner, for you were sojourners in the land of Egypt." In Prov 29:7, as Michael Fox (2009, 836) explains, the instruction "demands that one actively seek to know the rights of the poor." In Exod 23:9, the Israelites are exhorted to avoid treating others in their midst with the sorts of exploitative measures that characterized Egyptian domination of the Hebrews prior to the exodus. Instead, they should seek to respond empathetically and responsibly to others in their midst, to ensure their well-being.

In light of Prov 29:7 and Exod 23:9, the just person's interactions with the nonhuman other in Prov 12:10—the knowing the soul of the animal—should be imagined as empathic, responsible, and just relations, perhaps not identical to but also not unlike that which humans owe other humans in their efforts to secure a good and flourishing existence. The just person who knows the soul of their animal is thus not one who is simply shrewd enough to know that by taking minimal care of one's animal one might ultimately reap from the creature the material benefit of agricultural output. Indeed, the wicked surely know how to profit economically from their animals too. But like the "sinners" of Prov 1:10–19 who crassly pursue riches by unjust and violent means, the wicked might well be thought to misunderstand the place of wealth in securing human flourishing and so overvalue it. They are thus happy to seek material advantage through sheer domination of their animals. The minimal provision—"kindness"—they offer their animal is subsequently, and ironically, reckoned as a form of cruelty. It has little to do with establishing just, empathetic, and responsible relations with the nonhuman creature and is not integrated into a broader wise vision for human flourishing in a niche that people share with animals.

Proverbs 14:4

If Prov 12:10 has gestured to the sort of dispositions—typical attitudes and modes of action—that just humans should display toward nonhuman animals, Prov 14:4 suggests something similar. The advantages for humans that the domestication and agricultural use of nonhuman animals—large cattle—provide is not something that accrues absent any human obligation to the nonhuman creatures.

> Where there are no oxen, there is no grain;
> abundant crops come by the strength of the ox. (NRSV)
>
> bəʾên ʾălāpîm ʾēbûs bār / vərab-təbûʾôt bəkōaḥ šôr

The first half of the line can be interpreted in two different ways. Verse 4a might be read as saying, "Where there are no oxen, [there exists] a *trough* ['ēbûs] of grain [bār]." Or it might be rendered as, "Where there are no oxen, the stall ['ēbûs] is bare/clean [bār]" (Fox 2009, 573). On the first reading, the absence of the large animals means an agriculturalist is not obligated to expend resources on the maintenance of the creature; there is no need to hand over to the nonhuman animal as fodder a portion of the yield of grain for which one might have toiled significantly. Instead it can be consumed by others in the household, preserved for seed, sold, or bartered for other goods. The second reading of the line may hint that the absence of large bovines means not only that an animal's stall may be bare in the sense of containing no fodder, but it may also be free of manure, which would otherwise need to be removed. With this reading, there is no need to labor to maintain the ox's stall; without an animal it is already clean.

The irony that the second half of Prov 14:4 produces with the first verse half, however, is significant. Although the absence of oxen means part of one's yield need not be slated to maintain the animals and there is no need to clean stalls, without large cattle there is not much possibility for much agricultural gain. Without these nonhuman animals that are owed maintenance or care—appropriate feeding and stabling—the possibility for the flourishing of even relatively small-scale, settled human communities in the agriculturally challenging central highlands of Syria-Palestine is diminished. The harnessing of the power of draught animals would have facilitated the difficult tasks of tilling soil and transporting harvested crops, while animal manure would have fertilized fields. Both the preservation of the ox's grain feed and the absence of ox dung in the stall are relatively small advantages when compared with the abundant crops that an agriculturalist might produce with the ox's aid. The nonhuman coinhabitant of the human niche contributes to human flourishing and so is owed some care from humans to ensure the animals' well-being.

Intriguingly, aspects of the rhetoric of Prov 14:4 might also indirectly evoke something of the intimacy of human-nonhuman animal relationships. The term for oxen or cattle (*'elep*), of course, is well-related to the word for "thousand" (*'elep*). That conceptual linking may lead readers to imagine the line as one that addresses large cattle operations, arrangements designed primarily to increase the social-economic advantages of (some) humans—the owners of the herd. Yet when the more modest social milieu of households and small village farming is imagined as a legitimate context for interpreting the verse, the term might evoke other connotations of the consonants '-l-p too. For example, '-l-p (I) in the Hebrew Bible means "to learn" or "become familiar with," and the term *'elep* can refer to a tribal or clan unit of specific size, a kinship group perhaps "loosely equivalent to *mišpāḥâ family* (1 Sam 10:19-21)" (*DCH* 1:300, emphasis original). The adjective *'allûp*, moreover, means "tame" or "docile," and Ps 144:14 uses the plural form to speak of cattle. But *'allûp* also can describe a person's friend or "intimate companion," as it does on three occasions in Proverbs (2:17; 16:28; 17:9). The rhetoric of Prov 14:4, then, might gesture to the fact that if both humans and nonhuman animals are not only to survive but also (in some sense) flourish in their shared niche—in part through enjoying the benefits of increased agricultural production—close interspecies cooperation, understanding, and even a kind of companionship is required.

Proverbs 27:23-27

Proverbs 27:23-27 is a further passage that underscores the close relationship of humans with some nonhuman animals in a context where humans depend on animals to enhance their own [human] well-being. Like Prov 12:10 and 14:4, it makes clear that nonhuman animals are owed an exercise of human virtue. But the passage's rhetoric, perhaps more forcefully than the other verses, indicates that the value of the coinhabitants of the human niche ought not to be narrowly limited to the utilitarian or economic profit they provide humans.

> Know well the condition of your flocks,
>   and give attention to your herds;
> for riches do not last forever,
>   nor a crown for all generations.
> When the grass is gone, and new growth appears,
>   and the herbage of the mountains is gathered,
>   the lambs will provide your clothing,
>   and the goats the price of a field;
> there will be enough goats' milk for your food,
>   for the food of your household
>   and nourishment for your servant girls. (NRSV)

As with a minimalist reading of Prov 12:10, a simple reading of this passage might suggest that "knowing" one's flocks and attending to one's herds is a form of basic prudence, as it results in a genuine economic advantage for the human. The nonhuman animals provide people with valuable clothing, capital, and food—all necessary for the maintenance and flourishing of the ancient household. There is no need to deny this aspect of the instruction. Proverbs knows well the worth of a "good" such as wealth, and how—when it is appropriately pursued and its value rightly understood—it legitimately contributes to human well-being. However, in the context of the book's broader instruction, one might again say more about the moral implications of the passage.

First, notice the rhetoric that Prov 27:23 and 12:10 share. Proverbs 12:10, recall, insists that the "just person" is one who "knows" the "soul" of one's animals; such a person is empathetically and responsibly attuned to what is owed nonhuman creatures. In 27:23, the addressee is, similarly and emphatically, exhorted through the use of the infinitive absolute + imperfect construction to "know" "the faces of" (*pənê*) his animals; one subsequently is commanded to set one's "mind" (*lēb*), one's intellect and affect, to one's herds.

The unique expression "to know the faces of" underscores the line's moral point regarding human obligation to deal responsibly and empathetically with their domesticated animals. Although to know the faces of one's livestock probably most basically means to attend to the general "conditions" of one's flocks, a close parallel to the expression is found in Deut 34:10. In this verse Adonai is said to have known Moses (*yədāʿô*) "face to face" (*pānîm ʾel pānîm*), a locution that is regularly understood as expressing the depth and intimacy of their relationship of mutual concern.

The rhetoric of Prov 27:23 thus invites readers to more robust hermeneutical exploration of what "knowing the face" of one's animals might (come to) mean. It may, for instance, evoke for some Emmanuel Levinas's reflections on the ethical and social significance of the "face" of the Other. For Levinas (1969, 198, 201), the face of the Other "speaks to me and thereby invites me to a relation"; it "opens the primordial discourse whose first word is obligation." Indeed, "the Other faces me and puts me in question and obliges me" (207). "The face presents itself, and demands justice" (294). Levinas, of course, was concerned primarily with human others, with the face that represents not an object to be possessed but the living presence of another human being. Yet might not Levinas's concepts be critically and constructively extended to the living presence of nonhuman creatures (so Atterton and Wright 2019), which the Bible also sometimes simply calls "living beings" (*ḥāyâ/ôt*)?

Levinas's reflections on the face, when applied to Prov 27:23, in fact sit well with the sorts of moral conclusions that might also be drawn out from verses such as 12:10 and 14:4. If humans for Proverbs owe something to the nonhumans in their midst, this obligation to the living Others in their midst becomes clearer when humans are exhorted to look not merely on the conditions of their animals—for example, as simple means to economic advantage—but authentically consider the faces of animal Others. Reading Prov 27:23 in light of Levinas might thus constructively spur further reflection on the nature and contours of the justice owed to at least some nonhuman animals, both for Proverbs itself and in contemporary contexts of interpretation. As Levinas (1990, 294) says, "In front of the face, I always demand more of myself."

Wealth's Worth, Animal Value

Besides insisting, evocatively, that humans ought "to know the faces of" their animals, Prov 27:23–27 importantly also distinguishes between valuable material goods that one might simply accumulate and possess, and the worth of nonhuman animals whose faces humans encounter. The passage, that is, intimates that the telos of paying attention to one's flocks is not simply to ensure material gain. "Riches" (and a "crown"; v. 24) are not equivalent to livestock. The lines, moreover, make clear that the salient distinction between the value of material goods and that which nonhuman animals offer turns on the ephemeral or enduring quality of each. "Riches do not last forever, nor a crown for all generations." Indeed, the fleetingness of material goods is underscored by the evocation in the next line (v. 25) of a well-known biblical metaphor for the brevity of life—the regular disappearance of vegetation (e.g., Job 14:1; Ps 102:11; Isa 40:7–8). By contrast, the worth of one's flocks and herds is more permanent. When that which is ephemeral disappears—whether riches or the grass of the fields—the contributions of lambs and goats to human well-being remains.

The enduring value that the nonhuman creatures of Prov 27:23–27 hold for humans also finds an intriguing conceptual parallel to the worth Wisdom itself holds for people. Throughout the book's early chapters images of material wealth are deployed to speak metaphorically of the incomparable worth intangible wisdom holds for humans. First, wisdom is said to be valuable *like* material goods in Prov 2:4–5; next Wisdom is described as *more valuable* than material goods (3:14–16) and is even said to be so valuable that, if one could literally buy Wisdom, one should use whatever material wealth one has in order to acquire her (4:5–9). Subsequently, in 8:10, Wisdom herself exhorts one to "Take my instruction, and not silver." Finally, in 8:18 personified Wisdom claims to possess not only a material good, riches, but a social good, honor (v. 18a; possibly "honorable wealth"; see Fox, 2009, 277).

> Riches and honor are with me,
> enduring wealth and justice.

ʿōšer-vəkābôd 'ittî / hôn ʿātēq ûṣədāqâ

What is clear from the movement of the rhetoric of riches in Prov 1–9, and from the fact that in 8:18a a personified figure now speaks, is that the wealth Wisdom possesses, and presumably offers those who find her, should primarily be reckoned as a kind of symbolic wealth; it is not in the first place a promise of real riches. The rhetoric of 8:18b likewise suggests that the riches and honor that Wisdom holds (in v. 18a) is a figurative wealth. In verse 18b what Wisdom possesses is not real, "precious wealth" (hôn yāqār), like that which the robbers in 1:10–19 promise those who follow their vicious way. Instead, it is hôn ʿātēq and ṣədāqâ —enduring wealth and justice. Although sometimes efforts are made to achieve a parallelism of economic terms in the verse by construing ṣədāqâ as a synonym for wealth, these proposals are not convincing (Fox 2009, 278). Since justice is a key virtue in Proverbs, its appearance at any point in the book should not be surprising, while the waw of ûṣədāqâ might well be understood epexegetically. Wisdom holds "enduring wealth, that is, social virtue" (ṣədāqâ), which itself is probably a metonym for all of the virtues of wisdom's way.

Within the larger symbolic economy of the book's rhetoric of riches and morality, then, the lasting advantage for humans that the nonhuman animals of Prov 27:23–27 hold over ephemeral wealth is analogous to the enduring worth wisdom holds for people. What is of central concern to Proverbs is the establishment and maintenance of stable, thriving human communities. For this, wisdom, especially social virtue, is needed. But flourishing communities in the ancient niche also required a basic material prosperity and so entailed appropriate human relations with animals too. That, itself, required an exercise of wisdom or social virtue, the knowledge and desire to provide what is due to the animal Other in one's midst. By genuinely knowing the faces of one's animals, and authentically setting one's intellect and affect (one's heart) to one's animals, the addressees of Proverbs might not only be genuinely moved to fulfill their basic obligations to certain animals with whom they exist; they also might recognize more fully the place of nonhuman creatures in an economy of human flourishing.

Of course, modern readers of Proverbs, especially those for whom the Bible carries some normative authority, do well to question critically verses such as Prov 12:10, 14:4, and 27:23–27. It should not be forgotten that the texts presume significant human control over domesticated animals, including the power to slaughter them for sacrifice and food. Proverbs 15:8, 21:3, 27; and 23:20, for instance, all assume the practice of sacrifice and/or meat consumption. What is more, Proverbs emerges from, and originally spoke to, social and ethical contexts where human institutions (e.g., the patriarchal household, the monarchy) were predicated on fundamental inequalities. Although through the addressee's wisdom with animals—that is, his ability to ensure the thriving of nonhuman others in his environs—some benefit might accrue to even the most marginalized human members of a community (e.g., "life" to the female servants or slaves of Prov 27:27), it is difficult to imagine how anyone besides the male head of a household might genuinely flourish in such a context. The text does little to question the validity of the social or gender and sex inequalities that it presupposes. Hermeneutically, much critical and constructive work is left to contemporary interpreters of Proverbs.

Still, Proverbs does intimate that humans have particular moral obligations to some nonhuman animals in their midst and that the well-being of these creatures is related to human well-being. The animals that are entangled with people in a shared niche, and the conditions of their existence, are bound up with possibilities for achieving human flourishing. That constitutes an insight that also demands further critical reflection by ethically concerned readers of the Bible today, even as the paternalistic, patriarchal, and hierarchical components of the book's discourse are not ignored.

Conclusion: Niche Construction, Domestication, Morality, and Proverbs

The quip "humans did not domesticate dogs, dogs domesticated humans" has become a popular way to underscore the intimacy and complexity of many human-canine relations. The contemporary proverb points to the fact that the presence of dogs in the human niche can, evolutionarily, be accounted for not only in terms of the benefits that domestication of dogs provides humans but how the relationship constitutes an advantage for canines too. The outlines of the story of early canine-human relations, sometimes called predomestication (of wolves), are well known, though some matters remain disputed (see Gailbert et al. 2011, 191). In prehistoric contexts, canines would come to feed on food scraps associated with human communities. In so doing, however, they would serve humans by eliminating that waste; they also could signal with their barking the approach to a settlement of other, sometimes dangerous animals—human or otherwise. Subsequently, of course, over centuries canines were selected and bred by humans for more specialized activities and relations with both humans and other animals. The point is, however, that in this account of early canine domestication, the canines and not only the humans "get something" from domestication. The relations between humans and the domesticated animals that Proverbs imagines can be understood to have arisen similarly; both humans and nonhuman animals likely benefited, evolutionarily speaking, from their interspecies interactions, even if not in precisely equal fashion.

It may well be objected that a story of human domestication of animals, which speaks of mutual advantages to humans and nonhumans, is too sanguine, eliding too much of the genuinely negative aspects of human domination of nonhuman creatures in domestication processes. Tim Ingold, for example, contends not merely that human hunter-gatherers understood the hunting of nonhumans as part of a broader set of cooperative relations of trust between humans and animals. He also notes that later human efforts at domestication, understood as akin to human manipulation of tools, certainly did entail the exercise of controlling power over nonhumans—though still not the sort of sheer domination of animals that the modern epoch would come to know (Ingold 2011, 72–74).

However, anthropologist Pat Shipman (2011), in her book *The Animal Connection*, puts forth a somewhat different thesis about humans, animals, and domestication, which is more like the dog story sketched above and which may prove helpful for understanding Proverbs' moral discourse. Shipman contends that humans have a deep and ancient connection to animals that survives today and that the domestication of other species by humans was an important moment in the forging of this connection. As Shipman puts it, "We have evolved to be connected to animals.... We still have a deep need to be involved with animals" (271). But more than this, she argues that humans "have co-evolved with the ones we have domesticated, and both species in the process have reaped benefits from the arrangement" (267). In this process, she says, "Humans who were more successful at handling and living with animals accrued a selective advantage." But she also contends that "the animals undergoing domestication were effectively selecting for particular traits in humans" too (258). Humans looked for nonhuman animals that possessed, among other traits, sociality and cooperativeness, and who were not aggressive. For their part, the nonhuman animals, according to Shipman, selected for humans who possessed the "vital skills," or what one might call the virtues, of compassion, "empathy, understanding, and compromise," and who were able to draw on these skills or virtues to cooperate effectively with nonhuman others.

Shipman's arguments resonate rather fully with some niche-construction perspectives on domestication. As Melinda Zeder (2016, 326) intimates, the niche construction efforts of humans and some nonhuman animals in essence is a work of coconstruction that can result in "co-evolutionary relationships" that either humans or nonhumans might initiate. Niche-construction activities, that is, can influence "selection pressures on humans and emergent domesticates that evoke demonstrable evolutionary responses in both." Animals, for instance, might "experience selection for reduced reactivity to humans that enhance the[ir] reproductive success," which itself can encourage "more intervention by humans in their care, protection and breeding" (326). However, "In order for niche-construction to result in domestication, a sustained, multi-generational relationship must develop from which both humans and target species gain mutual, though not necessarily symmetrical benefits" (328). The human sharing of traditional ecological knowledge, including across generations, is a primary mechanism for extending "the dependence of one or both partners on the other" and for "deepening mutualisms between humans and emergent domesticates" (328, 332). Traditional ecological knowledge, in other words, serves "as an enduring cross-generational user's manual that contains essential information on where and when resources can be found and how to maintain the modified environments and management strategies needed to ensure their continued productivity" (332).

The moral vision developed by Proverbs was developed and passed down across generations by people who lived in niches in which some nonhuman animals were prominent and which surely coevolved with humans. Consequently, the book's instruction might thus plausibly include aspects of traditional ecological knowledge related to the human-domesticate relationships that over long ages developed in the central highlands of what became ancient Israel and Judah. Intriguingly, both the traits that humans sought out in nonhumans and those that nonhumans sought out in people in the scenario Shipman articulates sound a lot like the sorts of social virtues that the wisdom tradition places at the center of moral life as it attempts to guide humans to the good of a flourishing existence (see Deane-Drummond 2014, 123). Individuals who exercised the virtues necessary to attend well to the nonhuman animals with whom they lived—those who knew the soul of animals and who acknowledged the faces of their flocks—enjoyed an evolutionary advantage. Through their relations with nonhuman animals, they were able to enhance the benefits to human households in their ecological niche. The traditional wisdom of biblical texts such as Prov 12:10, 14:4, and 27:23–27 (with their embedded traditional ecological knowledge) perhaps reveals the far end of this process. The verses recognize not only as shrewd or pragmatic those who know how the domestication and care of nonhumans can bring real material benefits to humans. They more fundamentally acknowledge as wise and just those who understand, desire, and act well on their obligations to ensure the well-being of the nonhuman others in their niche—a virtuous mode of being that contributed to long term human flourishing.

In the end, then, the attitudes, actions, and obligations toward some nonhuman animals that Proverbs occasionally promotes for its addressees as components of a wisdom designed to enable human flourishing might be said to constitute the moral distillation of an evolutionary process whereby successful individuals—both human and some nonhuman animal—were able to cooperate well with one another in a shared ecological niche in ways that benefited each. One might thus also say that the moral vision developed by Proverbs, especially its concern with cooperative social virtue, owes at least something to some of those nonhuman animals with whom humans shared their ecological niche. It might be regarded as the wisdom not merely of the big-brained "super-cooperator," *Homo sapiens sapiens*, but also the wisdom of cooperating, social, nonhuman animals too.

Works Cited

Atterton, Peter, and Tamra Wright, eds. 2019. *Face to Face with Animals: Levinas and the Animal Question*. Albany: State University of New York Press.

Deane-Drummond, Celia. 2014. *The Wisdom of the Liminal: Evolution and Other Animals in Human Becoming*. Grand Rapids: Eerdmans.

Fox, Michael V. 2009. *Proverbs 10–29: A New Translation with Introduction and Commentary.* AB 18B. New Haven: Yale University Press.
Fuentes, Agustín. 2017. "Human Niche, Human Behaviour, Human Nature." *IntF* 7:1–13.
Galibert, Francis, Pascale Quignon, Christophe Hitte, and Catherine André. 2011. "Toward Understanding Dog Evolutionary and Domestication History." *CRB* 334:190–96.
Ingold, Tim. 2011. *The Perception of the Environment: Essays on Livelihood, Dwelling, and Skill.* London: Routledge.
Levinas, Emmanuel. 1969. *Totality and Infinity: An Essay on Exteriority.* Pittsburgh: Duquesne University Press.
———. 1990. "Signature." In *Difficult Freedom: Essays on Judaism.* Baltimore: Johns Hopkins University Press.
Shipman, Pat. 2011. *The Animal Connection: A New Perspective on What Makes Us Human.* New York: Norton.
Wennberg, Robert N. 2002. *God, Humans, and Animals: An Invitation to Enlarge Our Moral Universe.* Grand Rapids: Eerdmans.
Zeder, Melinda A. 2016. "Domestication as a Model System for Niche Construction Theory." *EE* 30:325–48.

Mark's Parabolic Aviary: Reading Mark's Parabolic Birds Ecologically with and against Mark's Jesus

Brian James Tipton

Introduction: Ubiquitous Birds and the Gospel of Mark

> Birds did not just present themselves as physical objects of curiosity and study, but also populated people's minds and imaginations and then re-emerged in their language, legends, and patterns of thought in some symbolic form.
>
> —Jeremy Mynott, *Birds in the Ancient World*, 245

Wherever you go, there *they* are. Our winged counterparts that are seemingly always in our midst, yet far too often ignored or not taken into account as our fellow creatures. Birds are everywhere we go, everywhere we inhabit, and everywhere we think. From our lofty skyscrapers to our lowly apartments and single-story houses, from our origin myths to our favorite chocolate bars, our feathered friends flutter and coo their way through our daily lives, cracking their loud cock-a-doodle-doos, caw-caws, or chirps throughout our days and nights. As I researched the topic of birds in antiquity for this chapter, I was reminded of how close birds are when a hummingbird burst into our home, making its way through our living room, flittering, fluttering, and humming until it found its way out.[1] Birds. Wherever you go, there *they* are. And so it is in this chapter. They will flutter in and out as winged words that traverse through the sacred texts I analyze, interpret, and explore, forcing me to acknowledge

---

1. For a video of the encounter, see Tipton 2018.

their presence in metaphor, simile, and simply birds-as-birds in the narrative world.

This chapter explores the ways in which birds enter Mark's Gospel, roosting in its branches until they are shooed away and condemned for simply being birds. That is, in this chapter I use critical animal studies as my hermeneutical lens for interpreting and analyzing the various episodes in the Gospel of Mark that incorporate parabolic birds—Mark's parabolic aviary. Much of the work to date on the birds of Mark focuses on individual passages, not taking into account the varying ways in which the gospel's author employs or uses birds throughout the gospel as a whole (1:9–11; 4:4, 15, 30–32; 11:15–19; 14:26–31, 68–72). Nor does this previous analysis proceed with an eco-theological or ecocritical lens in mind—critically reflecting on what this use means and how it functions. This chapter fills that gap, comparing, analyzing, and interrogating the ways in which Mark's parabolic birds are employed. I use J. Donald Hughes's (2014) *Environmental Problems of the Greeks and Romans: Ecology in the Ancient Mediterranean*, which, as the title suggests, provides the backdrop for the lived reality of disrupted environments within the Greco-Roman world. I also use Rosi Braidotti's (2018, 70) approach to nonhuman animals, wherein animals are read as and for animals and not just as symbols, a neologism termed "neoliteral," as a means of deciphering the dynamics between human and nonhuman animals in order to move beyond the "signifying system that props up the humans' self-projections and moral aspirations."[2] These resources provide a means of attending to those creatures not often addressed by critical animal study nor biblical scholars—birds.[3]

While human animals make their way through every pericope in the Second Gospel, the nonhuman animal graces many of these stories as well (seventeen in total),[4] and by far the dominant creatures (beyond humans) within these narratives are birds, comprising five episodes. Yet, as I will illustrate below, these narratives do not present birds as a singular, mechanistic,

---

2. I will also engage Braidotti 2009, 2011.

3. As opposed to the most common animals addressed by animal scholars: primates, dogs, horses, and cats; see Bach 2018, 9–10.

4. One finds locusts (Mark 1:6), pigeons/doves (1:10; 11:15–19), wild beasts (1:13), birds (4:1–20, 30–32), swine (5:1–20), sheep (6:34), fish (6:30–44; 8:1–10), dogs (7:24–30), worms (9:44, 46, 48), a camel (10:17–31), a colt (11:1–11), a Passover lamb (14:12), a cock/rooster (14:26–31, 66–72), and, finally, snakes (16:18).

instinct-driven beastly grouping; rather, Mark's Gospel displays various rhetorical and didactic uses for our feathered friends, illumining the varied ways that birds were thought about, interpreted, and interacted with in the ancient world. At the core of my analysis and interrogation will be the work of critical animal studies, where Cartesian assumptions about our animal Others are minimalized or rejected, allowing space for *difference* within the creaturely continuum and even within specific species.[5] That is, the singular categories of animal or bird will, by and large, be rejected when interpreting Mark's parabolic aviary, yet I will also explore how the nonhuman animal, the bird, is *used* by the author of Mark and/or the Markan Jesus as a didactic tool throughout the Second Gospel.[6] I will work within the erudite framework provided by critical animal studies scholars such as Braidotti and Colleen Glenney Boggs to (re)consider how Mark or the Markan Jesus uses various creaturely categories, *why* those rhetorical strategies for teaching may have been effective for the early receiver of these narratives, and *how* our own assumptions about animals and animality may pigeonhole our interpretations of the gospel and Mark's aviary.

The goal in this work will be an interrogation of the Markan narrative alongside a neoliteral reading of our nonhuman animal counterparts, reading birds-as-birds, valuing them in a way that provides insights into how one can read them differently, while also considering what it would look like to read nonhuman animals and Mark's aviary with a critical animal studies philosophical axiom in mind—that difference matters. In this sense, my readings are not just about human animals, nor simply about our nonhuman animal counterparts, but rather about both, providing

---

5. As Jacques Derrida (2008, 34) notes, the modern concept of "the animal," "within the strict enclosure of this definite article ('the Animal' and not 'animals')," razes this difference in spite of its asininity. Though my work largely resides within the *indistinction* approach to animality, much of my thinking combines indistinction and difference. My goal within here is to address the radical singularity, or radical difference, within the nonhuman animal kin-dom as well. As Walker-Jones and Millar point out in the introduction to this volume, "There is no single dividing line between humans and animals but many dividing lines between and within species, many of which cut across each other." Thus, a working assumption and foundation within my work is that *difference* matters and that difference *within species* matters *and* creates space for new ways of being in relation to our nonhuman animal counterparts.

6. For more on this in antiquity, see Babette Pütz's (2014) discussion on animal imagery in classical comedies (specifically Aristophanes) and animals as didactic tools through laughter.

insight through a decentering of the human, using the indistinction model (Calarco 2015) of animal studies by "remov[ing] the human as the starting point for ethical reflection ... to find new ways of thinking and doing that promote the mutual flourishing of all species" (see the introduction). This flourishing comes from thinking "about human beings and animals in deeply relational terms," by positioning nonhuman animal counterparts as siblings in the kin-dom of God, *not* as animal Others—what I am calling a *sibling hermeneutic* (Calarco 2015, 56).[7] These winged creatures are ubiquitous, fluttering, flittering, humming, and gliding throughout people's lives. Ever present, always coming into contact, yet, so often, never fully recognized. My hope is that this work will illuminate why it is important to interact with animals-as-animals. This is true now, as it was in the time of Jesus and, I will show, in the Gospel of Mark.

Jesus's Parable of the Sower: Birds as Symbolic Satan

> A parable is a short narrative fiction that expresses a moral or religious lesson. It is a cousin to the proverb, which, as Miguel de Cervantes once said, is a "short sentence founded upon long experience."
> —Alyce M. McKenzie, *The Parables for Today*, 4–5

> And as he sowed, some seed fell on the path, and the birds came and ate it up.... These are the ones on the path where the word is sown: when they hear, Satan immediately comes and takes away the word that is sown in them. (Mark 4:4, 15)[8]

We begin our journey into Mark's parabolic aviary lakeside, standing in a boat while Jesus teaches a large crowd about a sower, the sower's seed, and what happens to that seed. Studies on the parable of the sower vary

---

7. For a full discussion on and development of sibling theology and a sibling hermeneutic, see Tipton 2022, 106–24. Calarco (2015, 50) notes, "Indistinction theorists attempt to develop ways of thinking about human beings, animals, and ethics in a manner that radically displaces human beings from the center of ethical reflection." He goes on, stating that this "helps us to think about animals and human-animal relations outside a strictly human vantage point and to decenter subjectivity in a radical way" (61), which is what I attempt within this chapter and with sibling theology and a sibling hermeneutic more broadly. For more on kin-dom language, see Isasi-Díaz 2010.

8. The NRSV translation is used here and throughout, unless otherwise noted.

greatly, and each of these approaches plays a crucial role in painting an expansive interpretive picture of a short parable—a scholarly exploration of long experience leading to a short story, as it were. While this variety of approaches has led to relatively consistent conclusions, much of the previous scholarship on the parable barely mentions or largely ignores one key aspect: the rhetorical use of birds by Mark's author.[9]

With that said, some previous scholarship does expressly analyze the rhetorical use of birds within the parable, reflecting on why it was effective in its ancient rhetorical context and how the ancient audience may have understood Jesus's construction of the symbolic relationship between the birds of the parable and his allegorical interpretation of them as Satan. William Herzog (2012) reads the parable in light of a hypothetical Galilean village where peasants reflect on Jesus's words and the component parts of the parable, using their lived experience to unpack Jesus's message of exploitation and oppression by the Roman elite. Herzog frames the parable as one about *both* the agrarian livelihood of the peasants *and* how the Roman system of taxes, tributes, and rent affected their ability to survive off of the land. In this fabled depiction the birds symbolize or transform into the Roman masters of the peasants, devouring that which the peasants worked so hard to sow.[10] Ernest Van Eck and Meshack Mashinini (2016, 1) read the parable in terms of the reality of the political, social, and economic world as a symbol of social transformation, where Jesus provides a "critique on food insecurity systems in urban townships." Van Eck and Mashinini reach the same conclusion as Herzog, reading the birds as a symbol for the evil and satanic Roman Empire and the systems of exploitation that it had constructed—systems that had a disproportionate effect on peasant farmers.

While Herzog, Van Eck, and Mashinini all engage Mark's use of the birds within the parable of the sower, each interpreting them in terms of the Roman imperial system,[11] both studies lack two major features: an ecocritical analysis of the *use* of the birds as well as an analysis of

---

9. For example, Adela Yarbro Collins (2007), in her lengthy commentary on the Gospel of Mark, fails to make any comments on the birds whatsoever.

10. For more on the relationship between peasantry, hunger, poverty, and Jesus's existence as a peasant and his response to that socioeconomic status, see Hendricks 2011, 64–67. As Hendricks (64) notes, "In the Gospels Jesus speaks about poor people and the effects of poverty on their lives more often than any single subject except God."

11. An interpretation of the passage I generally agree with.

the relationship between the birds of the parable and those birds found throughout the rest of the gospel. While these readings are effective in elucidating some key components of the passage, as well as employing methods of interpretation that make space for both a social justice–oriented and ecocritical reflection on the parable, these interpretations do not take the step of partaking in such ecocritical reflection. That is, each attempts to further elucidate what the parable and Jesus's allegorical interpretation mean but does not interrogate *how that meaning was constructed* and how the nonhuman animal was used and framed. While it may have been fully justified for Jesus or the author of Mark to criticize the economic practices of the Roman Empire and the damage they caused, it is necessary to acknowledge that Jesus symbolically links the birds with Satan through his use of the parable for didactic purposes. Something powerful occurs in the use of the birds (*peteina*) as a didactic tool, and it is this use that biblical scholars ignore but animal scholars find a place for interrogation and analysis. As Boggs (2009, 535) notes, "The fictional use of animals for didactic purposes," which is what this portion of the parable is constructed on, "is not interested in animals as such" but rather is simply using them as a means of instructional teaching. Consequently, the author of Mark neither recognizes, nor is interested in, the animal, in the *peteina*, as such but rather is simply using them as a means of instructional teaching.

Furthermore, in this passage birds are being used as symbolic teaching tools against the economic evils of the Roman Empire. Birds are being portrayed *as the evil empire*—as the Roman participants in the grabbing, taking, and consuming of the sown seed. Braidotti (2009, 527) notes that there is an ethical response, a critical reading, that pushes back against the "metaphoric habit of composing a sort of moral and cognitive bestiary in which animals refer to values, norms, and morals"—in the case of this parable, as the evil associated with the Roman Empire. Braidotti suggests that in order to resist this rhetorical technique and metaphoric habit, in order to "move beyond the empire of the sign," one must move toward a "neoliteral relation to animals, anomalies, and inorganic others," to read animals-as-animals as a means of taking part in a "deep bioegalitarianism, a recognition that we humans and animals are in this together" (528). In this type of reading, Braidotti suggests that "animals are no longer the signifying system that props up humans' self-projections and moral aspirations" and that having been approached literally, they become "entities framed by code systems of their own" (528). I take my cue from Braidotti and attempt a neoliteral reading of these birds as a means of deciphering the human-animal relations in the parable, all the while attempting to partake in a deep *zoe*-egalitarianism[12] that sees the needs of the birds on a par with, related to, and/or entangled with the needs of humans. Which, after all, is what the parable is about: the need to survive and thrive.

If the parable *is* about the oppressive Roman practices of land ownership and taxing as well as the peasant farmers' ability to have access to their crops and traditional farming practices—thus, the ability to avoid starvation and becoming destitute, to survive—the point is made through a parable that critiques the birds' actions in relation to farming practices. That is, if one reads the parable neoliterally, shifting focus away from Jesus's allegorical reading of it, then one begins to see that the narrative pits the nourishment needs of the peasants over against the nourishment needs of the birds. The parable depicts hungry birds scavenging for food as the sower throws seeds, somewhat recklessly, across his fields. In this sense, it is the hungry bird versus the tired, exploited, hungry human.[13] In the parable of the sower it is the hunger of the birds that is employed as a means of critiquing the evil, satanic practices of the Roman imperial economic and tax systems—a hunger that leads to the characterizing of the birds *as symbolic Satan*.

Reading with a Sibling Hermeneutic:
Experiencing Birds and Peasants in Solidarity

And yet, thinking ecocritically with and for the birds, the parable depicts them simply being birds, eating when seed is thrown, acting on the need to survive in a harsh landscape where most environmental resources have been plundered away by the greedy and exploitative economic and agrarian

---

12. Braidotti (2018, 71; see also 60) alternatively calls deep bioegalitarianism a "deep *zoe*-egalitarianism between humans and animals. The vitality of their bond is based on sharing this planet, territory, or environment on terms that are no longer so clearly hierarchical, nor self-evident." Here and throughout I use the term *zoe-egalitarianism* to recognize the shift in Braidotti's own approach, though when citing Braidotti I will leave her original terminology.

13. One could also argue, viewed from the perspective of the birds, that the scene depicts not a destitute gardener or farmer but rather a human *feeding* the birds. If one puts oneself in the feet, or rather claws, of the birds, one sees a human throwing seed in the air, is if to say, "Come and get it, hungry ones. Come get your breakfast. The early bird gets the seed."

practices of the Roman Empire. As Hughes (2014, 110–28, especially 121–28) argues extensively, poor husbandry and farming practices, oppressive taxation leading to extensive depletion of land resources, harmful military practices, monocultural production, and overgrazing, among other issues prompted by the Roman Empire, led to severe agricultural decline and a lack of access to natural resources for nonhuman animals. This led to a lack of food for wild creatures such as this parable's birds, and thus the persecution of these wild winged creatures due to their competition for resources with humans and domesticated animals alike (94).[14] That is, the birds that come swooping down on the field, doing so simply to sustain themselves, are responding to the same oppressive problems caused by the Roman Empire that wreak havoc on the peasant farmers and their companion species alike.[15] In this sense, the birds are more like the peasant farmers than they are like the Roman Empire, and that is where the fissure of the metaphoric use of birds in Jesus's parable ruptures. As Susan McHugh (2009, 491) notes, "Contrived metaphoric breakdowns and other ostentatiously mismanaged animal representations invite critique," since they contain "[built-]in gaps, fissures, or ruptures," and Jesus's metaphoric use of the birds in the parable of the sower is no exception.

While the parable may have been used to critique the Roman Empire, this was through using birds as a didactic tool, associating them with the evil and satanic forces of the Roman Empire; meanwhile, outside the para-

---

14. In my region of southern California this looks, contemporarily speaking, like coyotes wandering the streets of suburbia while household pets disappear, which in turn leads to a particular ending for those coyotes.

15. Issues surrounding resources are greatly important to scholars of critical animal studies, race/ethnicity, and the postcolonial. For example, colonized groups (here peasants) often have their land and resources stripped away, leaving a dearth of resources available, for which they are pitted against their nonhuman animal counterparts to fend for themselves for what little is left. In these situations, the human and nonhuman colonized subjects are often imagined as animals looking to fulfill their basest needs. In turn, this causes resentment by the colonized subjects for their nonhuman animal Others, thus reinstilling a sense of human/animal binary among the marginalized groups—human and nonhuman alike. In this scene, it leads to the birds being imagined as Satan. For more on this approach, see Huggan and Tiffin 2010, especially 18. This issue, of course, has its roots in previous approaches to marginalization and oppression and the way power brokers pit groups against each other in competition for carefully controlled resources and power (e.g., Ruether 1972; Guenther 2012, 51). For more on the term "companion species," see Haraway 2003, 2008, and for a brief summary of the term, see Calarco 2021, 48–51.

bolic and allegorical world, outside the empire of the sign and back in the real world, the experience of birds in antiquity was more in line with peasant farmers—abused, exploited, marginalized, and taken advantage of. The lived experience of these birds matches the lived experience of the farmers, a lived experience that Jesus could have recognized as a Jewish peasant himself and should have taken into account when constructing his anti-imperial parable. Jesus, in critiquing the Roman Empire, loses sight of the full magnitude of the empire's destructive practices and how those practices shaped and affected the lives of the peasants and birds alike, each attempting to survive in a harsh landscape with little to offer. A deep *zoe*-egalitarian turn away from these practices would have seen the lived experience of peasant farmers as on a par with the winged creatures that inhabit Jesus's parable. It would have seen them as companion species, as co-constitutive Others, as *siblings* within the kin-dom, each in the thick of it. Braidotti (2018, 72) argues for a deep *zoe*-egalitarianism, a recognition that animals and we humans (as animals) are in this together and our bond is "based on sharing this planet, territory, or environment on terms that are no longer so clearly hierarchical"[16]—a deep *zoe*-egalitarianism that Jesus constructs in the next parable to be analyzed, that of the mustard seed.

Jesus's Parable of the Mustard Seed: Birds as Birds, or as the Nations

> He also said, "With what can we compare the kingdom of God, or what parable will we use for it? It is like a mustard seed, which, when sown upon the ground, is the smallest of all the seeds on earth; yet when it is sown it grows up and becomes the greatest of all shrubs, and puts forth large branches, so that the birds of the air can make nests in its shade." (Mark 4:30–32)

While most previous scholarship focuses on the initial words of the Markan Jesus,[17] dealing solely with the kingdom of God (*tēn basileian tou*

---

16. A solidarity that comes to displaced expression in the baptismal scene, in which the power that will propel Jesus through his mission is symbolized by none other than a pigeon.

17. Studies on the parable of the mustard seed do not vary as greatly as that of the sower. Most analysis revolves around what the parable means and what the use of the mustard seed represents. See Perkins 2002; Marcus 2000, 324; Collins 2007, 255–56; Funk 1973; Scott 1981, 71–73; Schellenberg 2009.

theou) and the growth of the mustard plant, most scholars largely ignore the final stretch of the parable: the birds of the air/heavens taking refuge in the branches of the mustard plant. That said, some scholars do comment on Jesus's statement about the birds, interpreting them in one of two ways: as birds being birds, and thus not needing extensive comment, and as a representation of all the nations taking refuge within the kingdom of God. For both Adela Yarbro Collins (2007) and Ryan Schellenberg (2009), there is not enough evidence to read the birds as anything more than birds resting in the shade of the mustard shrub, as a part of the scenery—birds as birds. Yet, other scholars comment on and analyze the rhetorical use of birds, reflecting on how the ancient audience may have understood what the Markan Jesus was pointing to in his comment at the end of the parable. While the parable could have been complete without this addendum, alluding to the large nature of the kingdom of God and its insignificant or paltry beginnings, the addition of Jesus's statement on the "birds of the air" (or more precisely, the "birds of the heavens," *ta peteina tou ouranou*) prompts the audience to understand the kingdom of God as one that provides shelter and shade—one that protects against outside elements. For both Pheme Perkins (2002) and Joel Marcus (2000), the birds that take shelter in the shade of the parabolic mustard shrub are not mere birds-as-birds but rather symbolize the ancient inclusive roots of the Israelite faith, where the nations (*ta ethnē*) are brought in and given shelter by God.

Thus, one sees a potential for two options for the birds within the Markan parable of the mustard seed: birds-as-birds, finding shade under the branches of the mustard to make nests in, yet being written out of commentaries and biblical scholarship, or birds as a symbolic stand-in for their human counterparts, for gentiles being brought into the kingdom of God. As with the parable of the sower, I will once again take my cue from Braidotti, resisting the empire of the sign, reading the parable neoliterally while allowing the birds to function as birds as a means of deciphering the logic of the parable and human/nonhuman animal relations within it. In this sense, I will read with Collins and Schellenberg, allowing the birds to be birds, yet I will further their analysis by taking seriously the nonhuman animals in the scene—the *peteina*.

In my analysis of the parable of the sower, I made clear that the nourishment needs of the birds are not taken into account by Jesus. Rather, the birds are set up as symbolic representatives of Satan, symbolizing the evil and extractive nature of the Roman Empire. In this parable Jesus performs an astonishing *zoe*-egalitarian pivot where not only is the birds' need for shade taken into account; it is wholly accepted and used as a means for propping up the *basileia tou theou* as a place of refuge and irenic possibility. That is, like their human counterparts, who cannot last long in the baking sun of the Mediterranean climate, in this scene Jesus portrays the birds' comparable need for shelter from the Mediterranean sun. The question then arises: Why set up shop in the shade of the mustard plant? As Perkins points out, any gardener will be able to point out the unlikelihood of seeing a bird nesting in a mustard plant.[18] From a horticultural and ornithological standpoint, the parable's construction is nonsensical. Birds in their natural habitat and state would not nest or rest in the mustard plant. Yet, in his work on the environmental impact and problems caused by the Greeks and Romans, Hughes notes the massive deforestation project caused by the technological breakthroughs in antiquity. He notes that the amount of lumber needed for the projects of the Greeks and more so the Romans was monumental. The major Greek and Roman monuments fueled great destruction and—set alongside the daily need for "fuels in ancient households, public facilities such as baths, and industries, producing heat and light," as well as the need to clear land for agriculture—created an intense need for and extraction of timber (Hughes 2014, 69, and more broadly 68–87). The impacts of this major deforestation were many, ranging from the creation of deserts where forests once stood, to erosion, siltation, flooding, and drought, among other major climactic shifts.[19] All this led to the loss of habitat for the nonhuman animals that inhabited these nature spaces. This, of course, had an impact on how and where birds nested, and one could imagine seeing birds beginning to nest in a mustard plant where once stood their forest habitat, Mediterranean scrubland, or other shrubs.[20] In this regard it appears that Jesus is taking into account the lived experience of the birds in this parable, using

---

18. "Building nests in the bush? 'Never seen that,' the gardener remarks" (Perkins 2002, 312).

19. As Cohen points out in this volume, some of our ancient contexts parallel modern deforestation and changing wildlife habitats, and this is no different.

20. This, of course, would give new meaning to Jesus's reference to the cedars of Lebanon. What would one do with this reference if the cedars no longer stood, having been used as lumber for the purposes of the empire? Here we see overlap with Waters's contribution to this volume on Jer 9, which highlights the results of great land degradation in Judah, where the birds have fled their usual environments. Well, they have to end up somewhere if they flee, right? In this case, it appears it was to the shelter of a mustard plant.

that lived experience, accepting the notion that the birds, along with their human counterparts, need access to shade in order to survive in a harsh, unforgiving world, even more so when one's home, one's habitat, has been disrupted or destroyed.[21]

Taking a Deep *Zoe*-Egalitarian Turn: Siblings in the Struggle to Survive

When reading the parable of the mustard seed alongside the parable of the sower[22] and thinking about each in relation to *real birds*, by attempting a neoliteral reading of each story, a distinct contrast unfolds. Read neoliterally, the parable of the mustard seed indicates an abrupt about-face by Jesus in relation to his winged words, where he accepts the notion that birds have needs too. While it appears that the need for food in the parable of the sower *was not* considered (and was even used as a means of deriding the birds and their symbolic counterparts, the Roman Empire), the need for shelter *was* considered. In this sense, it appears that the Jesus character constructed in this narrative (whose relationship to the historical Jesus is necessarily oblique) has himself taken a deep *zoe*-egalitarian turn, seeing the needs of the birds on a par with the needs of humans, understanding that we are all in this together, siblings in the struggle to survive, siblings in the kin-dom. Birds *as* birds need rest, too, a place in the shade, where they can nest and continue in life. While no scholars point to this as a conclusion for the parable, a neoliteral reading of the passage opens that door.

Conclusion: Mark's Aviary as a Didactic Tool and Symbol

Using critical animal studies to explore and analyze the two avian parables in Mark's Gospel provides insight into how the gospel's author employs our feathered friends, and as Jacob Evers notes in this volume, returns one to

---

21. In a tip of the hat to Waters's contribution to this volume, a recognition of the interconnectedness of the earth community. In a similar, yet non-neoliteral reading of the passage, Hendricks (2011, 119) declares that the "significance of the mustard seed for Jesus' parabolic purposes ... is that despite its devalued stature and its lack of commercial value in such settings, the mustard plant offers what traditionally valued plants do not: a home to those whom Jesus calls 'the birds of the air,' those without fields of their own or who, for whatever reasons, are unable to care for themselves."

22. A practice that is likely intended, as they are separated by just ten verses, and each employs motifs of sowing and birds.

the question of whether an allegorical reading may be the most useful for reflection, exposing the enshrined human interests that underlie biblical texts and interpretation. Not only does one see that the Markan Jesus uses birds to think with; one sees that this use of birds illustrates multiplicity in the way that birds were understood and/or interpreted in the ancient world. That is, birds were thought of as associates of the evil empire, and thus their nourishment needs were not taken into account, yet birds were also protected under the shade of the *basileia tou theou*, where their need to avoid the baking Mediterranean sun was justified and even celebrated as a means of propping up the kin-dom of God—they became siblings within God's kin-dom. In these readings one sees the potential of a neo-literal approach and that approach's ability to unpack the human/animal relationships, assumptions, and dynamics that are exhibited within biblical narrative(s) and their subsequent interpretations. This method leads to a *zoe*-egalitarian ethic that enables the interpreter to critically engage biblical text(s) with an ecocritical method and ethic—to see that human and nonhuman animals alike are in this together, siblings in the struggle to survive. The need to move beyond the empire of the sign, to move beyond nonhuman animals as mere didactic tools, is the foundation for seeing animals as animals, not just symbolic representations or metaphorical stand-ins for Other(ed) humans. That is, recognizing that there are no (re)presentations of birds for birds' sake in the gospel allows one to critically engage and ecocritically reengage these narratives. Even when analyzing birds represented as birds, one sees that they are in fact feathered constructions for the purpose of teaching the audience a lesson—a lesson one can look beyond to see the human/animal relationships constructed within the parables.

There is much to be gained by taking birds as birds seriously in the Gospel of Mark, and Mark's aviary (1:9–11; 11:15–19; 14:26–31, 68–72) is ripe for further analysis and exploration in the vein of critical animal studies—as is the rest of Mark's bestiary. Though Mark's creaturely world has already begun to be explored (Moore 2011; Jeong 2023), there is still plenty of work to do that both takes into account the methodological focus of animal studies and addresses interdisciplinary approaches to animality and Mark, including work around animality and race/ethnicity, postcolonial theory, gender, sexual orientation, disability, class, and socioeconomic status, among other analytic trajectories. Mark's bestiary, as well as the rest of the biblical bestiary, is ripe for exploration and interrogation.

However, I want to return briefly to aspects of these constructions that speak to the contemporary world humans inhabit alongside our nonhuman animal counterparts. These readings make clear that, too often, humans ignore the plight of nonhuman animals in the midst of land degradation as well as land and wildlife depletion. Moreover, humans portray animal Others as the enemy. Yes, coyotes roaming the streets of suburban Southern California are a distinct reality—same with bears and wolves reaching into our neighborhoods as they look for food, or birds turning to farm-fields for sustenance. Yet, we all know the problem is larger than that. Deforestation is one thing. Monoculture farming is another. But the havoc of climate change and its far-reaching consequences are, well, somewhat unconscionable. Just ask Cody Petterson, who has been attempting to fight the deforestation of the Cuyamaca Forest, a place I used to camp at during my undergraduate years and where we enjoyed the snow next to the lake, snow that now falls less often and in decreasing amounts (Rannard 2019). Petterson worked, alongside various agencies, for fifteen years to restore the conifer forest, yet in April 2019 broke down at the realization that a beetle was now destroying the trees he was attempting to save, trees that could have survived if it not for prolonged drought—deforestation on a massive scale (Petterson 2019). Yet, that beetle, one must be reminded, was and is not Satan. Neither are the birds of the fields, the bears of backyards, or the coyotes of cities. Neither, of course, are the tired *human* immigrant kin who cross the southern border to work fields and who, time and again, are abused, exploited, marginalized, taken advantage of, and portrayed as predators and animals (much like the peasant farmers of the ancient world and this Markan parable). They were pushed out of their environment and home context by the effects of city sprawl, global climate change, and loss of water access and rights, all effects that folks north of the border caused and that all feel the effects of.

These readings and situations remind us that a *zoe*-egalitarian approach to biblical interpretation *and* living posits that we should not pit ourselves against nature but rather realize that our experience, as we confront climate change, is actually more in line with our animal siblings than we may realize. Because, after all, we are all in this together, and wherever we go, there they are: our nonhuman animal Others.

Works Cited

Bach, Rebecca Ann. 2018. *Birds and Other Creatures in Renaissance Literature: Shakespeare, Descartes, and Animal Studies*. New York: Routledge.
Boggs, Colleen Glenney. 2009. "Emily Dickinson's Animal Pedagogies." *PMLA* 124:533–41.

Braidotti, Rosi. 2009. "Animals, Anomolies, and Inorganic Others." *PMLA* 124:526–32.

———. 2011. *Nomadic Theory: The Portable Rosi Braidotti*. New York: Columbia University Press.

———. 2018. *The Posthuman*. Malden, MA: Polity.

Calarco, Matthew. 2015. *Thinking through Animals: Identity, Difference, Indistinction*. StBR. Stanford, CA: Stanford University Press.

———. 2021. *Animal Studies: The Key Concepts*. New York: Routledge.

Collins, Adela Yarbro. 2007. *Mark: A Commentary*. Hermeneia. Minneapolis: Fortress.

Derrida, Jacques. 2008. *The Animal That Therefore I Am*. Edited by Marie-Louise Mallet. Translated by David Wills. PCPS. New York: Fordham University Press.

Funk, Robert. 1973. "The Looking-Glass Tree Is for the Birds: Ezekiel 17:22–24; Mark 4:30–32." *Int* 27:3–9.

Guenther, Lisa. 2012. "Beyond Dehumanization: A Post-humanist Critique of Solitary Confinement." *JCAS* 10:46–68.

Haraway, Donna. 2003. *The Companion Species Manifesto: Dogs, People, and Significant Otherness*. Chicago: Prickly Paradigm.

———. 2008. *When Species Meet*. Minneapolis: University of Minnesota Press.

Hendricks, Obery M. 2011. *The Universe Bends toward Justice: Radical Reflections on the Bible, the Church, and the Body Politic*. Maryknoll, NY: Orbis.

Herzog, William R. 2012. "Sowing Discord: The Parable of the Sower (Mark 4:1–9)." *RevExp* 109:187–98.

Huggan, Graham, and Helen Tiffin. 2010. *Postcolonial Criticism: Literature, Animals, Environment*. New York: Routledge.

Hughes, J. Donald. 2014. *Environmental Problems of the Greeks and Romans: Ecology in the Ancient Mediterranean*. Baltimore: Johns Hopkins University Press.

Isasi-Díaz, Ada María. 2010. "Kin-dom of God: A Mujerista Proposal." Pages 171–89 in *In Our Own Voices: Latino/a Renditions of Theology*. Edited by Benjamín Valentín. Maryknoll, NY: Orbis.

Jeong, Dong Hyeon. 2023. *Embracing the Nonhuman in the Gospel of Mark*. SemeiaSt 102. Atlanta: SBL Press.

Marcus, Joel. 2000. *Mark 1–8: A New Translation with Introduction and Commentary*. AB 27. New York: Doubleday.

McHugh, Susan. "Literary Animal Agents." *PMLA* 124:487–95.

McKenzie, Alyce M. 2007. *The Parables for Today*. Louisville: Westminster John Knox.

Moore, Stephen D. 2011. "Why There Are No Humans or Animals in the Gospel of Mark." Pages 71–94 in *Mark as Story: Retrospect and Prospect*. Edited by Kelly R. Iverson and Christopher W. Skinner. RBS 65. Atlanta: Society of Biblical Literature.

Mynott, Jeremy. 2018. *Birds in the Ancient World: Winged Words*. Oxford: Oxford University Press.

Perkins, Pheme. 2002. "Mark 4:30–34." *Int* 56:311–13.

Petterson, Cody. 2019. "Requiem for the Trees." San Diego County Democrats for Environmental Action, 22 April. https://tinyurl.com/SBL06107i.

Pütz, Babette. 2014. "Good to Laugh With: Animals in Comedy." Pages 61–72 in *The Oxford Handbook of Animals in Classical Thought and Life*. Edited by Gordon Lindsay Campbell. Oxford: Oxford University Press.

Rannard, Georgina. 2019. "Climate Change: One Man's Fight to Save a California Tree." 19 May. https://tinyurl.com/SBL06107j.

Ruether, Rosemary Radford. 1972. *Liberation Theology: Human Hope Confronts Christian History and American Power*. New York: Paulist.

Schellenberg, Ryan S. 2009. "Kingdom as Contaminant: The Role of Repertoire in the Parables of the Mustard Seed and the Leaven." *CBQ* 71:527–43.

Scott, Bernard Brandon. 1981. *Jesus, Symbol-Maker for the Kingdom*. Philadelphia: Fortress.

Tipton, Brian. 2018. "Hummingbird Visitor, February 15th, 2018." YouTube, 15 February, 0:14. https://tinyurl.com/SBL06107h.

———. 2022. "The Markan Bestiary: Ecology, Animality, and the Second Gospel." PhD diss., Drew University.

Van Eck, Ernest, and Meshack Mandla Mashinini. 2016. "The Parables of Jesus as Critique on Food Security Systems for Vulnerable Households in Urban Townships." *HvTSt* 72:1–10.

The Pasture and the Battlefield: Domesticated Animals in the Song of Songs

Jared Beverly

No other book in the Hebrew Bible demonstrates so much celebration of sexuality, so much freedom for a woman, and such a rich menagerie of animal images as the Song of Songs. There are indeed positives here: Hendrik Viviers (2001) calls the Song a book of "eco-delight," and many feminist scholars herald the Song's relative liberty for women. Cheryl Exum (2000, 25) points out that this book "can be hazardous to your critical faculties" due to its inviting sex positivity and seeming proto-feminist tendencies. But the story is not so simple, and interpreting the Song's evocative metaphorical imagery can get complicated quickly. As Exum (2005, 158) notes, "No scholarly consensus exists concerning what principles should be followed in interpreting the images." In his book on the Hebrew Bible and animal studies, Ken Stone (2017, 24) introduces into biblical studies Aaron Gross's (2015, 15) call for a "multifaceted, critical 'animal hermeneutics,'" that is, a study of how human animals interpret nonhuman animals as well as how they interpret themselves by means of those nonhuman animals. I propose that for the Song of Songs, replete as it is with animal metaphors, this animal hermeneutics is an especially valuable tool in understanding the poem, both in its original context and today.

In this essay, I examine the Song's domesticated animals, which include in particular sheep and goats (often treated together) as well as horses. Sheep and goats first appear in 1:7–8, which is one of many passages in the Song that relate a theme of one lover's searching and longing for the other. In verse 7 the woman asks,

Tell me, you whom my being loves,
Where do you graze?

> Where do you make your sheep lie down at noon?
> For why should I be like one who is veiled
> Beside the flocks of your friends?[1]

Verse 8 provides the man's reply:

> If you do not know for yourself,
> Most beautiful among women,
> Follow for yourself
> In the footprints of the sheep.
> And pasture your kids
> Beside the tents of the shepherds.

Here, one or both of the lovers are figured as shepherds, one looking for the other. Sheep and goats again appear in 4:1–2, toward the beginning of a poem in which the man is describing the woman:

> Your hair is like a flock of goats
> That is flowing from the mountain of Gilead
> Your teeth are like a flock of shorn ewes
> That are coming up from washing,
> All of which bear twins
> And none among them is bereaved of children.

These comparisons are repeated almost verbatim in another descriptive poem in 6:5–6. Finally, the horse appears in one brief but exegetically fascinating verse. In 1:9, the man says to the woman, "To a mare among the chariots of Pharaoh I compare you, my lover." Scholars constantly remark on the oddity of lovingly referring to one's romantic partner as a horse, but there may be some interesting things to unpack here.

With these sheep, goats, and horses in mind, these images can be read as, first, challenging the stability of the line dividing human from animal, as well as, second, challenging normative gender expectations. Finally, however, in spite of these positive critical moves, the Song's domesticated animal metaphors are still founded on the subjugation of these domestic animals and their use for human purposes. Though the book might be eco-delightful, the Song cannot be read simply as a pro-animal text—it is far more complex than that.

---

1. Unless otherwise noted, all translations are my own.

First, the structure of these metaphors is often unstable—it is frequently difficult to tell where the vehicle ends and the tenor begins. Human and animal blend together in these metaphors. Referring to the shepherding imagery of 1:7–8, Elaine James (2017, 36) says, "The young man becomes part of the landscape as he drives the flock, but in so doing he blends together with the sheep he cares for." Likewise, Yvonne Thöne (2017, 392) argues, "The Song's animal imagery has the effect of animalising the human as well as humanising the animal." Viviers (2001, 149) sees "humans 'becoming' Nature and Nature 'becoming' human." Such a blurring of lines could cohere well with what Matthew Calarco (2015, 56) calls the indistinction approach to animal ethics, which can allow one to "think about human beings and animals in deeply relational terms that permit new groupings and new differences to emerge, such that 'the human' is no longer the center or chief point of reference." The Song in this animal imagery recognizes the entanglement of human and nonhuman. In this vein, one also might recall Gilles Deleuze and Félix Guattari's concept of becoming-animal, in which the word *metaphor* no longer applies as it gives way to metamorphosis, as human becomes animal and animal becomes human (see Calarco and Atterton 2004, 99–100). The lines dividing human and nonhuman can get rather fuzzy.

Furthermore, domesticated animals can represent something of a middle ground between nature and culture and thus pose a challenge to this binary. For a horticultural comparison, as James (2017, 61) says of the Song's garden imagery, "while it is distinctly natural, is also distinctly cultural." Gardens take wild organisms and proceed to contain and fashion them for human purposes, and the Song's domesticated animals are no different. Sheep, goats, and horses were then and continue to be bred for the benefit of humans. They would not be what they are were it not for human intervention. At the same time, however, as animals, there will always be a wildness to them, an unpredictability in how they may cooperate with humans' bidding or resist their captivity and control by humans (Calarco 2015, 62). Unlike their wild counterparts, they live in close proximity to humans, and yet they are not humans. Under these circumstances of domestication, it is not always clear where culture ends and nature begins.

In addition to blurring the lines human and nonhuman and the lines of nature and culture, the Song's animal imagery can also be read as disrupting traditional gender hierarchies in ancient Yehud. This can be seen specifically in the placing of the woman in a role of greater authority or control than the man in the shepherding metaphor in 1:7–8 and the horse metaphor in 1:9. The shepherd imagery in Song 1:7-8, with its mentions of grazing and lying down, is frequently attributed sexual meaning; Tremper Longman (2001, 99-101), for instance, calls their union here a "tryst" and compares it to "playful, sensual game of hide-and-seek" (see also Pope 1977, 328-29; Fox 1985, 103; Exum 2005, 106-8). The lovers are meeting up outside civilization and its cultural expectations of propriety, free to explore their love in an idyllic and peaceful setting, one in which there is, as Jill Munro (1995, 87) says, "harmony between human and beast."

I have already observed that the boundaries between human and nonhuman here can be tricky to navigate, but scholars offer a number of possible interpretations to weather these waters with regard to these verses. Many commentators see the man alone as the shepherd here (e.g., Pope 1977, 329; Weems 1997, 385), and some suggest that *both* the man and the woman are depicted as shepherds in these verses (e.g., Ginsburg 1857, 136; Murphy 1990, 171; Munro 1995, 87-88). There is a grammatical oddity here, however, that leads other scholars to admit that there could be another interpretation. The woman's question to the man in 1:7—which the NRSV and most other modern translations render as something like "Where do you pasture your flock?"—actually has no direct object in the Hebrew. Most commentators suggest that the object "your flock" is implied here (e.g., Pope 1977, 328); perhaps the reader is meant to reasonably infer that sheep are being grazed here, or perhaps the object is just missing because poetry tends to be terse. However, because the Hebrew verb "pasture" or "graze" (r^ch) in actuality lacks an object, it is entirely feasible that, as James (2017, 36-37) notes, "the lover himself could be understood as the grazing animal" (see also Huwiler 1999, 252). In this reading, the woman's question to the man is *not* one shepherd asking another, "Where do you, as a shepherd, lead your flock to graze?" Instead, it could be a shepherd (the woman) asking a sheep (the man), "Where do you yourself, as a sheep, graze?" M. L. Case (2017, 173) points out that this intransitive use of the verb r^ch also appears in 2:17, where the man is imagined as a gazelle or deer that "grazes [r^ch] among the lilies." As Case notes, the use in 2:17 is frequently read as sexual innuendo, with the man's grazing indicating his oral pleasuring of the woman, and it is just as likely that r^ch in 1:7 should carry this same sexual subtext. Patrick Hunt (2008, 145) also acknowledges the possibility of this translation but goes further to ponder its interspecies implication. He is clearly uncomfortable with the possibility that this is a romantic scene between a shepherd and her sheep, deeming it "an almost unnatural copulation." Despite his reservations, though, as multiple commentators have pointed out, it is possible that the woman is imagining herself as a shepherd, loving the man whom she imagines as a sheep.

And if she is the shepherd and he the sheep, this clearly puts her in a position of authority over him. She, as his caretaker, controls his movements, leads him to food, and protects him from predators. Of course, when one considers the amorous context of the Song and the real-world work of those who work with animals, one might say she even intervenes in his breeding, recalling Jacob's breeding practices in Gen 30 as well as the interventions of modern farmed animal-husbandry practices. If she is his shepherd and he her sheep, then the text is imagining the woman with an unusual amount of power over the man.

Another metaphor of a domesticated animal, the horse, is applied to the woman in 1:9. This comparison troubles many modern commentators, who find it "bewildering" and strain to explain how calling one's lover a horse could possibly be complimentary (Garrett 2004, 144). It is perhaps easy to remark on "the beauty of the horse" in general, but identifying particular traits in one's lover as equine does not usually invite a positive response among Western readers today (Delitzsch 1891, 33). As a result, a number of scholars suggest that the poet's goal for this metaphor is not to provide a representation of her physical characteristics but rather to make a more conceptual connection. That is, it is not that she literally looks like a horse but rather that she bears herself with grace and nobility (Oettli 1889, 173), or perhaps that she is ordained in jewelry in 1:10–11 as a royal horse might be (Murphy 1981, 108–9).

These are not the only views, however. Marvin Pope (1970, 1977) is often credited with resurrecting for modern scholarship one interpretation, first seen in earlier rabbinic texts (e.g., Song. Rab. 1.9.2.2A–C; Avot R. Nat. 27; Pirqe R. El. 42), that positions this horse metaphor within the thought-world of the military. Horses in biblical texts are often associated with "military use" (Rimbach 1972, 146–48; see Exod 15:1, 21; Isa 2:7; 31:1; Jer 6:23; 46:9; 50:42; Ezek 38:4, 14; 39:20; Amos 4:10; Nah 3:2; Zech 10:3; Ps 20:8; Prov 21:31; Job 39:18–25), so perhaps the same usage is implied here in biblical love poetry. Pope suggests that only *stallions* were used in the Egyptian military to pull chariots, so the Song's mention of an Egyptian *mare* in 1:9 must be drawing on a military reference of a different sort. In his view, the mare plays a part in a defensive strategy, as she is set loose to distract the stallions and thus to trip up the opposing army's chariots (Pope 1977, 338–39). Pope grounds this reading in an Egyptian account in which a soldier killed this distracting mare, "thus preventing a debacle before the excited stallions could take out after the mare" (338). The meaning of the Song's horse metaphor, then, would be that in the same way that a mare in heat may distract stallions, so also the woman in the Song distracts the man with her attractiveness (Longman 2001, 103; LaCocque 1998, 78; Keel 1994, 57–58). This would not be the only place in the Song where she has such an effect on the man, as he claims to be overwhelmed by her gaze in 6:5. Elsewhere in the Hebrew Bible, there is a similar animal metaphor in Jer 2:24, where a male onager is used as a symbol of passion and lack of restraint.

In Pope's understanding of the horse metaphor, the woman has the potential to stop whole armies in their tracks. Figured as a horse, Carol Meyers (1986, 217) explains, she "does violence to the military effectiveness of the charioteers." While the Hebrew Bible is no stranger to women in military positions (e.g., Deborah in Judg 4–5), it is certainly not the most common role that women in these texts fulfill. The woman in this reading, then, is understood as a powerful force on the battlefield. The heat of estrus overcomes and disrupts the heat of battle. What is more, within this metaphor, the stallions (and with them, the man of the Song) are stripped of self-control as they are driven by hormones alone. In contrast to the traditional Western line of thinking that portrays men as guided by reason and women as guided by emotion and their bodies, it is the males here who are positively overtaken by desire and hormones. As a result of this horse imagery, the woman, whose presence overwhelms her beloved, is depicted in a way that according to Meyers runs "counter to stereotypical gender conceptions."

Nevertheless, in spite of the blurred boundaries that these metaphors might produce, and in spite of the surprising gender dynamics they entail, the Song's animal imagery still provides little freedom to the actual animals imagined here; in fact, these metaphors depend on the ownership and subjugation of domesticated animals. This is not to say that domestication in and of itself is wholly bad. Animal studies scholars have shown that domestication is not simply a one-sided exchange in which one party dominates the other, as it is often characterized. Donna Haraway (2003, 32) in particular, one of Calarco's (2015, 51) indistinction theorists, speaks of "co-constitutive companion species," that is, species that become what they are in relation to other species. In her example, it is not the case that humans merely trapped wolves and over time formed dogs out of them; rather, humans and dogs coevolved, each affecting and forming the other.

Humans would not be who they are without dogs, which evolved alongside us. Furthermore, Stone applies her concept of companion species to biblical studies in describing the animals in the stories about Jacob and Esau in Genesis. Without the goat skin to fool Isaac, for instance, Jacob could not have stolen his brother's blessing. A goat therefore has a profound effect on Jacob's future, and I have already mentioned Jacob's own breeding practices that certainly affected his flock's future. Stone (2017, 28) comments, "Israel's narrative emergence is inextricably intertwined with domesticated animals." In the Hebrew Bible's stories, the Israelite ancestors and their animals form companion species, each influencing and forming the other in their relations.

The Song of Songs would be a much less colorful series of poems without its animals, and clearly these animals have shaped the thoughts of the poet and the world this poet inhabits. Nonhuman animals provide these lovers a rich vocabulary of imagery in describing each other's bodies and desires. Without sheep, goats, and horses, the Song of Songs as we know it simply would not exist. However, even as it is possible to read moments of recognition for animals and even indistinction in the aforementioned verses, the metaphors of the Song typically use these creatures in ways that emphasize merely their use for human purposes rather than any intrinsic value they might have. The reader is never privy to the perspectives of the Song's beasts—instead, domesticated animals appear merely as beings that serve human functions.

In 4:1–2, for instance, goats and sheep stand in as symbols for the woman's flowing hair and white teeth. The latter in particular are signified with reference to a product from the sheep—her teeth are "like a flock of shorn ewes." The presence of these sheep, therefore, is dependent only on the wool they can provide to humans. Earlier, regarding 1:7–8, if one accepts the interpretive possibility of reading the man as sheep to the woman's shepherd, then one would perhaps have an instance of imagining an animal's perspective. As I mentioned, however, this possibility has been noted by relatively few people; most scholars do not follow this view and instead cast either the man or both lovers as shepherds. In this more common reading, the focus is entirely on the animals' caretaker(s) rather than on the animals themselves.

The horse metaphor is even more precarious for the animal. While the shepherding imagery places the characters in a serene pasture, if Pope's insight on Egyptian military customs is correct, then the horse metaphor imagines the lovers on a battlefield. The humans who serve as the tenor of this metaphor do not appear to endanger each other in 1:9, but the vehicle, the mare that serves as a distraction for an opposing army's hormonal stallions, is risking her life. Indeed, the Egyptian source on which Pope (1977, 338) bases his reading says the offending mare is killed. What signifies Eros for the lovers eventually spells Thanatos for the mare. In addition, while it might be true that this metaphor figures the woman as strong and overpowering, Thöne (2017, 397) points out that the mare is not simply interfering with human warfare of her own accord—she is dominated and directed by soldiers who care for battle tactics more than her own well-being.

The Song's instrumental portrait of domesticated animals under human control is particularly ironic given the meaning that some scholars give them. Specifically, many scholars point to these animals' associations with rural settings, to places apart from the strictures of city life. For instance, Hunt (2008, 141) suggests that this imagery "show[s] nature without interference from a human conscience, where innocent and wild creatures are unencumbered by sexual inhibitions that impede humans." What then can represent freedom from the sexual norms of culture for the human characters is founded on the domestication and ownership of nonhuman animals. The lovers can frolic and play without the watchful eye of authority, but these metaphors presume human authority over animals. Moreover, while the poet often blurs human and animal together, and while the boundary between nature and culture can become fuzzy, the very existence of these metaphors relies on a very clear divide between human and animal, between owner and owned. Without these preexisting discourses of domestication and without the beings whose lives are controlled by this discourse, these metaphors would not exist.

One can see a similar dynamic at play with the woman's greater degree of agency in the Song. Her role as a shepherd, this role that gives her authority over other beings, is again dependent on the domestication and ownership of nonhuman animals. This is not to pit women's liberation against animal liberation—if Carol Adams's (1990) work has taught us anything, it is that the fate of women and animals is intertwined in a patriarchal world that consumes meat and sex. The Hebrew Bible is no stranger to this entanglement (e.g., Bathsheba as an eaten lamb in 2 Sam 12). In the case of the Song's domesticated animals, however, it remains the case that they are subjugated. One sees, again ironically, that human freedom is expressed by means of animal subjugation.

Where, then, does this leave readers? The Song of Songs is not a feminist text; it is not an anthem to sexual anarchy; it is also not an animal liberation manifesto. Thus, for the reader concerned with nonhuman animals, the Song provides a complicated picture of gender and species constructions that can be read as unstable, but simultaneously these constructions are based on the human control of and domination over other animals.

Works Cited

Adams, Carol J. 1990. *The Sexual Politics of Meat: A Feminist-Vegetarian Critical Theory*. New York: Continuum.

Calarco, Matthew. 2015. *Thinking through Animals: Identity, Difference, Indistinction*. StBr. Stanford, CA: Stanford University Press.

Calarco, Matthew, and Peter Atterton, eds. 2004. *Animal Philosophy: Essential Readings in Continental Thought*. New York: Continuum.

Case, M. L. 2017. "Cunning Linguists: Oral Sex in the Song of Songs." VT 67:171–86.

Delitzsch, Franz. 1891. *Commentary on the Song of Songs and Ecclesiastes*. Edinburgh: T&T Clark.

Exum, J. Cheryl. 2000. "Ten Things Every Feminist Should Know about the Song of Songs." Pages 24–35 in *The Song of Songs*. Edited by Athalya Brenner and Carole R. Fontaine. Sheffield: Sheffield Academic.

———. 2005. *Song of Songs: A Commentary*. Louisville: Westminster John Knox.

Fox, Michael V. 1985. *The Song of Songs and the Ancient Egyptian Love Songs*. Madison: University of Wisconsin Press.

Garrett, Duane A. 2004. "The Song of Songs." Pages 1–265 in *Song of Songs/Lamentations*. Nashville: Nelson.

Ginsburg, Christian D. 1857. *The Song of Songs, Translated from the Original Hebrew, with a Commentary, Historical and Critical*. London: Longman, Brown, Green, Longmans, and Roberts.

Gross, Aaron S. 2015. *The Question of the Animal and Religion: Theoretical Stakes, Practical Implications*. New York: Columbia University Press.

Haraway, Donna J. 2003. *The Companion Species Manifesto: Dogs, People, and Significant Otherness*. Chicago: Prickly Paradigm.

Hunt, Patrick. 2008. *Poetry in the Song of Songs: A Literary Analysis*. New York: Lang.

Huwiler, Elizabeth. 1999. "The Song of Songs." Pages 219–90 in *Proverbs, Ecclesiastes, Song of Songs*. Peabody, MA: Hendrickson.

James, Elaine T. 2017. *Landscapes of the Song of Songs: Poetry and Place*. Oxford: Oxford University Press.

Keel, Othmar. 1994. *The Song of Songs*. Minneapolis: Fortress.

LaCocque, André. 1998. *Romance She Wrote: A Hermeneutical Essay on Song of Songs*. Harrisburg, PA: Trinity Press International.

Longman, Tremper, III. 2001. *Song of Songs*. Grand Rapids: Eerdmans.

Meyers, Carol. 1986. "Gender Imagery in the Song of Songs." *HAR* 10:209–23.

Munro, Jill M. 1995. *Spikenard and Saffron: The Imagery of the Song of Songs*. Sheffield: Sheffield Academic.

Murphy, Roland E. 1981. *Wisdom Literature: Job, Proverbs, Ruth, Canticles, Ecclesiastes, and Esther*. Grand Rapids: Eerdmans.

———. 1990. *The Song of Songs: A Commentary on the Book of Canticles or the Song of Songs*. Minneapolis: Fortress.

Oettli, Samuel. 1889. "Das Hohelied Und Die Klagelieder." Pages 153–224 in *Die Poetischen Hagiographen (Buch Hiob, Prediger Salomo, Hohelied Und Klagelieder)*. Nördlingen: Beck'schen Buchhandlung.

Pope, Marvin H. 1970. "A Mare in Pharaoh's Chariotry." *BASOR* 200:56–61.

———. 1977. *Song of Songs: A New Translation with Introduction and Commentary*. New Haven: Yale University Press.

Rimbach, James A. 1972. "Animal Imagery in the Old Testament." PhD diss., Johns Hopkins University.

Stone, Ken. 2017. *Reading the Hebrew Bible with Animal Studies*. Stanford, CA: Stanford University Press.

Thöne, Yvonne Sophie. 2017. "Female Humanimality: Animal Imagery in the Song of Songs and Ancient Near Eastern Iconography." *Journal for Semitics* 25:389–408.

Viviers, Hendrik. 2001. "Eco-delight in the Song of Songs." Pages 143–54 in *The Earth Story in Wisdom Traditions*. Edited by Norman C. Habel and Shirley Wurst. Sheffield: Sheffield Academic.

Weems, Renita J. 1997. "The Song of Songs." *NIB* 5:361–434.

The Donkey as Tamasoaalii: A *Fāgogo* Reading of Balaam and the Donkey in Numbers 22:22–35

Brian Fiu Kolia

Fāgogo: A Samoan Decolonial Pedagogy

Fāgogo is the Samoan art of storytelling. It invites listeners to a world of fantasy, a world where impossible feats are possible, where humans do extraordinary things, where humans and animals coexist in harmony. It is a coexistence that extends beyond the normalcy of the real world, as humans and animals converse and have relations. Yet, behind the mystical world of *fāgogo* lies a reality communicated through pedagogy. It ranges from the significance of cultural customs, to the moral fiber of Samoan village life, to the significance of animals, which in pre-Christian times were seen as equals, given respect reserved for chiefs, and worshiped as gods.

Fāgogo also points to a reality of lands and oceans that are being endangered due to rising sea levels and global warming. Indeed, *fāgogo* is a lived metaphor, and the one I tell in this essay is no different. *Fāgogo* is also decolonial, as it seeks to maneuver the mentality of its listeners away from the colonial attitudes of the islands being perceived as insignificant dots on the map, toward a macroscopic view of island existence, where immortal beings jump from island to island, hurling spears into outer space, while creator gods draw huge boulders out of the sea to create islands. This is the world of *fāgogo*.

Fāgogo as a Hermeneutical Lens

The aim of this chapter is to use *fāgogo* as a hermeneutical framework in order to highlight the pedagogical character of the story of Balaam and the donkey. The historicity of such stories is often questioned, which I believe misses the point of such tales. The art of storytelling is ignored when the real question should center on what it is these stories are trying to tell us and what sort of theological message they are pointing us toward. Stories like Balaam and the donkey communicate *a* truth as opposed to *the* truth.

In Samoan storytelling, *fāgogo* implies that the story is a *tala*. *Tala* can be a noun and a verb, and both forms are important here. As a noun, *tala* refers to the story itself. As a verb, *tala* means "to open" or "to unpack." So, when a *fāgogo* is told, it is a package layered with meanings that needs to be *tala*, to unpack, to unfold in order to unveil everything to be seen. So *tala* is not only story; it is also the act of telling the story. Let me elaborate on *tala*. The process of *tala* does not mean discarding the packaging, but like the presentation of an *ie toga* (a traditional Samoan "fine mat"), *tala* denotes the action of opening up, that is, to open so that the whole thing can be seen in its complete state. The packaging therefore is part of the final product. This is to expose the *tala* in order to give the opportunity to the storyteller to tell the whole story, for the audience to hear the whole story.

More importantly, *fāgogo* is decolonial, as it gives indigenous readers the opportunity to read the story in light of their own context, to highlight oppressive and colonizing voices, and thus raise their own questions of the text. The hope is that indigenous readers can locate the liberating message in the text (see Bible and Culture Collective 1995, 284). Significantly, *fāgogo* seeks to move beyond the Western binaries between human and nonhuman animals and tell stories of mutual flourishing. This aligns with the intentions of indistinction theorists such as Matthew Calarco (2015, 50), who states that "indistinction theorists attempt to develop ways of thinking about human beings, animals, and ethics in a manner that radically displaces human beings from the center of ethical reflection and that avoids many of the exclusions associated with lingering forms of anthropocentrism." Reading the text this way also allows for one to read the text from indigenous and native perspectives as a way of subverting Western perspectives. Colonial subjects are overtly and covertly pressured to forget their culture's stories and modes of thought. For Samoans, this pressure often came from European missionaries, who "made attempts to purge or suppress the more pagan elements of the ancient religion" (Peteru 2009, 380). However, as Aumua Clark Peteru continues, the missionaries "were not as successful in this regard and elements of the old religion survived and continue to persist in the modern Samoan mindset" (380–81).

The process of *tala* guides *fāgogo* for the storyteller. It is the process by which the hearers can approach the biblical text with the intent to see and hear the whole *tala*, as it unfolds.[1] Through this process of *tala*, one is also mindful of other possibilities for interpretation, as directed by the elements of the *fāgogo*. This may seem simple, but as Tui Atua Tupua Tamasese Efi (2003, 59) stresses, "it is not, because its value to the Samoan Culture is deep. Because it is the process of weaning, of nurturing, of sharing stories, values, rituals, beliefs, practices and language. It helped sustain and could still sustain a nation." This is the essence of *fāgogo*, for it is as Efi says, a process.

Here I will revisit the story of Balaam and the donkey to highlight the pedagogical significance of the story through a Samoan *fāgogo* known as the story of Tamasoaalii.[2] The story of Tamasoaalii is a tale from the Samoan village of Fagafau, where Pupu Luki, one of its legendary fishermen, went to fish the shark species known as the *naiufi*. Intriguingly, there are questions raised from this story that I wish to pursue in dialogue with the story of Balaam and the donkey. Can the story of Balaam and the donkey be read as *fāgogo*? Could we see the donkey as Tamasoaalii? The purpose of this chapter is to enhance the reading experience by canoeing past Western binaries between human and nonhuman animals so as to explore other possibilities beyond into a space where humans and nonhuman animals coexist in mutual flourishing. Such an approach follows the waves of an indistinction approach to the text, which seeks to tell alternative stories in order to hear marginalized voices. In doing so, I hope to shed further light on the relationship between the donkey and Balaam from a Samoan perspective.

Fāgogo: The Story of Tamasoaalii

On the Samoan island of Savaii, in the village of Fagafau, there lived the legendary fisherman Pupu Luki. He was renowned for fishing the shark species known as the *naiufi*. But fishing was of a special nature. Instead of trying to hunt the *naiufi* using fishing tools and weapons, the *naiufi* swims

---

1. I use the term *hearing* interchangeably with *reading* to account for the indigenous *readers* who, as is common in indigenous communities, are part of oral cultures.
2. In majority of cases in the Samoan language, like most Polynesian languages, there are no diphthongs like in the English language, so each vowel in this word is pronounced independently as Ta-ma-so-a-a-li-i.

close to shore to greet the fishermen and offer itself in honor of the village high chief.

The village held high hopes for Pupu Luki as he embarked on his fishing expedition. In support, Pupu's family and the village would hold prayer vigils to the gods, to grant protection for Pupu. As mentioned, this was not fishing that involved "luring, trapping and killing mercilessly" (Efi 2014, 46). Rather, it involved "inviting the fish to honour the village chief's mana by being an equal adversary and then ultimately by gifting himself to the chief to help bolster or sustain the chief's status" (46).

So, as Pupu and his companion went out to sea, they would leave close to midnight. Pupu would use a shark rattle made from coconut shells tied to a branch from an orange tree to attract the *naiufi*. Pupu would put the rattle into the water and twist it around to resemble a moving bonito while chanting:

> *Afio maia oe le manaia*
> Welcome to you the *manaia*—the head of the untitled men's guild
>
> *Afio maia oe le tausala*
> Welcome to you the *tausala*—the head of the ladies' guild
>
> *Afio maia oe le tamasoaalii*
> Welcome to you the *tamasoaalii*
>
> *O loo ou faatali atu*
> I await your coming. (Efi 2014, 46–47)

In these words, the *naiufi* is perceived by Pupu as his equal. The *naiufi* is being greeted as the *manaia* or the *tausala*, who are the head and finest of the *aumaga* (untitled men's guild) or *aualuma* (women's guild) respectively, who are afforded enormous respect in the village. With this, the *naiufi* swims towards the boat, as if the *naiufi* is respectful. In a similar manner, Pupu places a lasso around the *naiufi*'s neck with enough slack so as to not capsize the boat should the *naiufi* struggle.

For the whole night, there is a struggle between Pupu and the *naiufi* as the *naiufi* senses the rope around its neck, and in the struggle the *naiufi* leads Pupu and his companion on a chase across the ocean for many hours. Ultimately, the *naiufi* tires from the struggle and succumbs to Pupu's persistence. During this whole ordeal, Pupu is never the aggressor, as he only responds to the *naiufi*'s struggle. Pupu is always respectful, and as the *naiufi* is eventually caught, the village acknowledges the "worthy struggle" as they understand that the *naiufi* is a gift from the god Tagaloa (Efi 2014, 48). As a result, the village honor the *naiufi* with the title Tamasoaalii (lit. *Tama* [young man] *Soa* [aide] *Alii* [high chief]), meaning "the aide to the high chief." The story speaks of the interconnectedness between humans and sea life/animals. It also highlights the importance of service, respect and honor, as the service by Tamasoaalii provides a key lesson in service for young women and men in the village.

The story of the *naiufi* is therefore a lived metaphor, as the name Tamasoaalii epitomizes the notion of *fa'aaloalo* (respect) in village life but also in the practice of culture in Samoa and in diasporic communities. In one such custom, when a distinguished guest or *aiga* is honored with Samoan gifts, a representative, usually a *taule'ale'a* (young, untitled male), of the recipient in response would honor the gifts by chanting the names of the four ancient kingly families of Samoa (known as the *Tafa'ifa*). Included alongside those four royal families is the name of the *naiufi*: Tamasoaalii. The *taule'ale'a* would be standing outside chanting the name of the *naiufi*: *Tamasoaalii e, Tamasoalii e!* (Oh Tamasoaalii, oh Tamasoaalii!) (Tauiliili 2010, 34).

Reading Numbers 22:22–35 as *Fāgogo*

I want to reread Num 22:22–35 in the manner of *fāgogo*, in order to focus readers' attention on its pedagogical significance, much in the same way the *fāgogo* of Tamasoaalii depicts. I seek to *tala* the *tala* of Num 22:22–35, to highlight some of the themes that can be heard. Specifically, I wish to highlight service (*tautua*), respect (*fa'aaloalo*), and the significance of chants.

Service: *Tautua*

Tautua is the Samoan word for service and toil. The service varies from hard labor in the plantations, to fishing, to serving the *matai* (chiefs) in various tasks and situations. *Tautua* is a significant part of Samoan life, as *tautua* is performed in every facet of life in the village, from the family (*aiga*), to the village (*nu'u*), to the church (*lotu*). In Samoa, *tautua* is performed in honor of the *matai* (chiefs), who consist of *alii* (high chief) and *tulafale* (orator). *Tautua* also consists of sacrifice and commitment of the highest order. The *fāgogo* of Tamasoalii, however, teaches that *tautua* is not restricted to humans, as nonhuman animals and sea creatures also perform *tautua*. As depicted in the story of Tamasoaalii, the *naiufi* performs *tautua* in honor of the high chief. The *naiufi* in its *tautua* performs also the greatest sacrifice, by offering itself to the high chief.

The sacrificial undertones of *tautua* might be construed as being oppressive, particularly to women and marginalized groups within the village context. In the Samoan village, *tautua* is performed mainly by able-bodied young men, as much of the work consists of hard physical labor. However, *tautua* in the village context must also be understood within the context of *feagaiga* (roughly translated as "covenant"). In the Samoan context, *feagaiga* refers to the most elementary expression of *fa'aaloalo* (commonly translated as "respect"), that is, the kinship relationship between brother and sister. *Feagaiga* is also used to refer to either party of that relationship: the brother is the *feagaiga* to the sister, the sister is *feagaiga* to the brother. The protection of the *feagaiga* is paramount in this relationship, and so in the village context the brother must respect and protect his sister at all costs. Thus, most of the physical labor is left to the brother to perform, while the sister-*feagaiga* is assigned lighter house duties. In essence, the performance of *tautua* should be framed by *feagaiga*, given that *feagaiga* represents the fundamental demonstration of *fa'aaloalo*.

In reading the Numbers story as *fāgogo*, the donkey also performs *tautua*. However, the value of the donkey's *tautua* is not immediately acknowledged by Balaam, and one wonders what would have happened if only Balaam had treated his relationship with the donkey as *feagaiga*. The donkey reminds Balaam of her *tautua* in 22:30 when she claims: "Am I not your donkey, which you have ridden all your life to this day? Have I been in the habit of treating you this way?"[3] The donkey's bray eventually leads to her *tautua* being recognized by Balaam. Not only does the donkey provide endless service in carrying Balaam, but she also provides *tautua* through protection. It was the donkey who saw the angel of YHWH, yet Balaam and his two servants remained oblivious. Ironically, the servants who were expected to provide *tautua* failed Balaam in this instance, as it was the donkey who stalled Balaam's mission in order to save him from the impending danger ahead. It is here that the donkey provides the *tautua* of the Tamasoaalii. Where Balaam's human *tautua*-servants had failed, the donkey—the animal-*tautua*—becomes the aide (*tama soa*) to the chief

---

3. Unless otherwise noted, biblical translations follow the NRSV.

(*alii*), that is, Balaam, as the donkey rescues her *matai* (chief) Balaam from the angel of YHWH.

Respect: *Fa'aaloalo*

One of the many lessons that *fāgogo* teaches is that of *fa'aaloalo*. But the idea of *fa'aaloalo* lies in its root word, *alo*, which literally means "to face." *Fa'aaloalo* implies a face-to-face relationship as an ideal platform to show one another respect, as if to say, "If you respect me, you will say it to my face!" *Fa'aaloalo* is most definitely implicated in the Tamasoaalii *fāgogo*, between Pupu Luki and the *naiufi*. Sadly, Balaam shows no such respect toward his trusted animal-*tautua*. As the donkey maneuvers her master out of the way of the angel of YHWH, Balaam becomes furious and strikes her.

In relation to *fa'aaloalo*, I want to mention the significance of *va* (space). *Va* can be physical, psychological, emotional, temporal, or spiritual. More importantly, the space is relational, and in Samoa, the *va* is protected by *tapu* (sacred boundaries) to ensure humility and grace between all creatures in creation (Efi 2019). *Va* therefore does not seek to separate but to ensure harmony and interconnectedness between all humans and animals. The *va* between Pupu Luki and the *naiufi* is sacred, as Pupu neither threatens nor hesitates.

Yet while the relationship between human and nonhuman animal may be deemed sacred, one cannot deny the underlying reality, that is, the *naiufi* still dies. In light of this reality, *fa'aaloalo* constitutes trust, which according to Tim Ingold (2000, 69–72) is a vital element in the relationship of hunter-gatherers with their prey. As Ingold argues, humans, in the view of hunter-gatherers, consist of only a small part of the environment and thus exist in a sharing relationship with other animals within the environment. This view means that "unlike the individual in modern Western society who always wants more than he can get, however well-off he may be, the wants of the hunter-gatherer ... are very limited. What one has, one shares, and there is no point in accumulating material property that would only be an impediment, given the demands of nomadic life" (65). Intriguingly, the hunter-gather relationship of trust with the species they hunt applies to the story of the *naiufi* and also to the Cree of Canada, of whom Ingold (2000, 67; see also Walker-Jones 2020, 67) writes.

> Suppose that animals intentionally present themselves to the hunter to be killed. The hunter consumes the meat, but the soul of the animal is

released to be reclothed with flesh. Hunting here, as among many northern peoples, is conceived as a rite of regeneration: consumption follows killing as birth follows intercourse, and both acts are integral to the reproductive cycles, respectively, of animals and humans. However, animals will not return to hunters who have treated them badly in the past. One treats an animal badly by failing to observe the proper, respectful procedures in the processes of butchering, consumption and disposal of the bones, or by causing undue pain and suffering to the animal in killing it. Above all, animals are offended by unnecessary killing: that is, by killing as an end in itself rather than to satisfy genuine consumption needs. They are offended, too, if the meat is not properly shared around all those in the community who need it. Thus, meat and other usable products should on no account be wasted.

The fishing of the *naiufi* also follows this model. As one hears in the story, the *naiufi* offers itself as the Tamasoaalii in honor of the village high chief and the village community. The consumption of the *naiufi* reciprocates the *fa'aaloalo* by the *naiufi*, through utilizing of all the meat and distributing it among the villages. In fact, the way the *naiufi* is distributed follows a *fa'aaloalo* structure, which may seem hierarchical but in the context of the *naiufi's* offering highlights the significance of the *naiufi's fa'aaloalo* to the village. The most important part of any fish, including the *naiufi*, is its head, which is given to the high chief and the high chief's family. The other parts of the *naiufi* are then distributed to the next rank in chiefs and their families, and if there is any part of the *naiufi* left, it is distributed among the young untitled men, known as *taule'ale'a*. No part of the *naiufi* goes to waste, as even the internal organs are seen as a delicacy in most fishing villages. Indeed, the fishers of the *naiufi* would not fish more than they need, nor would they kill for sport, and in response to the *naiufi* offering itself, the village utilizes every part of the *naiufi*. This reciprocity is a key aspect of *fa'aaloalo*, a relationship built on face-to-face (*alo-to-alo*) trust.

The *fa'aaloalo* between *naiufi* and fisher is also relevant to understanding the ancient Israelites. Jonathan Klawans (2006, 74) argues that the shepherd metaphor is key to grasping that ancient Israelites had a relationship of compassion and empathy with their domestic animals, especially at the moment of sacrifice. While nonhuman animals still suffered and died, killing was limited and ideally humane, which is better than modern factory farming and slaughterhouses. A similar contrast in Oceania would be between traditional Samoan fishing in villages and the methods and impact of the giant trawlers and other factory-fishing vessels. According to the World Wildlife Federation (2021), one hundred million sharks and rays are killed a year by fishing and by-catch, so that a quarter of the world's species are threatened and a third of European species are at risk of extinction (Green 2015, 718).

The question of *fa'aaloalo* has further implications in rereading this dialogue between Balaam and his donkey. Taking the root meaning of *fa'aaloalo*, *alo* (to face), the lack of respect by Balaam could be said to result from their lack of face-to-face interaction. Balaam, after all, is on the back of the donkey and cannot see the donkey's face. Pupu Luki and the *naiufi* are constantly face to face in their interaction, which reflects the interconnectedness between humans and animals.

The face-to-face interaction does however occur between the donkey and the angel of YHWH, and in this instance the donkey demonstrates *fa'aaloalo* when she sees the angel of YHWH. The manner in which the donkey shows *fa'aaloalo* is uncannily similar to that of the *naiufi*. Like the *naiufi*, the donkey moves respectfully and carefully, so as not to disrespect the angel of YHWH. Within this framework of *fa'aaloalo*, the *naiufi* offers itself to Pupu, while the donkey surrenders herself before the angel of YHWH in 22:27 as "it lay down under Balaam." The motion of lowering is paramount to *fa'aaloalo*, as it is a visual cue for respect and humility. The response to such humility in Samoan exchanges is never domination by the other party but a reciprocation of humility and respect. Pupu and the villagers honor the *naiufi* through the celebration and later full consumption and distribution of the *naiufi*. Sadly, although Balaam is humbled, he never apologizes to the donkey, as he only expresses remorse to the angel of YHWH. Ironically, the lessons of interconnectedness between humans and animals are provided by a divine being, the angel of YHWH, as the donkey connects with the angel. In this connection, the donkey becomes the "seer" that Balaam fails to be (Way 2011, 185).

Chants

Fāgogo as pedagogy often involves song in the form of chants (Kolone-Collins 2010, 57). They are sung in honor of the main character in the *fāgogo*, who displays an extraordinary trait worthy of such praise. The chant's theme is therefore honor, but the tune is a rather tantalizing melody that breaks the narrative and sends the listener into a warmhearted mood. In the case of the *naiufi*, Pupu Luki's chant honors the great sacrifice of the fish to the village. People who display great service and prestige are often labeled Tamasoaalii as a mark of honor. When sung, the tune is one of celebration.

Every *fāgogo* has a chant. Does the story of Balaam and the donkey have a chant? Perhaps not in the traditional sense. From a *fāgogo* perspective, however, the *fāgogo* teller chants, and the *fāgogo* hearer hears it. This is perhaps the essence of *fāgogo* as a Samoan decolonial pedagogy, that islander and indigenous readers or hearers of the text do not have to read through Western eyes but can read through their own (Kolone-Collins 2010, 31; see also Smith 2012). As an islander, when I hear the Balaam and the donkey *fāgogo*, I can hear a *fāgogo* chant when YHWH opens the mouth of the donkey. The donkey's chant is not one of celebration but of lamentation. If one were to imagine the tune, it would be one of melancholy. The donkey laments the mistreatment: "What have I done to you, that you have struck me these three times?" (22:28). The chant is significant that the angel of YHWH repeats the chant: "Why have you struck your donkey these three times?" (22:32). Intriguingly, Balaam hears her too, as if he is accustomed to hearing her, as though the donkey has chanted before (Alter 2004, 800)! The chants prompt reconciliation, as Balaam responds to the chants in remorse. He realizes his error in judgment but especially his lack of *fa'aaloalo* to his animal-*tautua*. It is through the chant that Balaam reconciles himself with his donkey. It is through the chant that Balaam is reconciled with his calling as a prophet. It is through the chant also that one can view the donkey as the Tamasoaalii, to both Balaam and YHWH.

Conclusion: Balaam and the Donkey as *Fāgogo*

When reading Balaam and the donkey as *fāgogo*, one becomes aware of a different reality that is not constituted through objective reasoning but is in resonance with one's own reality. *Fāgogo* takes readers to mystical worlds not to remove them from reality but to revisit their own life settings. The experience of reading *fāgogo* therefore is magical but can also be somewhat tragic. Tragedy comes in all forms, and what the *fāgogo* of Balaam and the donkey reminds readers is that tragedy can come from one's own hands. While the angel of YHWH moves to block the impending danger to Moab, reading as *fāgogo* makes us aware of the danger to the donkey. The *fāgogo* makes readers aware of the animality of the scene in Num 22. Jacques Derrida asks us to consider the animal-Other in our thinking, and I move that we consider the same in our reading. Derrida

(2008, 113) writes: "For a thinking of the other, of the infinitely other who looks at me, should, on the contrary, privilege the question and the request of the animal. Not in order to put it in front of that of man, but in order to think that of man, of the brother and the neighbor from the perspective of an animal." The mistreatment of animals breaks the interconnectedness between humans and the animal-Other. Balaam failed to see the angel of YHWH, and one could argue that this was because he did not see things through the perspective of an animal. But YHWH reconciles the interconnectedness, by giving the donkey a voice, for her chant to be heard.

The *fāgogo* can at the same time be liberating and reconciling. Pupu Luki and the villagers sing the chant in honor of the *naiufi* that has been killed. They celebrate the *naiufi*'s sacrifice and honor it with the title Tamasoaalii. In further honor of the *naiufi*'s great service, the honorific is offered to those humans who perform great deeds in the village. Balaam for many years had not acknowledged the great service of the donkey. It is a relationship that threatens to break following Balaam's constant cruelty. But the relationship is reconciled when YHWH opens the donkey's mouth, while Balaam's eyes are opened. When reading *fāgogo*, hearers enter into a separate realm only to come back to reality with a renewed purpose to reconcile broken relationships and their own brokenness. This is why the chant is important, as it is one of the more memorable components of *fāgogo*, and in it both the *fāgogo* teller and *fāgogo* reader can participate. Interestingly, this togetherness reflects the interconnectedness of all beings in creation. Reading Balaam and the donkey as *fāgogo* ensures that listeners remember the donkey's bray as a chant, one that listeners may embrace as a point for reconciliation.

I must admit that, in the current climate, many islanders often migrate to other lands as they seek economic stability, well-being, and education. Samoans, in particular, often lose aspects of their culture and indigenous identity; sadly, *fāgogo* is one of those aspects that is often lost on diasporic Samoans. As a Samoan decolonial pedagogical tool, *fāgogo* seeks to establish connection between beings but also between generations. It can provide a vital point for Samoans in the diaspora to link with indigenous knowledge of their ancestors. It also calls for a reading of the biblical text from a perspective that gives voice to island and indigenous realities. The failure of Balaam to see the angel of YHWH reflects our own failures to see past colonial attitudes that push us to neglect our own islander and indigenous views. A *fāgogo* reading of the text instead provides a platform to hear the many voices, to unsilence the chants of war and victory and the chants of pain and reconciliation.

Works Cited

Alter, Robert. 2004. *The Five Books of Moses: A Translation with Commentary*. New York: Norton.
Bible and Culture Collective. 1995. *The Postmodern Bible: The Bible and Culture Collective*. Edited by Elizabeth A. Castelli, Stephen D. Moore, Gary A. Phillips, and Regina M. Schwartz. New Haven: Yale University Press.
Calarco, Matthew. 2015. *Thinking through Animals: Identity, Difference, Indistinction*. StBr. Stanford, CA: Stanford University Press.
Derrida, Jacques. 2008. *The Animal That Therefore I Am*. Edited by Marie-Louise Mallet. Translated by David Wills. PCPS. New York: Fordham University Press.
Efi, Tui A. T. T. 2003. "More on Nuance, Meaning and Metaphor." *SPJNZ* 20:49–63.
———. 2014. "Whispers and Vanities in Samoan Indigenous Religious Culture." Pages 37–36 in *Whispers and Vanities: Samoan Indigenous Knowledge and Religion*. Edited by Tamasailau M. Suaalii-Sauni, Maualaivao Albert Wendt, Vitolia Mo'a, Naomi Fuamatu, Upola L. Va'ai, Reina Whaitiri, and Stephen L. Filipo. Wellington, NZ: Huia.
———. 2019. "An Ethic of Responsibility in Samoan Customary Law." In *Responsability: Law and Governance for Living Well with the Earth*. Edited by Betsan Martin, Linda Te Aho, and Maria Humphries-Kil. Abingdon: Routledge.
Green, Crystal. 2015. "An International SOS (Save Our Sharks): How the International Legal Framework Should Be Used to Save Our Sharks." *PILR* 27:701–24.
Ingold, Timothy. 2000. *The Perception of the Environment: Essays on Livelihood, Dwelling and Skill*. London: Routledge.
Klawans, Jonathan. 2006. "Sacrifice in Ancient Israel: Pure Bodies, Domesticated Animals, and the Divine Shepherd." Pages 65–80 in *A Communion of Subjects: Animals in Religion, Science, and Ethics*. Edited by Paul Waldau and Kimberley Patton. New York: Columbia University Press.
Kolone-Collins, Su'eala. 2010. "Fagogo: 'Ua Molimea Manusina': A Qualitative Study of the Pedagogical Significance of Fagogo—Samoan Sto-

ries at Night—for the Education of Samoan Children." Master's thesis, Auckland University of Technology.

Peteru, Aumua C. 2009. "Where You Live, Who You Are." Pages 365–82 in *Su'esu'e Manogi: In Search of Fragrance Tui Atua Tupua Tamasese Ta'isi Efi and the Samoan Indigenous Reference*. Edited by Tamasailau M. Suaalii-Sauni, I'uogafa Tuagalu, Tofilau N. Kirifi-Alai, and Naomi Fuamatu. Wellington, NZ: Huia.

Smith, Linda Tuhiwai. 2012. *Decolonizing Methodologies: Research and Indigenous Peoples*. 2nd ed. London: Zed Books.

Tauiliili, Pemerika. L. 2010. *Anoafale o le Gagana ma le Aganuu*. 2nd ed. Milton Keynes, UK: AuthorHouse.

Walker-Jones, Arthur. 2020. *Psalms Book 2: An Earth Bible Commentary "As a Doe Groans."* London: T&T Clark.

Way, Kenneth. C. 2011. *Donkeys in the Biblical World: Ceremony and Symbol*. Winona Lake, IN: Eisenbrauns.

World Wildlife Federation. 2021. "Shark." https://tinyurl.com/SBL06107k.

Miss Piggy and the Pretty Woman of Proverbs 11:22: Beauty, Animality, and Gender

Anne Létourneau

Nezem zāhāb bəʾap ḥăzîr / ʾiššâ yāpâ wəsārat ṭāʿam
A golden ring in a pig's snout / A pretty but tasteless woman. (Prov 11:22, my translation)

Building off the recent scholarship on the Bible, gender, and animal studies, this essay investigates the metaphorical association of femininity and animality in Prov 11:22. In a 2008 article, Knut Heim reassesses the "traditional" equation made between the pretty woman and the pig. Through a syntactic and structural analysis of the parallelism of this proverb, he emphasizes that the comparison is actually between the pretty woman and the piece of jewelry, the nose ring (*nezem*), and not the pig itself. Moreover, taking into consideration the literary context of Prov 11:22, he argues that the pig is to be identified with the husband stuck with a beautiful but senseless wife (Heim 2008, 25–27; Fox 2009, 539–40). This clever interpretation is particularly appealing since it contends that, for once, it is not the woman but the man who is animalized through a negative association with the pig. However, while a very compelling exegesis of the verse, it discards too easily the connection that exists between the two clearly identified sentient beings, pig and woman, in favor of a man nowhere to be found in verse 22. I suggest that this poetic association deserves further exploration. In this chapter, I demonstrate that woman and swine can be understood as linked through the beauty motif. The pig's item of jewelry belongs indeed to the world of feminine beautification in the ancient Levant (Limmer 2007). I propose that the golden ring, even when considered as a stand-in for the beautiful woman in the parallelism (Fox 2009; Heim 2008; Quick 2021), blurs the frontier between human and nonhuman animals (Stone 2017).

The aesthetic and intimate connection[1] between the two characters needs to be appraised anew. I contend that beauty—and its props—constitutes the metaphorical bridge joining the two parts of verse 22, a bejeweled pig and a misbehaving pretty woman.

First, I explore how the *nezem* relates to the aesthetic self-presentation of women, the different contexts in which their bodies are adorned from betrothal to seduction scenes, and how it contributes to the feminization of the pig. This section gives me the opportunity to reflect on the social function of this item of adornment in the context of the ancient Near East. I examine how the contrasting display of a golden ring in the middle of a pig's face and a pretty woman deviating from discernment draws attention to cases of misplaced or misused beauty. Furthermore, this provides me with the opportunity not only to reflect on the inner workings of the metaphor in Prov 11:22 but also to adopt the decentering perspective that indistinction (animal studies) theorists advocate for in order to make space for the pig's *standpoint* (Calarco 2015, 56).

Second, I turn to the animalizing effects of the pig on the woman in the second part of the simile. In the wake of recent zooarchaeological scholarship (Sapir-Hen et al. 2013), I reappraise the idea of the pig taboo (Lev 11:7, Deut 14:8) as an ethnic definer possibly shedding light on Prov 11:22. Multiple and complex relations existed between pigs and humans in ancient Israel. In his book *Pig*, Brett Mizelle (2011, 15) notes the suids' "malleability ... which gives them a wider range of possible relationships with humans than other domesticated animals." In this short study, I explore how the swine imagery disqualifies the woman by association, while also presenting an opportunity to highlight both estrangement and closeness between human and nonhuman animals at stake in this verse.

Third, I study how the woman's "turning away" from *ṭā'am* can be associated with the suid species. While acknowledging proximity between human and pig, verse 22 could also be building off a certain ambivalence toward humans' "deep identity with [this] animal life" as they exchange their respective features and behaviors (Calarco 2015, 61).

This essay offers a close reading of Prov 11:22, informed by the insights of material studies, zooarchaeology, and animal studies more generally to

---

1. As Calarco (2015, 52) writes about the indistinction approach in critical animal studies, quoting Donna Haraway: "Instead of stressing abyssal differences, many indistinction theorists instead emphasize and 'affirm the pleasure of connection of human and other living creatures.'"

provide a new perspective on the poetic partnership of pig and woman, highlighting how the verse blurs the characters' experiences and bodies as well as our readerly expectations.

The *nezem*: The Pig and the Case of the Misplaced Adornment

The *nezem* is an item of jewelry worn by both men and women in the Hebrew Bible. Archaeological excavations of burials confirm that all members of the family—including children—wore such adornments in the Levant (Golani 2013, 70; Quick 2021, 133). The word *nezem* designates different types of "rings" that decorate the ears and/or the nose—and possibly the fingers[2]—of the wearer. I count sixteen occurrences of the word *nezem* in the Hebrew Bible. The majority of these rings are made of gold,[3] a sign of wealth and prestige (see Hartwell 2017, 48; Limmer 2007, 289–90; Fischer 2019, 548). In two occurrences, the weight of the precious metal in shekels is also emphasized (Gen 24:22; Judg 8:26). For this reason, Abigail Limmer (2007, 69) contends that some of these rings work as "wealth storage" and are exchanged, offered, or looted as such. It is also worth noting that many rings are associated with or transformed into—sometimes melted—religious objects (Gen 35:4; Judg 8:24–26; Exod 32:2–3; 35:22). These biblical connotations may shed light on the ring-wearing pig.

Six *nəzāmîm* are said to adorn specific body parts of biblical characters: nose or ears.[4] Apart from the pig of Prov 11:22, only women's noses are decorated in such a way in the biblical texts. In Gen 24, Rebecca receives a betrothal gift from Abraham's servant, on a quest to find the perfect wife for Isaac. The golden ring is mentioned three times (vv. 22, 30, 47) and accompanies another item of jewelry, namely, a pair of *tsəmîdîm*, or bracelets. In verse 47, the expected location of the adornment is specified as the servant recalls how he performed the selection of Rebekah through the

---

2. Hair rings are also to be found (Golani 2013, 129).

3. Seven out of sixteen occurrences are golden rings: Gen 24:22; Exod 32:2–3; 35:22; Judg 8:26; Prov 11:22; 25:12; Job 42:11.

4. The first two occurrences of the word in Gen 24:22, 30 come with no precise location. Rebecca's nose is clearly identified only in verse 47. Specific locations are also missing in Exod 35:22, Judg 8:24–26, Hos 2:15, Prov 25:12, and Job 42:11. In the case of Exod 35:22, Judg 8:24–26, and Job 42:11, these items of jewelry are offerings, spoils, or gifts. In Hos 2:15, Gomer uses her jewelry to perform her adulterous/idolatrous behaviors.

bedecking of the woman's nose and arms. In Ezek 16:12, young Jerusalem is adorned by God. After entering into a bǝrît ("covenant") with the young female personification (v. 8), YHWH performs a series of gestures confirming her new status as his bride (Gansell 2014, 62; Quick 2019, 221 n. 34, see also 135–37): he bathes her, dresses her, and adorns her with multiple items of jewelry, including a nose ring, earrings, and a crown (Ezek 16:12–13). In Isa 3:21, nose rings are part of the long list of items of dress of which the proud daughters of Zion will be stripped for their ostentatious behaviors (see Létourneau, De Doncker, and Roy-Turgeon 2022). As can be gleaned from each of these examples, all nose ring wearers are women in the Hebrew Bible. Ancient Egyptian and Mesopotamian iconography, depicting mostly men, seems to confirm this trend. This brings Limmer (2007, 70; see also Platt 1979, 77–78) to "suggest … that nose-rings were specifically a female ornament." In Hos 2:15, the *nezem* of the prophet's adulterous wife, worn to seduce her lovers, can be understood as another (unspecified) nose ring. Gomer could therefore be considered in the midst of other nose-ring wearers. As noted by Limmer and Amir Golani, one needs to keep in mind that the same ring could decorate the ear or the nose of a woman.[5] Archaeological finds support the idea of *interchangeable* jewelry in ancient times (Golani 2013, 128–29; Limmer 2007, 277–78).

I suggest that this biblical intertextual mapping of women who own nose rings allows for an interesting discovery: they are all involved in beautifying practices. Jerusalem and the daughters of Zion wear especially regal outfits in addition to their rings (Limmer 2007, 290; Platt 1979). According to Golani (2013, 71–72; see also Green 2007, 295–97), an archaeologist, ancient women often wore more physically and symbolically limiting jewelry than men, revealing their socio-sexual status. As Laura Quick (2019, 217) notes in a recent article on cosmetics in the book of Judith and the story of Susanna, "sexual intention is heavily coded through dress and adornment." I would add that these intentions can also be narratively imposed on the fabric and ornament mostly worn by female characters. Jewelry can function as a gendering device, also displaying sexual information about the wearer.

In the biblical texts, the (man)handling of jewelry in pre- and post-wedding scenes gives precious information about the gender relations

---

5. See the Late Bronze Age burial at Megiddo where an (ear)ring was found on the nose of a skeleton (in Golani 2013, 109, 128; Platt 1979, 78).

in Gen 24 and Ezek 16. Indeed, Rebekah and personified Jerusalem do not adorn themselves;[6] a servant—in the name of Abraham and Isaac—or God, places the jewelry on the bride's body. Contrary to this, both Isa 3:21 and Hos 2:15 suggest instances of self-adornment by overdressed and adulterous women. In each case, they are indeed punished—stripped—for their agentive and disobedient behavior. The nose ring could be understood as being misused or misplaced, on the wrong bodies, by both Gomer and the daughters of Zion.

Thus, where might one situate the pig of Prov 11:22 among this network of precious-metal wearers? When considering the other occurrences of the word *nezem* and *'ap*, it seems difficult to entirely reject associating the pig with women, the sole wearers of this item of jewelry. Even Heim (2008, 25–27; see Prov 12:4a; Fox 2009, 540) cannot escape a certain feminization of the animal through the nose ring since he contends that this object metaphorically represents the wife who is "worn" proudly by her husband. According to Heim (2008, 21), and in agreement with Gen 24 and Ezek 16, the issue at stake would here again be the selection of a *good* bride/wife, truly an important task in the book of Proverbs. Other scholars express a similar opinion. For example, as Quick (2021, 138) contends, "In the book of Proverbs, the nose-ring itself is utilized as a metaphor for a bride." The item of jewelry informs readers of the female characters' conjugal status,[7] which can in itself be understood as a type of male appropriation (see 138). However, *nəzāmîm* can also carry other nonmarital meanings, as is the case in Isa 3 and possibly Hos 2, where women are punished for the self-display of their adorned bodies. Bringing the bejeweled pig closer to Gomer and the daughters of Zion creates the opportunity for a different kind of interpretation: the three texts can be understood as cases of misplaced or misused beauty, escaping the control of men, husbands, and God. Similarly, in an article reflecting on the translation of biblical proverbs, Suzanna Millar (2020, 94) points out how the golden ring (*nezem zāhāb*) is "misplaced" in the prophetic texts (Isa 3:21, Ezek 16:12, Hos 2:15): on the wrong bodies and used for the wrong purposes. Proverbs 11:22 can also be understood as a case of beauty done

---

[6]. As Quick (2021, 138) notes, Rebekah still demonstrates power over her own life by accepting both the jewelry and the marriage proposal.

[7]. Quick (2019, 221 n. 34) even argues that, in the book of Judith, the heroine's *enotia* (Jdt 10:3–4) cannot be translated by nose rings, since she is a widow and not a married woman or a bride-to-be.

wrong. The tiny and shiny piece of jewelry, lost in the cylindrical and flat snout of the swine (cited in Fox 2009, 541),[8] evokes the diverse feminine traits of its usual wearers: from the perfect bride-to-be to the cheating wife and wealthy urban ladies. The meanings refracted through the animal's ring are multiple and should not be limited to conjugal appropriation, as the aesthetic spark of feminine disobedience adorns a new character.

To better understand the simile of Prov 11:22, one needs to go beyond the strict parallelism of the verse and pay attention to other aspects of the syntax. Indeed, the images of the pig and woman cannot be fully apprehended through neat parallel equations. While I absolutely do not intend to reject parallelism as a fundamental structure of biblical Hebrew poetry as suggested by Robert Holmstedt, I do think that Holmstedt's proposal to focus on apposition is worth considering when analyzing Prov 11:22. He contends that "nonrestrictive apposition *creates* the association between words such that the poet forces the linked terms to be interpreted in light of each other" (Holmstedt 2019, 15; emphasis original). Following this idea, one could understand the first half-line with the ornamented snout of the swine as a contrasting but proximate reformulation of the "tasteless" ʾiššâ yāpâ in the second half-line. However, is one necessarily to understand the woman (ʾiššâ yāpâ) as the anchor in the poetic line? The indistinction approach in critical animal studies leads one to also challenge the anthropocentrism and human/animal binaries in poetics. What if the woman is also reformulating the pig? In a 1987 review article in biblical poetics, Francis Landy (1987, 176) mentions Song of Songs' "reversible metaphors" of lovers, animals, and waters. He also highlights the dynamics of reciprocity at play between the terms of biblical poetic devices (merismus, hendiadys; 167). Similarly, in Prov 11:22, pig and woman are figuratively shaping each other, even partially amalgamating. As Millar (2020, 94-95) proposes: "an evocative general comparison emerges without exactitude

---

8. From a contemporary perspective, it is also the "wrong" ring for a rooting pig. The animal's digging will not be stopped by such a little piece of metal. As Hartwell (2017, 49) rightly states, a nose ring is not usually an adornment for a pig but a way to control better the animal and prevent a specific behavior: rooting and its destructive effects. Psalm 80:14 does mention the devastating impact of a wild boar on a vine representing Israel. While nose rings were used for cattle and equids during an early period in antiquity (Borowski 1998, 90), zooarchaeologist Lidar Sapir-Hen (2021, personal communication) confirms she has never found any evidence for the use of nose rings with domesticated pigs. I thank her for this precious insight.

which leads to imaginative blending processes." Swine and feminine aesthetics merge with each other.

Ancient Pigs: Companionship amid Aversion

I now wish to turn to the piggish traits that the simile brings into the portrayal of the beautiful woman, which engender both a grotesque impression and a sense of closeness between human and animal. Most scholars associate the pig imagery with ideas of uncleanness, impurity, and taboo.[9] As is clearly stated in Lev 11:7 and Deut 14:8, the consumption of pig meat is forbidden. Moreover, in Isa 65:4b and 66:3, 17, the sacrifice and consumption of pigs' flesh are assimilated to idolatrous practice (Forti 2008, 51). According to Tova Forti (51), "the use of the pig in the simile depends primarily on the cultic-religious tradition that reflects a longstanding aversion to swine." She also builds her argument on later Hellenistic and rabbinic texts (1 Macc 1:44–50; b. Sotah 49b; B. Qam. 82b; Forti 2008, 51–52 n. 80). However, nothing in the simile of Prov 11 refers to this religiously motivated revulsion for the animal. The simile is built first and foremost on physical appearance and behaviors: the pig's face is emphasized in the first half-line, while the pretty woman's erratic and tasteless behavior is highlighted in the second. As Amy Gansell (2014, 51) suggests, "with regard to feminine beauty, biblical descriptions tend to focus on the head through discussion of women's eyes, hair adornment, and veils." Like the women depicted on ivory plaques in the Levant, the pig's face—especially the nose—is at the center of verse 22, suggesting that this is the body part at work in the metaphor.

Building on the zooarchaeological scholarship of Lidar Sapir-Hen and others, I suggest that Prov 11:22 might not—or not only or mainly—reflect the idea of the pig taboo. There are other possibilities. In the southern Levant, the pig was never bred in high numbers, contrary to other farm animals such as cattle, goats, and sheep (Sapir-Hen et al. 2013, 2; 2019, 53). Since pig consumption was higher in Iron Age Philistine towns, for years, the absence of pig bones in the region of the ancient kingdoms of Israel and Judah was identified as an ethnic marker, a way for Israelites to differentiate themselves from the Philistines. However, in recent research,

---

9. On the historical development of the pig taboo in ancient Israel, see Price 2020, 116–41.

Sapir-Hen (2019, 52) convincingly argues that "until proven archaeologically—pigs cannot be used as an ethnic marker." Recent discoveries of domesticated pig bones from the Iron Age IIB (precisely the first half of the eighth century BCE) in the lowlands of the ancient northern kingdom of Israel could undermine the idea of a shared eternal and normative aversion to pigs in both Israel and Judah (Sapir-Hen et al. 2013, 9). Sapir-Hen and colleagues (12–13) suggest that the population increase in the north might have brought the need for a fast production of meat, provided by domesticated pigs. I do think that this zooarchaeological data sheds a fascinating light on the bejeweled pig and her human counterpart in the second half of verse 22. Without getting into the extremely slippery issue of dating Prov 10–29,[10] I suggest understanding the relationship of pig and woman from the perspective of the Northern Kingdom, outside—or at least in tension with—the prohibition and the disgust implied in the biblical legal texts. From this point of view, the pig-human relationship could first and foremost be defined as mixing both closeness and distance. Ancient Israelites lived in closed quarters with their domesticated animals. The skeleton of a small pig found among broken vessels in an Iron Age IIB room in Jerusalem, near the Gihon Spring, while a unique discovery, especially for the kingdom of Judah, testifies to this proximity (Sapir-Hen, Uziel, and Chalaf 2021).

Following Ken Stone (2017, 21–44; see also Haraway 2003) in his discussion of goats, sheep, and cattle as companion species, I suggest thinking also of pigs as rare but possible companions under the right circumstances in the Northern Kingdom. While the pig might have had a bad reputation as garbage eater, the "trash" they ate was mostly human food scraps, which testifies to their living in close quarters and their very similar omnivore palate (Mizelle 2011, 13). Both closeness and distance between pig and woman are key to the metaphor's dynamic. One can interpret the proximity between the human and this nonhuman animal as enabling a negative emphasis on some of the physical features of the animal and their transfer to the woman, undermining her humanity.

Irene López Rodríguez provides interesting insights on animal metaphors in an article about their use to designate women in English and Spanish. She notes that in these languages "pig and its female counterpart

---

10. I follow Fox (2009, 499) on this matter, who contends that Prov 10–29 was "composed and edited during the monarchy, probably in the eighth to seventh centuries B.C.E." For this text, I lean toward the eighth century BCE.

sow/cerda are metaphorically used as terms of opprobrium for a woman, implying fatness, dirtiness, ugliness and even promiscuity" (López Rodríguez 2009, 88). Since the pig's face and nose are emphasized in Prov 11:22, the animal's excellent sense of smell and its rooting habits especially come to mind (Mizelle 2011, 94). One can imagine—even for the Iron Age period—an urban pig scavenging through human leftovers and garbage. While this animal has a long-held reputation as dirty, Mizelle rightly points out that they "are actually quite clean animals if left to their own devices" (140). It is the breeding for meat imposed by humans that is responsible for that unclean reputation (Berger, in Mizelle 2011, 116).

In the same way that the pig acquired the female human nose ring, the woman is clearly stained by her association to the foraging swine. One can read her as othered, disqualified through this metaphoric animalization of her body. One could also understand the adorned pig as contributing to the cultural ostracizing of the woman by identifying her with the kingdom of Israel and specific eating practices. According to Sapir-Hen, Meirav Meiri, and Israel Finkelstein (2015, 313), the pig taboo might have its roots in a conflict between Judahites and Israelite migrants coming to the south after the destruction of the kingdom in the north. Proverbs 11:22 could be partly reflecting some of these tensions. However, the woman is not simply dirtied in her association with the pig. As I will now demonstrate with the analysis of the second half-line, she is quite simply becoming a pig.[11]

Is She Pretty or Piggish? Running Away from Tasteful Things

Turning to the second half-line, especially the words *wəsārat ṭāʿam*, it becomes clear that the simile of verse 22 does not simply produce a clash through the combination of its two half-lines. Each one of them puts a paradoxical being on display. On the one hand, the pig is feminized through its adornment, while on the other, a pretty woman is piggified through her lack of taste/discernment. Again, one cannot simply stick to the Lowthian parallelism in one's analysis. The ring and the lack of taste/discernment have to be related to each other, since they disrupt the depictions of both human and nonhuman animals. Their features are exchanged and blended between them as readers now face a prettied pig and a good-looking

---

11. I have purposely left aside Deleuzian and Guattarian perspectives in this piece. However, the agencement at play in Prov 11:22, with the woman's becoming pig and the pig's becoming woman, would definitely be worth exploring further.

woman acting like a swine. Many scholars mention how beauty is not in itself evaluated negatively in the Hebrew Bible (Fox 2009, 541; Schipper 2019, 406). While this notion needs to be revised, especially for biblical women who are often endangered by their characterization as pretty (see Létourneau 2018), I agree that the ʾiššâ yāpâ, in Prov 11:22, just like the gracious woman in 11:16, is depicted positively until the second part of the half-line hits and engenders a clash with her beauty.

I now move to the words wəsārat ṭāʿam. The verb sûr is often used in the book of Proverbs to signify "turning away" from evil (e.g., Prov 3:7; 13:19; 14:16; 16:6, 17), "avoiding" death (13:14; 14:27) and the descent into Sheôl (15:24). The use of this verb is of course closely linked to one of the main metaphors of the book: the "path" (derek; Létourneau 2015, 664–70). According to Michael Fox (2000, 128), the path is closely associated with ethical behavior. While the ʾiššâ yāpâ is not located on a road, she is depicted as *deviating* from something: ṭāʿam. In the absence of the preposition *min* between the participle and the noun, Fox (2009, 541) suggests a different understanding of the end of the second half-line with another subject: he argues that the ṭāʿam is "leaving" the woman.[12] However, I suggest sticking with the idea of the pretty woman as the one turning away from taste, since it locates her in the context of the fools (pətāʾîm) invited to turn toward Woman Wisdom or Folly. She is in good company with these individuals who risk taking the wrong turn in the maze that is the book of Proverbs, especially Prov 1–9. While she was not invited by anyone—she is not a son, after all—the pretty woman is also judged as taking a wrong turn.

Most scholars translate ṭāʿam as "discernment," "discretion," or "sense" (Forti 2008, 52; Heim 2008; Fox 2009, 540–41). The majority of occurrences of the root ṭāʿam, in both its verbal and nominal forms, actually designate the more concrete idea of "taste," the act of "eating," often in association with a temporary food prohibition. For example, in 1 Sam 14:24, 29, 43, Jonathan eats the forbidden honey; in 2 Sam 3:35, David refuses to eat bread; in Jonah 3:7, animals and humans have to fast and wear sackcloth in Nineveh. In each of these cases, interestingly, a judgment call is made to respect an oath or a decree. The concrete meaning of ṭāʿam is certainly associated with the more abstract idea of discernment. Is tasting

---

12. Fox (2009, 541) refers to Muraoka (1977) to argue, "The genitive *taʿam* is semantically the subject of the const. ptcp. *sārat*, in spite of the gender agreement between the ptcp. and *ʾiššāh*. In other words, the woman's *good sense* has departed."

not always the act of discriminating among flavors? In her monograph *The Senses of Scripture*, Yael Avrahami (2012, 95) notes that "the sense of taste is a critical sense with which we learn about and analyse the world." Many biblical passages testify to the sense of judgment involved with tasting: in 2 Sam 19:36, old Barzillai tells David that both his ability to discriminate between good and bad and his capacity to taste food and drink have left him (Avrahami 2012, 100). Similarly, in Job 12:11, the ear discriminating between words is compared to the palate tasting food. Since food is often used to symbolize wisdom or folly in the book of Proverbs, especially through the invitations of both personifications in Prov 9:1–6, 13–18, similarly, the lack of discernment of the pretty woman in Prov 11:22 should be connected to the materiality of food tasting. This character deviates from *ṭāʿam* by locating herself at the other end of the spectrum across from two women with great taste: the *woman of worth*[13] (*ēšet ḥayil*, Prov 31:18) and Abigail (1 Sam 25:33), David's wife-to-be. Both women are endowed with "discernment" (*ṭāʿam*). However, the expression *wəsārat ṭāʿam* also connects the woman closely with the pig. Victor Hurowitz (2013, 98), Bernd Schipper (2019, 407), and Max Price (2020, 134) all mention the existence of an Akkadian tablet with a telling anecdote about a pig:

> The dirty pig has no sense. [?]
> He lie[s] [in the m]ud, eating food.
> The[y (the pigs)] do (var. He] does) not say: "Pig, what respect do I get[14]?"
> But he sa[ys to him]self: "I (only) trust in the pig." (Streck 2012, 790)

The same semitic root is used in Akkadian and Biblical Hebrew to talk about the lack of *sense* of the pig and the woman, *ṭēma* and *ṭāʿam*. In the Akkadian tablet, the pig's senselessness is connected to its specific eating and cooling down behaviors, its self-preservation as a swine. As previously mentioned, the Hebrew *ṭāʿam* can be used to talk about discernment on different levels: food and wisdom. While the verb *sûr* seems to be set aside for human beings, taste is something they have in common with nonhuman animals. Pigs are known to have an acute sense of smell—and taste—however, humans tend to deny and misunderstand this pig quality

---

13. On the idea that Prov 11:22 has to do with spousal ideals, see Heim 2008.
14. According to Streck (2012, 790), the pig in the Akkadian text (Lambert 1960, 215, ll. 5–8) represents a self-absorbed person.

to marginalize these animals.[15] The pretty woman is precisely assigned this pig flaw as a lack of taste for what is good—whether food or wisdom. She wanders away from sense and discernment. Her beauty hides bad taste and terrible decision-making. So, is she also smelly, eating trash, and taking mud baths? The Syriac version (Peshitta) goes even further in suggesting animalization of the woman at the end of the *mashal*. Fox's (2009, 990; emphasis added) translation is as follows: "Like an ornament of gold in the nose of a sow, this is a beautiful woman *stinking* of sense." It clearly brings one back to the pig and its dirty reputation. In the MT, there is definitely a blending of characters in Prov 11:22 as woman and pig share and exchange some of their main features: a ring and a reputation for tastelessness. While she roots away from good sense, the pretty woman becomes a pig and is also brought closer to the strange and the foolish women described as groaning like wild animals in Prov 7:22; 9:13 (Létourneau 2015, 628–929; 2022; see also 2021). Conversely, the misplaced ring turns the pig into a lady, in tune with Levantine fashion.

Conclusion

Through this brief analysis of Prov 11:22, I hope to have shown that, contrary to what Heim argues, keeping the connection alive between the adorned pig and the pretty woman brings forth many fruitful interpretative possibilities. I offer to go beyond the tendency to limit the meaning of a proverb to its parallelistic structure in order to consider appositional tensions as well as reversible metaphors at play. There is a game of reverberations going on with the different words of this proverb: between ring and beauty, pig and woman, tastelessness and ring, and so on. On the one hand, the pig is feminized through its accessorizing; the nose ring evokes married, as well as seductive and wealthy, women and brings to the front cases of misused beauty. On the other, the pretty woman is animalized through her association with the pig. I tried to think through the animal-woman relationship—outside the realm of the pig taboo—with the help of zooarchaeology. I opened a potential space of proximity for an animal that was not always vilified in the northern kingdom of Israel and a woman who could have encountered pigs daily, including in the vicinity of her very own house. However, the simile still is a way to denigrate the

---

15. On the ambivalence toward pigs, see Mizelle 2011, 116–37.

woman. Pig features are clearly being thrust upon her to create grotesque effects. She might also be vilified through association with the old kingdom of Israel and its problematic (food) ways from a Judean point of view. The lack of taste of the pretty woman can also be analyzed in the midst of the colliding images of pig and human woman. An Akkadian tablet confirms the ancient perception of pigs as senseless, a feature now applied to a woman. Their exchange of characteristics highlights their closeness and how they both escape the sages' control. The human and nonhuman metaphorical partners in Prov 11:22 could be interpreted as sapiential and aesthetical counterexamples, a way to pronounce that female beauty[16] needs to be set in the right context in order to be enjoyed by its—of course—male recipients.

To conclude, and in order to step out of this logic, I suggest a way to follow in the steps of the adorned pig and tasteless woman and disobey the very cautionary proverb that stages their performance. I connect Prov 11:22 with another wisdom intertext where another animal/woman is adorned with jewelry: the mare/beloved in Song 1:9–11. As Francis Landy and Maria Metzler (2019) suggest in a very poetic piece about this passage, the mare brings chaos among the stallions. She is also out of control. However, contrary to the pig/woman of Prov 11:22, the horse is appraised as the beautiful female beloved. In Song 1:9–11, the beautifying adornments, as the reversible metaphoric bridge from woman to animal, work in favor of aesthetic pleasure and desire. Could we look at the bejeweled pig in the same way? It would be worth exploring further this idea of opening a redeeming space for both pig and woman, their beauty and disobedient ways, in the vicinity of the Song's mare.

Works Cited

Avrahami, Yael. 2012. *The Senses of Scripture: Sensory Perception on the Hebrew Bible*. London: Bloomsbury T&T Clark.

Borowski, Oded. 1998. *Every Living Thing: Daily Use of Animals in Ancient Israel*. Walnut Creek, CA : AltaMira Press.

Calarco, Matthew. 2015. *Thinking through Animals: Identity, Difference, Indistinction*. StBr. Stanford, CA: Stanford University Press.

---

16. On the idea of a disconnection between beauty and wisdom pronounced in Prov 31:10–31 about the *woman of valor*, which favors "acquired wisdom," see Vayntrub 2020.

Fischer, Stefan. 2019. "Women's Dress Codes in the Book of Proverbs." Pages 543–56 in *Clothing and Nudity in the Hebrew Bible*. Edited by Christopher Berner et al. London: T&T Clark.

Forti, Tova. 2008. *Animal Imagery in the Book of Proverbs*. Leiden: Brill.

Fox, Michael V. 2000. *Proverbs: A New Translation with Introduction and Commentary*. New York: Doubleday.

———. 2009. *Proverbs 10–31: A New Translation with Introduction and Commentary*. New Haven: Yale University Press.

Gansell, Amy Rebecca. 2014. "The Iconography of Ideal Feminine Beauty Represented in the Hebrew Bible and Iron Age Levantine Ivory Sculpture." Pages 46–70 in *Image, Text, Exegesis: Iconographic Interpretation and the Hebrew Bible*. Edited by Isaak J. de Hulster and Joel M. LeMon. London: Bloomsbury T&T Clark.

Golani, Amir. 2013. "Jewelry from the Iron Age II Levant." PhD diss., University of Zurich.

Green, Jack. 2007. "Anklets and the Social Construction of Gender and Age in the Late Bronze and Early Iron Age Southern Levant." Pages 283–311 in *Archaeology and Women: Ancient and Modern Issues*. Edited by Sue Hamilton, Ruth D. Whitehouse, and Katherine I. Wright. Walnut Creek, CA: Left Coast.

Haraway, Donna J. 2003. *The Companion Species Manifesto: Dogs, People, and Significant Otherness*. Chicago: Prickly Paradigm.

Hartwell, Jeanette M. 2017. "Mannen, vrouwen en rijkdom: Herinterpretatie van Spreuken 11:16 en 11:22 in het licht van genderverhoudingen." *ACEBT* 31:41–50.

Heim, Knut M. 2008. "A Closer Look at the Pig in Proverbs xi 22." *VT* 58:13–27.

Holmstedt, Robert D. 2019. "Hebrew Poetry and the Appositive Style: Parallelism, *Requiescat in pace*." *VT* 69:617–48.

Hurowitz, Victor. 2013. "Unsavory Personalities in the Book of Proverbs in Light of Mesopotamian Writings." *HS* 54:93–106.

Lambert, Wilfred G. 1960. *Babylonian Wisdom Literature*. Oxford: Clarendon.

Landy, Francis. 1987. "Recent Developments in Biblical Poetics." *Prooftexts* 7:163–78.

Landy, Francis, and Maria Metzler. 2019. "Deconstructing Horses, in Love and War." Pages 151–66 in *The Song of Songs: A Fresh Perspectives on a Biblical Love Poem*. Edited by Stefan Fischer and Gavin Fernandes. Sheffield: Sheffield Phoenix.

Létourneau, Anne. 2015. "Femmes étrangères dans la bible hébraïque: de la douceur du nourrir à la violence du mourir." PhD diss., Université du Québec à Montréal.

———. 2018. "Beauty, Bath and Beyond: Framing Bathsheba as a Royal Fantasy in 2 Sam 11,1–5." *SJOT* 32:72–91.

———. 2021. "From Wild Beast to Huntress: Animal Imagery, Beauty, and Seduction in the Song of Songs and Proverbs." *BibInt* 31:67–93.

Létourneau, Anne, Ellen De Doncker, and Olivier Roy-Turgeon. 2022. "A Parade of Adornments (Isa 3:18–23): Daughters (of) Zion in the Light of Gender and Material Culture Studies." *Open Theology* 8:445–59.

Limmer, Abigail Susan. 2007. "The Social Functions and Ritual Significance of Jewelry in the Iron Age II Southern Levant." PhD diss., University of Arizona.

López Rodríguez, Irene. 2009. "Of Women, Bitches, Chickens and Vixens: Animal Metaphors for Women in English and Spanish." *CLR* 7:77–100.

Millar, Suzanna R. 2020. "Openness, Closure, and Transformation in Proverb Translation." *BT* 71:79–100.

Mizelle, Brett. 2011. *Pig*. London: Reaktion Books.

Muraoka, Takamitsu. 1977. "Status Constructus of Adjectives in Biblical Hebrew." *VT* 27:375–80.

Platt, Elizabeth E. 1979. "Jewelry of Bible Times and the Catalog of Isa 3:18–23." *AUSS* 17:71–84.

Price, Max D. 2020. *Evolution of a Taboo: Pigs and People in the Ancient Near East*. New York: Oxford University Press.

Quick, Laura. 2019. "'She Made Herself Up Provocatively for the Charming of the Eyes of Men' (Jdt. 10.4): Cosmetics and Body Adornment in the Stories of Judith and Susanna." *JSP* 28:215–36.

———. 2021. *Dress, Adornment and the Body in the Hebrew Bible*. Oxford: Oxford University Press.

Sapir-Hen, Lidar. 2019. "Food, Pork Consumption, and Identity in Ancient Israel." *NEA* 82:52–59.

Sapir-Hen, Lidar, Guy Bar-Oz, Yuval Gadot, and Israel Finkelstein. 2013. "Pig Husbandry in Iron Age Israel and Judah: New Insights Regarding the Origin of the 'Taboo.'" *ZDPV* 129:1–20.

Sapir-Hen, Lidar, Meirav Meiri, and Israel Finkelstein. 2015. "Iron Age Pigs: New Evidence on Their Origin and Role in Forming Identity Boundaries." *Radiocarbon* 57:307–15.

Sapir-Hen, Lidar, Joe Uziel, and Ortal Chalaf. 2021. "Everything but the Oink: On the Discovery of an Articulated Pig in Iron Age Jerusalem and Its Meaning to Judahite Consumption Practices." *NEA* 84:110–19.

Schipper, Bernd U. 2019. *Proverbs: A Commentary on the Book of Proverbs*. Minneapolis: Fortress.

Stone, Ken. 2017. *Reading the Hebrew Bible with Animal Studies*. Stanford, CA: Stanford University Press.

Streck, Michael P. 2012. "The Pig and the Fox in Two Popular Sayings from Assur." Pages 789–92 in *Leggo! Studies Presented to Frederick Mario Fales on the Occasion of His Sixty-Fifth Birthday*. Edited by Giovanni B. Lafranchi, Daniele M. Bonacossi, Cinzia Pappi, and Simonetta Ponchia. Wiesbaden: Harrassowitz.

Job and the Maggots

Suzanna R. Millar

Job is intimately acquainted with maggots (*rimmâ*). He relates to them personally, as he announces "maggots clothe my flesh" (*lābaš bəśārî rimmâ*; 7:5), and imagines "call[ing] the maggot 'my mother' and 'my sister'" (*qārā'tî ... 'immî va'ăḥōtî lārimmâ*; 17:14).[1] He ruminates on them generally, describing the maggots associated with dead bodies; indeed, "maggots cover them" (*vərimmâ təkasseh 'ălêhem*; 21:26), and "the maggot finds him sweet" (*mətāqô rimmâ*; 24:20). Bildad, too, speaks of maggots, finding in them a symbol for the pitiful human state. Not even the moon and stars are pure; "How much less the human, who is a maggot?" (*'ap kî 'ĕnôš rimmâ*; 25:6).

Although Job attends to these maggots, scholars resolutely ignore them, even when they consider other nonhuman life forms.[2] We humans have little inclination to think of maggots. They are not our companions, like dogs or cats, nor our foodstuff, like cows or sheep. They have neither economic nor religious value. They do not earn the respect due the predator, nor the sympathy due the prey. If we think of them at all, it is with disdain and disgust. In their unbreachable difference from humans, we consider them unbreachably below humans. Connoting the festering and putrid, their heaving bodies squirm and pulsate, and so we too heave or squirm, repulsed. When we encounter them in literature, we squash or sanitize them from our minds, reasoning that their little bodies are little more than symbols for bigger concerns. Maggots are symbols for human death, and human death should be our concern, not maggots.

---

1. Unless otherwise noted, all biblical translations are my own.
2. Several monographs consider nonhuman animals in Job but only give fleeting mention to maggots, e.g., Doak 2014, 159–60, 169, 276; Hawley 2018, 116; Schifferdecker 2008, 101. See also Riede 2002, 51–54, 127–28; Millar 2021.

However, some recent eco-critics have challenged this tendency (e.g., Bertoni 2016; Schwartz 2012). Small life deserves consideration in its own right, maggot-as-maggot, worm-as-worm. Small life is fundamental to the eco-entanglements that perpetually destroy and create possibilities for all life. If the maggot entails death, then death entails fertilization and compost, and I, with Donna Haraway (2016, 32), "jump ... into that wormy pile." Maggots can help to birth vermiform modes of thought that twist the inflexible structures of Western rationalism, and new ways of relating that wriggle upward through the gaps of kyriarchal, anthropo-dominant models. This is in line with what Matthew Calarco (2015, 48–69) calls an indistinction approach to nonhuman animals (see introduction to this volume). Drawing on indistinction theorists (notably Haraway, Deleuze, and Plumwood), this chapter searches for new modes of interspecies being, thinking, and relating.

In this essay, the maggots in Job will be uncomfortable companions. I do not profess to unearth the original meaning of the text but rather to follow the maggots as guides in ecocritical reflection. I will treat the textual body as they treat the human body, ingesting and digesting, finding it fecund with possibility. As we tunnel together—I into the corpus and they into the corpse—we will confuse and cross boundaries, between the individual and the corporate, between life and death.

Individual and Corporate Bodies

The Individual Body

The maggots on/in Job's body trouble and violate ancient Israelite ideals of bodily integrity. It is against this background that their activity must be viewed. The ideal body is whole and fully integrated (Basson 2008). Coconstitutive with the self, the body indexes moral state. Those with a physical impairment may have been cursed by God (Deut 28:21–22, 27–28, 35, 59–61), been foolish and sinful (Ps 38:4 [3], 6 [5]), or perverted what is right (Job 33:27). Of particular importance was the skin, the protective barrier separating the self from the outside world, and an obvious visible marker for a curse (Deut 28:35). Disintegrating skin speaks to Bildad of an individual's wickedness (Job 18:5, 13), while Leviathan's tightly fused and integral scales are an object of God's delight (41:7–9 [15–17]).

Though Job begins his story as a man of both moral and physical integrity (an *'îš tām* in both senses; 1:1), he is quickly stricken with physical suffering (2:7). Like the lamenting psalmist, he cries out in bodily affliction (e.g., Job 6:10–12; 9:17; 16:8; 17:7; 30:17; see Pss 22:15–18 [14–17]; 31:10–11 [9–10]; 38:1–12 [1–11]). This is taken to indicate his guilt, his shriveled and lean condition witnessing to his moral corruption (Job 16:8; Erickson 2013). Particularly stricken is Job's skin (van der Zwan 2017), which suffers as though under a divine curse—covered with "grievous sores from the sole of his foot to the crown of his head" (*šəḥîn rāʿ mikkap raglô vəʿad qodqŏdô*; Job 2:7; see Deut 28:35). Job scrapes these sores with a potsherd (2:8), which may be intended as a counterirritant but further enacts his skin's breakdown. Ultimately, his skins sticks to his bones, turns black, and falls from upon him (19:20; 30:30).

Job's condition is apparently worsened by a case of myiasis—maggot infestation. In myiasis, flies lay their eggs in wounds or orifices (around two hundred eggs per fly), the eggs hatch into larvae, and the larvae feed on available tissue or bodily fluids (Fleischmann, Grassberger, and Sherman 2011). Accordingly, Job describes his flesh as "clothed with maggots and clods of dust" (*lābaš bəśārî rimmâ vəgûš ʿāpār*; 7:5).[3] Clothing—that which should distinguish human from nonhuman life—is now constituted by nonhuman life (see Gen 3:21). Like a garment, the maggots spread over him, intimate in their physical touch. What is more, clothing is costume, announcing personal identity. Clothing may indicate social status (Job's crown is stripped from his head, 19:9; see 1 Sam 18:4), virtues and morals (righteousness and justice are his robe, Job 29:14; see Pss 93:1, 104:1, 132:9), and bodily health (he wastes away like a moth-eaten garment, 13:28; see Quick 2020). The maggots may hatch in this manifold semiotic potential, bringing implication of low status, poor morals, and ill health.

Elsewhere, Job sews sackcloth onto his skin (*śaq tāpartî ʿălê gildî*; 16:15), perhaps to bandage its shriveled and ruptured state (16:8, 13). Here, the maggots are not clothes that protect his skin but clothes that replace his skin, directly covering the flesh. In an uncomfortable restitching of metaphorical components, there is not here wounded skin protected by a garment, nor even skin like an insect-eaten garment (see 13:28); rather, a garment of insects, which eats the skin.

---

3. The *qere* is *gûš* and the *ketiv* is *gyš*. *Gûš* seems to be a hapax meaning "clod" (cf. Aramaic *gvšʾ*). Driver (1969, 73–74), followed by Clines (1989, 163), takes this to have a "figurative medical connotation" meaning "pustules," "scabs." But this does not work with the subsequent word, *ʾāpār* ("dust"), and they resort to convoluted explanations.

The maggots threaten the integrity of the skin and by extension the integrity of the self (in its social, ethical, and physical dimensions). Using mouth-hooks, maggots burrow into and feed off open wounds, deepening and enlarging them (Soler Cruz 2008). The perpetual motion of their multiple bodies unstitches the skin, threatening fragmentation. As Steven Connor (2004, 242) puts it, "The dream of worms does not destroy or deny the skin so much as reconstitute it, as a thing of holes, passages." The "clods of dust" (*gûš ʿāpār*) that clothe Job alongside the maggots offer little hope of integrity. Unlike clay, which clings together (10:9a), dust disintegrates (10:9b).

As maggots bore the skin, it begins to leak. The later Testament of Job is effusive: "I wet the earth with the moistness of my sore body, for matter flowed off my body, and many worms covered it" (T. Job 5.7). In the biblical account, Job complains: "my skin congeals and flows" (*ʿôrî rāgaʿ vayyimmāʾēs*; Job 7:5b).[4] As though the healing process is stuck on loop, his suppurating sores scab over, only to reopen to flows of fluid.

The maggots allow for this leakage, feed off it, and even become part of it. Maggots seem to ooze, unskeletoned, from the sores. They are precarious formations of otherwise formless slime, asserting a troublesome existence, resistant to proper categorization as solid or liquid. Ruminating on "the being of the slimy," Jean-Paul Sartre (2003, 631) notes the "vague, soft effort made by each to individualize itself" (here, each maggot squirms to the surface) "followed by a falling back and flattening out that is emptied of the individual" (the squirming maggot mass). This maggot-slime seems to suck in Job too, whose own skin is caught in a solid-fluid flux of hardening (*rgʿ*) and melting (*mʾs*). Job is thus clothed by maggots, a slimy solid-becoming-liquid, and by clods of dust, a precarious solid-becoming-granular. No wonder that he anticipates the complete dissolution of the self: "your eyes are on me and I am gone" (*ʿênêkā bî vəʾênennî*, 7:8; see 7:21).

The Social Body

If Job's physical body is threatened, so too is his place in the social body, for unwhole bodies violated social norms, taboos, and regulations around

---

4. With most interpreters, I take *rgʿ* as "to harden, congeal," cognate with Ethiopic *ragaʾa* (so BDB). Some scholars (e.g., Dhorme 1967, 100) note that *rgʿ* occurs in Job 26:12 parallel to *mḥṣ*, "to shatter," and hence translate it as "to crack." *Mʾs* is probably a by-form of *mss*, "to melt" (as has also been suggested for *mʾs* in Job 7:16; 42:6; e.g., Clines 2011, 1207, 1219).

purity (Basson 2008). Particularly troublesome were breaches to bodily boundaries, such as Job's diseased skin (see Lev 13) and physical discharges (see Lev 15). The "matter out of place" produced by such unruly, leaky bodies could contaminate and pollute the community (Douglas 2003). And the worms that infest Job are themselves impure. As the "prototype and model of the swarming things," they are not easily placed in proper categories of form or motion (Lev 11:41–44; Douglas 2003, 57). As common inhabitants of decaying flesh, they carry a reminder of the pollution of death (e.g., Num 19:11–20).

Job's personal disintegration threatens social disintegration. In a society tightly structured by kinship relationships, the physical body receives identity through its position within the social body, and the social body receives identity through the physical bodies positioned within it (Basson 2008, 289). The individual body functions as a concentrated semiotic manifestation of society as a whole (Erickson 2013, 298). Thus, unruly, unwhole bodies bring disorder and disruption. If the maggots are matter out of place for Job, Job is matter out of place for society.

Maggots elicit disgust, from both the readers and other actors in Job's society. Chapter 7 draws attention to the intense divine gaze on Job, encouraging readers to picture the repulsive scene (7:8, 19–21). Readers, like God, will not look away from Job, even as he swallows his spittle (*lōʾ-tišʿeh mimmennî ... ʿad-bilʿî ruqqî*; 7:19). Disgust is typically elicited by things that threaten disease/contamination or suggest human mortality (Kasperbauer 2015). Maggots—known to provoke disgust cross-culturally—burrow into both these concerns (Davey et al. 1998). In Job 7:5, they are also entangled with other disgust elicitors. People are disgusted by violators of bodily boundaries: substances that might enter into them and cause disease (like maggots clothing the flesh; Rozin et al. 1995). They are disgusted by bodily fluids (such as pus and blood leaking from sores) and by that which resembles them (such as slimy invertebrates; Rozin, Haidt, and McCauley 2018, 818). People are disgusted by death and decay, and by their denizens (worms eating dead flesh; McGinn 2011, 13–18).

Job thus repels society and is expelled from society in return. He is marginalized and ostracized, publicly humiliated as passers-by spit at him (17:6; 30:10). Even his family rejects him: his brothers are far away (19:13); his relatives have failed (19:14); he is a stench to his wife and siblings (19:17). Accordingly, Job seeks his family elsewhere.

The Ecological Body

As though answering Donna Haraway's (2016, 102) ecological invitation to "Make Kin Not Babies!" Job positions himself within the nonhuman community. He declares himself "a brother of jackals and a companion of ostriches" (30:29) and imagines "call[ing] the maggot 'my mother' and 'my sister'" (*qārā'tî ... 'immî va'ăḥōtî lārimmâ*; 17:14). David Clines (1989, 399) notes the "legal ring" to this language, suggestive of formal adoption into a family (citing parallels in Hos 2:4 [2]; Ps 2:7; Jer 2:27; Prov 7:4). Here, the adoption is only hypothetical and is apparently rejected ("if ['*im*; v. 13] I call ... where then is my hope [*vǝ'ayyēh 'ēpô tiqvâtî*; v. 15]?"). However, it is a suggestive possibility, inviting ecocritical exploration.

The maggot is feminized as mother and sister. As mother, she may nurture and care for Job. As sister—a possible idiom for "lover" (see Song 4:9–10, 12)—she may offer affection and intimacy. Job might join with the speaker of the Middle English Disputation Betwyxt the Body and Wormes, who declares to the maggots "Let us be friends ... let us kiss and dwell together forever" (Steel 2013, 108). Or, he might speak with Shakespeare's Cleopatra, who plays on the alternative meaning of "gentle" (as "maggot"), longing for a "gentle grave," and calling the asp's love-bite "As sweet as balm, as soft as air, as gentle" (act 5, scene 2; Martin 2015, 138).

As a child of mother-worm, Job is a subordinate in the ecological family. This is a powerful challenge to human exceptionalism; as Erasmus Darwin puts it, "Stoop, selfish Pride! survey thy kindred forms, / Thy brother Emmets, and thy sister Worms!"[5] (cited in Schwartz 2012, 116). Such a challenge is sounded throughout Job. For example, Ps 8 is repeatedly invoked and subverted (Job 7:17–18; 15:14–16; 25:4–6; see also 4:17–19; Kynes 2012, 63–79). This psalm asks, "What is man?" (*mâ 'ěnôš*; Ps 8:5 [4]) in comparison to the glorious stars and divine beings (8:4 [3], 6 [5]). The answer comes as an affirmation of human status above all nonhuman animals (8:7–9 [6–8]). In Job, neither stars (Job 25:5) nor heavenly beings (4:18; 15:15) are pure. How much less the human, "who is crushed like a moth" (4:19). Indeed, says Bildad, "how much less the human, who is a maggot, or the child of humanity, who is a worm" (25:6; *'ap kî-'ěnôš*

5.. This line is taken from Darwin's final long poem, "Temple of Nature" (3:433–34), which traces his ideas of evolution from microorganisms to organized human society. "Emmets" means "ants."

rimmâ ûben-ʾādām tôlēʿâ). Far from their vertiginous position above other creatures, the human is identified with the vermicular.

Indeed, this has biological backing. Based on a major study of gene expression, for example, Mark Gerstein and colleagues (2014) comments on the "deep similarities" of humans with flies and worms (quoted in Hathaway 2014). Bildad, of course, intends his remark as a degradation, assuming that the worm lacks worth. This assumption is pervasive and undergirds common structures of dehumanization. "I am a worm and not a man," laments the psalmist, "the reproach of humanity and despised by a people" (Ps 22:7 [6]). The assumption is even written into the English language: despicable creatures we call "vermin" (from Latin *vermis*, "worm"). But scrutinized with an ecocritical gaze, which refuses a priori devaluation of other life forms, the identification of human and maggot might not be lamentable. As theorists of human-animal identity have taught, observing the similarities between humans and nonhumans provides a corrective to human exceptionalism and offers resources for ethical relating (Calarco 2015, 6–27).[6]

However, an important corrective is sounded here from theorists of human-animal difference (Calarco 2015, 28–47). In many meaningful ways, this maggot is not like me; I am not like this maggot. The encounter may be structured instead by an ethics of radical Otherness, such as that proposed by Emmanuel Levinas (e.g., 1969). For Levinas, ethical resources are primarily found in the face-to-face encounter with the Other. However, even this assumes similarity. What if the Other does not have a face? What if, unlike Derrida's (2008, 3–4) cat, it does not meet your gaze? What if what you mistook for eyes are in fact its posterior respiratory spiracles?[7] The ethics of Otherness are pushed to their limits here, further than many would want to go.

Perhaps an alternative mode of relating is needed, one not focused solely on identity or difference. Calarco's (2015, 48–69; see also Bunch 2014) indistinction theorists can help here. Gilles Deleuze and Félix Guattari (1988, 232–48) suggest a "becoming-animal" emerging between heterogeneous beings. This entails "inhabiting zones of indistinction where traditional binary distinctions between human beings and animals

---

6. For discussion of identity, difference, and indistinction approaches, see the introduction to this volume.

7. Fleischmann, Grassberger, and Sherman (2011, 9) note that these are often mistaken for eyes in maggots.

break down" (Calarco 2015, 57). As the maggots bore into Job, dissolving his individual self, they and he co-become into something else. To willfully misinterpret Bildad's syntax, they co-become the "man of maggots" or even the "man-maggot" (*'ĕnôš rimmâ*; 25:6). For Deleuze and Guattari (1988, 233, 237–38, 241–42), the relationship of becoming does not proceed by resemblance, filiation, or identity but is better understood as "a hideous pact," a "contagion," an "unnatural participation."

In this heterogenous assemblage, distinctions break down between inside and outside, subject and object, agent and patient. We cannot speak of a singular subject (Job) confronting external objects (maggots), for the maggots are inside him and, as they ingest his flesh, he is inside them. Within this hybrid becoming, agency is distributed. The debilitated, disintegrating Job can no longer imagine himself a powerful independent actor. As Jane Bennett (2010, 96) describes, agency now "has no single locus, no mastermind, but is distributed across a swarm of various and variegated vibrant materialities."

Indeed, the maggot is encountered as a swarm, a teeming. Ethical reflection may come most naturally if one imagines the individual maggot; perhaps the "single worm" that later tradition depicts being placed on Job's body (T. Job 5.8), perhaps the *rimmâ* (conceived as singular noun) whom Job calls "my mother" or "my sister" (Job 17:4). But all lives are entangled in codependent and mutual becomings, thus challenging pretensions to singular identity—the *rimmâ* (conceived as collective noun) who cover the dead with their teeming mass (21:26). Though Deleuze and Guattari (1988, 243, 239) refuse to neglect the "exceptional individual," they contend, "A becoming-animal always involves a pack, a band, a population, a peopling, in short, a multiplicity." The man-maggot multiplicity constitutes a dynamic ecological entanglement of "manifold and makeshift relatings," not reducible to individual man or maggot parts (Bertoni 2016, 11).

Death and Life

Maggots and Death

As interpreted above, the maggots participate in myiasis—infestation of a still-living organism. But maggots are also symbols of death, known for habitually feeding off corpses (e.g., Isa 14:11; 66:24; Sir 7:17, 10:11). Thus Gilgamesh laments his rotting friend Enkidu: "I would not give him up for burial … until a worm fell out of his nose" (*ANET*, 90). Death is a major preoccupation of both Job (e.g., 3:11–23; 7:6–10; 9:22–23; 10:18–22; 14:1–14; 17:13–16; 21:23–34) and his friends (4:7–11, 17–21; 15:17–35; 18:5–21; 20:4–11). The maggots tunnel into these reflections.

First, maggots attest death-in-life. In ancient Israelite understanding, death was probably not a one-time event, experienced when breathing and circulation ceased. Rather, the powers of the grave could reach the realm of the living, dragging individuals toward death-in-life, entangling them in the cords of Sheol (Ps 18:5; see also 30:4 [3]; 49:15; 86:13; 88:4 [3]; 116:3; Mathewson 2006; Suriano 2018, 217–48). Thus Job is like one already dead, his friends participating in mortuary rituals upon seeing him (Job 2:12; Clines 1989, 61). A chthonic alliance of maggots and dust—which elsewhere claims those dead and buried (21:26; see also 17:13–16)—now clothes Job (7:5), shrouding him in life with the cling of the grave. The creatures feast on the necrotic tissue of his wounds, exposing the painful truth that parts of him are—and have always been—dying or dead. Indeed, all organic life experiences perpetual small deaths. At a microbial level, parts of us are always dying, always being consumed by uncountable others.

Second, maggots are caught in the tension between Job's conflicting desires to delay and hurry death. On the one hand, Job laments human transience (e.g., 9:25–26; 10:20–22; 13:28; 14:1–2). He depicts human death as a fragmentation of personal boundaries and a degeneration from solid to liquid to gas. Like heat that melts the snow, then evaporates the waters, so death claims the individual life (24:19). Maggots enact these metaphors, breaking up the skin, oozing from it as it melts away (7:5). Accordingly, Job's life is as fleeting as a weaver's shuttle, a breath, or a fading cloud (7:6–7, 9). What is more, maggots are themselves transient life—easily squashed and extinguished. So too the human, who is crushed like a moth (4:19), indeed, who is a maggot (25:6). On the other hand, though, Job longs for death "like a slave who longs for the shade" (7:2; see also 3:3–26; 6:8–9; 7:15; 10:18–19). Accordingly, Job imagines welcoming these vermicular denizens of the underworld, painting a macabre portrait of domestic and familial belonging with Sheol, darkness, pit, and worm (17:13–14).

Third, maggots epitomize and enact the chaos of death, which must be controlled. The teeming and self-generating maggot mass behaves to the individual body like death behaves to the social body—infringing on and violating boundaries, destabilizing and breaking down structures, eating what was once prized. Maggots and death are similarly indiscriminate:

everyone, Job says, "will die town together in the dust, and maggots will cover them" (21:26).

To control this chaos, Israelite society constructed systems, rituals, and institutions that separated a good death from a bad death. These were essential both for the deceased individual (whose postmortem existence was at stake) and for the community (for whom death was dangerous and polluting). The ideal death was curated through the ritual time and space of the bench tomb (Suriano 2018, 39–55). The cadaver was laid on a bench and provisioned with paraphernalia for the transition to the underworld (e.g., clothing, food, drink, amulets, and lamps). A stone was rolled over the entrance of the tomb, and the body left to decay. The troubling activity of maggots and other small life was sealed off within these ritual boundaries and stone walls. Thus enclosed, the collision of human and maggot life was simultaneously controlled and blocked from the consciousness. The bones, once free from multispecies flesh, could be gathered and collected alongside those of similarly unfleshed kinsmen in the repository.

This leads to a fourth point: maggots challenge the individual's postmortem belonging. They gnaw on and disintegrate human strategies to keep the deceased within their community. If kinship relations extend to the dead (Cook 2007), enacted through the bones being gathered to the ancestors, then maggots offer themselves as new kin, "mother" and "sister" of the deceased (Job 17:14). If memorialization keeps the deceased alive in society, then the worm-eaten corpse is "no longer remembered" (24:20). If a bad death is epitomized by the social abandonment of the cadaver to scavengers (e.g., Deut 28:26; Jer 16:4; Stavrakopoulou 2010, 71–76), then worms remind us that all bodies are consumed, sweet to maggots (Job 24:20).[8] And if a good death entails lavish funerary displays of human solidarity—such that "all mankind follows after" the deceased and "those who go before him are innumerable" (21:33)—then maggots counter that all deaths are alike, entailing the same postmortem company: all "will lie down together in the dust, and maggots will cover them" (21:26).

---

8. I translate *matāqô rimmâ* in Job 24:20 as "the maggot finds him sweet." The verb *mtq* usually means "to be sweet" (Job 21:33; Exod 15:25; Prov 9:17). The third-person masculine singular object suffix and the overall sense require a transitive meaning "to find sweet" here. Alternatively, *mtq* here might correspond to Aramaic *mtq*, "to suck." The subject (*rimmâ*) is feminine and the verb masculine, but this type of mismatch is not unprecedented (e.g., *rimmâ* in Isa 14:11; collective animal terms in Gen 12:16; 13:5; 30:43; 32:6).

Maggots and Life

For all their associations with death, however, maggots manifest, signify, and enable life. Maggots that infest the wounds of living subjects can clean the wound, kill harmful microorganisms, and stimulate healing (Fleischmann, Grassberger, and Sherman 2004, 26–27). Though he laments their presence, Job might be a preemptive recipient of this recently FDA-approved medical treatment, "maggot therapy."

If Job imagines his body as a decaying corpse, one might note that the decaying corpse is in fact a vital ecosystem, teeming with small life (Costandi 2015). Bacteria are rampant. When the immune system deactivates, aerobic bacteria from the microbiome begin to spread and multiply, digesting the body's tissue in a process of autolysis (Javan et al. 2016). They are soon joined by anaerobic bacteria, which further break down tissue into gases, liquids, and salts, effecting the body's putrefaction. Insects can smell the decay. Blowflies and flesh flies may lay their eggs in corpses within minutes of death (Carter, Yellowlees, and Tibbett 2007, 14). These eggs hatch into larvae—Job's maggots—that molt twice into increasingly larger forms. The maggots flourish, feasting on flesh, bodily fluids, and ingested foods. During the decomposition, diverse insect life may join the corpse-community (Lindgren et al. 2015).

Above, I discussed the man-maggot assemblage experienced by Job and his teeming vermicular companions. Here I add that this assemblage does not require all participants to be alive. Indeed, the birth and collaboration of maggots depend on necrotic tissue. Alliances are made possible through death (Bezan 2015). They thus challenge the absolute distinction between life and death as a structuring principle for ethics and society. The "necro-ecology" of the worm-infested corpse is internally generative (Bezan 2015). The dead flesh is reanimated through the crisscrossing, crowded, creative ecological interactions.

Within this eco-entanglement, the varied partners interrelate through consumption (Bertoni 2016). Job is described in later tradition as "worm-eaten" (T. Job 5.6; 8.2), and he describes the maggot finding the dead man "sweet" (*mətāqô rimmâ*; Job 24:20). Maggots ingest what we abject, taking in what we push away (Hovanec 2019, 89). Eating is transformative, at once destructive and creative. Job feeds the maggots and is diminished. The maggots feed on Job and are enlivened. This challenges the assumed human position atop the food pyramid, forcing us "to acknowledge our own animality and ecological vulnerability"

(Plumwood 1999, 91).[9] As Hamlet aptly puts it, "We fat all creatures else to fat us, and we fat ourselves for maggots" (*Hamlet*, act 4, scene 3; cited in Martin 2015, 141). Humans are but the diet of worms.

Job, though, depicts the interaction both ways. As maggots cover the corpse (21:26), consume it, and delight in its sweetness (*mtq*; 24:20), so the corpse is imagined to consume its grave soil—"the wadi's clods are sweet [*mtq*] to it" (21:33). This unhuman appetite for dirt may be well-founded for the fertility that decomposition can bring to the soil. Challenging the cultural ideal of entombment, the untombed cadaver participates in life-generating interactions. As Haraway (2016, 32) puts it, "human as humus has potential." The decomposing body provides localized fertilization, enlivening the surrounding ecosystem (a "cadaver decomposition island"; Carter, Yellowlees, and Tibbett 2007). Carbon and nutrients are released into the soil, microbial biomass and activity increase, and varied plant-life may grow. Biodiversity increases as the cadaver site is attended by insects and scavengers, themselves attended by a community of bacteria and organic matter.

Thus, though the dust of the earth may be closely associated with death (Job 10:9; 17:16; 20:11; 21:26; 34:15), it is also the stuff of creation. This includes human creation—*'ādām* comes from *'ădāmâ* (Gen 2:7; see also Job 10:9; 33:6). If Job will lie down in the dust at his death, this is no less than a return to the generative womb of the earth (1:21).[10] Death enables life for other beings. For many cultures, death has symbolic resonances of, and generative potential for, new birth (Bloch and Parry 1982). As for Job, the grave-maggot becomes his mother (17:14), a warm bosom of fertility and life. He may elsewhere declare that creative forces depart from the deceased—the "womb forgets" (*yiškāḥēhû reḥem*) those whom the worm finds sweet (24:20). But this departure from the individualized human life makes way for dispersed ecological vitality.

---

9. Plumwood's remarks were stimulated by her experience of almost being eaten by a crocodile. This encounter offered her a profound reconfiguration of the dualistic narrative in which humans are masters over nature.

10. In Job 1:21, Job says, "Naked I came from my mother's womb, and naked shall I return there." This verse is disputed. The deictic particle "there" (*šāmmâ*) apparently refers back to the "mother's womb" (*beṭen 'immî*), suggesting that the "mother" in question may not be the human mother but mother earth (see Ps 139:13–15; Qoh 5:14 [15]; Sir 40:1; Wis 7:1–6; Vall 1995). Alternative suggestions include that *šāmmâ* is a reference to the underworld (Gordis 1978, 78) or to the mother goddess (Hays 2012).

Indeed, life and death are closely related, the former made possible through the latter (Millar 2021). The divine speeches unflinchingly acknowledge this, cradling images of death and destruction in the language of birth and generation (38:9, 28–29). Fledgling life proliferates—young lions, ravens, goats, ostriches, and hawks (38:39, 41; 39:1–4, 14–16, 30). But this life depends on the death of others (38:39, 41; 39:15, 29–31). Indeed, the speech ends with young hawks feasting on a corpse, slain in battle (39:30). In all likelihood, the maggots got there first.

Conclusion

In this essay, we have peered with Job at maggots (7:5; 17:14; 21:26; 24:20; 25:6). We have furrowed with maggots through Job (they through flesh, we through text). As we have done so, we have been guided in new possibilities for ecocritical engagement.

The maggots have disturbed the divisions and interactions between individual and corporate bodies. They bore through Job's skin, perforating the boundary of his individuated body. Concomitantly, they contaminate and pollute him, provoking his expulsion from the social body. But they welcome him to the ecological body, offering dynamic entanglements—new modes of relating and becoming. The maggots have also squirmed through the divisions of life and death. As Job reminds us, maggots consume corpses. Chthonic and chaotic, they epitomize the teeming tumult of death. But they are nourished by death, transforming the cadaver into a vibrant and vital community of living, dying, and eating together.

What are the ethical implications of this? Western society is largely constructed on the myth of the rational, autonomous subject, whose goal is to acquire and dominate. This subject position is preserved for the truly human (typically, the male, white, elite). Small life is insignificant, precarious, even repulsive. Job's maggots may challenge this. Their agency is decentralized, manifested through messy bodily interaction rather than through pure rational logos. They enter human flesh and human flesh enters them, challenging strict divisions between self and other. The self has no clear boundaries; it is always and already implicated in collective becomings. For Deleuze and Guattari (see above), that which we become is always minoritarian. Indeed, it may entail an entanglement with that which unwarrantedly disgusts and repels—decay, maggots (immigrants, queer folk, the disabled—cast as vermin).

Job's maggots provoke us to acknowledge, even to embrace, such entanglements. Indeed, the disruption of our usual ontological categories of selfhood creates a space where novelty and creativity can occur (Brown 2007, 262). What if we let Job's maggots, wriggling upward through their human hosts, mangle interspecies hierarchies? What if we found their decay to be putrid and productive, fertilizer for new life and thought? What if, in short, we truly said "my mother" and "my sister" to the maggot?

Works Cited

Basson, Alec. 2008. "Just Skin and Bones: The Longing for Wholeness of the Body in the Book of Job." *VT* 58:287–99.

Bennett, Jane. 2010. *Vibrant Matter: A Political Ecology of Things*. Durham, NC: Duke University Press.

Bertoni, Filippo. 2016. *Living with Worms: On the Earthly Togetherness of Eating*. Amsterdam: Universiteit van Amsterdam.

Bezan, Sarah. 2015. "Necro-Eco: The Ecology of Death in Jim Crace's *Being Dead*." *Mosaic* 48:191–207.

Bloch, Maurice, and Jonathan Parry. 1982. "Introduction: Death and the Regeneration of Life." Pages 1–44 in *Death and the Regeneration of Life*. Edited by Jonathan Parry and Maurice Bloch. Cambridge: Cambridge University Press.

Brown, Lori. 2007. "Becoming-Animal in the Flesh: Expanding the Ethical Reach of Deleuze and Guattari's Tenth Plateau." *PhaenEx* 2:260–78.

Bunch, Mary. 2014. "Posthuman Ethics and the Becoming Animal of Emmanuel Levinas." *CTC* 55:34–50.

Calarco, Matthew. 2015. *Thinking through Animals: Identity, Difference, Indistinction*. StBr. Stanford, CA: Stanford University Press.

Carter, David, David Yellowlees, and Mark Tibbett. 2007. "Cadaver Decomposition in Terrestrial Ecosystems." *Natur* 94:12–24.

Clines, David J. A. 1989. *Job 1–20*. WBC 17. Dallas: Word Books.

———. 2011. *Job 38–42*. WBC 18B. Nashville: Nelson.

Connor, Steven. 2004. *The Book of Skin*. Ithaca, NY: Cornell University Press.

Cook, Stephen L. 2007. "Funerary Practices and Afterlife Expectations in Ancient Israel." *RC* 1:660–83.

Costandi, Moheb. 2015. "This Is What Happens after You Die." Ars Technica. https://tinyurl.com/SBL061071.

Davey, Graham C. L., et al. 1998. "A Cross-cultural Study of Animal Fears." *BRT* 36:735–50.

Deleuze, Gilles, and Félix Guattari. 1988. *A Thousand Plateaus: Capitalism and Schizophrenia*. ACET. London: Continuum.

Derrida, Jacques. 2008. *The Animal That Therefore I Am*. Edited by Marie-Louise Mallet. Translated by David Wills. PCPS. New York: Fordham University Press.

Dhorme, Edouard. 1967. *A Commentary on the Book of Job*. Translated by Harold Knight. London: Nelson.

Doak, Brian. 2014. *Consider Leviathan: Narratives of Nature and the Self in Job*. Minneapolis: Fortress.

Douglas, Mary. 2003. *Purity and Danger: An Analysis of Concept of Pollution and Taboo*. London: Routledge.

Driver, Godfrey R. 1969. "Problems in the Hebrew Text of Job." Pages 72–93 in *Wisdom in Israel and in the Ancient Near East: Presented to Harold Henry Rowley by the Editorial Board of Vetus Testamentum in Celebration of His Sixty-Fifth Birthday, 24 March 1955*. Edited by D. Winton Thomas and Martin Noth. VTSup 3. Leiden: Brill.

Erickson, Amy. 2013. "'Without My Flesh I Will See God': Job's Rhetoric of the Body." *JBL* 132:295–313.

Fleischmann, Wim, Martin Grassberger, and Ronald Sherman. 2004. *Maggot Therapy: A Handbook of Maggot-Assisted Wound Healing*. Stuttgart: Thieme.

Gerstein, Mark, et al. 2014. "Comparative Analysis of the Transcriptome across Distant Species." *Nature* 512:445–48.

Gordis, Robert. 1978. *The Book of Job: Commentary, New Translation and Special Studies*. MosS 11. New York: Jewish Theological Seminary of America.

Haraway, Donna. 2016. *Staying with the Trouble: Making Kin in the Chthulucene*. Durham, NC: Duke University Press.

Hathaway, Bill. 2014. "Evolution Used Similar Molecular Toolkits to Shape Flies, Worms, and Humans." YaleNews. https://tinyurl.com/SBL06107m.

Hawley, Lance R. 2018. *Metaphor Competition in the Book of Job*. JAJSup 26. Göttingen: Vandenhoeck & Ruprecht.

Hays, Christopher B. 2012. "'My Beloved Son, Come and Rest in Me': Job's Return to His Mother's Womb (Job 1:21a) in Light of Egyptian Mythology." *VT* 62:607–21.

Hovanec, Caroline. 2019. "Darwin's Earthworms in the Anthropocene." *VRev* 45:81–96.
Javan, Gulnaz T., Sheree J. Finley, Zain Eabidin, and Jennifer G. Mulle. 2016. "The Thanatomicrobiome: A Missing Piece of the Microbial Puzzle of Death." *FM* 7. https://doi.org/10.3389/fmicb.2016.00225.
Kasperbauer, Tyler J. 2015. "Animals as Disgust Elicitors." *B&P* 30:167–85.
Kynes, Will. 2012. *My Psalm Has Turned into Weeping: Job's Dialogue with the Psalms*. BZAW 437. Berlin: de Gruyter.
Levinas, Emmanuel. 1969. *Totality and Infinity: An Essay on Exteriority*. Pittsburgh: Duquesne University Press.
Lindgren, Natalie K., Melissa S. Sisson, Alan D. Archambeault, Brent C. Rahlwes, James R. Willett, and Sibyl R. Bucheli. 2015. "Four Forensic Entomology Case Studies: Records and Behavioral Observations on Seldom Reported Cadaver Fauna with Notes on Relevant Previous Occurrences and Ecology." *JME* 52:143–50.
Martin, R. 2015. *Shakespeare and Ecology*. OST. Oxford University Press.
Mathewson, Dan. 2006. *Death and Survival in the Book of Job: Desymbolization and Traumatic Experience*. LHBOTS 450. New York: T&T Clark.
McGinn, Colin. 2011. *The Meaning of Disgust*. Oxford: Oxford University Press.
Millar, Suzanna R. 2021. "The Ecology of Death in the Book of Job." *BibInt* 30:265–93.
Plumwood, Val. 1999. "Being Prey." Pages 76–92 in *The New Earth Reader: The Best of Terra Nova*. Edited by David Rothenberg and Marta Ulvaeus. Cambridge: MIT Press.
Quick, Laura. 2020. "'Like a Garment Eaten by Moths': (Job 13:28): Clothing, Nudity and Illness in the Book of Job." *BibInt* 30:46–65.
Riede, Peter. 2002. *Im Spiegel Der Tiere: Studien zum Verhältnis von Mensch und Tier im Alten Israel*. OBO. Freiburg: Universitätsverlag.
Rozin, Paul, Jonathan Haidt, and Clark McCauley. 2018. "Disgust." Pages 815–34 in *Handbook of Emotions*. Edited by L. F. Barrett, M. Lewis, and J. M. Haviland-Jones. 4th ed. New York: Guilford.
Rozin, Paul, Carol Nemeroff, Matthew Horowitz, Bonnie Gordon, and Wendy Voet. 1995. "The Borders of the Self: Contamination Sensitivity and Potency of the Body Apertures and Other Body Parts." *JRP* 29:318–40.
Sartre, Jean-Paul. 2003. *Being and Nothingness: An Essay on Phenomenological Ontology*. RC. London: Routledge.

Schifferdecker, Kathryn. 2008. *Out of the Whirlwind: Creation Theology in the Book of Job.* HTS 61. Cambridge: Harvard University Press.

Schwartz, Janelle A. 2012. *Worm Work: Recasting Romanticism.* Minneapolis: University of Minnesota Press.

Soler Cruz, Maria D. 2008. "Myiasis." Pages 2517–27 in *Encyclopedia of Entomology.* Edited by John L. Capinera. Heidelberg: Springer.

Stavrakopoulou, Francesca. 2010. "Gog's Grave and the Use and Abuse of Corpses in Ezekiel 39:11–20." *JBL* 129:67–84.

Steel, Karl. 2013. "Abyss: Everything Is Food." *Postm* 4:93–104.

———. 2019. *How Not to Make a Human: Pets, Feral Children, Worms, Sky Burial, Oysters.* Minneapolis: University of Minnesota Press.

Suriano, Matthew J. 2018. *A History of Death in the Hebrew Bible.* New York: Oxford University Press.

Vall, Gregory. 1995. "The Enigma of Job 1,21a." *Bib* 76:325–42.

Zwan, Pieter van Der. 2017. "Some Psychoanalytical Meanings of the Skin in the Book of Job." *VeE* 38:1–8.

Responses

From Jumping Viruses to Job's Leviathan: A Response

William P. Brown

The introduction to this groundbreaking volume opens with the editors' marveling over how the Bible teems with so many different animals. My response opens with marveling over the animals included in this volume: foxes and birds, Behemoth and Leviathan, dogs and lions, bears, birds, donkeys, and pigs, jackals, and ostriches, to name a few. Perhaps one could offer a friendly subtitle to this remarkable collection: "Lions and Tigers and Bears, Amen!" And maggots too.

I am also struck by the diversity of approaches adopted and adapted by the contributors. While the arrangement of essays is structured around Matthew Calarco's helpful delineation of approaches (i.e., difference, identity, and indistinction), rarely does any essay adhere exclusively to one or the other. Some contributors, moreover, rely on science to bring depth to the biblical text, while others draw from prosody and metaphor theory. As there is no need to cage animals in zoos, so there is no need to tie down practitioners of animal hermeneutics to one specific approach or another. Many of the essays featured in this volume are in various degrees free range.

I want to touch on two significant gaps in the volume, one methodological and the other textual. They are, in fact, tangentially related: (1) the significance of the COVID-19 pandemic for human and nonhuman animals, and (2) the most extensive litany of animals featured in the Hebrew Bible: Job 38–41. The first adds a hermeneutical twist to Calarco's triad of approaches; the latter integrates all three of his approaches in dialogue with a biblical text.

A Hermeneutic of Spatial Distancing

Given the timing of the volume's publication, I suspect many of the contributors to this volume labored under the dark cloud of the COVID-19 pandemic, and yet nothing of it is mentioned in any of the essays. The pandemic, one could say, adds a new twist, if not perspective, to the approaches represented in this volume, namely, a hermeneutic of spatial distancing, not unrelated to the practice of social distancing encouraged by health professionals to mitigate spread of the virus. As first suspected and despite later suspicions to the contrary, the transmission of SARS-CoV-2 was most probably a zoonotic leap, a jump to people from infected animals, at the Huanan Seafood Market in Wuhan, China, one that likely occurred not once but twice by the end of 2019 (Cohen 2022, 946). COVID, in fact, is not the only zoonotic disease to wreak havoc, historically or potentially, in human society. The Centers for Disease Control (2019) identify eight zoonotic diseases that are of "most concern" in the United States: zoonotic influenza (e.g., bat flu, avian flu, swine flu), salmonellosis (from, e.g., pet bearded dragons), West Nile virus (mosquito borne), plague (*Yersinia pestis*, from rodents and their fleas), emerging coronaviruses (e.g., MERS-CoV from camels in the Arabian Peninsula), rabies (from, e.g., bats, raccoons, skunks, and foxes), Brucellosis (from infected domesticated animals), and Lyme disease (from the blacklegged tick. All result from human-animal interaction, some specifically from human encroachment on the wild, deforestation, and poaching, not to mention raising animals for human consumption. In the case of COVID-19, human-to-animal transmission is well documented, particularly in zoos, in which several types of big cats, otters, and nonhuman primates have been particularly susceptible (Centers for Disease Control and Prevention 2023). To add urgency to the issue, climate change is forcing wild animals to relocate their habitats in unprecedented ways and to coexist with new neighbors, thereby allowing viruses to "spill over into unfamiliar hosts—and, eventually, into us" (Yong 2022, 1).

The prevalence of zoonotic diseases forces us to think twice about how humans should interact with their animal siblings in God's diverse "kin-dom" (see Brian Tipton's essay). The issue is not addressed by exploring issues of difference, identity, or indistinction, at least not directly. Most pertinent in the case of zoonotic diseases is the issue of distance and, more broadly, spatial relations. The value of keeping distance and thereby respecting the natural habitats of wild animals is paramount. I am reminded of the psalmist's way of describing the mutual but separated flourishing of lions and humans:

> You bring on darkness for there to be night,
> in which every animal of the forest moves about.
> The young lions roar for prey,
> seeking their food from God.
> When the sun rises, they withdraw,
> and to their dens they retire.
> Humans go forth to their work,
> to their labor until evening.
> How manifold are your works, YHWH!
> With wisdom you have made them all.
> The earth is full of your creations! (Ps 104:20–24)[1]

If one did not know any better, it would seem that the psalmist is claiming that the only difference between humans and lions is that the lions take the night shift while humans take the day shift, both earning their living. But when it comes to COVID and other epidemiological dangers that are zoonotic, this matter of indistinction recedes into the background while that of distance rises to the fore. Day and night are reserved for humans and lions, respectively. Lions, moreover, have their dens, and humans their own domiciles (left unstated in the psalm); they do not share living space, nor are they meant to. Such separation, both temporal and spatial, ensures their mutual flourishing. Distinction, in this case, requires distance and respect for habitations. Psalm 104 paints a picture of a planet that is irreducibly pluralistic in terms not only of species but also of habitation, all for the sake of mutual flourishing—a profound lesson for surviving the Pandemicene in which we live.

Job's Difference, Indistinction, and Identity vis-à-vis the Animals

Speaking of spatial relations, YHWH's answer in the book of Job redraws Job's own conceptual map about the wilderness and his place in creation, all from the collage of animals presented to him in 38:39–41:26[34]. The three approaches identified by Calarco provide a trifocal lens through which to read YHWH's answer to Job for its multileveled depth and

---

1. Unless otherwise stated, all biblical translations are my own.

wisdom. Although perhaps inspired by the genre of the catalog, YHWH's litany of animals (six pairs) is no dry, taxonomic list. Far from it, each animal is described in such poetic detail that Job is afforded a near-personal encounter. What is Job to learn from this zoological sweep of creation? Something about his own identity and relationship to the wild, both different and indistinct.

Difference

Through the power of divine poetry, Job discovers the wild in a radically new way and thereby discovers something new about himself. First, he discovers that the animals are utterly alien to him, not projections of his disdain or fear. They are subjects unto themselves, fully individualized, fully "selved" (Brown 2010, 128). The onager, for example, roams freely far and away from the "shouts of the driver" in the city, where its domesticated cousin resides (39:7–8). In Job's purview, the onager was a lowly scavenger that he likened to the impoverished (24:4–8). In YHWH's world, the onager is a quintessentially free creature. The same for the auroch, which YHWH describes as undomesticated and thus uncontrollable (39:9–12). For all its lack of wisdom, the ostrich fearlessly stands its ground before the hunter, laughing (vv. 16–19). Job, who in his prime once fancied himself as a "king among his troops," meets the true king on earth, Leviathan (41:26[34]). Most striking, YHWH reverses Job's antagonism toward the lion by asking him not to kill it but to provide for it (38:39). Everything that Job had projected on the wild is effectively dismantled in YHWH's discourse. The world of YHWH's kin-dom is a world suffused with alterity and inalienable dignity.

Indistinction

For all that is different between Job and these denizens of the wild, certain connections, both subtle and obvious, cannot be gainsaid. First and foremost, YHWH acknowledges a connection, if not affinity, between Behemoth and Job:

> Behold Behemoth, which I created with you;
> it eats grass like an ox.
> Behold its potency in its loins,
> and its power in the muscles of its belly. (Job 40:15–16)

The key lies in the prepositional phrase "with you" (*'immāk*), rife with possibilities. The text is tantalizingly unclear. Nevertheless, in light of Job's lament in chapter 30, in which he complains of being a "brother of jackals and a companion of ostriches" (v. 29), the preposition *with*, which links Behemoth and Job together, takes on a deeper relationship than that of temporal convergence. In his essay in this volume, Robert Seesengood notes, "Human and monster share an affinity in being, each, transcendent over the rudimentary animal." While most of the animals described by YHWH in Job could not be classified as rudimentary, Leviathan and Behemoth do stand out as mythically monstrous. Similarly, Job stands out among his friends as monstrously blasphemous.

Is there something shared indistinctly between Job and Behemoth? What connection do a potent, fearless monster and a tortured yet defiant human being share? It is no coincidence that Job is considered monstrous by his friends and even self-identifies as a monster at one point (Job 7:12). It is often noticed that Behemoth and Job do share some common traits, particularly strength and fearlessness in the face of danger: "Even if the river presses forth, it is not alarmed; it remains confident when the Jordan surges against its mouth" (40:23). Comparably, Job audaciously presses forth his case against God and his friends amid the onslaught of judgment and condemnation unleashed by his friends. Like the ostrich, Job stands his ground fearlessly, even though he lacks wisdom (38:2, 39:17–18). More broadly, in YHWH's speech, Job is counted an alien among the aliens of the wild, who shares marginalized status as an outcast. The company that he keeps with the jackals and the ostriches is in fact good company (see 30:29).

Identity

From the beginning to the end of the book, Job's own identity undergoes surprising changes, culminating in his encounter with the animals. In the first two chapters, Job is profiled as the upright and uptight patriarch who obsesses over his children's character and stoically accepts the disasters that befall him. But in the poetic dialogues that follow, Job turns indignant toward God and his friends, bitterly lamenting his suffering and audaciously charging God with wrongdoing. But in his encounter with the voice from the whirlwind, Job takes on a new character, forged from his newly conceived relationship with the wild, fashioned by the dialectic between difference and indistinction vis-à-vis the animals.

What one learns about Job in the end contrasts sharply with his depicted character at the beginning. In the epilogue, one finds Job doing something unprecedented within the scope of biblical tradition: he shares his inheritance with his three daughters, providing them the means of financial independence (42:15b; see Num 27:1–11). Job's patriarchal identity has changed, owing to his transformation in the wilderness with the animals. How so? The question of Job's transformed identity can be answered with a thought experiment. Given the twelve poetic portraits of the animals in YHWH's answer, one might wonder how Job's own poetic portrait might be construed in relation to them, as spoken by YHWH. Perhaps something such as this, beginning with YHWH's own boast to "the satan" in the prologue of the book but now extended to the animals:

> Behold my servant Job!
> A blameless and upright man is he.
> Among human beings no one is so fierce;
> among his peers he has no equal.
> Do you think you can chain his mouth shut?
> Will he make supplications to you?
> Argue with him and think of the dispute!
> You will not do it again.
> He scorns the tyranny of tradition,
> and refuses to heed the accusations of his detractors.
> Even if the dialogue is turbulent, he is not frightened;
> he remains confident amid a torrent of backlash.
> He goes forth and does not repent.
> Who has let this wild ass of a man go free?[2]

By bringing Job in relation to the animals of the wild, the poet affirms the patriarch's fearless character. What was emerging in Job's self-identity as a result of his dialogical exchanges with his friends finds its culmination in the wild. YHWH's answer to Job, it turns out, is an invitation for Job to gird up his loins and be the fearless creature he was meant to be in the face of adversity, like the ostrich standing its ground (39:18), like the warhorse charging into battle (vv. 21–24), like Behemoth's unwavering confidence before rushing waters (40:23), like Leviathan's assured victory in a contest of strength (41:1–3[9–11]), like the onager's scorn of human oppression (39:7), like the auroch's refusal to be tamed (vv. 9–12). Job's identity is

---

[2]. Adapted and abbreviated from Brown 2020, 265–66.

"be-wilded," thanks to his new companions. Difference, indistinction, and identity all have their say in accounting for Job's transformation.

Works Cited

Brown, William P. 2010. *The Seven Pillars of Creation: The Bible, Science, and the Ecology of Wonder*. New York: Oxford University Press.
———. 2020. "Job and the 'Comforting Cosmos.'" Pages 249–66 in *Seeking Wisdom's Depths and Torah's Heights: Essays in Honor of Samuel E. Balentine*. Edited by Barry R. Huff and Patricia Vesely. Macon, GA: Smyth & Helwys.
Centers for Disease Control and Prevention. 2019. "8 Zoonotic Diseases Shared between Animals and People of Most Concern in the U.S." 6 May. https://tinyurl.com/SBL06107n.
———. 2023. "Animals and COVID-19." Updated 7 April. https://tinyurl.com/SBL06107o.
Cohen, John. 2022. "Studies Bolster Pandemic Origin in Wuhan Animal Market." *Science* 375:946–47.
Yong, Ed. 2022. "We Created the 'Pandemicene.'" *The Atlantic*, 28 April. https://tinyurl.com/SBL06107p.

Biblical and Other Cultural Zoontologies

Robert McKay

As a snail which melteth, let every one of them pass away.
—Psalm 58:8 KJV

In his 1869 work *Bible Animals*, a six-hundred-page concordance of biblical animals and sui generis example of what I will call here biblical cultural zoontology, English clergyman and amateur zoologist James G. Wood says what the psalmist got wrong about snails. The idea apparently went among the ancients that a snail's slime trail was subtracted from the substance of their body "until at last it wasted entirely away" (Wood 1869, 589).[1] Without ever quite saying so, Wood lets it be known that this popular belief is a bit daft, but that even so, "a snail which melteth" served the author very well as a simile in their "terrible denunciations" of the wicked. And that is Wood's point. Zoological or ethological truths about the being of snails—the biology or behavior of this species of mollusk in general, let alone of this or that particular snail—are rather beside the point; Wood says nothing specific about these things. But the spiritual meaning of the snail as rhetorical device certainly is the larger point, and one can be assured of this all the more if one sees it against a background of systematic and accurate scientific knowledge about the snail that gives the ancient dissolution theory the lie. This is zoology as biblical cultural zoontology: an intertwined story of the reality of animal life and of biblical meaning, circulating as a cultural text with its own priorities. The term "cultural zoontology," as I use it here, is designed to capture the understanding that—perhaps most especially in the arena of nonhuman animal life—seemingly factual

---

1. I am grateful to Tom Tyler for alerting me to this book. A recent cultural zoontological narrative account of snail slime that gives rather more time to the idea of the animal's disappearance can be found in van Dooren 2022.

accounts of the embodied being of animal others (zoologies) are always also situated accounts of the existential being of those others, or lack of it.[2]

In the preface to *Bible Animals*, Wood makes a pronouncement that, perhaps surprisingly, points toward this idea.

> Owing to the conditions of time, language, country, and race under which the various books of the Holy Scriptures were written, it is impossible that they should be rightly understood at the present day, and in this land, without the aid of many departments of knowledge. Contemporary history, philology, geography, and ethnology must all be pressed into the service of the true biblical scholar; and there is yet another science which is to the full as important as either of the others. This is Natural History, in its widest sense. (Wood 1869, n.p.)

The objectionable era of high racial Orientalism is writ large in these words, of course. The ideal they offer is of animal life itself rightly falling under the full and knowing purview of the "true biblical scholar," along with the pasts, languages, places, and peoples converted without remainder into objects of knowledge, so as to serve the project of understanding the Bible "rightly." Natural history, as with the other disciplines, is imagined to be a positive science, delivering an enlightening knowledge that illuminates scripture. Nonetheless, hiding there in plain sight, in that "widest sense" in which natural history is invoked and in the recognition that the meanings at work in biblical texts are indeed products of their culture, are reasons why we might find at least some of the lineaments of Wood's approach in their very different visage in the current volume. "The importance of Zoology in elucidating the Scriptures cannot be overrated," Wood (1869, n.p.) continues, "and without its aid we shall not only miss the point of innumerable passages of the Old and New Testament, but the words of our Lord Himself will either be totally misinterpreted, or at least lose the greater part of their significance."

---

2. In using the term *cultural zoontology*, I am influenced by important work by anthropologists, including Eduardo Kohn (2013), and in literary studies by David Herman (2019), which has elaborated the notion of "cultural ontologies" to make sense of the extent of the complex and varying ways in which societies invoke and recognize reality, personhood, and other fundaments of being. I am interested also in zoontologies, for the way that they offer a "disarticulation [of] the problem of … pluralism from the concept of the human," as initially proposed by Cary Wolfe (2003, xiii).

Ask the Animals has a very different theology of the text and interpretation, of course, but for all that, it *is* nevertheless a work of zoology "in its widest sense"—if by that we understand biblical cultural zoontology. For Wood, the meaning of Holy Scripture is the endpoint of hermeneutics, and zoological knowledge—or rather a quizzical ethnological understanding of ancient people's apparently quirky zoological ideas from the authoritative position of nineteenth-century natural-historical scientific orthodoxy—is one of the means to realize it. For a secular reader such as myself, it is straightforward enough to see through this, by reading with a "hermeneutic of suspicion," as the editors of this volume affirm is justified (see the introduction). Ideological critique allows one to see that Wood's is a motivated marshaling of scientific knowledge for theological ends. But his unguarded respect for the theological meaningfulness of erstwhile-authoritative zoological ideas, as he theologically reframes them in the light of his own then-authoritative zoological ideas, means that this analysis would be too simple. Much harder to do—but something that animal studies as an analytical project certainly should do—is to see how such suspicion spreads (as suspicion must) to worry about zoological knowledge itself. This is especially tricky when a solid ground of knowledge of what animals truly are or want—"insights into animal lives," as the editors put it (see the introduction to this volume)—is presumably the authoritative point on which ideological critique of the rhetorical deployments of animals and animality—in the Bible, or indeed by its interpreters—must stand.

Because this book is in the vanguard of animal-related inquiry in biblical studies, *Ask the Animals* is a significant part of a transdisciplinary endeavor of animal studies to redirect the humanities, a project whose all-encompassing affirmative role is often said to be to understand what it means to be human (if not divine). The aim is instead to explore what it means, for the more-than-human world, to keep reproducing this phantasm of the human by way of the intellectual and material ownership of animals and animality.[3] But there is a recalcitrant danger here, which is placing (albeit this time in a suspicious mode) too much analytical faith in the figure of the human. For to presume the absolute unknowability of animals by humans, as a basis for understanding biblical animals (or indeed

---

3. On the relationship between animal studies and the philosophical-anthropological project of the humanities, which has influenced these comments, see Wolfe 2015.

zoological facts) as resolutely human cultural documents, narrowly but inevitably misses the point. On the contrary, this book, by opening biblical studies onto biblical animal studies and so offering its own exercises in biblical cultural zoontology, shows that a humanist ideological critique of animal life—in which animal life simply is what it is, while zoontologies are nothing but endlessly significant embodiments of *human* multiplicity—resolves nothing. It is itself a cultural zoontology. The real question is what to do with this knowledge.

So what does reading *Ask the Animals* as biblical-cultural zoontology suggest for animal studies? Most importantly, I think, it asks one to attend seriously to the implications of the volume's revelation of the extent and the specifics of the many ways in which religious and zoontological forms of knowledge interpenetrate and are co-created in biblical texts and their interpretations, *including those found in this volume*. Let me give just one example. A stated rationale for the volume is that animal studies scholars, in developing anti-anthropocentric responses to animals' place in human cultures, have concentrated to the point of stereotype on the charismatic megafauna of theological ideas (moments such as those in Gen 1–9). And they have done so without due attention to the complexity of meanings at work therein or indeed elsewhere in the Bible's animal worlds. My own first published article is a perfect case in point; in it, I embraced a critical rewriting of Genesis, offered by novelist Alice Walker, whose work I was interpreting with approval, as an anti-anthropocentric tactic for imagining human affinity to (rather than essentialized difference from) animals (McKay 2001).[4] This hermeneutic misstep is happily redressed by the kind of wide-ranging and compendious analysis that this volume offers. But rather than simply correcting animal studies' limited exploration of biblical hermeneutics, the book's careful attention to the recent history of anti-anthropocentric strategies of biblical interpretation, as much as its acknowledged role in both supplementing and complicating their legacy, lays bare something else. This is the way in which biblical cultural zoontology indeed persists; it cannot simply be brought to a halt by authoritative zoological interpretation from whatever other sphere.

Another way of making this point is to stress the value of the volume's synoptic framing, inspired by Matthew Calarco. For—just like the book

---

4. A different but consonant approach is found in Habel and Wurst 2000.

as a whole—I am arguing here that animals and animal-human relations, in the Bible and elsewhere, should not be understood in terms of identity, difference, or indistinction *alone*. The question is rather, What does thinking about animals in terms of these or other cultural zoontologies allow one to know about more-than-human life? The demand now is to read the stories of animal being that they tell for what they say about how so-called animals have, might, should, or will live, and how so-called humans have, might, should, or will live with them. That is a genealogical-hermeneutic project to which animal studies can and should turn.

I would like, if I may, to end on a personal note. Privilege is enacted in many and sometimes surprising ways. In the course of writing this response, I have been privileged to read—ahead of and therefore, in part, for other readers—this book's exemplary account of how one might and should read the animals of the Bible. Welcome though this is, it is not anything I would have ever expected, and yet other privileges that have come to me have no doubt made it possible. I am in the privileged position (unusual, though as I read this volume I know not exceptional) of being an animal studies scholar with a background steeped in biblical inquiry and (Scottish Protestant Christian) religious practice: the child of a father who has been a Church of Scotland minister and religious broadcaster; a stepfather who is himself an emeritus Professor of Biblical Studies cited in this very book; a mother who was a laboratory biochemist, turned science teacher, turned Church of Scotland Minister, turned religious studies teacher, and finally awarded a personal chair by her university, also cited in this very book; and a stepmother who was a professionally trained singer and teacher and who stood alongside me in my formative years as a chorister of Paisley Abbey in Scotland. Indeed, my time in that ecclesiastical environment no doubt marked a sort of prebeginning of my time in animal studies. This was not only by teaching me the formative value of animal subculture over more august human-focused ideas, as I attended so much less dutifully to my father's preaching than to the handheld Nintendo game *Octopus*, which was coveted and begrudgingly shared between the choirboys during the Sunday service longeurs. No, it was my trying and failing, transfixed, confused, and frankly a little frightened, to understand what the contents *really were* of the communion cup and bread being mysteriously consumed by the adults behind me. I now realize this provided an introduction to the radical and irresolvable complexity not just of metaphor but of the relationship between word and object, and of metaphorical understanding and belief. That privileged opportunity may well have initiated me into the interpretation of biblical cultural zoontologies that *Ask the Animals* has helped me to understand.

Works Cited

Dooren, Thom van. 2022. "Snail Trails: A Foray into Disappearing Worlds, Written in Slime." Pages 53–67 in *Animal Remains*. Edited by Sarah Bezan and Robert McKay. London: Routledge.

Habel, Norman C., and Shirley Wurst. 2000. *The Earth Story in Genesis*. Sheffield: Sheffield Academic.

Herman, David. 2019. *Narratology beyond the Human*. Oxford: Oxford University Press.

Kohn, Eduardo. 2013. *How Forests Think: Towards an Anthropology beyond the Human*. Berkeley: University of California Press.

McKay, Robert. 2001. "Getting Close to Animals with Alice Walker's *The Temple of My Familiar*." *S&A* 9:253–71.

Wolfe, Cary. 2003. *Zoontologies: The Question of the Animal*. Minneapolis: University of Minnesota Press.

———. 2015. "Human Advocacy and the Humanities: The Very Idea." Pages 27–48 in *Species Matters: Humane Advocacy and Cultural Theory*. Edited by Michael Lunblad and Marianne DeKoven. New York: Columbia University Press.

Wood, John G. 1869. *Bible Animals*. London: Longman, Green, Reader & Dyer.

Afterword:
An Animal Hermeneutics?
Research Directions and Teaching Ideas

Arthur Walker-Jones and Suzanna R. Millar

Having traversed these many and varied chapters, what can we conclude about the features of an animal hermeneutics? As editors, we did not want to limit from the start either the contributors or future practitioners of animal hermeneutics by creating guidelines or principles. We do not advocate any singular method; indeed, the contributors navigated the fields of biblical and animal studies with a wide range of methods. Three philosophical approaches organized this volume—difference, identity, and indistinction. These approaches are not mutually exclusive, and many chapters combine elements from each. Each provides resources for rigorous analysis, and each has ethical ramifications. The chapters in this volume thus illustrate the potential of the interdisciplinary field of animal studies to generate new interpretations in biblical studies, and for biblical studies to contribute to animal studies.

Furthermore, this volume indicates certain issues and approaches that will probably remain part of animal hermeneutics going forward. At its most basic, an animal hermeneutics attends to the many nonhuman animals in the Bible and treats them as subjects and agents in the Bible's history and literature. This, of course, has implications for many methodologies and biblical books. For example, as demonstrated in part 1, studies in Christology (Gruen), divinity (Seesengood), the history of the human/animal binary (Atkins), and the nuances and complexities of human animality in the biblical corpus (Stone) benefit from new insights in biblical understandings generated at the interchange between posthumanism and animality studies (what we called the difference approach). Yet the emphasis in posthumanism and animality studies often tends toward anthropocentrism, and such studies have not yet motivated much engagement in animal politics, which may be an unrealized point of reference for animal hermeneutics and biblical studies going forward, as fields in the humanities strive to demonstrate their relevance for current affairs.

Beyond this, several recurring issues appeared in this volume that are worth naming explicitly. First, many contributors engage with research from other disciplines. For example, several make use of the extensive information available about animals from biology and zooarcheology (e.g., Evers, Létourneau, Millar, Sandoval, Tipton, Waters). Though Robert McKay rightly cautions against thinking science is neutral and objective (scientific zoontologies are themselves cultural), such information can more fully illuminate animal worlds. Furthermore, several contributors dialogue with literary and cultural theorists, especially Matthew Calarco (see introduction), Jacques Derrida (Atkins, Cohen, Kolia, Seesengood, Stone), and Donna Haraway (Beverly, Létourneau, Millar, Stone, Tipton), but also Rosi Braidotti (Tipton), John Coetzee (Gilmour), and Gilles Deleuze (Beverly, Millar).

Second, the contributors carefully and extensively interrogate the nature of metaphors. William Gruen shows that even when nonhuman animals are read as metaphors, attending to why certain species are chosen may be illuminating. Yet metaphors are informed by and inform lived relationships with real animals. An animal hermeneutics may therefore resist the hegemony of the logos, and (like Tipton) employ a neoliteral reading. Jacob Evers, however, discovers that such a literal reading of animals may raise ethical problems of its own. Anne Létourneau and Jared Beverly explore the ways tenor and vehicle intermingle. Létourneau reads the pig literally using science and archaeology but finds it difficult to retrieve a liberative interpretation of the metaphor. She concludes by proposing an intertextual mixing of metaphors, connecting the pig in Proverbs with the mare in the Song of Songs—a creature that Beverly so astutely analyzes. Dong Hyeon Jeong's paper shows how empires use animal metaphors to animalize the Other, metaphors that may be internalized by those so animalized.

Third, an animal hermeneutics shares much with ecological, feminist, and decolonial biblical hermeneutics. Evers, Margaret Cohen, and Jaime Waters relate their work to principles of ecological hermeneutics, and they (along with several others) make appeals for contemporary environmental action based on their studies of other animals, such as birds (Waters, Tipton). Yet there are also points of tension here. Evers's close reading of nonhuman animals in Isa 11 problematizes interpretations of this depiction as an ecologically paradisal peaceable kin-dom. Beverly shows how the aspects of Song of Songs hailed as liberative by ecologists and feminists depend on the subjugation of domestic animals. Létourneau explores the intersection of femininity and animality in Proverbs' depiction of the porcine woman. Such animalization can be a strategy for colonial dehumanization, as shown by Jeong, as he (along with Tipton and Evers) explores the shadow of empire on these texts. In a liberative move, Brian Kolia offers Samoan storytelling to produce a decolonial counternarrative.

Fourth, the contributors illustrate the complexities of identification. Ecological biblical hermeneutics has generally viewed identification with earth as positive. Similarly, identity theorists in animal studies have found resources for ethics by considering how animals display the same characteristics that humans value in themselves. Chapters in this volume illustrate that human identification with other species can contribute to ecocriticism (Cohen, Waters) and political movements for humane treatment of other animals (Gilmour). Yet Jeong shows how identification can lead to harm for the animalized. And indistinction theorists seek to move beyond the anthropocentrism of identification with human characteristics and find other "surprising ways that humans are like other species" (Calarco). Thus Ken Stone discovers in Qoheleth a sense of "common creaturehood" that includes mortality. Brian Tipton discovers that birds and humans in Mark are alike oppressed by the Roman Empire. And Létourneau shows that, instead of the pig animalizing the woman (Prov 11:22), they are alike in "their beauty and disobedient ways."

Further Research

Each of the four areas highlighted above deserves further study. There are also a few areas not so prevalent in this volume where more research is desirable. For example, Suzanna Millar invites consideration of small creatures, and Cohen shows the connection between animal studies and plant studies. Both of these are new frontiers in animal studies that open up possibilities for biblical research.

The volume explores texts of both the Hebrew Bible and New Testament, though there are significant lacks in both areas. There is not, for example, any consideration of the biblical legal material—texts that are of central importance to the Jewish canon. Equally, there are only three chapters focused on the New Testament (Gruen, Jeong, and Tipton). Gruen and

Tipton treat foxes and birds, but other species abound, and some (such as the dove and lamb) play central roles that could be fruitfully explored with animal studies. Biblical texts do not have, of course, a singular perspective on nonhuman animals. Rather, the diverse passages engaged in this volume offer a range of dialoguing voices that are complex and sometimes contradictory (so Cohen, Stone, Tipton).

It is ironic that one of the contributors who speaks most explicitly about theology and religious practice is not a biblical scholar but an English professor: McKay responds to the volume as a foundational thinker in animal studies. Elsewhere, Gruen discusses Christology, Peter Joshua Atkins analyzes the interpretive practice of John Calvin, and Michael Gilmour gestures toward a Christian biblical animal ethics. Other essays open up a space for mystery, the humility of confronting an Other whose being we cannot grasp (Seesengood). There will always be some wildness outside human control—the untamable chaos associated with the monstrous and the divine (Seesengood). Indeed, several essays note the connections and slippages between animality and divinity (Gruen, Seesengood). Multiple biblical texts present a connection between God and nonhumans, not mediated or regulated by humans (Cohen, Kolia, Waters). There is scope here for much more research on the biblical foundations for Jewish and Christian animal ethics and theologies.

Pedagogy

Finally, we hope that this volume will be a valuable resource for students and teachers, providing an example of robust animal hermeneutics. It offers a rich variety of approaches for students to develop, critique, explore, and use as a model for their own interpretive practice. Animal hermeneutics extends an invitation to allow other species into our teaching spaces. We mean this both conceptually and physically. Instructors might invite to class animal activists, representatives of the Society for the Prevention of Cruelty to Animals, humane societies, or animal sanctuaries. They might take field trips to zoos, animal sanctuaries, equine therapy programs, or the like. We humans—especially those in Western urban contexts—may have been schooled in anthropocentrism, separating ourselves off from other species. But many essays in this volume demonstrate the deep interconnectedness of human with nonhuman life. The essays provoke us to understand other animals as cocreators of our ecological niches (Sandoval), as fellow members of earth community (Waters), as companion species (Beverly, Létourneau, Stone), as kin (Millar, Tipton). This is all the more vital when we are mutually faced with the existential threat of anthropogenic climate crisis and mass ecological degradation (e.g., Cohen, Evers, Gilmour, Kolia, Tipton, Waters). What would it mean for our teaching practice if we took this seriously? What if we acknowledged and sought to dismantle our anthropocentric biases? And what if we and our students became attentive to the wisdom embodied and enacted by other species (Waters), going with the proverbialist to the ant, considering her ways and becoming wise (Prov 6:6)?

A course might begin, for example, with asking students what their relationship is with nonhuman species. Do they have pets? If they are from a city, what birds and animals have they encountered there? If they are from a farm, what relations with other animals, domestic or wild, have they had? Do they eat meat and dairy products? This could lead to a discussion of Western cultural zoontologies and the ethics of human relations with other animals. Here we suggest some teaching activities stimulated by chapters from this volume, before concluding with a pedagogical reflection.

Course: Animals and the Bible
Reading: Introduction and "From Jumping Viruses to Job's Leviathan"
Activity: Arthur Walker-Jones and Suzanna Millar explain three different approaches to animal hermeneutics: difference, identity, and indistinction. William Brown then shows how these three approaches could be applied to a single text (Job 38–41). Which perspective do you find most fruitful? Following Brown's example, choose a different biblical text and analyze it from these three perspectives.

Course: Animals and the Bible
Reading: "'Let Them Eat Straw'" and "Mark's Parabolic Aviary"
Activity: Jacob Evers offers an allegorical interpretation of Isa 11:1–6, while Brian Tipton gives a neoliteral interpretation of Mark's parables. Why do these scholars choose these seemingly opposite approaches, and how do ethical and historical considerations guide their readings? When we encounter animals in biblical texts, how might we decide whether to interpret symbolically or literally?

Course: Decolonial Approaches to the Bible
   Reading: "Like Dogs That Return to Their Own Vomit"
   Activity: Dong Hyeon Jeong describes the colonial neurosis and animalizing hate reflected in 2 Peter (esp. 2:12). Write three short imaginative responses to Peter's statements: one from a member of Peter's own community who may too be experiencing colonial neurosis, one from the "false teachers" whose bodies have become objects of animalizing hate, and one from someone advocating for the "irrational animals" who have become a vehicle for this hate.

Course: Decolonial Approaches to the Bible
   Reading: "The Donkey as Tamasoaalii"
   Activity: Brian Kolia reads the story of Balaam's ass in relation to a traditional Samoan story. Choose a story from your own culture in which animals have an important role and imaginatively explore its interactions with a biblical text.

Course: Ecological Approaches to the Bible
   Reading: "'Let Them Eat Straw'"
   Activity: Jacob Evers explains the problems with the apparently ideal future described in Isa 11. What are these problems, and what might a less ecologically harmful future look like? Rewrite Isa 11:6–8 as an eschatological vision more conducive to ecological flourishing.

Course: Ecological Approaches to the Bible
   Reading: "Attending to the Forest and Its Denizens in the Hebrew Bible"
   Activity: Discuss in groups: What are the relationships between humans, nonhuman animals, and plants in the texts Margaret Cohen describes? From an ecological perspective, are there ethically relevant differences in the way we should treat these three groups?

Course: Ecological Approaches to the Bible
   Reading: "Recognizing the Gen(i)us of Animals" and "Mark's Parabolic Aviary"
   Activity: Jaime Waters and Brian Tipton both describe ecological degradation and its effect on bird life, in the biblical world and

today. Research birds in your local area and how human activities have affected their lives. How could biblical texts enter conversation with these contemporary concerns?

Course: Feminist Approaches to the Bible
Reading: "The Pasture and the Battlefield" and "Miss Piggy and the Pretty Woman of Proverbs 11:22"
Activity: Discuss in groups: What is the connection between gender and animality in the texts analyzed by Jared Beverly and Anne Létourneau? Is there any tension/conflict between readings directed toward gender justice and those concerned with animal justice?

Course: Christian Theology
Reading: "He Differed in Nothing from the Beasts"
Activity: Peter Atkins analyzes Calvin's interpretation of Dan 4 and the reasons for it. Investigate another theologian's appraisal of Dan 4, considering how they are interpreting the texts and the theological presuppositions underlying their interpretation.

Course: Biblical Reception
Reading: "Biblical Studies Meets the Humane Society"
Activity: Michael Gilmour examines how biblical animals have been received in works of fiction. Read a selected passage from *Black Beauty, Beautiful Joe,* or *Dr. Doolittle.* Consider how it is interpreting and using biblical texts. What is the value of imagination and storytelling for a biblically informed animal ethics?

We hope that teachers will use this volume critically and creatively and will be sensitive to the deep epistemological and pedagogical ramifications of animal hermeneutics. The Western education system prizes the rational *logos*. A rational-irrational dualism has been constructed, frequently mapped against the human-animal binary (Atkins). Nothing that is "irrational" or animal can be a site of genuine knowledge. As this book shows, this is false and reductive. The volume problematizes the categories through which we think (preeminently human and animal categories), challenging the very structures of Western thought. Animal hermeneutics invites alternative knowledges, alternative stories, as we have put it. It values storytelling (Gilmour, Kolia), bodies and affect (Jeong), and indigenous knowledges from communities who learn from and with other species (Kolia).

Furthermore, animal hermeneutics places epistemology and pedagogy in close connection with ethics and justice. It raises core questions of value and moves beyond thinking into being, becoming, and doing. Many essays stress the interlocking oppressions facing nonhuman animals and marginalized humans (such as women, queer folk, and foreigners), with animal hermeneutics' methodological correlate in its connection with feminist, queer, and postcolonial approaches (Beverly, Jeong, Kolia, Létourneau, Stone). Solidarity and alliance are possible across such lines of difference (Jeong, Tipton). Our classrooms could become sites where such intersectional and interspecies differences are acknowledged and celebrated but also complexified through recognizing fundamental points of identity. They could even become sites where these differences no longer structure our ethics and epistemology, as we nurture indistinction and imagine alternative ways of being and knowing conducive to the mutual flourishing of all individuals and species.

Contributors

Peter Joshua Atkins is a teaching fellow in Old Testament and Hebrew Bible at the University of Edinburgh. He is the author of *The Animalising Affliction of Nebuchadnezzar in Daniel 4* (Bloomsbury T&T Clark, 2023) as well as articles "Praise by Animals in the Hebrew Bible," *JSOT* 44 (2020): 500–513, and "Mythology or Zoology: A Study on the Impact of Translation History in Isaiah 13:21," *BibInt* 24 (2016): 48–59.

Jared Beverly is a PhD student at Chicago Theological Seminary and faculty associate at Graceland University. He has written an article titled "Nebuchadnezzar and the Animal Mind (Daniel 4)," *JSOT* 45 (2020): 144–57.

William P. Brown is William Marcellus McPheeters Professor of Old Testament at Columbia Theological Seminary and author of many books and articles, including *The Seven Pillars of Creation: Bible, Science, and the Ecology of Wonder* (Oxford University Press, 2010), *Wisdom's Wonder* (Eerdmans, 2014), and *Sacred Sense* (Eerdmans, 2015).

Margaret Cohen teaches at the University of Arizona and is the author of numerous journal articles, book chapters, and encyclopedia entries focusing on the Hebrew Bible and the archaeological realia of ancient Israel.

Jacob R. Evers is an independent scholar of the Hebrew Bible/Old Testament in the Pacific Northwest. His research and writing focuses on Isa 1–12 and ecological hermeneutics. He is an ordained minister in the Foursquare Church and teaches at a university associated with the denomination (Life Pacific University).

Michael J. Gilmour is associate professor of English literature and New Testament at Providence University College. He is a fellow of the Oxford

Centre for Animal Ethics and the author of *Eden's Other Residents: The Bible and Animals* (Cascade, 2014), *Animals in the Writings of C. S. Lewis* (Palgrave Macmillan, 2017), *Creative Compassion, Literature and Animal Welfare* (Palgrave Macmillan, 2020), and a number of other books and articles.

William "Chip" Gruen is professor of religion studies and director of the Institute for Religious and Cultural Understanding at Muhlenberg College. He is the author of a number of articles on material culture and animal symbolism in ancient Christianities. Most recently, he published a chapter on the Christian catacombs at Rome in *The Reception of Jesus in the First Three Centuries* (Bloomsbury T&T Clark, 2019).

Dong Hyeon Jeong is assistant professor of New Testament interpretation at Garrett-Evangelical Theological Seminary. He is the author of *With the Wild Beasts, Learning from the Trees: Animality, Vegetality, and (Colonized) Ethnicity in the Gospel of Mark* (SBL Press, 2023). He has also published numerous articles on the intersections of posthumanism, race and ethnicity, and postcolonialism.

Brian Fiu Kolia is a lecturer in Hebrew Bible/Old Testament at Malua Theological College in Samoa and an adjunct lecturer at Trinity Theological College, Naarm (Melbourne) Australia. He is the author of "Eve, the Serpent, and a Samoan Love Story: A Fāgogo Reading of Genesis 3:1–19 and Its Implications for Animal Studies," *BCT* 15 (2019): 156–63, and "Lifting the Tapu of Sex: A Tulou Reading of the Song of Songs," in *Sea of Readings: The Bible in the South Pacific* (SBL Press, 2018), 85–102

Anne Létourneau is assistant professor at Université de Montréal and the author of a number of peer-reviewed articles, including "From Wild Beast to Huntress: Animal Imagery, Beauty, and Seduction in the Song of Songs and Proverbs," *BibInt* 31 (2021): 67–93; "Culture du viol et poil castrateur: Tamar, fille de David, dans le traité Sanhédrin 21a du Talmud de Babylone," *SR* 49 (2020): 36–252; "Beauty, Bath and Beyond: Framing Bathsheba as a Royal Fantasy in 2 Sam 11,1–5," *SJOT* 32 (2018): 72–91; and "Jézebel: Généalogie d'une Femme Fatale," *ScEs* 66 (2014): 189–211.

Robert McKay is professor of contemporary literature at Sheffield University. His research focuses on the representation of animals and the ethics of human-animal relations in literature, film, and culture since 1945. He has published numerous articles and book chapters and was a member of the Animal Studies Group that wrote the seminal work in animal studies, *Killing Animals* (University of Illinois Press, 2004).

Suzanna R. Millar is a chancellor's fellow in Hebrew Bible/Old Testament at the University of Edinburgh. She is the author of *Genre and Openness in Proverbs 10:1–22:16* (SBL Press, 2020) and is currently working on a monograph about power dynamics and nonhuman animals in the books of Samuel.

Timothy J. Sandoval is associate professor of Hebrew Bible at Brite Divinity School. He is the author of *The Discourse of Wealth and Poverty in Proverbs* (Brill, 2006) as well as edited volumes and peer-reviewed journal articles.

Robert Paul Seesengood is professor of religious studies at Albright College. His recent publications include *Jesse's Lineage: The Legendary Lives of Jesus, David and Jesse James* (Bloomsbury/Continuum, 2013), cowritten with Jennifer L. Koosed; *Paul: A Brief History* (Wiley-Blackwell, 2010); and *Competing Identities: The Athlete and the Gladiator in Early Christianity* (Continuum, 2006).

Ken Stone is professor of Bible, culture, and hermeneutics at Chicago Theological Seminary. He is the author of *Reading the Hebrew Bible with Animal Studies* (Stanford University Press, 2018) and *Practicing Safer Texts: Food, Sex and Bible in Queer Perspective* (T&T Clark, 2005) as well as many other peer-reviewed books and articles.

Brian James Tipton is an adjunct faculty member in New Testament and early Christianity at Drew Theological School, and is founder and teaching pastor of Connectional Teaching Ministries in Southern California. He holds a PhD from Drew Theological School, where his dissertation focused on animality and the Gospel of Mark, exploring its various nonhuman creatures in metaphor, metonymy, simile, and simply animals-as-animals.

Arthur Walker-Jones is professor of religion and culture at the University of Winnipeg and the author of a number of books and articles, including *Psalms Book 2: An Earth Bible Commentary; "As a Doe Groans"* (T&T

Clark, 2019), *The Green Psalter: Resources for an Ecological Spirituality* (Fortress, 2009), and *Hebrew for Biblical Interpretation* (SBL Press, 2003).

Jaime L. Waters is associate professor of Old Testament at the Boston College School of Theology and Ministry. She is the author of *Threshing Floors in Ancient Israel: Their Ritual and Symbolic Significance* (Fortress, 2015) and *What Does the Bible Say about Animals?* (New City, 2022).

Ancient Sources Index

Hebrew Bible/Old Testament

Genesis

Ref	Page
1–9	266
1–11	7
1:1	124
1:11–12	125
1:21	41
1:24–26	108
1:26–28	7, 93–94
1:29–30	111
1:31	108
2–3	13
2:7	95, 108, 246
2:19	108, 112
3:19	95
3:21	237
3:24	111
9:1–7	93–94
9:2–3	108
9:3	107
9:9–10	1
12:10–13	72
12:16	85, 244
13:2	85
13:5	244
13:5–7	85
19	55
19:1–9	72
21:27–30	85
22:22–30	1
24:10	85
24:22	221, 223
24:25	72
24:30	221, 223
24:32	72
24:47	221, 223
26:1–7	72
30	199
30:43	244
32:6	244
35:4	221
49:9	71
49:17	74

Exodus

Ref	Page
7	55
7:11–12	56
14:9	89
14:23	89
15:1	89, 199
15:19	89
15:21	89, 199
15:25	244
19:4	31
20:10	110, 127
20:17	85
22:1–40	151
22:30 [ET 22:31]	88
23:5	71
23:9	166–67
23:19	119
32:2–3	221
34:26	110
35:22	221

Leviticus

Ref	Page
11:7	220, 225
11:41–44	239
13	239

Ancient Sources Index

Leviticus (cont.)
15   239

Numbers
13:23   123
19:11–20   239
21:6–7   134
22   214
22:1–40   151
22:22–30   1
22:22–35   209–14
27:1–11   260

Deuteronomy
5:21   85
14:8   220, 225
14:21   119
20   119, 122–23, 126
20:19   127
20:19–20   118
22:6–7   105, 119
22:10   164
22:22–35   205–16
22:27   213
22:28   214
22:30   210
22:32   214
24:10   170
25:4   107, 110
25:24   110
28:21–22   236
28:26   244
28:27–28   236
28:35   236–37
28:59–61   236
29:18   140

Joshua
13–22   123
17   122–26
17:6–7   124–25
17:8   123
17:14   124
17:15   124
17:15–18   124
17:18   123–24

Judges
4–5   200
8   221
8:24–26   221
8:26   221
14:5–6   88
19:19   72
25:4   107

1 Samuel
6:14   121
8:16–17   85
10:19–21   169
14:24   228
14:29   228
14:43   228
17:34   121
18:4   237
24:14   88
25:33   229

2 Samuel
3:8   88
3:35   228
9:8   88
12   202
15:1   89
16:9   88
17:8   70, 122
19:36   229

1 Kings
4:22–28   85
4:26   89, 164
4:28   89
5:8   72
8:62–64   85
10:26   85
10:26–29   89
14:11   88
16:4   88
20:1   89
20:20   89

Ancient Sources Index

21:23–24	88	7:21	238
22:38	88	9:17	237
		9:22–23	243
2 Kings		9:25–26	243
2:21	122	10:9	238, 246
2:23–24	121	10:18–19	243
2:24	122	10:18–22	243
5:22	122	10:20–22	243
6:2	122	12:11	229
6:4–6	122–23	13:28	237, 243
9:10	88	14:1	171
9:24	52	14:1–2	243
9:35–37	88	14:1–14	243
		15:14–16	240
Esther		15:15	240
6:7–11	164	15:17–35	243
		16:8	237
Job		16:13	237
1:1	236	16:15	237
1:21	246	17:4	242
2:7	237	17:6	238–39
2:8	237	17:7	237
2:12	243	17:13–14	243
3:3–26	243	17:13–16	243
3:8	40	17:14	235, 240, 244, 246–47
3:11–23	243	17:16	246
4:7–11	243	18:5	236
4:17–19	240	18:5–21	243
4:17–21	243	18:13	236
4:18	240	19:9	237
4:19	240, 243	19:13	239
6:8–9	243	19:14	239
6:10–12	237	19:17	239
7:2	243	19:20	237
7:5	235–39, 243, 247	20:4–11	243
7:6–7	243	20:11	246
7:6–10	243	21:23–34	243
7:8	237, 239	21:26	243–47
7:9	243	21:33	244, 246
7:12	259	24:4–8	258
7:15	243	24:20	245–46
7:16	238	25:4–6	240
7:17–18	240	25:6	243
7:19	239	24:19	243
7:19–21	239	24:20	235, 244, 246–47

Job (cont.)

25:5	240
25:6	240, 242, 247
25:26	235
26:12	238
29:14	237
30:10	239
30:17	237
30:29	240, 259
30:30	237
33:6	246
33:27	236
34:15	95, 246
38–41	255
38:2	259
38:9	247
38:26	108
38:28–29	247
38:39	247, 258
38:39–41:26[34]	257
38:41	1, 247
39:1–4	247
39:2–3	1
39:7	1, 260
39:7–8	258
39:9–12	258, 260
39:14–16	247
39:15	247
39:16–19	258
39:17–18	259
39:18	260
39:18–25	199
39:19–25	164
39:21–24	260
39:22	1
39:29–31	247
39:30	247
40:7–41:26	40
40:15–16	258
40:23	259–60
41:1–3[9–11]	260
41:7–9[15–17]	236
41:26[34]	258
42:6	238
42:11	221
42:15	260

Psalms

2:7	240
8	240
8:4[3]	240
8:5[4]	240
8:5–8	93–94
8:6[5]	240
8:7–9[6–8]	240
9:17	244
18:5	243
20:7	164
20:8	199
22:7[6]	241
22:15–18[14–17]	237
23	101
30:4[3]	243
31:10–11[9–10]	237
32:9	164
38:1–12[1–11]	237
38:4[3]	236
38:6[5]	236
49:15	243
50:10	116
58:4	74
58:8	263
74	41, 46
74:13–23	40
83:15	116
86:13	243
88:4[3]	243
93:1	237
102:11	171
103:14	95
104	94–96
104:1	237
104:10–30	108
104:17	1
104:20–22	70
104:20–24	257
104:21	1
104:26	40
104:27	1
104:29	94–95

104:30	94	15:8	173
116:3	243	15:18	165
120:5–7	72	15:24	228
132:9	237	15:25	165
139:13–15	246	16:6	228
144:14	169	16:11	165
		16:17	228
Proverbs		16:28	169
1–9	228	17:5	165
1:3	161, 165	17:9	165, 169
1:10–19	167, 172	17:12	70, 122
2:4–5	171	17:17	165
2:17	169	18:15	52
3:7	228	18:24	165
3:14–16	171	20:3	165
4:5–9	171	20:10	165
6:6	273	20:23	165
7:4	240	21:3	173
7:22	230	21:12	165
7:23	91	21:13	165
8:10	171–72	21:15	165
8:18	172	21:27	173
9:1–6	229	21:31	199
9:13	230	22:6	103
9:13–18	229	22:9	165
9:17	240	22:13	162
10–29	161, 226	22:22	165
10:1–22:16	161	23:9	166
10:11	165	23:10–11	165
10:20	165	23:20	173
10:21	165	23:32	74
10:31–32	165	25–29	161
11:1	165	25:12	221
11:9	165	25:26	165
11:16	228	26:11	151
11:22	219–31, 271, 275	26:13	162
12:4a	223	27:10a	165
12:10	104, 163–70, 173, 176	27:23	170–71
12:26	165	27:23–27	164, 169–73, 176
13:14	228	27:24	171
13:19	228	27:25	171
14:4	167–69, 173, 176	27:26	164
14:16	228	27:27	164, 173
14:27	228	28:1	165
14:31	165	28:5	165

Ancient Sources Index

Proverbs (cont.)
28:15	162
28:27	165
29:7	166–67
29:27	165
30:19	74
31:10–31	231
31:18	229

Ecclesiastes
1–2	89
1:12	84
1:14	94
2	86
2:3	85
2:7	85
2:15–16	93
3	94
3:1–8	92
3:9–15	92
3:16–22	92–93, 95
3:21	94
3:18	93
3:19	93–94
3:21	94
4:2	88
4:4	94
5:10	86
5:14[15]	246
7:15–17	93
8:8	87
9:1–4	87
9:4–6	88
9:7–10	88, 90
9:12	91
9:18	86–87
10	89
10:1	86–87
10:5	90
10:6–8	89
10:7	91
10:8–9	90
10:11	90
10:20	90
12:4–5	92

Song of Songs
1:7	198
1:7–8	195–98, 201
1:9	196, 198–99, 201
1:9–11	231
2:17	198
4:1–2	196, 201
4:9–10	240
4:12	240
6:5	200
6:5–6	196

Isaiah
1–12	77, 79
1:2–3	78, 137
1:4	78
2:7	199
2:13–15	78
3:21	222–23
5:1–7	77
5:8–17	79
5:29	77
6:11–13	79
7:14	77
7:18–25	78
9:5	77
9:17	116
10:1–11	78
10:12–19	78
10:18–21	79
11	10, 271
11:1	78
11:1–5	75, 77
11:1–6	273–74
11:1–9	112
11:4b	78
11:6–8	67–79
11:8	74
11:9	78
11:9–10	77
11:10	78
11:12–16	78
11:15–16	75
14:11	242, 244
14:30	71

27:1	40	16:12	222–23
31:1	199	16:12–13	222–23
34:11–15	135	19:1–9	75
34:14	41	38:4	199
40:7–8	171	38:14	199
44:14	123	39:20	199
56:11	88		
65	74	Daniel	
65:4b	225	4	10, 51–64, 275
66:3	225	4:1–14	52
66:17	225	4:13	52
66:24	242	4:16–24	52
		4:25–30	52
Jeremiah		4:30	52, 62
2:24	200	4:31	52
2:27	240	4:31–34	52
6:23	199	4:33	52
8–9	12, 131–42	7	46
8:4–9:11	131–42		
8:6b	133	Hosea	
8:7–9	136	2:4[2]	240
8:14–15	133	2:15	221–23
8:17	134	2:18	1
9:2–8[1–7]	139	13:8	70, 122
9:9–10	141		
9:10[9]	135	Amos	
9:12[11]	139	4:10	199
9:15b[14b]	140	5:19	74
10:3	116	9:3	40
10:22	135		
14:1–6	140	Joel	
15:3	140	1:17–18	1
16:4	244	1:20	1
23:15	140		
23:28	72	Jonah	
46:9	199	3:7	72, 228
49:33	135	4:7–9	1
50:42	199	4:11	108
51:37	135		
		Nahum	
Lamentations		3:2	199
3:10	121		
		Zechariah	
Ezekiel		10:3	199
16:8	222–23		

Deuterocanonical Books

Judith
- 10:3–4 — 223

Wisdom of Solomon
- 7:1–6 — 246

Sirach
- 7:17 — 242
- 10:11 — 242
- 40:1 — 246

1 Maccabees
- 1:44–50 — 225

Pseudepigrapha

Testament of Job
- 5.6 — 245
- 5.7 — 238
- 5.8 — 242
- 8.2 — 245

New Testament

Matthew
- 3:16 — 30
- 8:19–21 — 23
- 8:19–22 — 25
- 9:57–59 — 23
- 9:57–62 — 26
- 10:16 — 25
- 10:19 — 1
- 10:29–31 — 110
- 12:6 — 1
- 14:26 — 32
- 16:5 — 32

Mark
- 1:6 — 180
- 1:9–11 — 180, 191
- 1:10 — 30, 180
- 1:13 — 180
- 4:1–20 — 180
- 4:4 — 180, 182–87
- 4:15 — 180, 182–87
- 4:30–32 — 180, 187–90
- 5:1–20 — 180
- 6:4 — 32
- 6:30–34 — 180
- 6:34 — 180
- 6:49 — 32
- 7:24–30 — 180
- 8:1–10 — 180
- 8:27 — 32
- 9:44 — 180
- 9:46 — 180
- 9:48 — 180
- 10:17–31 — 180
- 11:1–11 — 180
- 11:15–19 — 180, 191
- 14:12 — 180
- 14:26–31 — 180, 191
- 14:68–72 — 180, 191
- 16:18 — 180

Luke
- 3:22 — 31
- 9:18 — 32
- 9:57–59 — 23
- 9:57–62 — 26
- 10:4 — 27
- 12:6 — 1
- 13:32 — 28
- 24:13 — 32
- 24:51 — 33

John
- 1:32 — 31
- 3:13 — 33
- 6:62 — 33
- 20:17 — 33–34
- 20:19 — 32

Acts
- 1:9–11 — 33

Romans
- 8:22 — 104

8:34	34	2:22	151
		3:1–2	149
1 Corinthians		3:3–5	149
6:12	149	3:7	152
9:9–10	109	3:8	147
		3:10–13	152
		3:14	147
Ephesians		3:17	147, 150
1:19	34	3:18	149
4	34		
4:9–10	34	1 John	
		4:8	103
Philippians			
2:9–10	29	Jude	
		10	151
Colossians		11	151
3:1	34	22–23	151

Early Christian Writings

1 Timothy			
3:16	34	Gospel of Nicodemus	
		5	34
1 Peter			
3:22	34	Gospel of Peter	
4:6	34	41–42	34
2 Peter		Gospel of Thomas	
1:1	147–48	86	26, 28
1:2–3	149	22–23	151
1:3–4	147		

Rabbinic Works

1:4	148		
1:5–7	148–49	Avot of Rabbi Nathan	
1:8	149	27	199
1:10	148		
1:12	149	b. Bava Qama	
1:12–15	148	82b	225
1:15	149		
1:16	149	b. Sotah	
1:19	149	49b	225
2:2	149		
2:10b–22	151	Pirqe Rabbi Eliezer	
2:12	144, 151	42	199
2:15–16	151		
2:18	149		
2:19	149		
2:20–21	148–49		
2:21	150		

Song of Songs Rabbah
    1.9.2.2A–C   199

Greco-Roman Literature

Apthonius, *Progymnasmata*
    2–4   27

Plutarch, *Praecepta gerendae reipublicae*
    5   151

Sallust, *Bellum Iugurtinum*
    18.1   153

Strabo, *Geography*
    5.2.7   153

Modern Authors Index

Adams, Carol J.	4, 7, 86, 109, 202	Bodenheimer, Friedrich	8
Agamben, Giorgio	13	Bodner, Keith	121
Ahmed, Sara	143–45, 147–48, 150–54	Boer, Roland	73
Aichele, George	10, 150, 153	Boggs, Colleen Glenney	181, 184
Albertz, Rainer	123	Böhl, Franz	124
Alderman, Isaac	11	Borowski, Oded	8, 135–36, 224
Allen, Barbara	6	Braidotti, Rosi	13, 78, 180, 184–85, 187
Allen, Leslie	132, 134, 139	Bray, Karen	147
Alter, Robert	214	Brinkema, Eugenie	147
Angell, George T.	104, 106	Brintnall, Kent L.	146
Armstrong, Philip	6	Brown, Lori	248
Asay, Amanda Karlene	126	Brown, William P.	83, 90–91, 93
Asma, Stephen T.	46	Brueggemann, Walter	69, 134
Atkins, Peter Joshua	9, 63	Bultmann, Rudolf	27
Atterton, Peter	170, 197	Burnett, Joel S.	121
Avrahami, Yael	229	Bunch, Mary	241
Bach, Rebecca Ann	180	Calarco, Matthew	8–9, 11, 13, 24, 58–59, 63, 68, 83–84, 95, 108–10, 117, 126, 136–37, 182, 186, 197, 200, 206, 220, 236, 241–42, 255, 257, 266–67
Balabanski, Vicky	68		
Balentine, Samuel	40		
Baluška, František	126		
Balvanera, Patricia	76	Callan, Terrance	151
Balz, Horst	36	Canlis, Julie	61–62
Basson, Alec	236, 239	Cansdale, George S.	8
Bauckham, Richard	101, 150	Carr, David M.	126
Beal, Timothy	41, 45–46	Carroll, Noel	46
Beard, Brady Alan	121	Carter, David	245–46
Beauchamp, Tom L.	101	Case, M. L.	198
Beers, Diane L.	106	Cavalieri, Paola	11, 108
Bennett, Jane	242	Chalaf, Ortal	226
Bertoni, Filippo	236, 242, 245	Chan, Michael	75
Bezan, Sarah	245	Childs, Brevard S.	67
Bickerman, Elias	83	Clements, Ronald E.	76
Black, Fiona C.	146	Clines, David J. A.	78, 237–38, 240, 243
Bloch, Maurice	246	Clough, David	7, 101
Bochart, Samuel	40	Clough, Patricia T.	146

-291-

Coetzee, John	106–7	Fornberg, Tord	150
Cohen, John	256	Forti, Tova	8, 84, 86–87, 96, 225, 228
Collins, Adela Yarbro	46, 183, 187–88	Foucault, Michel V.	46
Collins, Billie Jean	8	Fox, Michael	83–84, 87, 93, 96, 161, 164, 166, 168, 172, 198, 219, 224, 226, 228–29
Connell, Martin	34		
Connor, Steven	238		
Cook, Stephen L.	244	Franklin, Eric	26–27
Costandi, Moheb	245	Freud, Sigmund	46
Crenshaw, James L.	84	Frey, Ray G.	101
Davey, Graham C. L.	238	Fudge, Erica	3–4, 6–7, 137
Davids, Peter H.	149	Fuentes, Agustín	ix, 162
Davis, Ellen F.	96	Funk, Robert	187
Davis, Janet M.	102	Gailbert, Francis	174
Day, John	40	Gansell, Amy Rebecca	222, 225
Deane-Drummond, Celia	ix, 7, 176	Garrett, Duane	199
Deleuze, Gilles	13, 197, 236, 241–42, 247	Gerstein, Mark	241
Delitzsch, Franz	199	Gilmour, Michael	12, 108
Dell, Katharine	84	Ginsburg, Christian D.	198
Demsky, Aaron	124	Golani, Amir	221–22
Derrida, Jacques	4, 7, 9, 13, 40, 44, 47, 58–59, 61–63, 86, 125–26, 181, 214–15, 241	Goldingay, John	77
		Gordis, Robert	246
		Gowler, David	27
Desjardins, Michel	150, 154	Grassberger, Martin	237, 245
Dhorme, Edouard	238	Graybill, Rhiannon	10, 120
Dickson, Keith	31	Gregg, Melissa	146
Doak, Brian	235	Green, Crystal	213
De Donker, Ellen	222	Green, Jack	222
Donovan, Josephine	109–10	Gross, Aaron S.	2, 7, 125, 127, 195
Dooren, Thom van	263	Guattari, Félix	16, 197, 241–42, 247
Douglas, Mary	239	Guenther, Lisa	186
Driver, Godfrey R.	237	Habel, Norman C.	68, 131–32, 139, 266
Dozeman, Thomas B.	117	Haidt, Jonathan	239
Dunning, Benjamin	10	Halpern, Baruch	120
Efi, Tui Atus Tupua Tamasese	207–9, 211	Haraway, Donna	7, 13, 85, 186, 200, 220, 226, 236, 240, 246
Eliade, Mircea	28–30		
Engel, Mary P.	57	Harrison, Peter	2
Epstein, Heidi	10	Hartwell, Jeanette M.	221, 224
Erickson, Amy	239	Hathaway, Bill	241
Exum, J. Cheryl	195, 198	Hawley, Lance	235
Fanon, Franz	143–45, 151–53	Hays, Christopher B.	246
Feldt, Laura	120–21	Heide, Martin	8
Finkelstein, Israel	227	Heim, Knut M.	219, 228–29
Fischer, Stefan	221	Herman, David	264
Fleischmann, Wim	237, 245	Hendricks, Obery	183, 190
Fogg, Brandy R.	1–2	Hernandez, Rolando	76

Herzog, William R.	183	Lewis, C. S.	105–6
Hobgood-Oster, Laura	7	Liddell, Henry	46
Hoggett, Paul	146	Limmer, Abigail Susan	219, 221
Holladay, William Lee	132	Lindgren, Natalie K.	245
Holmstedt, Robert	224	Linzey, Andrew	106
Hope, Edward R.	8	Lofting, Hugh	110–13
Horrell, David G.	151	Longman, Tremper III	198, 200
Hovanec, Caroline	245	Lorde, Audre	152
Huet, Marie-Helene	46	López-Rodrígez, Irene	226–27
Huggan, Graham	186	Lundbom, Jack R.	134, 137
Hughes, J. Donald	180, 186, 189	Lutz, Cora E.	151
Hultkrantz, Ake	30–31	Luz, Ulrich	26
Hunt, Patrick	198, 202	MacDoland, George	105–6
Hurowitz, Victor	229	Mailahn, Klaus	31
Huwiler, Elizabeth	98	Marchal, Joseph A.	146
Ingold, Timothy	163, 174, 211–12	Marcus, Joel	187–88
Inoue, Sana	3	Marlow, Hilary	75, 137
Isasi-Díaz, Ada María	182	Martin, R.	240, 246
Jabr, Ferris	3	Mashinini, Meshack Mandla	183
Jackson, Deirdre	6	Mathewson, Dan	243
James, Elaine T.	197	Matsuzawa, Tetsuro	3
Javan, Gulnaz T.	245	Mbuvi, Andrew M.	149
Jeong, Dong Hyeon	9, 191	McCance, Dawne	6, 7
Jones, Henry	46	McCauley, Clark	239
Kalof, Linda	6	McConville, J. Gordon	117–19
Kang, Xiaofei	31	McGinn, Colin	239
Kasperbauer, Tyler J.	238	McGrath, Alister	105
Keel, Othmar	200	McHugh, Susan	6, 186
Kelly, John N. D.	149	McKay, Heather	11, 89
Kimber Buell, Denise	9	McKay, Robert	265
King, Shelley	105	McKenzie, Alyce M.	182
Klawans, Jonathan	212	McKenzie, Stephen	120
Knauf, Ernst Axel	123	Meiri, Meirav	227
Knoppers, Gary N.	117–18	Metzler, Maria	75, 231
John, Eduardo	264	Meyer, Eric	10
Kolone-Collins, Su'eala	213–14	Meyers, Carol	200
Koosed, Jenifer L.	9, 45, 83, 94, 146	Midgley, Mary	127
Kotrosits, Maria	146–47, 154	Midson, Scott	14
Kynes, Will	240	Miller, J. Maxwell	120
LaCocque, André	100	Millar, Suzanna	13–14, 181, 223–25, 235, 247
Lambert, Wilfred G.	229		
Landy, Francis	224, 231	Mizelle, Brett	220, 226–27, 230
Létourneau, Anne	228, 230	Moore, Stephen D.	10, 44–45, 146–47, 154, 191
Levi-Strauss, Claude	27		
Levinas, Emmanuel	170–71, 241	Morgan, Jonathan	73

Munro, Jill	198	Römer, Thomas	117–18
Muraoka, Takamitsu	228	Rosenblum, Jordon D.	12
Murphy, Roland	198–99	Roudinesco, Elisabeth	58, 61
Mynott, Jeremy	179	Roy-Turgeon, Olivier	222
Nelson, Richard	124	Rozin, Paul	239
Neyrey, Jerome H.	149	Ruether, Rosemary Radford	186
Niesel, Wilhelm	57	Runions, Erin	146
Nietzsche, Friedrich	47	Russell, Nerissa	75
Ninkovic, Velemir	126	Santos, Maurício	74
Niven, Charles D.	107	Sallustius Crispus, Gaius	153
Noth, Martin	123	Sapir-Hen, Lidar	220, 224–26
Oettli, Samuel	199	Sasson, Aharon	8
Olley, John W.	69	Satre, Jean-Paul	238
Olyan, Saul M.	9, 12	Saunders, Margaret Marshall	104–5, 107–8
Oswalt, John N.	76		
Otto, Rudolph	46	Schaefer, Donovan O.	146
Parry, Jonathan	246	Schellenberg, Ryan	187–88
Patton, Kimberley	7	Schifferdecker, Kathryn	84, 235
Peng, Jun Zhang	126	Schipper, Bernd	228–29
Perkins, Pheme	187–89	Schlobin, Roger C.	40, 46
Peters, Joris	8	Schmid, Konrad	117
Peteru, Aumua Clark	206	Schmidt, Gary D.	112
Petterson, Cody	192	Schwartz, Janelle	236, 240
Pierce, John B.	105	Scott, Robert	46
Pierotti, Raymond John	1–2	Scott, Bernard Brandon	87
Pitkin, Barbara	53	Seesengood, Robert	9, 12, 45, 144–45
Platt, Elizabeth E.	222	Seigworth, Gregory J.	146
Ploeg, Johannes van der	124	Seitz, Christopher R.	77
Plumwood, Val	13, 236, 246	Seow, Choon-Leong	87, 89, 91, 92–93
Pope, Marvin H.	40, 198–200, 202	Sewell, Anna	103–5
Price, Max D.	225, 229	Shacter, Jay F.	119
Pury, Albert de	118	Sherman, Phillip	83, 117
Pütz, Babette	181	Sherman, Ronald	237, 245
Pyper, Hugh	10	Sherwood, Yvonne	10, 78, 125
Quick, Laura	219, 221–23, 237	Shih, Shu-Ying	61
Radford, Benjamin	43	Shine, Richard	74
Rannard, Georgina	192	Shipman, Pat	174–76
Raymond, Erik	76	Singer, Peter	7, 11, 108
Regan, Tom	11, 108	Slifkin, Natan	40–41, 46
Riede, Peter	8, 235	Smiley, Jane	103
Rimbach, James A.	199	Smith, Gary	67
Robbins, Vernon	27	Smith, Jonathan Z.	25
Roberts, J. J. M.	67, 71	Smith, Linda Tuhiwai	214
Robinson, Michael J.	76	Sokoloff, Michael	52
Roller, Duane W.	153	Soler Cruz, Maria D.	238

Modern Authors Index

Spencer, F. Scott — 146
Stavrakapoulou, Francesca — 244
Steel, Allan — 41
Steel, Karl — 240
Stone, Ken — 9, 12, 14, 83–86, 88, 94–95, 117, 125, 195, 201, 219, 226
Strawn, Brent — 8, 88
Streck, Michael P. — 229
Strømmen, Hannah — 10, 83, 117, 125–26
Stulman, Louis — 132
Suriano, Matthew — 243–44
Talbert, Charles H. — 149
Taussig, Hal — 146
Tauiliili, Pemerika — 209
Thompson, Simon — 146
Thöne, Yvonne — 197, 202
Tibbett, Mark — 245–46
Tiffin, Helen — 186
Tipton, Brian — 182
Trudinger, Peter L. — 131–32, 139
Tull, Patricia K. — 67
Turner, Marie — 83–84, 94
Turner, Ralph V. — 34
Uval, Beth — 118
Uziel, Joe — 226
Vall, Gregory — 246
Vanderhooft, David — 120
Van Eck, Ernest — 183
Van Ee, Joshua J. — 67
Van Seters, John — 118
Viviers, Herndrik — 195, 197
Voorster, Nicolaas — 57
Wagner, Lloyd — 42
Waldau, Paul — 6, 7
Walker, Alice — 266
Walker-Jones, Arthur — 8, 14, 181, 211
Walsh, Carey — 84
Waters, Jaime L. — 9
Watson, Duane F. — 145
Watts, John D. W. — 74
Way, Kenneth — 8, 213
Webb, Stephen H. — 109
Weems, Renita J. — 198
Wennberg, Robert N. — 165
Whitaker, Patrick B. — 74
White, Lynn, Jr. — 7, 137
Whitekettle, Richard — 8
Wildberger, Hans — 67
Williams, David — 101
Williamson, Hugh G. M. — 75
Wolde, Ellen van — 124
Wolfe, Cary — 93–94, 264–65
Wolfe, Lisa Michele — 83, 89–90, 93
Wolff, Hans Walter — 52
Wood, James G. — 263–65
Wright, Jacob L. — 119
Wright, Tamara — 170
Wurst, Shirley — 266
Yellowlees, David — 245–46
Yong, Ed — 256
Young, Edward — 73
Zachman, Rachman — 60
Zeder, Melinda — 162, 175
Zoran, Debra — 73
Zwan, Pieter van der — 237

www.ingramcontent.com/pod-product-compliance
Lightning Source LLC
Chambersburg PA
CBHW021936290426
44108CB00012B/858